The Global-Local Interface and Hybridity

MIX
Paper from
responsible sources
FSC® C013056
FSC
www.fsc.org

Full details of all our publications can be found on http://www.multilingual-matters.com, or by writing to Multilingual Matters, St Nicholas House, 31–34 High Street, Bristol BS1 2AW, UK.

The Global-Local Interface and Hybridity

Exploring Language and Identity

Edited by
Rani Rubdy and Lubna Alsagoff

MULTILINGUAL MATTERS
Bristol • Buffalo • Toronto

Library of Congress Cataloging in Publication Data
The Global-Local Interface and Hybridity: Exploring Language and Identity/Edited by Rani Rubdy and Lubna Alsagoff.
Includes bibliographical references and index.
1. English language—Globalization. 2. English language—Foreign countries. 3. English language—Study and teaching—Foreign speakers. 4. English language—Standardization. I. Rubdy, Rani, editor of compilation. II. Lubna Alsagoff, editor of compilation.
PE1073.G56 2013
420–dc23 2013023706

British Library Cataloguing in Publication Data
A catalogue entry for this book is available from the British Library.

ISBN-13: 978-1-78309-085-3 (hbk)
ISBN-13: 978-1-78309-084-6 (pbk)

Multilingual Matters
UK: St Nicholas House, 31–34 High Street, Bristol BS1 2AW, UK.
USA: UTP, 2250 Military Road, Tonawanda, NY 14150, USA.
Canada: UTP, 5201 Dufferin Street, North York, Ontario M3H 5T8, Canada.

The policy of Multilingual Matters/Channel View Publications is to use papers that are natural, renewable and recyclable products, made from wood grown in sustainable forests. In the manufacturing process of our books, and to further support our policy, preference is given to printers that have FSC and PEFC Chain of Custody certification. The FSC and/or PEFC logos will appear on those books where full certification has been granted to the printer concerned.

Typeset by Techset Composition India (P) Ltd., Bangalore and Chennai, India.
Printed and bound in Great Britain by TJ International Ltd.

Contents

Contributors

Lubna Alsagoff is Associate Dean, Office of Education Research, at the National Institute of Education, Nanyang Technological University (Singapore). Her research interests reside within the context of language teacher education and include investigating English as a local-global language, with a particular focus on grammar as a means of investigating the relation between language practice and identity. She is co editor (with McKay, Hu and Renandya) of *Principles and Practices for Teaching English in an International Language* (Routledge, 2012), and has authored and edited books and contributed numerous journal articles and book chapters on these topics.

Rakesh M. Bhatt is Professor of sociolinguistics in the Department of Linguistics at the University of Illinois. He specializes in sociolinguistics of language contact, in particular, issues of migration, minorities and multilingualism, code-switching, language ideology and world Englishes. He has authored/co-authored two books, and is the author of essays in the *Journal of Sociolinguistics, Annual Review of Anthropology, International Journal of the Sociology of Language, International Journal of Applied Linguistics, Lingua, World Englishes, Studies in Second Language Acquisition, Second Language Research, English Language and Linguistics* and other venues. He is working on a book-length manuscript, under contract with Cambridge University Press, on the sociolinguistic patterns of subordination of Kashmiri language in diaspora.

Ofelia García is Professor in the PhD programs of urban education and of Hispanic and Luso-Brazilian literatures and languages at The Graduate Center, City University of New York. She has been Professor at Columbia University's Teachers College and Dean of the School of Education at Long Island University. Among her recent books are: *Bilingual Education in the 21st Century; Bilingual Community Education and Multilingualism* (with Zakharia & Otcu); *Handbook of*

Language and Ethnic Identity, I & II (with J.A. Fishman); *Educating Emergent Bilinguals* (with Kleifgen) and *Additive Schooling in Subtractive Times* (with Bartlett). She is the Associate General Editor of the *International Journal of the Sociology of Language.*

Christina Higgins is a sociolinguist whose research explores the relationship between language and identity with reference to local and global forces, resources and affiliations. In East Africa she has researched code-switching in the workplace, the intersection of popular culture and multilingualism, and HIV/AIDS education. She is the author of *English as a Local Language: Post-Colonial Identities and Multilingual Practices* (Multilingual Matters, 2009), co-editor (with Bonny Norton) of *Language and HIV/AIDS* (Multilingual Matters, 2010) and editor of *Identity Formation in Globalizing Contexts: Language Learning in the New Millennium* (Mouton de Gruyter, 2011).

Laurel D. Kamada is a Lecturer at Tohoku University in Japan. Her publications are in bilingualism and multiculturalism in Japan, gender and ethnic studies, marginalized (hybrid and gendered) identities in Japan, and discourses of ethnic embodiment and masculinity. Her other interests include discourse analytic approaches to the examination of identity. Her most recent book is *Hybrid Identities and Adolescent Girls: Being 'Half' in Japan* (Multilingual Matters, 2010).

Beatriz P. Lorente is a Lecturer in English linguistics at the Department of English at the University of Basel (Switzerland). She has a PhD in language studies from the National University of Singapore. She has conducted and published research on the role of language in transnational labor migration, especially in relation to the Philippines. She is currently working on a book manuscript entitled *Scripts of Servitude: Language and Transnational Domestic Work*, which will be published by Multilingual Matters.

Elizabeth Martin is Associate Professor of French at California State University, San Bernardino, where she teaches courses in business French, French advertising, commercial and technical French translation, and francophone business cultures through case studies. Her publications include a book on English in French advertising (Palgrave Macmillan) plus articles, book chapters and reviews on topics in sociolinguistics, advertising and languages for the professions. Her current research interests focus on language policy, code-mixed advertising, multilingual web localization and intercultural business communication.

Tope Omoniyi is Professor and Chair of Sociolinguistics at the University of Roehampton in London. His research interest is in language and identity broadly and narrowly conceptualized. He has explored it in the context of language-in-education, language policy and planning, physical and conceptual borderlands, popular culture, nation, religion and world Englishes. He is the Director of the Centre for Research in English Language and Linguistics (CRELL). He is a leading scholar in the new interdisciplinary field known as the sociology of language and religion. His publications which traverse these subjects have appeared in reputable academic journals.

Vincent B.Y. Ooi is an Assistant Dean at the Faculty of Arts and Social Sciences and Associate Professor at the Department of English Language and Literature, National University of Singapore. His research interests include computer-mediated communication, Asian discourses in English, the theory and practice of the lexicon, and corpus-based language studies. He is the author of *Computer Corpus Lexicography* (Edinburgh University Press, 1998), the editor of *Evolving Identities: The English Language in Singapore and Malaysia* (Times Academic Press, 2001), and the first lead editor of *Perspectives in Lexicography: Asia and Beyond* (K. Dictionaries, 2009). His articles have appeared in Oxford University Press, Routledge, John Benjamins, Rodopi, and IGI Global.

Emi Otsuji is a Senior Lecturer at the University of Technology, Sydney. Her research interests are: (1) language and globalization (metrolingualism and multilingualism), (2) performativity in language, culture and identity, (3) critical discourse analysis and (4) critical pedagogy in language teaching. She explores language use in contemporary urban environments that seek to move away from ascriptions of language and identity along conventional statist correlations between nation, language and ethnicity. Instead her studies favor an interest in how boundaries and distinctions are the results of particular language ideologies, and how language and space are managed and constructed through local interactions.

Alastair Pennycook is Professor of Language Studies at the University of Technology Sydney. His best known work has been on the global spread of English (*The Cultural Politics of English as an International Language*, Longman, 1994; *English and the Discourses of Colonialism*, Routledge, 1998; *Global Englishes and Transcultural Flows*, Routledge, 2007) and critical applied linguistics (*Critical Applied Linguistics: A Critical Introduction*, Lawrence Erlbaum 2001). His most recent research has focused on language practices, mobility and multilingualism (*Language as a Local Practice*, Routledge, 2010; *Language and Mobility: Unexpected Places*, Multilingual Matters, 2012).

Anjali Gera Roy is Professor in the Department of Humanities of Social Sciences at the Indian Institute of Technology Kharagpur. She has published several essays in literary, film and cultural studies. Her publications include a co-edited volume (with Nandi Bhatia) *Partitioned Lives: Narratives of Home, Displacement and Resettlement* (Pearson Longman, 2008) and a monograph *Bhangra Moves: From Ludhiana to London and Beyond* (Aldershot: Ashgate 2010). She has recently co-edited (with Chua Beng Huat) an anthology *The Travels of Indian Cinema: From Bombay to LA* (OUP, 2012) and edited *Magic of Bollywood: At Home and Abroad* (Sage, 2012).

Rani Rubdy is Associate Professor at the National Institute of Education, Nanyang Technological University, Singapore. Her research interests are in world Englishes, globalization and its social, sociolinguistic and educational consequences, transculturality and language planning and policy. Her publications include the co-edited volumes: *English in the World: Global Roles, Global Roles* (Continuum, 2006) with Mario Saraceni, *Language as Commodity: Global Structures, Local Marketplaces* (Continuum, 2008) with Peter K.W. Tan and *Asian Englishes: Changing Perspectives in a Globalised World* (Pearson, 2011) with Lawrence Jun Zhang and Lubna Alsagoff.

Mario Saraceni is a Senior Lecturer in English language and linguistics at the University of Portsmouth. His main academic interest is in the roles and the representations of English in the world. He wrote *The Relocation of English* (Palgrave, 2010) and, with Rani Rubdy, co-edited the volume *English in the World: Global Rule, Global Roles* (Continuum, 2006). He is now working on a book on world Englishes, to be published by Bloomsbury in 2014.

Peter K.W. Tan is Senior Lecturer in the Department of English Language and Literature at the National University of Singapore. His research interests include the development of Non-Anglo Englishes in South-East Asia, including their literary and computer-mediated forms and how they have influenced naming conventions. He is author of the book *A Stylistics of Drama* and has articles in journals (*Language Problems and Language Planning*; *Names: A Journal of Onomastics*; *Onoma*: *Journal of the International Council of Onomastic Sciences*; *World Englishes*; *English Today* and others), and chapters in various books.

T. Ruanni F. Tupas is an Assistant Professor of sociolinguistics at the National Institute of Education, Singapore. His research interests are in the interfaces between sociolinguistics and education, especially the politics of language in education in South-East Asia. From 2009–2012, he was Co-Director (with K.C. Lee) of a SGD$485,000 capability building curriculum development project funded by Temasek Foundation for selected tertiary institutions in Singapore, Indonesia, Vietnam and the Philippines. He was the 2009 Andrew Gonzalez Distinguished Professorial Chair in Linguistics and Language Education, awarded by the Linguistic Society of the Philippines (LSP) which recently has also elevated him to honorary membership.

Corazon D. Villareal is Professor at the Department of English and Comparative Literature, University of the Philippines Diliman. Her main publications are on translation and translational processes relating to Philippine literature and culture, among them, *Translating the Sugilanon: Reframing the Sign* (University of the Philippines Press, 1994), *Siday* (Ateneo de Manila University Press, 1997) and 'Translating Folklore in the Philippines' in Micaela Wolf (ed.) *Ubersetzen: Translating, Traduire: Towards a Social Turn?* (Lit Verlag, 2006). She was Fulbright Research Fellow at Columbia University (2006) and Associate at the Nida School of International Studies in Misano, Italy (2010).

1 The Cultural Dynamics of Globalization: Problematizing Hybridity

Rani Rubdy and Lubna Alsagoff

Introduction

Globalization is not just one of the most hotly debated concepts this century; it has become a social reality of contemporary importance – 'both as a social mode that we need to keep probing and as a focus for some new ways of understanding language in society' (Coupland, 2010: 2). Much has been written by globalization theorists (Castells, 1996; Featherstone, 1995; Giddens, 1990; Hall, 1991; Huntington, 1996; Inda & Rosaldo, 2008; Kraidy, 2002, 2005; Pieterse, 2004; Robertson, 1992; Tomlinson, 1999) on the nature and meaning of globalization, its causes and consequences, and its many contradictions and paradoxes. Indeed, globalization is best thought of as a multi-dimensional process that cuts across various spheres of activity in the realms of economy, politics, culture, technology and so forth that is transforming the world into a complex place – in the way it is imagined, represented and acted on by its inhabitants (Blommaert, 2010: 63). Furthermore, these transformations are so messy and unpredictable that we can only understand globalization as a complex of processes evolving and developing at different levels of scale, scope, speed and intensity, changing the world landscape in a number of ways.

Drawing on our insights from the voluminous literature on globalization, we suggest that the following characteristic elements of globalization have relevance for our engagement with the dynamics of language and culture in society.

- First of all, the development of worldwide modes of transport and communication has meant the speeding up of the flows of capital, people, goods, images and ideas across the world (Appadurai, 1996), thus pointing to a general increase in the pace of global interactions and processes (Inda & Rosaldo, 2008). National borders that were traditionally fixed have become increasingly porous and permeable, allowing more and more people to be cast into intense and immediate contact with each other. This is true not only in relation to trade, capital and information but also to ideas, norms, cultures and values.
- Second, the increased connectivity brought about by technological advances, and the unsurpassed speed with which events and messages can be transmitted to other parts of the world so that people located elsewhere experience them in real time, has erased the barriers of space and produced the experience of a 'shrinking world', of 'compressed time-space' (Harvey, 1989: 241–242).
- Third, globalization results in the intensification of worldwide social relations. As a result, happenings, decisions and practices in one area of the globe can come to have consequences for communities and cultures in other, often quite distant, locales around the world (Giddens, 1990).
- And finally, resulting from all this intensification of interconnectedness, driven by innovations in communication, media and technology, 'globalization also implies a heightened entanglement of the global and local such that, while everyone might continue to live local lives, their phenomenal worlds have to some extent become global as distant events come to have an impact on local spaces, and local developments come to have global repercussions' (Inda & Rosaldo, 2008: 11–12).

The image this evokes is of a world full of movement and mixture, contact and linkages, and persistent cultural interaction and exchange – a veritable 'global mélange' (Pieterse, 2004).

The social transformation triggered by globalization calls for profound changes in the way both language and culture have been traditionally conceptualized. Blommaert (2010), for instance, contends that the new forms of social interaction associated with globalization necessarily require that research reconsiders the earlier sociolinguistic frameworks and assumptions concerning the social nature of language. An engagement with globalization means cultures can no longer be conceived of as neatly bounded entities but rather 'as socio-cultural arrangements in terms of different forms of *mobility* or *flow*' (Coupland, 2010: 6) and that sociolinguistics must rethink itself as 'a sociolinguistics of mobile resources' (Blommaert, 2010: 1). Much like Pennycook (2007, 2010), Blommaert maintains that sociolinguistics and applied linguistics need to go beyond the traditional conceptual apparatus based on the idea of languages as autonomous codes in order to understand the complex ways in which linguistic and other semiotic resources act and interact in multilingual settings. More importantly, he argues that '(w)hat is globalized is not an abstract language, but specific speech forms, genres, styles, and forms of literacy practices' (Blommaert, 2003: 608). That is, people have *repertoires* – not the whole of any language, and they employ specific bits and pieces of language included in these repertoires for different purposes.

This characterizes, particularly well, the heterogeneous speech forms of many English-knowing bilinguals in the multilingual settings of former colonial countries and their diaspora communities, increasingly infiltrated by the spread of global English through film, television, popular music, the internet, advertising and youth culture. One key aspect of this heterogeneity is what Chouliaraki and Fairclough (1999) call *discoursal hybridity* – the intermixing of discourses and genres resulting from the unsettling of boundaries between different domains of social use of language in late modernity.

The concept of hybridity is intrinsically linked to the notion of identity for multicultural individuals and the present volume examines the ways in which language choice represents varying degrees of multiple identities and mixed cultural origins. The underlying theoretical position of this volume is that the English-based expressions of hybridity analyzed are a manifestation of such hybridized identities constructed at the intersection of global and local languages and cultures that are also embedded within broader discoursal and social practices. It focuses on hybridity as a natural principle intrinsic to processes of language choice and language practice in multilingual settings.

In the rest of this introductory chapter we present a more in-depth discussion of the dynamics of the global-local interface. First, we examine the three most influential paradigms proposed in accounting for the cultural dynamics of globalization in building a case for hybridity. We then discuss what it means for such hybrid lingua-cultural resources and practices to be part of the local, while they are part of the global. Next, we affirm the conceptual inevitability of hybridity as a construct in analyzing postmodern pluralist cultural identities, before mapping out the problematic of the notion of hybridity itself. Finally, we suggest the need to theorize the notion of hybridity and complicate it further in developing a more nuanced understanding of cultural exchange under translocal conditions of communication. Our engagement with hybridity in grappling with conceptualizations of cultural adaptation seeks to avoid a romanticized and celebratory valorization of hybridty/ization as symbolizing present-day linguistic and cultural diversity, and attempts a validation of its relevance as a theoretical and analytical construct in interpreting the impact of globalization in sociolinguistic research.

Globalization and Culture: Three Paradigms

Three theoretical positions in the literature on cultural globalization have been proposed, each with clearly distinguishable claims on this issue. The most common interpretation, the cultural imperialism thesis, is best expressed in the phrase the 'McDonaldization' of the world (Ritzer, 2000), associated with the acceleration of Western, particularly American, influence.

Implicit in the arguments of the cultural imperialism thesis is the assumption that global interconnectedness, equated with worldwide homogenization of societies through the impact of multinational corporations and the synchronization of technological, commercial and cultural influences emanating from the West, leads to the erosion of the culture of recipient nations – many of them in the developing world – by a single imposed culture, as in the global sweep of consumerism, or the hegemonic dominance of global English.

The second view is that of cultural polarization, expressed in terms of a 'clash of civilizations', which sees cultural difference as enduring and as generating rivalry and conflict between nations and groups (Huntington, 1996). From this perspective, the most salient feature of cultural globalization is not homogenization but heterogenization, in which local cultural and religious identities are being revived and revitalized mainly as a response to the threat, real or perceived, posed by globalization.

The third school of thought believes that 'cultural transmission is a two way process in which cultures in contact shape and reshape each other directly or indirectly' (Kumaravadivelu, 2008: 44). In this view, the forces of globalization are so complex and overlapping that they cannot be explained in terms of the narrow perspective of a center-periphery or East-West dichotomy. The two forces are in fact much like two sides of the same coin, with both homogenization and heterogenization operating in tandem and 'plunging the world in a creative as well as chaotic tension' (2008: 38) – a tension that is resolved through a process of hybridization. Sociologist Roland Robertson (1992) coined the term 'glocalization' to capture the essence of this intricate process in which 'the global is brought in conjunction with the local, and the local is modified to accommodate the global' (Kumaravadivelu, 2008: 45).

The Local in the Global, the Global in the Local

There is sufficient counterevidence to show that the entire world is not being swamped by Western cultural imperialism. For starters, cultural products are not simply passively consumed by periphery subjects, but periphery subjects creatively engage with these products in terms of their own local frameworks and dispositions, interpreting them according to their own cultural codes. There is overwhelming evidence that even 'cultural messages' which emanate directly from the US are differentially received and interpreted; that 'local' groups absorb communication from the 'center' not in a unidirectional manner but through 'selective incorporation' in a great variety of ways (Tomlinson, 1999).

Second, the major alleged producers of 'global culture' increasingly tailor their products to a differentiated global market (which they partly construct). Hollywood's attempt to employ mixed 'multinational' casts of actors and a variety of 'local' settings particularly to attract a global audience is a case in point. Similarly, there is much to suggest that seemingly 'national' symbolic resources are in fact increasingly deployed for differentiated global interpretation.

Third, cultural flows are not simply one way – a flow from the West to the rest. To be sure, 'there is substantial asymmetry in the flow of meaning in the world: the center mostly speaks, while the periphery listens' (Inda & Rosaldo, 2008: 20, citing Hannerz, 1992: 219). The claim about the one-sided dissemination of ideas and knowledge by a power elite, whether Euro- or US-centric, therefore needs to be tempered by empirical evidence about international cultural flows, and in particular, countervailing flows. Culture does move in the opposite direction, that is, from the rest to the West. The flow of ideas and practices – in religion, music, art, fashion, cooking and so on – from the so-called Third World to the dominant societies and regions of the world has been seriously underestimated. In the case of food, certain cuisines such as Indian, Chinese, Korean, Thai and Mexican, have become standard eating fare for many in the West. Music in the West now includes not only rock and roll and rhythm and blues (R&B), but also samba, salsa, reggae, *rai*, juju and so forth (Inda & Rosaldo, 2008: 21). In media entertainment, Latin American soap operas and *telenovelas*, Japanese Manga comics, Korean pop music and Indian Bollywood movies are famously exported to the US and Europe. Finally, the most visible sign of this reverse traffic is the millions of people from less affluent parts of the world 'who, largely as a result of poverty, economic underdevelopment, civil war and political unrest, are driven to seek a future in the major urban centers of the "developed" and "developing" nations' (p. 21), creating a marked presence of Third World peoples in the metropolises of the West.

Such globalized environments, characterized by increased movement and worldwide migration, and complicated further by the emerging new media and technologies of communication that facilitate access to local as well as translocal networks, are generating complex multilingual repertoires involving extreme forms of linguistic diversity and hybridity.

Several concepts have been suggested to describe the complexity of such new forms of diversity, or indeed 'super-diversity' (Vertovec, 2007), in multilingual settings, accompanying the perception that multilingualism itself is changing. The most widely used among these, *translanguaging*, refers to 'the act performed by bilinguals of accessing different linguistic features or various modes of what are described as autonomous languages' (García, 2009: 141, also Chapter 6, this volume). Other terms proposed include *metrolingualism* (Pennycook, 2010; Otsuji & Pennycook, 2010, also Chapter 5, this volume), *polylingualism* (Jørgensen, 2008; Møller, 2008), *transidiomaticity* (Jacquemet, 2005) and *translingual practices* (Canagarajah, 2013).

Essentially, all of these terms reflect 'a general dissatisfaction with the traditional enumerative and classificatory view of multilingualism [...] simply as a pluralisation of monolingualism' (Lähteenmaki *et al.*, 2011: 2). For instance, Pennycook rejects the 'multi' in multilingualism as 'a simplification in which multiplicity is made to consist of distinct, fixed and countable languages and cultures' (p. 4) in a way that does not capture the complex realities of contemporary language use. He proposes *metrolingualism* (Pennycook, 2010; Otsuji & Pennycook, 2010) as a concept that best captures the hybrid ways in which people in today's urban multilingual environments employ the resources at their disposal to play with and negotiate identities through language. A similar attempt to deconstruct such fixed notions as language and multilingualism characterizes Møller's (2008) and Jørgensen's (2008) concept of *polylingualism*, which refers to the way in which language users orient to a linguistic norm using all the linguistic resources available to reach their communicative goals (Møller, 2008: 218). Rather than languages, then, speakers and writers use features, selecting and combining them from more than one set of 'so-called languages' (Jørgensen, 2008). Like Otsuji and Pennycook, they view 'polylingualism as situated action, in that language users can and do negotiate the ways in which they orient to norms and values ascribed to different types of linguistic behavior in society at large' (Lähteenmäki *et al.*, 2011: 5). A related concept is Jacquemet's (2005) *transidiomatic practices*, 'the communicative practices of transnational groups that interact using different languages and communicative codes simultaneously present in a range of communicative channels, both local and distant.' Such practices are a result of the co-presence of multilingual talk and electronic media and are dependent on 'transnational environments', the mediation of 'deterritorialized technologies' and interaction 'with both present and distant people' (Jacquemet, 2005: 265). These reconceptualizations of conventional views of language all have their origin in the socio-constructivist paradigm, at the core of which lies a *practice* perspective for analyzing the way speakers create and negotiate meaning in social interaction. Although slightly varying in focus and/or emphasis, what is significant about these concepts is they have all been deployed to capture the manifest processes of lingua-cultural diversity and hybridity that characterize the nature of communication in today's globalizing world.

The Production of Locality and Hybridized Cultural Identities

Whereas traditional conceptions of culture assumed an isomorphism between place and culture, globalization has dislodged culture from particular locales. In a world of 'culture in motion', however, 'the deterritorialization of culture is invariably the occasion for the reinsertion of culture in new time-space contexts' (Inda & Rosaldo, 2008: 14). Hence, global cultural forms are not free-floating but are always reinscribed in new time-space contexts, relocated and relocalized in specific cultural environments. This means that globalized culture is never simply deterritorialized. It is also always reterritorialized, the two processes occurring simultaneously.

Relevant to the argument here is Bhabha's (1994) notion of a 'third space', the interstitial passage between fixed identifications, which 'opens up the possibility of a cultural hybridity that entertains difference without an assumed or imposed hierarchy' (Bhabha, 1994: 4). The third space is an *intercultural* space 'where difference is neither One nor the Other but *something else besides, in-between*' (1994: 219). Bhabha refers here to the liminal space between the cultures of the colonizer and the colonized, migrants and other (post)colonial subjects go through – a process that recasts their fixed sense of identity to generate an alternative hybrid subjectivity.

Intimately related to Bhabha's concept of third space is Bakhtin's (1981) notions of *heteroglossia, dialogism* or *double-voicedness*, which represent not only the coexistence of multiple speech styles and genres, but of a plurality of perspectives wherein utterly incompatible elements may be distributed within different perspectives of equal value. It is the incorporation of others' discourse into one's own frame that makes dialogue, and newness in language, possible. Hence, while traditional linguistics emphasizes only the centripetal forces that centralize and unify a language, Bakhtin also emphasizes the centrifugal forces that decentralize and disunify.

Theorizing Hybridity

Hybridity has been predominantly described as a boundary subverting, resistive and critical tool. Deployed as 'a term for a wide range of social and cultural phenomenon involving "mixing", it has become a key concept within cultural criticism and postcolonial theory' (Brah & Coombs, 2000: cover). Hybridity presents itself as an alternative discourse that subverts the very idea of a dominant culture and a unique canon, and invites a re-examination of power structures. Hence, it has been mobilized by postcolonial and postmodern thinkers as a strategy for dismantling unequal power relations that are inherent in such binary oppositions as East-West, local-global, modern-traditional and so on. Characterized as a site of democratic struggle and resistance against political and cultural domination, hybridity is viewed as a 'disruptive' and 'productive' category (Bhabha, 1994: 226; Joseph, 1999: 1) that challenges essentialism and resonates well with postmodern skepticism of essentialist understandings of culture.

With respect to cultural forms, hybridization is defined as 'the ways in which forms become separated from existing practices and recombine with new forms in new practices' (Rowe & Schelling, 1991: 231). In language, hybridity is a code for creativity and is used to describe not merely innovations in terms of linguistic features (creole, patois, pidgin), but increasingly the dynamics of mixed genres, styles, practices and discourses that make up the complex linguistic repertoires of people today. The main thrust of hybridity thinking today concerns cultural hybridity, as in recent cultural blends in art and music, but also in the diverse cultural influences in management techniques in business, and interdisciplinarity in sciences and education. Most common of all is everyday hybridity in identities, consumer behavior, lifestyle and so forth. Thus having been enlisted for various political and scholarly agendas, hybridity has emerged as a master trope, a privileged site for conceptualizing global/local articulations (Kraidy, 2005).

However, the notion of hybridity has also been brought into question and critiqued from various angles. In problematizing the concept, we will examine first some of the criticisms put forward against hybridity before going on to argue why it is still a helpful concept and merits a fuller articulation if we wish to gain a deeper understanding of global cultural (power) relations.

- The first concern involves the vexing issue of hybridity's conceptual ambiguity and the controversy over its meanings and its implications. Kraidy notes two paradoxes that hybridity is mired in: (i) Hybridity is understood as subversive and pervasive, exceptional and ordinary, marginal yet mainstream. (ii) The second paradox relates to it being polysemous and semantically open, partly owing to its different genealogies, allowing diverse interpretations and raising fears that the hybrid model can be appropriated by anyone to mean practically anything (Gómez-Peña, 1996: 12–13). Arguably, the detractors of hybridity view its conceptual slipperiness (but so is the term 'discourse') as weakening its theoretical rigor. To the contrary, we see hybridity's conceptual and interpretive openness as a strength that may render it potentially more powerful in its capacity to explicate the complex multidimensionality of global processes than a single-meaning model. Some of these multiple dimensions are operationalized and explored by the contributors to the present volume as they are played out in the specific contexts of their studies.

- A second objection to the concept of hybridity is its assumption that 'purity' precedes mixture. The very concept of language mix presupposes that languages are discrete and identifiable entities. Thus hybridity has been critiqued for its potential pre-supposition of languages in a pure, discrete state and of people as having fixed, ascribed non-hybrid identities even as it challenges essentialist ideas of culture and identity (Otsuji & Pennycook, 2010; also Chapter 5, this volume). However, notwithstanding its quotidian nature, hybridity is a helpful concept because it provides a profoundly reflexive perspective in transcending binary categories. It attests the point 'that boundaries are historical and social constructions and cognitive barriers whose validity depends on epistemic orders, which are ultimately of an arbitrary or at least contingent nature' (Pieterse, 2004: 52). As Pieterse observes, what is new is the recent acceleration of this awareness: 'mixing has been perennial as a process but new as an imaginary' (2004: 52).
- A third concern relates to the negative connotations surrounding the term, emerging partly from its perplexing and complex history linked with racial mixture and contamination (Young, 1995). In poststructuralist and postmodern analysis, however, hybridity and syncretism have become keywords, an antidote to essentialist notions of identity and ethnicity (Lowe, 1991), emerging as an important strand of postcolonial cultures and bringing a dimension of cultural renewal. In Bhabha's (1994) exploration of the postcolonial novel, hybridity is celebrated as the resilience of the subaltern and the subversion of imperial ideology, aesthetics and identity by natives writing back. Hybridity is thus dislodged from a position of weakness to one of strength in its ability to subvert and re-appropriate dominant discourses.
- Fourth, and perhaps the most conspicuous critique of hybridity, is that it skips over questions of power and inequality. Hybridity has been described as a strategy of liberation but it is not liberatory in itself. On the other hand, it has been accused of being appropriated or co-opted for furthering

various economic agendas of commercial and capitalist globalization and of lending legitimacy to a corporate logic and rhetoric (Hutnyk, 2005: 92). The revolutionary potential of hybridity thus seems to be undermined by its being mobilized to serve consumerist and commercial ends that may reproduce asymmetries or exclusions that we seek to move away from.

Admittedly, global culture, as well as most national and local cultures, is riven with relations of power and domination in which hierarchy and inequality abound. And sure enough, terms such as 'hybridity' and 'diversity' are usually employed to refer to the cultural and institutional positions of the weak and the disadvantaged, and rarely to the cultural mixture of the powerful. But this does not invalidate hybridity's potential to dismantle established power structures when such people, arguably the underdogs, use their agency to make their 'voice' heard. This is why, while recognizing hybridity as undoubtedly a key feature of many local and national cultures, and certainly global culture, it is important to articulate it in conjunction with the multiple forms of difference, oppression, hierarchy, struggle and hegemony, as well as cultural fusion and hybridization, occurring in specific contexts. We must be mindful also of Tomlinson's (1999: 141) reminder about the danger of expecting the concept of hybridity to do too much explanatory work.

Such are the contested themes often played out in hybridity talk. As Kraidy puts it, 'While some see hybridity as a site of democratic struggle and resistance against empire, others have attacked it as a neocolonial discourse complicit with transnational capitalism, cloaked in the hip garb of cultural theory' (2002: 316). Yet, 'in spite of the potential for antiprogressive appropriation and conceptual ambiguity', he asserts, 'hybridity is undeniable as a global existential condition' (Kraidy, 2002: 332, citing Hall, 1991; Joseph, 1999). He writes, 'I do not see any credible substitute to characterize the dual forces of globalization and localization, cohesion and dispersal, disjuncture and mixture that capture transnational and transcultural dialectics' (Kraidy, 2002: 316). Notwithstanding contestations surrounding its ideological implications, we believe an engagement with the hybridity perspective can offer valuable insights for sociolinguistic theory and method.

Concluding Remarks

We have argued that the centrality of hybridity in signifying the highly complex, processual and pervasive phenomena of cultural exchange and language mixing gives it considerable conceptual currency as a valid heuristic construct for analyzing the cultural dynamics of contemporary globalization.

New global cultural consciousness makes available new lifestyle choices which offer new possibilities and imaginaries for identity construction. This insight formed the impetus for inviting contributions to this book from authors representing a wide range of disciplinary backgrounds and approaches to the subject. Given the lack of a unified theory of hybridity, the book has benefitted more from the differences rather than the presumed similarities of the viewpoints which the authors have brought to bear on the concept of hybridity. Drawing from a variety of disciplines as well as ideological perspectives, the authors have come together to critically discuss, expand and challenge our understanding of the notion of hybridity. Hence, each of the chapters addresses a particular take on hybridity, using methodological and analytical tools from discourse analysis, code-switching, media studies, post-colonial studies, conversational analysis, and multilingual research to explore modes of English-based hybridization within the four sections on *Interrogating the Canon, Hybridized Discourses of Identity in the Media, Multilingual Diaspora and the Internet* and *Performing Hybrid Cultural Identities.*

In the first section of the book, *interrogating the canon,* authors Higgins, Rubdy, Lorente and Tupas, Otsuji and Pennycook, and García present a range of studies that explore hybridity's potential for subverting the canon of standard English from different viewpoints. Situating her study in East Africa, Higgins (Chapter 2) argues that hybridity should be re-perspectivized as a local phenomenon, in which the reterritorialization of English is best explained, not as a matter of adapting the global to the local, but rather in terms of both global and local flows within fluid shifting scapes. Rubdy (Chapter 3) sees hybridity as democratizing the canon of standard English through processes of localization, as evidenced in the commercial signage of three cities in the Indian state of Maharashtra that show the strategic and creative blending of English with Hindi and Marathi. In contrast, Lorente and Tupas' chapter (Chapter 4), which critically analyses the discourse of the website of a company that sells its services of training Filipinos to teach English as a foreign language, presents a cautionary unveiling of the deep entanglement of hybridity with capitalist globalization. Otsuji and Pennycook's (Chapter 5) analysis of multilingual repertoires in Australia, on the other hand, underscores the unremarkability of hybridity in which 'genres, styles, practices, and discourses are mobilised as part of everyday linguistic interaction'. García's chapter (Chapter 6) advocates hybridity and translanguaging as progressive pedagogy that is needed in place of monoglossic perspectives of bilingualism, and which is reflective of the 'fluidity of language practices and identifications in the 21st century'.

The four chapters in the next section focus on *the hybridized discourses of identity in the media.* Bhatt's chapter (Chapter 7) on the representations of contemporary Indian women through the use of Hindi in Indian English newspapers demonstrates how code-switching offers 'a third, *liminal*, space' for the construction of hybrid identities. Martin's analysis (Chapter 8) of French web-based advertising investigates the global and local fusion of identities and multimodal bilingual creativity and provides insights into the ways in which media distributed images, languages and music serve to construct the hybrid identity of today's online consumer. Roy's discussion (Chapter 9) of code-switching, along with haptic visuality, in crossover films in a highly transnationalized Bollywood explores how these offer affordances in the development of narratives of cultural differences and hybrid identities. Lee's chapter (Chapter 10) studies the hybridized *medialect* of Korean reality TV in which Korean entertainers exploit linguistic hybridization in the performance and marking of both self and others' identities.

In their examinations of *multilingual diaspora and the internet*, the chapters in the third section of this volume investigate hybridity in the linguistic practices of online communities. Saraceni's analysis, in Chapter 11, of Malaysian and Indonesian Facebook entries, suggests that discussions of hybridity require interrogation of the very concept of language. Next, in Chapter 12, Omoniyi examines data from YouTube and argues against the binarization of local and global in developing an understanding of the hybrid use of language in such e-borderland contexts. Ooi and Tan (Chapter 13) consider data from Facebook entries from Singapore, and argue that English, as the dominant language of the internet, has to accommodate the remaking of community as 'networked sociality' by developing a 'hybrid vernacular' as speakers forge identities and create different social relationships through code-mixing and code-switching.

In the last section on *performing hybrid cultural identities*, Kamada, Alsagoff and Villareal demonstrate language as the medium through which hybrid identities and agencies are constructed. In her chapter, Kamada (Chapter 14) investigates the hybrid linguistic and ethnic identities of mixed-ethnic girls of 'Japanese and "white/foreign" mixed-parentage in Japan who construct and perform a third ethnic identity that differs from either of their parents through "doing English" as part of their hybrid linguistic repertoire'. Alsagoff's chapter (Chapter 15) explores the dialogic of teacher identity construction in an online discussion forum which brings into focus the alignments between linguistic orientations and the construction of global and local identities. Villareal (Chapter 16) examines the heteroglossic personal narratives of the Philippine diaspora; she explores hybridity as subjectivity and observes how language functions as the 'intermediary' for narrators to develop the agency to manage the diasporic condition. In the concluding chapter (Chapter 17), we draw together critical points and common strands with the aim of providing a coherent synthesis of the various contributions to the book. In this way we seek to help illuminate, expand, and reframe current understandings of the interplay between textual and cultural hybridity and social identity within the continuing dialogue between the global and the local.

The English-based expressions of hybridity analyzed in these chapters not only represent the recruitment of local linguistic resources and practices in refashioning, recombining and reconstituting identities in a variety of cross-cultural and geographical contexts, they illustrate how the variegated manifestations of linguistic hybridity central to the thematic focus of the book are enactments of resistance, change, appropriation and creativity arising from the way English, a pre-eminently global language, has become deeply imbricated in the materiality of localities and social relations in these settings in ways that are of significant sociolinguistic interest in understanding the dynamics of mobile cultures and transcultural flows.

References

Appadurai, A. (1996) *Modernity at Large.* Minneapolis: University of Minnesota Press.

Bakhtin, M.M. (1981) *The Dialogic Imagination: Four Essays.* Austin: University of Texas Press.

Bhabha, H. (1994) *The Location of Culture.* London: Routledge.

Blommaert, J. (2003) Commentary: A sociolinguistics of globalization. *Journal of Sociolinguistics* 7 (4), 607–623.

Blommaert, J. (2010) *The Sociolinguistics of Globalization.* Cambridge: Cambridge University Press.

Brah, A. and Coombs, A.E. (2000) *Hybridity and its Discontents: Politics, Science, Culture.* London: Routledge.

Canagarajah, A.S. (2013) *Translingual Practices: Global Englishes and Cosmopolitan Relations.* New York: Routledge.

Castells, M. (1996) *The Rise of the Network Society.* Cambridge, MA: Blackwell Publishers.

Chouliaraki, L. and Fairclough, N. (1999) *Discourse in Late Modernity: Rethinking Critical Discourse Analysis.* Edinburgh: Edinburgh University Press.

Coupland, N. (2010) Introduction: Sociolinguistics in the global era. In N. Coupland (ed.) *The Handbook of Language and Globalization* (pp. 1–27). Chichester: Wiley-Blackwell.

Featherstone, M. (1995) *Undoing Culture: Globalization, Postmoderism and Identity.* London: Sage Publications.

García, O. (2009) *Bilingual Education in the 21st Century: A Global Perspective.* Oxford: Wiley Publications.

Giddens, A. (1990) *The Consequences of Modernity.* Stanford, CA: Stanford University Press.

Gómez-Peña, G. (1996) *The New World Border: Prophecies, Poems, and Loqueras for the End of the Century.* San Francisco: City Lights.

Hall, S. (1991) The local and the global: Globalization and ethnicity. In A.D. King (ed.) *Culture, Globalization and the World System: Contemporary Conditions for the Representation of Identity* (pp. 19–40). London: Macmillan.

Hannerz, U. (1992) *Cultural Complexity: Studies in the Social Organization of Meaning.* New York: Columbia University Press.

Harvey, D. (1989) *The Condition of Postmodernity.* Oxford: Blackwell.

Huntington, S. (1996) *The Clash of Civilizations and the Remaking of the World Order*. New York: Touchstone.
Hutnyk, J. (2005) Hybridity. *Ethnic and Racial Studies* 28 (1), 79–102.
Inda, J.X. and Rosaldo, R. (2008) Tracking global flows. In J.X. Inda and R. Rosaldo (eds) *The Anthropology of Globalization* (2nd edn) (pp. 3–46). Oxford: Blackwell Publishing.
Jacquemet, M. (2005) Transidiomatic practices: Language and power in the age of globalization. *Language and Communication* 25, 257–277.
Jørgensen, J.N. (2008) Polylingual languaging around and among children and adolescents. *International Journal of Multilingualism* 5 (3), 161–176.
Joseph, M. (1999) New hybrid identities and performance. In M. Joseph and J.N. Fink (eds) *Performing Hybridity* (pp. 1–24). Minneapolis: University of Minnesota Press.
Kraidy, M.M. (2002) Hybridity in cultural globalization. *Communication Theory* 12 (3), 316–339.
Kraidy, M.M. (2005) *Hybridity, or the Cultural Logic of Globalization*. Philadelphia: Temple University Press.
Kumaravadivelu, B. (2008) *Cultural Globalization and Language Education*. New Haven: Yale University Press.
Lähteenmäki, M., Varis, P. and Leppänen, S. (2011) Editorial, Special issue on Mediated multilingualism. *Apples – Journal of Applied Language Studies* 5 (1), 1–11.
Lowe, L. (1991) Heterogeneity, hybridity, multiplicity: Marking Asian American differences. *Diaspora* 1 (1), 24–44.
Møller, J.S. (2008) Polylingual performance among Turkish-Danes in late-modern Copenhagen. *International Journal of Multilingualism* 5 (3), 217–236.
Otsuji, E. and Pennycook, A. (2010) Metrolingualism: Fixity, fluidity and language in a flux. *International Journal of Multilingualism* 7 (3), 240–254.
Pennycook, A. (2007) *Global Englishes and Transcultural Flows*. London: Routledge.
Pennycook, A. (2010) *Language as a Local Practice*. New York: Routledge.
Pieterse, J.N. (2004) *Globalization and Culture: Global Mélange*. New York: Rowman and Littlefield Publishers Inc.
Ritzer, G. (2000) *The McDonaldization of Society*. Thousand Oaks: Pine Forge Press.
Robertson, R. (1992) *Globalization: Social Theory and Global Culture*. London: Sage.
Rowe, W. and Schelling, V. (1991) *Memory and Modernity: Popular Culture in Latin America*. London: Verso.
Tomlinson, J. (1999) *Globalization and Culture*. Chicago: Chicago University Press.
Vertovec, S. (2007) Super-diversity and its implications. *Ethnic and Racial Studies* 30 (6), 1024–1054.
Young, R.J.C. (1995) *Colonial Desire: Hybridity in Theory, Culture and Race*. London and New York: Routledge.

Part 1

Interrogating the Canon

2 When Scapes Collide: Reterritorializing English in East Africa

Christina Higgins

What is the mechanism that produces linguistic and cultural hybridity? In this chapter, I turn to the concept of *scapes* (Appadurai, 1990, 1996) as a way to explain how linguistic and cultural hybridities emerge and transform. I focus on the context of East Africa to explore how intersecting scapes produce new modes of meaning-making, not only in linguistic terms, but also in the form of new points of reference. The concept of intersecting scapes provides a way of explaining how English is encoded with new meanings in its local contexts. Drawing on data from the *mediascapes* of hip hop, advertising and the *ideoscapes* of politics and public health education, I show that rather than simply adapting English to fit local purposes, Kenyans and Tanzanians localize English again and again by exploiting the *multivocality* (Higgins, 2009) of the language to simultaneously index the multiple meanings associated with each scape.

Scapes and Linguistic Flows

A 2007 edition of the cartoon *Besela* (see Figure 2.1), published in Tanzanian comic books and newspapers, summarizes well what happens when various scapes (Appadurai, 1990) of social life collide. The three-frame cartoon depicts a middle-aged male teacher who is teaching a Swahili lesson on proverbs, a form of 'culture' teaching that is dominant in Tanzanian schools. The example depicts the fluid mediascape of popular culture (in the form of Tanzanian *Bongo Flava*, or already localized hip hop) within the mediascape of a popular magazine, *Mahaba ya Pwani*. The educational goal for the day, to teach Swahili

Figure 2.1 *Besela* by John Oscar
Source: *Mahaba ya Pwani* (2007), vol. 8.

proverbs, is thwarted not only by the intrusion of Bongo Flava into the orderly teaching of Swahili oral tradition, but also by the students' boisterous and unsolicited participation in the class, a behavior which is in reality uncommon, and which would be typically responded to with the prompt delivery of corporal punishment by teachers.

In the first frame, the teacher explains that his purpose is to help the students, and he asks if there are any questions. He expresses pleasure with the fact that the students are silent, which he takes to mean that they have understood his lesson perfectly thus far. In the second frame the teacher continues his proverb lesson and asks one of the students, Besela, to finish the proverb that begins with *Mficha uchi* ('One who hides their nakedness…'). This is one of the best-known proverbs in Tanzania, and every student would know that it finishes with *hazai* ('doesn't have children'), meaning that people should be willing to talk about their problems with others in order to find solutions or to cope with difficulties.

Though this proverb has been in use for many years, with its original meaning intact, the proverb has recently been incorporated into a popular Bongo Flava (Tanzanian hip hop) song by the artist Mchizi Mox, where it was given a strongly sexual nature. In the third and final frame of the cartoon Besela stands up, ready to answer the teacher's question. He says, *'Mbona ize hivyo?'* ('What such an easy one?'), thus making clear that he is an expert on such oral traditions, which he labels *'ize'* ('easy'). Instead of demonstrating his knowledge of traditional Swahili proverbs, however, he sings a verse of Mchizi Mox's song, leading the teacher to drop his Swahili book, clap his hand to his forehead and say *'Toba yarabi Bongo Flava kha! Mox, umeniharibia kazi. Aisee kamusi zote zimeekspiya sasa'* ('Good grief this Bongo Flava! Mox, you've destroyed my work. Now, all of the dictionaries have expired'). The cartoon is funny precisely because Bongo Flava-style language is in the 'wrong' context – in fact, even the students' body language is maladjusted to a Tanzanian classroom in the final frame. As those familiar with Tanzanian educational contexts know, such behavior would be impossible to find in an actual classroom, and the cartoon is presenting a situation that only exists in the imaginary. However, the point to be made here with this example is how the language in the scape of education can *ekspiya* 'expire' because it becomes *reterritorialized* (Deleuze & Guattari, 1972) in other domains of life – in this case, local hip hop music.

This sort of fluidity across the domains of education and popular culture illustrates how we can see hybridity as the product of global and local flows within shifting scapes. Appadurai (1990: 7) describes five scapes to establish the major 'building blocks of… the multiple worlds that are constituted by the historically situated imaginations of persons and groups spread around the globe', and refers to these sets of flows as the (1) *ethnoscape* (flows of people); (2) *technoscape* (flows of technology); (3) *financescape* (flows of money); (4) *mediascape* (flows of information and cultural expression); and (5) *ideoscape* (flows of ideas and philosophies). The scapes are amorphous due to their global spread (for example, the World Bank's funding scheme creates multinational, multilevel financescapes, which do not exist in one place), and

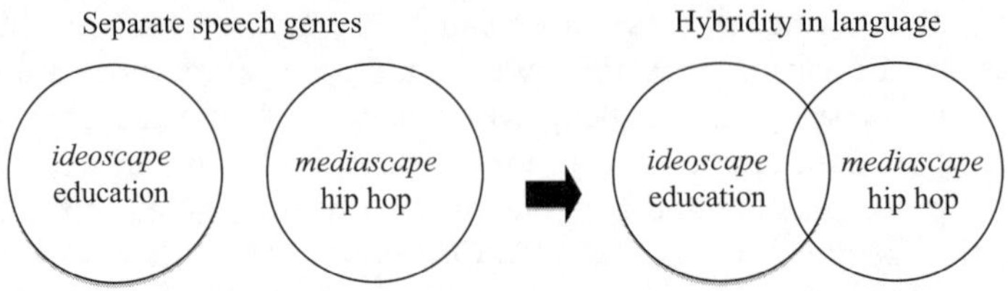

Figure 2.2 Linguistic hybridity as a result of scapes colliding

often take form only in the imagination (for example, popular culture can be a source of identification for young people in the form of a global hip hop youth culture in the mediascape).

When scapes collide, as is illustrated with the *Besela* example in Figure 2.1, the result is that the sociolinguistics of one scape (in this case, the mediascape) enter into that of another (the ideoscape of education). While these scapes may have previously exhibited more separation at the level of speech genres (Bakhtin, 1986 [1978]), their collision provides the necessary context for linguistic hybridity to emerge at the surface. This collision is depicted in Figure 2.2 to highlight the way in which previously separate scapes underneath language can produce hybridity at the linguistic surface:

Despite the abundant linguistic evidence to the contrary, most academic representations of global English depict English as a code that functions both linguistically and ideologically apart from other languages in local linguistic landscapes. Next, I briefly discuss this perspective before turning to the challenges that language use in East Africa present for such a stance.

English as Separate

Much academic work that describes the appropriation of English in local contexts treats English as a separate code, entirely distinct from other local languages in both form and function. English is frequently presented as a part of *extended diglossia* (Fishman, 1967), for it is described as an institutional language of schools, international business and parliaments, far removed from other more 'localized' contexts such as the home, the marketplace or popular culture (*cf.* Kachru *et al.*, 2006; Kirkpatrick, 2007). English is also ideologically constructed as a language that does not belong to the local context, for it is argued to be a largely instrumental language and, hence, is referred to in relatively distant terms in catchphrases such as a language of 'wider communication', a language for 'global competitiveness', and, most obviously, a 'foreign' language (Kachru & Nelson, 2006; Murata & Jenkins,

2009). It is presumed to mark an international point of view, or to act as a reference point to global/Western identities, rather than to construct a sense of the local. In terms of identity construction, it is held at arm's length, rather than seen as a local language.

Nonetheless, actual contemporary manifestations of English in the world challenge these dominant conceptualizations of this 'global' language (*cf.* Pennycook, 2003, 2007). Though it is most frequently described in monolectal ways in world Englishes literature, thus providing ease of comparison with center and periphery varieties, English often intersects with other languages, forming amalgalms such as Hinglish, Franglais, Spanglish and Japlish. English is mixed with other languages on the street in advertisements, in the consumption of popular culture and in everyday conversations. Because it occurs in a hybrid manner, however, it is not usually recognized as 'English' due to the impact of the centripetal forces of linguistic purity.

Furthermore, English does not constantly retain a foreign quality. Instead, it can create new ways for people to comment on local societal changes that result from global and local flows. Another cartoon from Tanzania illustrates the double-voice that English can provide for people to comment on local realities (Figure 2.3). Here we see a foreigner greeting a Tanzanian woman in

Figure 2.3 *Hawa yu Mama!* ('How are you mother?')
Source: *Kingo* (2001).

(apparent) English, exclaiming *'Hawa yu mama!'* ('How are you, mother?'). The woman responds in Swahili, stating *'We mzungu vipi mie sio Hawa'* ('What's wrong with you, foreigner, I'm not Hawa'), pointing out that he has mistaken her for someone else named Hawa, which is the East African name for 'Eve', originally derived from Arabic. The cartoon comments on the ethnoscape of tourists, missionaries and foreign workers, and its impact on the linguistic landscape of Tanzania.

The cartoon is funny not because the two fail to understand each other, but because the reader, who is expected to know both English and Swahili, can see that the utterance *Hawa yu mama!* can be taken as English and Swahili at the same time, and this *bivalent* (Woolard, 1998) meaning is the foundation of this cartoon's joke. *Hawa* works both as a Swahili name and as English 'how are', and *yu* can be taken as a shortened Swahili copula (*yuko*), thus meaning 'You are Eve, Mother!', an arguably odd thing to exclaim to an older woman one does not know; alternatively, *yu* can be read as the English 'you'. The simultaneity of meanings that this utterance produces for the bilingual reader is what makes this cartoon effective. Such humor that relies on knowledge of English as a way to critically and humorously interrogate local identities in relation to global flows is also found in Kenya (Higgins, 2009), South Korea (Park, 2009) and Hong Kong (Tsang & Wong, 2004).

Looking Underneath Language

In order to better understand hybridity, it is helpful to consider how the intersection of scapes may explain changes in linguistic and cultural forms of expression. In this way, looking *underneath* language at the social, political and economic forces which act on language is a useful approach for identifying how hybridity can emerge. Taking the case of advertising in Tanzania, we can examine how hybrid languages involving English have become a legitimate form of language for selling goods and services, and, more importantly, for selling consumer identities. In Dar es Salaam, these hybrid languages originate from the ethnoscape of the *kijiweni* ('street corner') where people, and especially the young and underemployed, congregate to pass the time. *Lugha ya mitaani* ('street language') has now become reterritorialized by the array of heavily competitive mobile phone companies' advertising campaigns in the mediascape. For example, the mobile phone company Tigo started running their *Longer Longa* advertisements in 2009, juxtaposing the street term *longa* ('chat') next to 'longer' as a way to draw attention to the cheap rates offered (see Figure 2.4). Since *longa* can be heard as a Tanzanian r-less pronunciation of the English word 'longer', the result is a bivalent, double-voiced reference to the lengthy amount of time

Figure 2.4 Tigo's 2010 advertisement announcing a rate of 1 shilling per second, 24 hours a day

Tigo provided their customers, at least for those who recognized the interplay of street language and English.

Despite the usual stigma associated with street language in other scapes (that is, the ideoscape of education, the mediascape of mainstream journalism), mobile phone companies have been using this non-standardized language for the past decade in an attempt to capitalize on the power of the mediascape and its key player, hip hop. Hence, street language has become commodified, corporatized and marketed back to those who produced it in the first place. This process is especially clear in recent advertisements starring Tanzania's Bongo Flava stars such as AY (see Figure 2.5), an artist who co-produced an album titled *Habari Ndio Hiyo* ('This here is what's new') in 2007 with fellow rapper Mwanafalsafa. The mobile phone company Vodacom re-scaped the album title for their slogan *Habari ndio hii* ('this is what's new').

Of course, singers, actors and others in the public eye have long been paid to market products. Moreover, how such individuals talk has long been of interest to young people, especially as one way to fashion cool, streetwise identities (*cf.* Alim, 2006). However, what is of note here is that the language that is associated with the spheres of the 'underclass' is being elevated to the

Figure 2.5 Bongo Flava artist AY on a mobile phone advertisement for Vodacom in 2010 (*Tsh 1 kwa sekunde* '1 Tanzanian shilling per second')

status of commodity because of shifting scapes. As Lorente and Tupas (Chapter 4, this volume) point out, this hybridizing of scapes is part and parcel to global capitalism. In making use of street language in their multilingual campaigns, Vodacom and Tigo are not changing the power relations between affluent people who can afford smart phones and the underclass. Indeed, it can be argued that these companies are exploiting the underclass's language for their own benefit. However, at the same time, and at the very least, this new intersection of scapes (hip hop, advertising and the street) creates new meanings in all three scapes: hip hop is increasingly commercialized, advertising is increasingly cool and the street becomes a less unknown or underground place. One could even go so far as to suggest that the sociolinguistic overt prestige of Tanzanian street language may be raised through the commodification process – although its covert prestige suffers in response, due to the commercialization of the linguistic forms.

Next, I turn to examples of shifting scapes that explore how hip hop language in East Africa has become altered through its movement from the sphere of the mediascape to the ideoscapes of politics and HIV/AIDS awareness. I present examples from both Kenya and Tanzania to show the range of altered meanings that such shifts can produce.

Hip Hop Intersects with Politics in Kenya

In 2002, Kenyan rappers Gidi Gidi Maji Maji released 'Who Can Bwogo Me?', and the song quickly became the number one song on Kenya's radio charts. Though first titled 'Who Can Bwogo Me?', the song came to be known as 'Unbwogable', a Sheng word that comprises the Dholuo word *bwogo* ('to be shaken') inside an English frame, thus meaning 'un-scare-able'. The song was written as Gidi Gidi Maji Maji's 'comeback' effort after the commercial failure of their first album due to corrupt music industry producers (Nyairo & Ogude, 2005). The first verse of the song voices the rappers' frustration with the music industry, but the lyrics seemed to voice the feelings of many Kenyans who faced daily encounters with bureaucracy, corruption and a decayed economy. In the verse, Maji Maji, one of the singers of the group, asserts his ethnic identity as Luo, and this characteristic is presented as an aspect of perseverance in the lyrics.

'Who Can Bwogo Me?', Gidi Gidi Maji Maji (2002)

What the hell is you looking for
Can a young Luo make money any more
Shake your feet baby girl enango ('what is it'?)
Majimaji nyakwar ondijo ('Maji Maji grandchild of Ondinjo, I am Luo')
Am a Luo but who are you?
What are you?
Who the hell do you think you are?
Do you know me?
Do I know you?
Get the hell out of ma face because hey I am unbwogable
I am unbeatable
I am unsueable
So if you like ma song sing it for me I say

CHORUS
Who can bwogo me
I am unbwogable

The third verse of the song provides Gidi Gidi, the other member of the group, with the chance to advertise his own determination in the face of challenging obstacles. He declares himself to be well known and his music to be lucrative, like a 'hot pepper'. Then, he turns to Dholuo to pronounce his greatness, stating that no one in Kanyamwar or Homabay (Luo-populated districts of Kenya) compares to him.

Listen, nobody can bwogo me
Neither nobody can bwogo this
Gidigidi big name, am saleable
Kama pilipili, yes am terrible ('Like hot peppers')
Kanyamwa homabay ng'ama chalo koda ('in Kanyamwar, Homabay, who is like me?')
Do you know Gidigidi is unbwogable

While this self-praise could be identified as a form of conceit often found in Western-based hip hop and ultimately derived from African American storytelling traditions, Nyairo and Ogude (2005: 237) explain that the Luo group is performing *pakruok* ('self praise'), the act of 'inject[ing] one's social credentials and authority' into a musical performance in order to receive the attention one deserves from the audience. This is a case of what Pennycook and Mitchell (2009) describe as the indigeneity of hip hop when they write, 'It is not so much the case that hip hop merely takes on local characteristics, but rather that *it has always been local*' (Pennycook & Mitchell, 2009: 30). In the case of 'Unbwogable', it becomes impossible to know to what degree the acts of self-aggrandizement are influenced by Western-based hip hop, or how much they represent the indigenous cultural practices of the Luo people.

This multivocality is what seems to have allowed the song to become an anthem for opposition to the ruling party in 2002. That year, Mwai Kibaki, the leader of the opposition parties known as the National Rainbow Coalition (NARC), led a presidential campaign that garnered great optimism as it promised real reforms in a country that had experienced a high degree of corruption under the ruling party, the Kenyan African National Union (KANU). In a pre-election rally, Kibaki shouted to the audience 'We are unbwogable!', and in the months that followed, *Unbwogable* became the slogan for Kibaki's campaign. In an analysis of why a song that promoted the Luo so clearly was politically successful in a nation that has endured decades of tribal politics, Nyairo and Ogude (2005: 239) explain 'This fusing of tongues – English and Luo – is a testament to a new Kenya, one that breaks with the earlier constructed Kenyan past in the sense of separate ethnic identities, and instead attests to the multiple and fluid identities that are increasingly defining postcolonial, particularly urban, Kenya.'

After the song became associated with Kibaki's campaign, the government-regulated radio station (which was overseen by KANU officials) stopped playing the popular song. It moved out of its mediascape, where it was a 'comeback' song for Gidi Gidi Maji Maji and moved into the ideoscape of politics, where it became a 'we will overcome' song for the NARC coalition. Gidi Gidi Maji Maji signed a licensing deal with NARC and the multivocality of *unbwogable* continued to gain new voices. The band produced remixes of the song that rewrote KANU's history, pointing out the corruption of the ruling party during the pre-election months (Nyairo & Ogude, 2005). They also marketed t-shirts and other paraphernalia with the slogan *unbwogable* on it, and these became a very popular way of expressing opposition to the ruling party.

While the word was identified as Sheng and as Luo in its earlier incarnations, *unbwogable* became classified as a form of English due to its circulation (and value) in political spheres of life. In December 2002, Daniel Arap Moi, the nation's long-standing leader, lost to Kibaki. After being sworn in as Kenya's president, Kibaki continued to use the term to praise the *unbwogable* character of the Kenyan people in political speeches. Once the new government was in power, *unbwogable* found its way into parliamentary proceedings, and when the word was questioned by the Speaker as 'unparliamentary language', Vice-President Michael Wamalwa defended its use, arguing that the 'English language is a growing language... Unbwogable captures the mood and soon it will be acceptable' (*East African Standard*, 20 February 2003, cited in Nyairo & Ogude, 2005: 244).

Hip Hop Intersects with Politics in Tanzania

Importantly, when scapes collide, semiotic resources flow in multiple directions. And of course, hip hop lyrics have long been political. In Tanzania, rappers have often criticized government policy and leaders for failing to address the needs of the people in favor of their own reputations and wealth (Perullo, 2005). In one of Tanzania's earliest rap songs, Mr II critiqued the government led by President Benjamin Mkapa. His songs were meant to speak to the average citizen, and so it is no surprise that his lyrics were entirely in Swahili, with some street Swahili expressions.

'Hali Halisi', Mr II (1998)

Naona sura zile zile, viongozi wale wale	I see the same faces, the same leaders
Toka wakati nipo shule mpaka sasa	From primary school until the present
Usicheze na siasa,	Do not play with politics

Siasa ni mchezo mchafu	Politics is a dirty game
Wanataka umaarufu	They just want to be famous
Wanasiasa wa Bongo wengi waongo	Lots of Tanzanian politicians are liars

In July 2010, Mr II (now known as Sugu) filed his papers to run as a member of parliament in the upcoming elections in October 2010, representing Mbeya, his home region (he later won the seat). It is not too surprising that his latest album title also embodied his interest in taking part in social change from a political angle (see Figure 2.6), using the English word VETO to refer to his stance on the state of politics in Tanzania. Though a Swahili expression for 'veto' has been invented by the National Swahili Council of Tanzania (*kuru ya turufu*), it makes sense that Sugu chose the more commonly used English word VETO to title his album, given this word's wide circulation in the area of politics, a domain in which English and Swahili-English code-switching is commonly used. Though his album was already very political due to his critique of the nation's policies and the government, his official act of running for office placed the mediascape of hip hop and the ideoscape of politics more squarely in the same space.

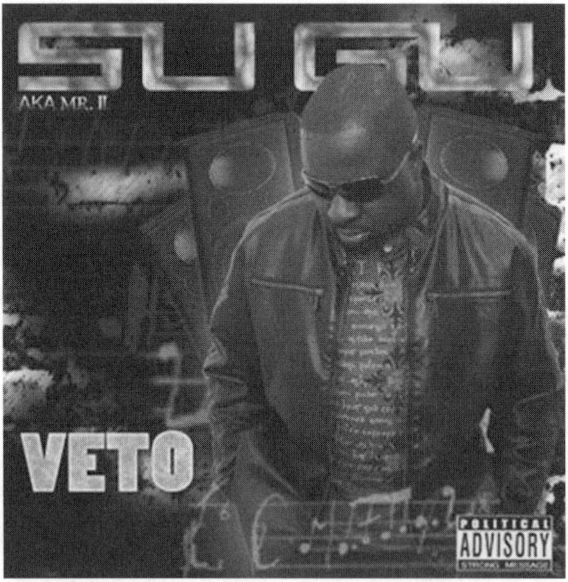

Figure 2.6 Sugu's 2009 album cover

Hip Hop Intersects with HIV/AIDS Education in Tanzania

A final example I will discuss in this chapter is how the already localized language of hip hop has become more hybrid due to being re-scaped through its affiliation with the ideoscape of HIV/AIDS awareness in Tanzania. To illustrate this, I discuss the reterritorialization of English-derived words that refer to young women in Bongo Flava lyrics. I first briefly illustrate how these English-derived terms are used to relate to a man's fantasy world where women are mostly sex objects. Then I explore how male artists use these terms within Swahinglish lyrics to critique these lifestyle choices due to the intersecting scape of HIV/AIDS education.

Masista du and *mademu* as sexual starlets in Bongo Flava

The content of Bongo Flava lyrics vary according to the goals of the artists. Artists such as Mr II/Sugu, Professor Jay and Mwanafalsafa ('Mr Philosopher') sing about social problems like corruption and poverty, while others such as Mchizi Mox, Ngwair and Dully Sykes are best known for songs celebrating drugs, alcohol and sex. In this latter strand of Bongo Flava, known as party music, the lyrics tend to focus on living the 'high life', characterized by the enjoyment of material and sexual pleasures. The language varieties that appear in Bongo Flava include Street Swahili, appropriated forms of African American English (AAE), appropriated forms of Jamaican Creole and various types of blending with English, including code-switching, often referred to by Tanzanians themselves as Swanglish.

One of these words, *sista*, is actually bivalent, or even multivalent, since it can be heard as a Tanzanian English word for 'nun', or as a way to refer to a young woman in Tanzanian English, Swahili or street language. *Sista* is obviously a reterritorialized form of the English word 'sister', but it has more recently acquired the connotations of African American English (AAE) 'sistah', and it can also be interpreted as a calque of Swahili *dada* ('sister'), a common vocative for young women in East Africa. If it comes along with *du* (an interjection particle meaning 'oh'), it immediately becomes Street Swahili, meaning 'hottie' or 'beautiful towngirl' (Reuster-Jahn & Kießling, 2006). The phrase *sista du* is very similar to another English-derived word for young women, *demu* ('dame'). In my observations, *demu* is used in less respectful ways than *sista* or *sista du* and is typically not used to refer to a woman who is within earshot. Nevertheless, young men often use the word to refer to their (non-present) girlfriends or to point out someone else's embarrassing lack of having a girlfriend. Significantly, the word *demu* also gets used in gossip-oriented newspapers involving scandalous stories about sexually loose women.

Rapping about living it up

A great deal of Bongo Flava has used the terms *sista, sista du* and *demu* to sing about a certain kind of modern young woman whose (always urban) lifestyle is marked by spending a great deal of leisure time in nightclubs and expensive bars, seeking the company of well-to-do men, dressing in tight, Western clothing and being sexually liberated. Ngwair's 2005 song 'She Gotta Gwan', whose title makes use of appropriated Jamaican Creole, employs the word *masista du* (pluralized with Swahili plural marker *ma-*) to exalt the beauty of a young woman who stands out in the crowd at a dance club. She is prized for her sexuality, and by the end of the song she is portrayed as willing to go home with a man from the club.

'She Gotta Gwan', Ngwair (2005)

Tukianzia uzuri tu she gotta gwan	If we start with the best, she got it goin on
Tabia, heshima ndio duh she gotta gwan	Personality, respect, yes, she got it goin on
Mpaka kwa **masista du** yeeh nabaki tu kusema	Of all the **sisters**, yeah, I still say,
uuh she gotta gwan	uhh she got it goin on
Sitojali ashatembea na wangapi	I won't care that she's been with many
Kuwa nawe maishani naona bahati	Being with you in life is lucky
. . .	
Nionyeshe zaidi ya nguo zako ulizovaa	Show me more than the clothes you wear
Nionyeshe zaidi ya ngozi yako ya kung'aa	Show me your skin that glistens
Nioneshe kile ambacho kitanipa raha	Show me everything that gives me pleasure
Hey hey hey hey	Hey hey hey hey

Similarly, in Dully Sykes' song 'Ladies Free', *demu* and *sista du* are characterized as sexually aggressive women who enjoy their leisure time in Dar es

Salaam's nightclubs and who take advantage of men with means, such as Sykes himself. The *demu* and *sista du* are part of a hip urban scene in which rappers (Kebi, Jerry & Mr II) and modern living intermingle. Sykes' song makes heavy use of Swahinglish and Street Swahili, two language varieties that strongly convey a cosmopolitan indexicality.

'Ladies Free', Dully Sykes (2004)

Ladies free, wala sijakosa Friday hii	Ladies free, and I haven't missed a Friday
Tena kulikucha wiki hii	Again it's coming this week
Hey yo **mademu** wanajazana kila kona	Hey yo **dames** are packed in every corner
Billicana na Mambo Club	Club Bilicanas and Mambo Club
Hey! hey oh! natoka kaunta ya chini	Hey! Hey oh! I leave the lower counter
nakwenda ya juu	And head upstairs
Nawaona Kebi na Jerry wapo na Mr II	I see Kebi and Jerry who are with Mr II
Kwenye makochi meusi wapo **masister du**	On black couches are some **hot sisters**, oh!
Mmoja ananibomu nimnunulie redbull	One of them asks me to buy her a redbull
Nikaona safi tu ah! mbona poa tu	I thought it was best, so just do it
Nikajiminya mwanaume nikatoa blue	I stopped complaining, and pulled out a blue
Nikamwambia keep change oh baby	I told her keep the change oh baby.

Here, the club scene, the linguistic choices and references to urban commodities like Redbull entextualize *demu* and *sister du* in a particular kind of context. This urban and freewheeling setting is established through the expression 'Ladies Free', through the surrounding thematic content of being in the club and through the juxtaposition of *mademu* and *masister du* with other Street Swahili expressions such as *ananibom* ('she keeps asking me') and *blue* (a 10,000 Shilling note, blue in color) whose meanings are not at all transparent from the English components alone. It is significant that Sykes can tell the young woman who keeps 'bombing' him for a drink to keep the change on a 10,000 shilling note (approximately $9), as this helps to construct Sykes' life of leisure. Even in the expensive club she would have kept at least half of the money as the change, a substantial amount for most Tanzanians.

Interviews with residents of Dar es Salaam confirmed that these words would be used in a positive way if the singers were singing about love, lust and pretty girls. When asked to consider the use of the words that reference women, one young man in secondary school said the following:

> *Mimi nikisema ni demu wangu kwa sisi vijana inamaanisha kwamba fulani ni mpenzi wangu. Halafu tukiongelea 'masista,' sijui, sababu masista ni wale wa kanisani au ni masista duu ambao ni wasichana wale wa club ambao ni wasichana wa kujirusha. Kwa wasichana hawa, wanasema kuna 'kiloose.'*
> For me, if I say my *demu*, for us young people it means something, it means my girlfriend. And if we're saying *masista*, then I don't know, *masista* are those people of church, or there are *masista du* who are the women who go to clubs and dance. To refer to these girls, we say they are 'loose'.

When I asked about the meanings behind these songs, one 25-year-old woman remarked that they did not seem to be very relevant to the current context of Tanzania, given the threat of HIV/AIDS:

> *Nyimbo zao hazilengi jamii yetu ya sasa hivi, kwa mfano hiyo ya Ngwair ya 'She Gotta Gwan'. Kama hapo anaposema kuwa yeye hajali huyo msichana ametembea na wanaume wangapi. Hiyo sidhani kama inatufundisha katika jamii yetu, hasa kwa sasa hivi kuna hili janga la UKIMWI na magonjwa mengi tu ya zinaa.*
> These songs don't target our society of today, for example, Ngwair's song 'She Gotta Gwan'. Like here when he says that he doesn't care that the girl has been with however many men. I don't think that this teaches our society anything, especially now that there is the calamity of AIDS and lots of sexually transmitted diseases.

HIV/AIDS in Tanzania has indeed shifted the social context of Bongo Flava, and this has had an impact on the way that some artists sing about women and sexual relationships. In the next section, I examine the impact of these shifting contexts from 2000–2006, when the Tanzanian government's attention to HIV/AIDS prevention focused a great deal of its efforts on changing behaviors known to spread HIV. I also explore more recent lyrics about women in 2009–2010, when messages about stigma and living positively with HIV had become prevalent in public health campaigns.

Hybridity due to shifting contexts

Party songs focusing on enjoying the good life are still big hits in Bongo Flava, but this use of *sista du* and *demu* now competes with another context which uses these words within a context of critique. Increasing HIV rates in Tanzania and calls from the government and public health sector for hip hop artists to do what they can to battle the disease have paved the way for the mediascape of hip hop to become an educational zone. Public discourses about HIV/AIDS have become much more possible in Tanzania since 1999, when the Tanzanian government declared AIDS a national crisis. It is not surprising that the first popular song to focus on HIV/AIDS in Tanzania, 'Sister Sister' by King Crazy GK, was released in 2000. Other macro-contextual changes during this time promoted public discussions of the disease, including the formation of a governmental organization called the Tanzanian Commission on AIDS that would implement a multisectoral campaign to fight the transmission of HIV.

Next, we see how street-conscious terms for young women become reterritorialized in a context of critique. The new indexicalities are created through using these terms to critique, rather than to celebrate, women's sexual behaviors. In producing and interpreting lyrics, then, artists and their fellow audiences re-entextualize utterances from one set of discourses to another in order to create new meanings.

Masista and *mademu* re-entextualized as behaviors for critique: 2000–2006

In contrast to songs that focus on leisure time and nightlife are songs by artists such as King Crazy GK, whose song titled 'Sister Sister' characterizes *masista* as the target of criticism instead of symbols of desire. In the first part of the song, we see the words 'sister sister' to describe a 'nice girl who got lost' and a 'dear who became disabled', expressions that depict the 'sister' as wayward while also entextualizing the Standard Swahili references for 'nice girl' (*msichana mzuri*) and 'dear' (*mpenzi*) as preferred ways of being. The actions of the sister of turning her back on her parents are described as *akasacrifice* (she then sacrificed), a Swanglish word that shows judgment on the part of the lyricist.

'Sister Sister', King Crazy GK (2000)

Maisha umeyachezea sasa	You've played around with your life
mpenzi unalia	now you cry
Sister sister!	**Sister sister!**

Eeh yo! Nakamata microphone rap	Eeh yo! I grab the microphone (to) rap
Na safari hii Crazy GK	This is the journey of Crazy GK
Siyo kama naimba bali nalia	It's not that I'm singing, I'm crying out
Namlilia **msichana mzuri** aliyepotea	I cry for a **nice girl** who got became lost
Akaitoa shule sadaka sababu ya starehe za muda mfupi	She left school for the offer of good times
Halafu akasacrifice wazazi wake	And then she sacrificed her parents
ili awafuate mabwana	to follow men
Bwana akamkimbia	Her man left her
Mpenzi akawa kiguru na njia	**The dear** became disabled on the way (w/o a man)

The song continues, and the outcome of 'sister' cutting ties with her parents follows. As a result of quitting school and leaving home she gets pregnant again and again, actions which are described in Swahinglish as *amepunch mpenzi, mashine akatega tena* ('She had sex with her lover and she got pregnant again'). The grim consequences of AIDS follow and 'sister' becomes entextualized with a negative set of behaviors as King Crazy GK laments 'Oh, sister sister'.

Wazazi nyumbani akawasusia	She stopped visiting her parents
Akajiona amepunch mpenzi	She punched (had sex) with her lover and the
mashine akatega tena	machine got her (she became pregnant again)
Ni watoto watano sasa anao	She's got five children now
UKIMWI juu ameambulia	and AIDS too
Ohh **sister sister**	Oh **sister sister**

Another popular rapper, Noorah, also critiqued the actions of young, urban women who enjoy the high life in his song 'Ukurusa wa Pili' ('Page two'). The lyrics relate to the female groupies who fawn over him because of his success. A fellow MC chimes in as well, offering comments on Noorah's tale at the end of most verses.

'Ukurasa wa Pili', Noorah (2006)

Attention please

This is another public announcement from MJ Records

Yo ndani ya gari navinjari	Yo in the car I'm hangin
na Prince Dully Sykes	with Prince Dully Sykes
Namuona du! White, simjui	I see her, hey! Light-skinned, I don't know her
Amevaa glasses	She's wearing shades
'Eti mambo!' Safi. 'Samahani,	'What's up?' Nothin. 'Excuse me,
naomba lifti'	can I get a lift?'
Unataka lifti? 'Eeh.' Kapande	You want a lift? 'Yes.' Then take
kitega uchumi	an elevator
'Ai kaka mbona unanijibu majibu	'Oh fella why do you talk to me
ya kihuni'	like a hooligan?'
Hebu toka hapa mtakufa na UKIMWI	From this you will die from AIDS,
nyie **mabinti**	you **daughters**
MC: Jaman	MC: C'mon, people

Here we see the use of AAE 'yo' mixed with Street Swahili such as *navinjari* ('I'm hangin') alongside Swahinglish such as *amevaa glasses* ('wearing (sun)glasses'). The *demu* in this case uses Swahinglish *naomba lifti* herself to ask for a 'lift', an expression which is quite common in Dar es Salaam. Here and throughout the song, Noorah depicts himself as smarter than these girls, using language that is either over their heads because of its streetwise quality, or through simply making fun of them. Like King Crazy GK, Noorah gives advice at the end of the verse to all young women, using the respectful Swahili word *mabinti* ('daughters') to warn them about the threat of HIV/AIDS.

The song continues with explicit critique of *demu*. Like the young woman asking for a lift, these are women who pester Noorah with their interest in him, which he depicts as disingenuous since they only call him when he has just been on tour (and likely to have money). He jokes around with one woman who calls him on the phone, responding to the question *Mbona siku hizi huonekani?* ('Why don't I see you these days?') in a playful manner ('Have I gotten too dark (skinned)?'), and also by pretending that his female caller has confused him with his fellow rapper Ngwair, implying that the woman has relationships with many rappers who she cannot keep straight.

'Halafu kuna **demu** huwa anapenda	Then there's another **dame** who
sana kunizingua	really likes to bug me

Huwa hanitafuti mpaka asikike	She doesn't look for me until she hears
nimetoka tour	I'm off tour
(Rings) Hallo! 'Mbona siku hizi	(rings) Hello? 'Why don't I see you
huonekani?'	these days?'
Nimekuwa mweusi? 'Ah we acha utani.'	Have I gotten too dark? 'Ah, stop joking'
Hivi unajua kwanza unaongea na nani?	Do you know who you called?
'Si Noorah?' Ni Ngwair. 'Basi samahani'	'Not Noorah?' This is Ngwair. 'Excuse me'

Finally, Noorah explicitly ties *mademu* behaviors and HIV/AIDS by ridiculing such *demu* for their actions. In his lyrics he shows his exasperation with young women by stating *Kama ana ngoma unamuongezea gitaa na keyboard na kila kitu* ('If she has AIDS, you can give her a guitar, a keyboard, everything'). Here, *ngoma* literally means 'drum', but it also is a Street Swahili euphemism for sex and also for HIV/AIDS. Noorah exploits this double meaning to mock *mademu* who get infected with HIV by singing about how he'll give them musical instruments to go along with their *ngoma*.

Aaah! Nishajua **mademu** wa	Aah! I know about the **dames**
siku hizi bwana	these days, my friend
Ukitokea nao eti wanakuambia aah!	If you go with them they tell you,
'Mi nna ngoma'	'I have the drum (AIDS)'
Kama ana ngoma unamuongezea gitaa	If she has the drum (AIDS), you can give her aguitar
na keyboard na kila kitu	and a keyboard, everything
Halafu anafungua bendi au vipi	so she can start a band, what do you think?

From 2000–2005 the critique of women's behaviors had become increasingly dominant among hip hop artists. This trend fit well with the many themes in Tanzanian hip hop which have served to critique societal corruption, disarray and change for the worse, which development and modernization seem to have brought about. Perhaps because hip hop is dominated by men, there is a prevalence of discourses in these socially responsible lyrics that puts the burden of sexual morality and sexual health on women's shoulders. Such responsibility is also seen in HIV/AIDS education events in discussions of women's clothing as a major source of lust (*cf*. Higgins, 2010). However, the past few years have seen some changes with regard to discourses of responsibility, at least at the level of public health discourse. While there seems to be little changing in terms of patriarchy or women's rights in Tanzania, this discourse is starting to appear in the realm of popular culture in the form of hip hop lyrics.

Singing about HIV/AIDS in 2009–2010

A survey of 10 top Bongo Flava hits in the past two years that discuss sexual morality and HIV/AIDS shows that women still feature strongly as the main characters in many songs, hence promulgating the indexicality between promiscuous women and the spread of HIV that was established in the earlier years. 'Marehemu' (Jebby, 2010), is a good example of a recent song that fails to challenge this linkage.

Marehemu' ('The deceased'), Jebby (2010)

Dunia haina siri	The world doesn't have any secrets
Leo nimegundua	Today I've discovered that
Wanaopenda ngono	People who like having sex
Mzichunge tabia	They have to control their behavior
Demu ameshaondoka	The **dame** has already left ('died')
Mtaani kuna utata	On the street there is chaos
Ngoma inaonyesha **warembo**	Drum ('AIDS') is targeting the **beauties**
wa huku swazi	of Swahilini here
Idadi ndefu inasubiriwa	There are many more that are expected (to die)
Sijui ni nani, wenyewe mnajijua	I don't know who, they know themselves
Idadi ndefu inasubiriwa	There are many more that are expected (to die)

On the other hand, Z Antony's lyrics in 'Kidole Kimoja' ('One finger'), for example, ask those who cast blame on women to reflect on their own actions as well, and hence, are a refreshing departure from a sole focus on women's behaviors. Moreover, it battles the problem of stigma in Tanzania that is directed toward people living with HIV/AIDS. This stigma is a major focus of more recent public health campaigns in the country (see Figure 2.7 and Figure 2.8).

Figure 2.7 Public service advertisement against discrimination for people living with HIV/AIDS (PLWHA). ('I have HIV. I like to sit at the same desk with my fellow students. Don't ostracize me')

Figure 2.8 A poster which reads, 'Stigma and AIDS. "Let's not ostracize her" so that she can live with hope' (Note, the girl's t-shirt reads 'I am living with hope')

'Kidole Kimoja' ('One finger'), Z Antony (2009)

Alikuwa **msichana** mdogo mzuri	She was a young pretty **girl**
juu yenu	above all
Alikuwa anapenda dini	She liked religion
Anaitwa Sophie	She was called Sophie
Ni mzuri mamii	She was really beautiful
Siku ya kifo chake huyu Sophie	The day she died, Sophie
Alituliza wengi	Left many people speechless
...	
Tulipopata habari mbaya	When we got the bad news
Inasemekana	It was said
Yule **changudoa**, eti ni **miwaya**	That **prostitute**, doesn't she have **'wires' ('AIDS')**
Chakula chabo sana	(Weren't there) many Peeping Toms (watching her have sex)?
Kidole kimoja kwa mwenzako	(Pointing) one finger at your friend
Vidole vitatu kwako	Three fingers (should point at) you
Jichunge mwenyewe	Look after yourself

Similarly, Mrisho Mpoto's song 'Bora Ukapime' ('You better get tested') aligns with many public health campaign efforts to encourage Tanzanians to get tested for HIV in order to prevent the further spread of the disease. 'Bora Ukapime' is essentially Mpoto's advice to his fans to learn their sero-status in order to prevent spreading HIV unknowingly and so that they take good care of themselves. The song is also missing woman-centric themes, which is likely due to the main message of the song being that knowing one's status will lead to less risky behavior (such as having sex with sexually promiscuous women).

'Bora Ukapime ('You better get tested'), Mrisho Mpoto (2009)

Twende ukapime	Let's go get tested
Ili kuhusu mashaka uliyonayo	In order to address your worries
Ukipata mafua unaugua mara mbili	If you get a cold you'll get sick twice as badly
Ukipungua uzito kwa ajili ya	If you lose weight
Kufululiza night	Night after night
Na kutokula vizuri unachanganyikiwa	And (if you) don't eat well you'll be confused

Kwa kuwa hujijui	Because you won't know your condition
...	
Ni kheri ndugu yangu	It's a blessing my friend
Usipokuwa na virusi	If you don't have the virus
Lakini ukikutwa navyo	But if you find that you have it
Si shari, si mwisho wa uhai	It's not evil, it's not the end of (your) life
...	
Bora ukapime	(You) better get tested
Ujue	So that you know
Uwe huru	So that you can be free

The point to be made in examining the shifts in language across one decade of hip hop songs penned about HIV/AIDS is not so much to explore how different kinds of English or Swahili relate to social changes, but to highlight how intersecting scapes from elsewhere bring with them new foundations for making relevant certain types of language. In the world of East African hip hop, artists continue to struggle economically due to difficulties with their producers and limited opportunities to tour. Therefore, it is not hard to see that their art may sometimes be 'compromised' by opportunities to compose a song for World AIDS Day, and to be disseminated on a CD sponsored by an international non-governmental organization. Songs about living responsibly are also looked upon favorably by many radio stations, and hence may receive more airtime than songs that are too risqué for the relatively conservative government agencies which regulate the airwaves. Perhaps more than in the wealthier parts of the world, the financescape of producing music in East Africa clearly contributes to artists' decisions about lyrics, musical styles and video content.

Conclusion

In spite of increasingly narrow language policies around the world that focus on the utility of Standard English as the language of globalization, language users in East Africa and all corners of the globe continue to create new forms of expression through reterritorializing and re-localizing English. Instead of focusing on language as the starting point for theorizing and describing the use of English, however, this chapter has argued that sociolinguists need to pay more attention to the ways that new spatial flows of people, ideas, monies and technology surrounding language create new constellations for English. This means that hybridity can better be explained by examining the flows *underneath* language, where intersecting scapes produce new contexts which then have an effect on language.

In exploring hybridity underneath language, it is important to remember that these new formations are not necessarily the first instances of localization, however. In each case, reterritorialization of Western-based hip hop had already taken place in East African hip hop before this mediascape intersected with other scapes. What will be fascinating to see is what future hybridities will emerge when these scapes continue to collide.

References

Alim, H.S. (2006) *Roc the Mic Right: The Language of Hip Hop Culture*. New York and London: Routledge.

Appadurai, A. (1990) Disjuncture and difference in the global cultural economy. *Theory, Culture, and Society* 7 (2–3), 295–310.

Appadurai, A. (1996) *Modernity at Large: Cultural Dimensions of Globalization*. Minneapolis: University of Minnesota Press.

Bakhtin, M.M. (1986 [1978]) *Speech Genres and Other Late Essays* (V.W. McGee, trans.). Austin: University of Texas Press.

Deleuze, G. and Guattari, F. (1972) *Anti-Oedipus* (R. Hurley, M. Seem and H.R. Lane trans.). London and New York: Continuum, 2004. Vol. 1 of *Capitalism and Schizophrenia*. 2 vols 1972–1980. Translation of L'Anti-Oedipe. Paris: Les Editions de Minuit.

Fishman, J. (1967) Bilingualism with and without diglossia; Diglossia with and without bilingualism. *Journal of Social Issues* 23, 29–38.

Higgins, C. (2009) *English as a Local Language: Post-Colonial Identities and Multilingual Practices*. Bristol: Multilingual Matters.

Higgins, C. (2010) Discursive enactments of the World Health Organization's policies: Competing cultural models in Tanzanian HIV/AIDS prevention. *Language Policy* 9 (1), 65–85.

Kachru, Y. and Nelson, C. (2006) World Englishes and language acquisition. In B.B. Kachru, Y. Kachru and C. Nelson (eds) *World Englishes in Asian Contexts* (pp. 79–92). Hong Kong: Hong Kong University Press.

Kachru, B.B., Kachru, Y. and Nelson, C. (eds) (2006) *The Handbook of World Englishes*. Malden, MA: Wiley-Blackwell.

Kingo (2001). Dar es Salaam, Tanzania: Gaba Ltd.

Kirkpatrick, A. (2007) *World Englishes:* Implications for International Communication and English Language Teaching. Cambridge: Cambridge University Press.

Murata, K. and Jenkins, J. (eds) (2009) *Global Englishes in Asian Contexts: Current and Future Debates*. London: Palgrave.

Nyairo, J. and Ogude, J. (2005) Popular music, popular politics: Unbwogable and the idioms of freedom in Kenyan popular music. *African Affairs* 104 (415), 225–249.

Oscar, J. (2007) Besela. In J. Oscar (ed.) *Mahaba ya Pwanis* (vol. 8, p. 24). Dar es Salaam, Tanzania: Full Talents High Quality Entertainment.

Park, J.S.Y. (2009) *The Local Construction of a Global Language: Ideologies of English in South Korea*. Berlin: Mouton.

Pennycook, A. (2003) Global Englishes, Rip Slyme, and performativity. *Journal of Sociolinguistics* 7 (4), 513–533.
Pennycook, A. (2007) *Global Englishes and Transcultural Flows*. London and New York: Routledge.
Pennycook, A. and Mitchell, T. (2009) Hip hop as dusty foot philosophy: Engaging locality. In S. Alim, A. Ibrahim and A. Pennycook (eds) *Global Linguistic Flows: Hip Hop Cultures, Youth Identities, and the Politics of Language* (pp. 25–42). New York: Taylor & Francis.
Perullo, A. (2005) Hooligans and heroes: Youth identity and hip-hop in Dar es Salaam, Tanzania. *Africa Today* 4 (51), 75–101.
Reuster-Jahn, U. and Kießling, R. (2006) *Lugha ya mitaani* in Tanzania. The poetics and sociology of a young urban style of speaking, with a dictionary comprising 1100 words and phrases. *Swahili Forum* 13, 1–196.
Tsang, W.K. and Wong, M. (2004) Constructing a shared 'Hong Kong identity' in comic discourses. *Discourse & Society* 15 (6), 767–785.
Woolard, K. (1998) Simultaneity and bivalency as strategies in bilingualism. *Journal of Linguistic Anthropology* 8, 3–29.

3 Hybridity in the Linguistic Landscape: Democratizing English in India

Rani Rubdy

Introduction

The advent of globalization, technological advances and India's 'satellite invasion', in conjunction with India's economic reforms in the 1990s, have engendered a massive social transformation. One consequence of economic liberalization and the opportunities it opened up for wealth production has been a growing middle class driven by intense social aspirations and consumerist orientations. The increasing presence of translocal billboards and signage advertising global as well as local products and services, semiotically packaged as global lifestyle products in the linguistic landscape of many of India's larger urban cities, is clear evidence of this social transformation, often characterized by the expanding use of English. Whereas traditionally the uses of English and the indigenous languages were kept fairly apart, the intriguing mix of languages, scripts and modalities in the domains of advertising, journalism and public signage in recent times has fostered an uninhibited and fertile expression of English-based hybridity in the linguistic landscape of these cities – a result, no doubt, of the penetration of English into most public domains of society. The increased use of multilingual signage involving English reflects, on the one hand, efforts to construct transcultural consumerist and cosmopolitan identities 'through symbolic displays of what selfhood or how selfhood is reflected' (Stroud & Mpendukana, 2009: 366) and, on the other, the operation of what has been termed English 'linguistic fetish' (Kelly-Holmes, 2005: 22), the symbolic use of English to invoke powerful associations of prestige, status, glamour, sophistication and modernity. While aspects of globalization and imperialism surely form part of these market-driven efforts, I suggest the local is quite resilient as well; the hybrid formations in fact manifest a refusal to buy too far into the logic of global commodification, in a move to both accommodate its transcultural flows and at the same time anchor its worldliness to local practices, values and worldviews.

Drawing on data from public signage and advertising in the linguistic landscape of three Indian cities, the chapter examines hybridization resulting from the strategic use of English alongside Hindi and Marathi as the cultural expression of an alternate reality, 'a third space' (Bhabha, 1994), a new class identity that is simultaneously local and global, traditional and modern, indigenous and cosmopolitan, enacted for and by the English-knowing bilingual middle class of people no longer bound by their traditions but free to creatively rework and remake their inherited sociolinguistic resources (Bhatt, 2008). Following Bhatt, I suggest that the third space is a discursive space which neutralizes the specific indexicalities of the participating languages, erases boundaries and erodes the colonial inflections in the 'Englishness' of Indian English (p. 185). Thus the hybrid formations (i) represent a toolkit for English-speaking Indian bilinguals to negotiate the global-local interface by enabling them to navigate between global identification and local cultural practices, and at the same time; (ii) function as a site for voicing the particular inclinations of middle-class youth towards subverting their disciplining in Standard English and breaking away from the habitus of its canons in ways that democratize and de-center English.

Conceptual Framework

The study is undertaken from the vantage point of Appadurai's (1996: 11) central argument that rather than being a story of cultural homogenization, 'globalization is a deeply historical, uneven and even *localising* process'. Indeed, globalization does not necessarily imply homogenization or Americanization because 'different societies appropriate the materials of modernity differently' (Appadurai, 1996: 17). This more nuanced view contends that people have the capacity to resist homogenization by engaging in what Pennycook (1994) has termed 'writing back', the process by which users of English around the world appropriate English and make it work for their various personal, professional and political purposes. In this view, transcultural flows unleashed by globalization are not so much processes of homogenization as part of a reorganization or reconstitution of the local. As

Canagarajah (1999: 2) puts it, '[T]he intention is not to reject English, but to *reconstitute* it in more inclusive, ethical, and democratic terms'.

A related perspective on the processes of cultural exchange triggered by transcultural flows comes from Homi Bhabha's (1994) discussion of 'hybrid identities' or 'third space', wherein postcolonial subjects by virtue of living in the slippage between dominance and subordination are said to possess a 'double vision' or 'in-betweenness' that results in the creation of new languages and new possibilities. As Papastergiadis (2000) explains it:

> ... hybridity ... invariably acknowledges that identity is constructed through negotiation of difference, and the presence of fissures, gaps and contradictions is not necessarily a sign of failure ... the concept also stresses that hybridity is not the combination, accumulation, fusion or synthesis of various components, but an energy field of different forces. Hybridity is not confined to a cataloguing of difference. Its 'unity' is not found in the sum of its parts, but emerges from a process of opening up what Homi Bhabha has called a 'third space', within which other elements encounter and transform each other. (Papastergiadis, 2000: 170)

It has been suggested that the third space opened up by such cultural encounters is a 'third culture in its own right' (Kramsch, 1993: 9). Bhatt (2008), for instance, finds the concept especially relevant in the context of postcolonial and (late-)modern India, as a theoretical construct

> to refer to a semiotic space between competing cultural collectives – e.g., colonized-colonizer, indigenous-foreign, local-global, traditional-modern – where cultural identity across differences of class (English bilinguals-other bilinguals), gender roles (male-female), and cultural values (traditional/local-modern/global) is negotiated, setting up new structures of sociolinguistic authority and new socio-political initiatives. (Bhatt, 2008: 178)

Specifically, he argues that the third space is a discursive space 'where two systems of identity representation converge and are co-modified and commodified in response to the global-local tensions on the one hand, and the dialogically constituted identities, formed through resistance and appropriation, on the other' (Bhatt, 2008: 178). Hybridity thus challenges and problematizes essentialist dichotomies and identities and so leads to the restoring of agency and enfranchisement.

These insights into the complex and dynamic two-way flow between the local and the global are captured well by Robertson's (1992) concept of 'glocalization', which emphasizes 'an understanding of globalization as a process which is grounded in the local even while taking into account global perspectives and actions' (Alsagoff, 2010: 110). Initiated as a Japanese business practice, *dochakuka*, which involves the customization of a standardized product in the global market to suit local cultures, glocalization is characterized by the simultaneity – the co-presence – of both universalizing and particularizing tendencies which operate to create a fluid push-pull effect. In other words, glocalization 'foregrounds the understanding that in the dichotomies of the global-local, universalist-particularist, homogeneity-heterogeneity, *indigenization* is [simply] the other side of the coin of the *homogenizing* aspects of globalization' (Alsagoff, 2010: 110, citing Robertson 1997, emphasis in original).

The concept of 'glocalization' highlights the new direction that speakers are taking using the resources of English in its global and local forms – namely, enacting hybrid cultural identities deriving simultaneously from the connectedness of English to global 'imagined communities' (Anderson, 1991) and its entanglement in local conditions – in a way that provides a heuristic 'that takes into account the local, national, regional and global contexts of intercultural communicative processes' (Kraidy, 1999: 472). It follows then, as Appadurai reminds us, that locality is produced, not given, a result of particular ways of construing identity, 'a phenomenological property of social life, a structure of feeling that is produced by particular forms of intentional activity and that yields particular sorts of material effects' (Appadurai, 1996: 182).

Given the intentional, agentive nature of the way locality is constructed, the study attempts to explore the following: in what ways do the hybridized signs and texts in the data constitute enactments of locality performed by global and local actors seeking to appropriate, negotiate or resist global transcultural flows? Furthermore, what affordances in terms of the symbolic system of signifiers available in the local linguistic environment facilitate the enactment of such (re)appropriation and negotiation?

Methodology and Research Context

It has been suggested that the contextual features of situations, the different interactions and identities that are possible within them, and the way they shape and are shaped by textual practices are what contribute to translating *space* into (particular) *place*, that is, 'real, material and symbolic spaces in which people anchor a dense complex of symbolic and material practices' (Blommaert *et al.*, 2005: 206, cited in Stroud & Mpendukana, 2009). One way in which *place* is constituted is through the language used in signage, in speakers' public displays, performances and interactions – that is, *the linguistic landscape (LL)*, defined by Landry and Bourhis (1997: 25) as

> [T]he language of public road signs, advertising billboards, street names, place names, commercial shop signs, and public signs on government buildings ... of a given territory, region or urban agglomeration.

Adopting Landry and Bourhis' definition and drawing inspiration from previous and ongoing studies in the now flourishing field of LL (Gorter, 2006; Shohamy & Gorter, 2009; Jaworski & Thurlow, 2010), the study examines hybrid language use in the LL in three cities in the Indian state of Maharashtra: Mumbai, a metropolitan city and India's largest business and entertainment capital, Pune, an educational hub fairly cosmopolitan in character, and the smaller, more provincial town of Kolhapur. The data for this study, most of which were gathered between 2009–2011 for a larger study on multilingual signage to ascertain the differential patterns of English language presence in these cities, comprise an eclectic range of text types representing linguistic and cultural hybridity and come from photographs of shop signs, billboards and advertisements drawn from the main commercial streets in these cities; excepting the Amul butter advertisements which were taken from online sources. Unlike the predominantly survey-based quantitative approaches initiated in earlier work, however, the study adopts a more qualitative, discourse/genre- and context-specific analysis of language in landscape text. Content analysis of the signage comprised two stages: the first stage involved analyzing texts in relation to their linguistic features; the second stage analyzed the content – both informational and visual – with reference to the specific sociocultural knowledge assumed on the part of sign producers and consumers at an interpretive level.

Landscapes are not simply physical spaces but are discursive and often ideologically charged constructions. Studies of LL therefore generally start with the assumption that signage is indexical of more than just the ostensible message of the sign. Of particular relevance to our analysis of hybrid language use as a response to globalization is the role of signage as the discursive terrain across which the struggle between different codes of meaning construction takes place in a way that forges links between landscape and identity, social order and power. Although few studies have explored hybridity as the central focus of their analysis of LL, several studies, (Bhatia, 2000; Piller, 2001; Reh, 2004; Martin, 2006; Higgins, 2009), some more critical in approach than others, have examined how global and local identities are constructed in multilingual advertisements and media texts that reveal, reproduce and sometimes resist social order. In approaching the questions I have raised around the dynamics of hybrid language practices in the LL of the three cities under consideration, I build upon such current and ongoing work in the evolving field of LL that critically reviews theorizations and methodologies of space in the construction of global and local identities.

A discussion of the linguistic context of data collection becomes necessary for understanding the role of hybrid codes in landscape signage. The local language of the state of Maharashtra is Marathi. Although both Hindi and English are official languages of India and appear together with Marathi in official signs provided by governmental organizations, in line with India's language policy known as the Three Language Formula, it is English that has a stronger presence in the commercial streets of these cities, particularly Mumbai and Pune, which have a larger consumer base of English literate bilinguals than Kolhapur. English appears alongside Marathi in a large volume of *duplicating* writing, in which identical information is presented in both languages, as well as *complementary* signage, in which different parts of a text are presented in different languages, thus presuming individual multilingualism in the target readership (Reh, 2004). Whereas English-only signage is abundant in the commercial streets, the curious positioning about Hindi is it has little presence in non-official signage in these cities. With the exception of billboards advertising Bollywood movies, the exclusive use of Hindi is rare, indicating higher status and acceptance of English over Hindi among the Indian middle class. Marathi-only signs, on the other hand, are prevalent in many non-official sites. In bilingual shop signs and street signs, the use of English alongside Marathi is more common, indicative of a functional allocation of the languages in the production of locality. However, Hindi becomes very visible when used in conjunction with English, particularly in advertisements associated with products of multinational brands targeted at a wider pan-national clientele, and in producing a flavor of youth culture through *Hinglish*, widely spoken by Indian youth on college campuses and in informal talk on the streets, as reflected in much of the data in our study.

Constructing Locality in the Linguistic Landscape

A marketing strategy that has gained immense popularity in metropolitan cities in India, such as Mumbai and Pune, is that of language mixing, mainly in the form of code-switching to appeal to urban youth by using the language they use – a mix of English with Hindi or Marathi. This trend has been especially prevalent in advertising, with some of the major international brands having moved away from the exclusive use of English in non-English dominant countries in what is termed 'diversity marketing'

(Piller, 2003: 177), as well as in an effort to curb what is perceived as Western influence through global media in certain markets (Bhatia, 2000).

English matrix with Hindi words

A common manifestation of English-based hybridity in advertising is the seamless juxtaposing of Hindi lexical items or morphological elements within an English matrix construction. As noted also in Piller (2001) and Higgins (2009), such multilingual advertising is often characterized by the combination of two or more languages that creates new meanings which are not simply the product of two monolingual capacities combined but tend to involve a greater degree of linguistic blending at the lexical and even morpho-syntactic levels, demanding hybrid literacies.

An interesting example of such a blend is the Virgin mobile advertisement posted in Mumbai seen in Figure 3.1, comprising an attention grabbing, alliterative caption 'bindass BUDDIES' in giant-sized fonts and a less ostentatious but equally provocative hybridized slogan printed below the brand name that urges the consumer to 'Think ***hatke***', that is, 'think out of the box' or 'dare to think differently' (in bold font and italicization for emphasis). The use of the Hindi slang 'bindass' ('cool and carefree', or 'with reckless abandon') as an adjective in an English [modifier + Head] noun phrase construction not only echoes the intimacy, solidarity and rapport of informal teen talk in the local context but simultaneously creates an image that is modern, irreverent and 'cool', clearly targeting a youthful audience.

The visual cues in the graphics, a set of pencils and a note pad, ostensibly bearing the conventional male and female symbols, reinforce this image of college-going youth and suggest that the 'buddies' referenced in the advertisement may not be 'just friends' in some platonic sense but most likely

Figure 3.1 Hindi-English code-mixing in a Virgin mobile advertisement in Mumbai

'boyfriends' and 'girlfriends'. The message implied in the advertisement is that by subscribing to Virgin mobile clients can chat 'bindass' ('to their heart's content' or 'with happy abandon') with their female/male 'buddies'. The bilingual coinage maintains the concept of 'friend' while adding the meaning of 'being in a romantic relationship that is fun and free of care', and, by implication, of indulging their proclivity to talk to their heart's content. The hybrid elements in the phrase 'bindass BUDDIES' thus acquire a new set of connotations when combined together than when used singly in each of the languages from which they are drawn.

Even more inventive is the Lay's potato chips advertisement in Figure 3.2, which exemplifies hybridization at the morphosyntactic level, wherein the slogan, 'Be a little Dillogical' has the Hindi noun 'Dil' as a prefix to the English adjective 'logical' in constructing the neologism, 'Dillogical' (on the analogy of 'illogical'). Not least because it inverts the canonical [Adjective + Noun] structure of English noun phrases, but because of the ingenious way it exploits the emotional appeal of 'Dil' ('heart'), a word that has powerful affective connotations associated with 'young love' in the Indian consciousness, deriving from its sumptuous use in Bollywood song lyrics and the passionate *gazals* of Hindi and Urdu poetry. The incorporation of the prefix 'Dil', then, is meant to convey a simple message: 'Listen to your heart and let it win over your head for a change!' The linguistic hybridity in this coinage maintains the concept of 'illogical' while adding the subtle nuance of 'being guided by one's heart'. Consumers are thus artfully persuaded to suspend hard logic and rational thought and give in to what their heart tells them through this slogan which currently appears on every bag of Lay's potato chips in the Indian retail market. Drawing on Bakhtin's (1981, cited in Piller, 2001) notion of dialogism

Figure 3.2 Hindi-English fusion in the pan-Indian Lay's brand advertisement

or double-voicedness, the 'voice' of reason may be said to come in English, while the 'voice' of the heart comes in Hindi. As Higgins notes (2009: 122), such texts not only demand literacy among consumers in both languages, but they demand hybrid literacies to interpret the dialogical relationship that the use of the two languages produce.

Hindi matrix with English words

Quite the opposite trend, of English lexical elements in a Hindi matrix, though still in roman script, has also been gaining ground, as displayed in Figure 3.3. The advertisement of a lifestyle product, McDonald's Happy Price Menu, photographed in a shop window in Mumbai, closely mimics the code-switching practices characteristic of Hinglish, the seamless blending of English words with Hindi, used by many school and university students as a 'cool' way to speak. The body copy comprises three statements, each describing a scenario warranting the celebration of the reader's achievement of some sort, by consuming the food items displayed on the menu.

(1) Girlfriend se pehli baar argument jeeta.
('Won an argument with my girlfriend for the first time')
(2) Pehli baar bina copy kiye pass hua.
('Passed (the exams) for the first time without copying/cheating')
(3) Aaj pehli baar perfect parking ki
('Parked perfectly for the first time today')

The message highlighted (in capitals) by the slogan in the last panel 'Har chhoti khushi ka celebration' ('Celebration of every small pleasure') translates as McDonald's meals being 'a great way to celebrate every small joy of life'.

Figure 3.3 The use of Hinglish in a McDonald's advertisement in a shop window in Mumbai

In the slogan, Hindi fulfills the informational function by carrying the message; English plays an identity enhancing role through its associations with quality, modernity, glamour and being cool. It should be noted that the English words embedded in the text ('argument', 'pass', 'copy', 'parked', 'perfect' and 'celebration') do not cover lexical gaps but are now well-established loanwords that have found their way into most Indian languages and are an inherent part of a bilingual's creativity. Besides asserting the advertiser's creativity and playfulness, this strategy fosters inclusiveness by ensuring that the message is intelligible to the large groups of Indian consumers for whom English is not a dominant language.

The references to passing exams reinforces the image of the reader as a college student who also has the affluence to live a desirable lifestyle, expressed in terms of having a girlfriend and a car as well as a passion for enjoying the good things of life.

Expression of cultural hybridity through conceptual content

A good example of the kind of fusion between global cosmopolitan trends and local processes and practices engendered by cultural interchange is the billboard advertising a TV show in Figure 3.4, photographed alongside a bustling shopping mall in Pune. The TV show, titled 'Kaun banegi Shah Rukh ki favourite cheerleader?' ('Who wants to be Shah Rukh's favourite cheerleader?'), pertains to a competition held for cheerleaders aspiring to participate in the cricketing events hosted by the Indian Premier League (IPL) known as *Twenty20*. Twenty20 is a relatively recent improvisation of the game of cricket, which limits each team to a set of 20 overs (an over is a set of six balls) instead of the 50-over World Cup and traditional five-day test matches. A major attraction of the highly commercialized Twenty20 game is the endorsement of the teams by well-known Bollywood actors, which has boosted spectator interest, increased the excitement and glitz and intensified the star status of both cricket players and its Bollywood star sponsors. It is to icons from these two platforms that the Indian youth has begun to look to for inspiration, lifestyles, trends and so on. In this particular case, the sponsor in question is no less a national icon than the popular Bollywood actor Shah Rukh Khan. The competition winner is the cheerleader he picks as his favorite.

The billboard not only depicts a coalescence of India's two main obsessions – cricket and Hindi commercial cinema, popularly known as Bollywood – it also reflects an interplay of global-local dimensions at a number of levels of contemporary Indian culture that transcends these dichotomies. For one thing, as a sport that is English in its origin, cricket epitomizes the most powerful condensation of Victorian elite values. Yet the

Figure 3.4 A billboard in Pune advertising a cheerleader competition on India's NDTV

sport has become profoundly indigenized and decolonized in India, 'unyoked' as it were from its Englishness by the way its terminology has been drawn into the world of the vernacular languages, helped no less by the media. At the same time, the vernacularization of cricket in this manner has played a crucial role in socializing non-urban Indians into the cosmopolitan culture of cricket, leading to the growth of cricket consciousness and cricket excitement among Indians of all classes and interests (Appadurai, 1996).

A further layer of internationalization has been introduced into the 20-over cricket format, itself a modern morphology of the sport, by the recent incorporation of cheerleaders (even though hotly debated as the importing of American-style razzmatazz) in a world of competitive and commoditized sport, lending new power to the spectacle of this global sport by sensationalizing events surrounding it. What it does, in Appadurai's (1996: 103) words, is to 'place cricket in a splendid world of semi-cosmopolitan glitz, in which cricket provides the textual suture for a much more diverse collage of materials having to do with modern lifestyles and fantasies'. The billboard in Figure 3.4 thus embodies a multiple layering of global-local, cosmopolitan-regional, modern-traditional and new-old interfaces, representing a fine tension between global cultural reproduction and forces of indigenization.

Bilingual aural rhyming

Another favored strategy in advertising, especially jingles, is that of bilingual rhyming, which typically involves rhyming between an English lexical item and a Marathi or Hindi word, as reflected in the slogan in Figure 3.5, posted by the National Egg Coordination Committee (NECC) at a roadside bus stop in Pune.

Figure 3.5 Advertisement of the NECC at a bus stop in Pune

The slogan, 'Sunday ho ya Monday, roj khao ande ...' ('Be it Sunday or Monday, eat eggs everyday') is in a Hindi matrix with 'Sunday' and 'Monday' embedded in English, rendered memorable by the rhyming of 'Monday' with the Hindi 'ande' (eggs). The slogan typifies common usage among most educated Indian speakers in their preference for English terms in referring to the days of the week (or the months of the year) even when communicating in the regional languages.

Barring the slogan, the rest of the advertisement is in English, obviously targeted at the English-educated middle-class homemaker ('Mother Nature's gift to mothers'), many of whom have adopted Western eating habits in their homes as part of their daily breakfast menu in place of local, regional breakfast meals that are more elaborate and take considerably longer to cook. The advertisement thus nicely balances the multiple identities of the middle-class working woman, employing English to appeal to the concerns of the health-conscious middle-class Indian homemaker open to modern cosmopolitan lifestyles ('The tastiest multi-vitamin capsule in the world'), while promoting the sale of eggs, a West-based food product, with a slogan grounded in Hindi that persuasively rhymes with the English words embedded within it as a localizing strategy.

The use of hybridized scripts to construct unconventional spellings

The code-mixing is not only of vocabulary and syntax but also of scripts, wherein elements from two distinct language scripts are combined into a single text or phrasal structure to produce unconventional spellings in various inventive ways. The Devanagari script, closely associated with Sanskrit, is the script used for writing both Hindi and Marathi. One of its characteristics is that the letters are strung together with a distinctive horizontal bar that is drawn across the top of each word. The examples that follow draw upon roman and Devanagari scripts to form a visible orthographic amalgam, distinctly stylized in a way that would not fail to catch the bilingual reader's attention.

Confining our analysis to the signboard at the lower right of Figure 3.6, we observe the eye-catching hybrid orthographic amalgam, 'Utsav' ('festival'), the Marathi name of a shop in Pune. As a cognate derived from Sanskrit, one would ordinarily expect the word to be transcribed in Devanagari; yet the resources of both the Devanagari and roman script are exploited in an attempt to construct a visible representation of the vernacular pronunciation through unconventional spelling. Only the first letter, representing the sound [u], is in Devanagari; the rest of the spelling uses lower case English letters, stylized according to Devanagari conventions – the horizontal bar drawn across at the top and the double vertical bars flanking the shop name further serving to localize the sign. The total image constructed is that of an entirely Marathi word, effectively 'de-Anglicizing' and 'domesticating' the English elements within it.

The fundamental principle of Devanagari is that each letter represents a consonant which carries an inherent vowel *a* [ə]. Vowels other than *a* [ə] are written with diacritics. Thus from क *ka* we get के *ke,* कु *ku,* की *kī,* का *kā,* and so on. Figure 3.7 depicts a shop front showing duplicated signage (Reh, 2004), that is, the shop name 'Mochi' is displayed in both English and Marathi. But

Figure 3.6 A stylized Marathi-English script on a shop sign in Pune (bottom right)

Figure 3.7 Fusion of Devanagari and roman script on a shop front in Pune

although the English version on the left is in the roman script and follows the conventions of English capitalization (the larger font used for 'm'), it is quite strikingly modeled on the Devanagari script, as is clear from the horizontal bar drawn across the top and the use of Devanagari diacritics that mimic the Marathi equivalent on the right. The resulting stylized version of the English language shop name is thus rendered a hybrid mix of the roman alphabetic system with Devanagari diacritics, in the process subverting both the orthographical conventions of English and the phonological principles underlying Devanagari.

The selection of the shop name itself is rather unusual for an upscale shoe shop located in an expensive commercial mall in Pune such as this one, considering that 'mochi' (meaning 'shoemaker' or 'cobbler') is an occupational term traditionally imbued with associations of lower caste status. In times of rigid caste-driven segregation, the humble 'mochi' sat by the dusty roadside in a makeshift shack plying his trade, approached solely for his pedestrian services. The choice of the term 'mochi' for an upscale shop name is clearly a deliberate marketing strategy to conjure up folk associations of the past in an attempt to juxtapose the glamour, chic and sophistication of the modern day products sold in the shop, symbolizing modernity and a cosmopolitan consumerist lifestyle, with the local ethnic authenticity of times gone by, for particular effect.

English lexical items transliterated in Devanagari script

A common form of localization is the transcribing of English shop names exclusively in Devanagari, without including the English version.

The Devanagari signage in Figure 3.8, which reads 'Video Junction', the name of a video shop in Kolhapur, exemplifies this form of localization. English shop names transliterated into Devanagari were particularly visible in the provincial town of Kolhapur compared to the cosmopolitan centers of Pune and Mumbai: 'Video Parlor', 'Beauty Parlor', 'Fashion Centre', 'Fashion House', 'Hair Cutting Saloon', 'National Light House', 'Sweet Corner', 'Cake Shop', 'Silver Palace', 'Jewelry Palace', 'Jewelry House', 'Delux Tools' 'Classic Video Games', 'Monarch Digital ', 'Jumbo Color Zerox', 'Nice Price', 'Right Choice', 'High Point', and many more. Yet other transliterated examples displayed a combination of English and Marathi words (for example, 'Kolhapuri Chappal (slip-ons) House', 'Utkrusht (Excellent) Leather Works'). This type of signage is obviously tailored for speakers who, though not literate in English, have sufficient passive knowledge of the language to recognize them in their spoken form and comprehend their meaning. The utilization of Devanagari, presumably to make the shop signs intelligible to a larger customer base, allows shop owners to still use the global resources provided by English, while reinforcing inclusiveness and locality.

This is in contrast to advertising that exhibits 'fake multilingualism', which fetishes languages for their idealized symbolic values (Higgins, 2009: 116), as reported in several studies where for advertising purposes consumers need not even understand the foreign language that is used, as long as they recognize the connotations that it is associated with. In such advertisements foreign languages are not used for their *communicative* value, but are purely emblematic, used for their *symbolic* value.

Figure 3.8 English shop name in Devanagari script on a signboard in Kolhapur

Figure 3.9 Localized English shop name in Devanagari in Kolhapur

The signboard in Figure 3.9, which reads 'Shri Jewel Palace', from a shop selling silverware and jewelry in Kolhapur, exhibits a strategy that further localizes and hybridizes the text. Localization in Figure 3.9 is achieved not just by the unique way in which the Sanskritized symbol 'Shri' is juxtaposed with the English 'jewel palace', but also by the prominence given to this symbol which has a deep-rooted significance as a harbinger of good fortune and a marker of auspicious beginnings in the Marathi cultural consciousness. Respectful of traditional Marathi textual practice, the symbol is accorded the initial position in the signage, the extra large font size magnifying its presence and foregrounding its special significance in the local ethno-cultural ethos.

The mixing of scripts to create unconventional spellings, the transliteration of English into Devanagari, and the use of ethno-cultural symbols in our data all produce locality by highlighting attachment to local identity while maintaining translocal orientations in much the same way as do the hybrid blends, neologisms and the Hinglish code-mixed texts in the international brand advertisements examined above.

Wordplay, allusion, irony and intertextuality: The Amul Ads

This section focuses on wordplay, allusion and intertextuality in Hindi-English hybrid advertisements by Amul, a leading Indian dairy production company whose genesis in a vast cooperative network has symbolized the triumph of indigenous technology, and whose billboard advertising campaigns provide many interesting, intelligent and amusing examples of hybridization.

The Amul butter advertising campaign, implemented primarily through the use of billboards at strategic places in India's urban and suburban landscapes, has been India's longest running campaign and forms part of the collective memory of a large number of Indians. Over the last 40 years, these advertisements have emerged as a communication tool that comments on a range of current events that include politics, television, films, celebrities, cricket, the economy, the environment, festivals, foreign affairs, the internet, kids, lifestyles, music, sports, strikes, and various other aspects of urban life.

The Amul advertisements have a simple template, comprising a header positioned at the top, a copy comprising a well-recognized visual cue and a tagline (which initially ran the slogan 'Utterly butterly delicious!') placed beneath the product brand name at the bottom. While the header typically references a contemporary global or local event that is mirrored in the visual cue, the tagline, usually in minimalist text, highlights some positive attribute of the product itself. The advertising strategy, which has its brand ambassador, the Amul butter girl, a round-eyed, chubby-cheeked girl in a polka dot dress playing the role of a social observer, serves various purposes, such as evoking humor, satire, irony and simple playfulness, and has been highly successful in connecting with the target consumer, thus enhancing the brand image. What is unique about these advertisements, though, is their use of Hindi-English code-switching, reminiscent of Hinglish, bilingual puns and wordplay, allusions, intertextual references and plain smart creativity.

The English part of the text is generally used as an intertext for creating bilingual word puns. Allusion, irony and wordplay nearly always involve stretching the meaning potential of English lexical items by blending them with partially homophonous indigenous items and fusing their meanings. For the pun to work successfully and the message to be interpreted correctly, the reader has to deduce the English word that is used as an intertext by deriving it from the Hindi word that has been exploited to create such wordplay, as illustrated in the advertisement in Figure 3.10.

It would be hard to miss the global dimension of the Amul advertisement in Figure 3.10, cleverly exploited by the semi-homophonic wordplay between the English 'Code' and the Hindi word 'Krodh' ('rage') in the header 'Da Vinci Krodh', which is used as an intertext to reference the worldwide furor raised over Dan Brown's novel *The Da Vinci Code* some years ago. The local word 'Krodh', connoting 'religious rage' in many a narrative of ancient Indian mythology, captures particularly well the allusion to the controversy and opposition raised by the book, whose phenomenal success had the church and Christians alike demanding that its copies be burned and its movie adaptation banned. A larger than life-size visual of Da Vinci's Mona Lisa and angry posturing by the public in the graphics conjure up the strongly negative reactions hurled at the author of the international best-seller. In contrast,

Figure 3.10 Amul advertisement alluding to Dan Brown's *The Da Vinci Code*

as the tagline implies, the products of Amul in the local market attract 'No opposition'.

Considering that fiction, like myth, is part of the conceptual repertoire of contemporary societies, the reference to Dan Brown's novel in fact provides an example of intergeneric intertextuality, thus constructing the reader as an intelligent, educated, well-informed Indian who has the necessary cultural capital (knowledge of Western popular culture, best-selling fiction, media news, and so on) to appreciate the underlying humor. The advertisement optimizes the fact that today's cosmopolitans combine experiences of various media with other forms of experience – cinema, video, restaurants, spectator sports, tourism, and so on – that have different national and transnational genealogies (Appadurai, 1996: 64). It also illustrates how images of the media are quickly absorbed into public discourse and moved into local repertoires of irony, humor and resistance, as does the advertisement presented in Figure 3.11.

The advertisement in Figure 3.11 draws on yet another international event by using wordplay to raise a laugh. The graphics closely resemble the slew of pictures that appeared in the international press at the time, showing President George W. Bush ducking a shoe thrown at him by Muntader al-Zaidi, an Iraqi correspondent during a press conference in Iraq. The humor is derived from the wordplay between the Hindi word 'joota' ('shoe') in the text, 'Joota Kahin Ka!', and the semi-homophonous word 'jhoota' ('liar') in the original idiomatic Hindi expletive, 'Jhoota Kahin Ka!', meaning 'You big fat liar!' or 'Liar! Liar!' – a social comment on Washington's invasion of Iraq, commandeered by George W. Bush under false allegations that it held weapons of mass destruction. The play upon the words 'joota' (shoe) and 'jhoota' ('liar') thus grabs the reader's attention by exploiting this double meaning

Figure 3.11 Amul advertisement alluding to the shoe episode with President George W. Bush

and adds to the satirical effect of the advertisement. Such double layers of meaning in the Amul advertisements are immediately accessible to bilingual Indian speakers but may not necessarily be comprehensible to those who do not understand Hindi.

Additionally, because the expletive 'Jhoota Kahin Ka!' conjures up rather frivolous, informal, highly localized contexts of use, deriving from its frequent utilization in Hindi commercial cinema, usually in verbal exchanges among intimates, for example, between lovers, communicatively its use would appear hugely out of place in contexts of serious international import. By invoking such frivolous localized usage to charge Bush with the responsibility for grossly misleading the world through his US foreign policy, it creates a sense of the absurd with a view to mocking and ridiculing, and holding Bush to shame.

The tongue-in-cheek 'Attack it' in the tagline below likewise has a double meaning contingent on how the reader interprets the ambiguous referent 'it': whether as the 'liar' (that is, Bush) inferred from 'jhoota', in which case the phrase 'Attack it' may be interpreted as sound and explicit approval of the act of shoe throwing perpetrated by Muntader al-Zaidi as shown in the graphics; or as 'the butter marketed by Amul', in which case 'Attack it' may be interpreted as simply urging the consumer 'to eat it with relish'. Such double layers of meaning underlying the intended ambiguity in these 'multi-voiced' texts are illustrative of what Higgins (2009), drawing on Bakhtin's (1981) concept of dialogism and his view of dialogue in making sense of identity construction, terms *dialogic multilingualism*, since they require readers to tap into more than their knowledge of both English and Hindi and 'rely on consumers' abilities to decipher third codes' (in this case, Hinglish),

Figure 3.12 Amul advertisement recording Mumbai's 'No TV Day'

indeed, 'to interpret the "voice" of English in these multilingual advertisements as the voice of global and local modernity' (Higgins, 2009: 124).

In contrast to the Amul advertisements above, the advertisement in Figure 3.12 draws exclusively on local knowledge relating to a recent initiative by one of Mumbai's leading daily newspapers, *The Hindustan Times,* which asked residents of Mumbai to do the unthinkable: switch off the TV and get out and enjoy the city. *The Hindustan Times* came up with the idea of a 'NO TV Day', scheduled for 29 January 2011, in order to promote family bonding time and encourage residents to take time out to appreciate the city. The hybrid header, 'Zindagi on. TV off' (literally, (Switch) 'Life on (Switch), TV off'), communicates this message in a pithy and attention-grabbing way, albeit in a form of fractured English. Yet, far from indexing inadequate language competence, the flouting of standard English grammar rules in the use of 'on' and 'off' as verbal elements and the blurring of the boundaries between the two languages in these fractured phrases contribute to the creativity and memorability of the advertisement for Indian audiences in a way that a monolingual advertisement would be incapable of achieving.

Reflecting on the challenge advertisers are presented with by savvy media-literate viewers grown too acclimatized to advertising's conventional messages and reading rules, Kuppens (2009: 119) notes that the advent of postmodern intertextual advertising is an attempt to appeal to a generation of critical, media-literate and skeptical viewers: 'The creativity, humour, and reflexivity that are typical of intertextual advertisements, constitute an exciting way of appealing to advertisement-literate viewers who "see through" classic advertising strategies' and, crucially, function as 'a source of ego enhancement' for viewers who recognize the intertextual references. By positioning the viewer as the holder of the necessary cultural capital, the advertiser 'appears to speak to the viewer as a peer' (Kuppens, 2009: 119, citing Goldman & Papson, 1994: 43). Kuppens further points out that, 'the enjoyment and pleasure that viewers derive from such advertisements, potentially contribute to positive attitudes towards the advertisement, and hence to the brand' (Kuppens, 2009: 119, citing Hitchon & Jura, 1997), 'rendering the viewer more permeable and responsive to the commercial message' (Kuppens, 2009: 119, citing Stam *et al.*, 1992: 2003).

Because the Amul advertisements embody themes and sensibilities that are both global and local and are redolent with allusions requiring considerable intelligent processing and inferring on the part of readers, it is clear they are tailored for a target group with the linguistic and cultural literacy to decode them. Their wide and continued popularity is an attestation of the cultural capital and linguistic sophistication of the middle-class Indians they largely target. Moreover, English is more than just an emblematic tool indexing status, prestige or modernity for this group; its use in hybrid multilingual advertisements serves not just communicative or utilitarian commercial purposes, but also satisfies the creative needs of advertisers and consumers alike, as evidenced by the presence of bilingual word puns, wordplay, code-switching, allusions and intertextuality, which capitalize on their knowledge of multiple languages and cultural resources. Texts are thus recontextualized, reinterpreted, adapted and 're-presented' to reflect orientations and identifications that are simultaneously local and global, that is, glocal.

Conclusion

The English-based expressions of hybridity in our study provide compelling evidence of how these texts, discourses and genres construct middle-class Indian consumers seeking to align themselves with globalization as modern, young, educated and cosmopolitan, while blending English with Indian languages to *reframe, reconstitute* and *re-signify* their complex, evolving subjective identities. Cosmopolitanism, imagined or real, is of course not a new experience for the elite among Indian bilinguals, for whom English has long been a preserve and a privilege. What the hybrid codes involving English do is open up avenues for other bilinguals to 'move out' of their unequal marginal positions and change the rules of an economy by which English no longer acts only as an agent of oppression or minoritization but also as a tool for transcending and transforming the limitations of their local resources in a less intrusive, more inclusive way. While English invokes cosmopolitan identities and access to the international world its fusion with the local Indian languages subverts the social hierarchy associated with English in

India as the prerogative of an elite minority and its adherence to a canonical standard.

Significantly, this *refashioning* of identities is achieved without doing damage to indigenous sociocultural values, traditions and practices. The processes of hybridization through Englishization are not unilateral; even as the local is reshaped as a result of adapting to new frames of reference opened up by the in-betweenness of a 'third space', in the ensuing two-way dialectical process the local also acts upon the global to de-Anglicize, domesticate and democratize English. By not only preserving the local, but actively valorizing and drawing upon it, hybridity in the Indian context works to re-center globalization and thus provides something of a contrapuntal to the homogenizing tendencies of global English.

References

Alsagoff, L. (2010) Hybridity in ways of speaking: The glocalization of English in Singapore. In L. Lim, A. Pakir and L. Wee (eds) *English in Singapore: Modernity and Management* (pp. 109–130). Hong Kong: Hong Kong University Press.

Anderson, B. (1991) *Imagined Communities: Reflections on the Origins and Spread of Nationalism.* London: Verso.

Appadurai, A. (1996) *Modernity at Large: Cultural Dimensions of Globalization.* Minneapolis, MN: University of Minnesota Press.

Bakhtin, M.M. (1981) *The Dialogic Imagination: Four Essays.* Austin: University of Texas Press.

Bhabha, H. (1994) *The Location of Culture.* London: Routledge.

Bhatia, T. (2000) *Advertising in Rural India: Language, Marketing Communication and Consumerism.* ILCAA Study of Languages and Cultures of Asia and Africa Monograph Series No. 36. Tokyo University of Foreign Studies, Tokyo, Japan.

Bhatt, R.M. (2008) In other words: Language mixing, identity representations, and the *third space. Journal of Sociolinguistics* 12 (2), 177–200.

Blommaert, J., Collins, J. and Slembrouck, S. (2005) Polycentricity and interactional regimes in 'global neighbourhoods'. *Ethnography* 65, 205–235.

Canagarajah, A.S. (1999) *Resisting Linguistic Imperialism in English Teaching.* Oxford: Oxford University Press.

Gorter, D. (ed.) (2006) Linguistic landscape: A new approach to multilingualism. *International Journal of Multilingualism* 3 (1), 1–6.

Higgins, C. (2009) *English as a Local Language: Post-Colonial Identities and Multilingual Practices.* Bristol: Multilingual Matters.

Jaworski, A. and Thurlow, C. (2010) *Semiotic Landscapes: Language, Image and Space.* London: Continuum.

Kelly-Holmes, H. (2005) *Advertising as Multilingual Communication.* Basingstoke and New York: Palgrave-Macmillan.

Kraidy, M.M. (1999) The global, the local, and the hybrid: A native ethnography of glocalization. *Critical Studies in Mass Communication* 16 (4), 456–477.

Kramsch, C. (1993) *Context and Culture in Language Teaching.* Oxford: Oxford University Press.

Kuppens, A.N.H. (2009) English in advertising: Generic intertextuality in a globalizing media environment. *Applied Linguistics* 31 (1), 115–135.
Landry, R. and Bourhis, R.Y. (1997) Linguistic landscape and ethnolinguistic vitality: An empirical study. *Journal of Language and Social Psychology* 16 (1), 23–49.
Martin, E. (2006) *Marketing Identities through Language: English and Global Imagery in French Advertising*. New York: Palgrave.
Papastergiadis, N. (2000) *The Turbulence of Migration.* Cambridge: Polity Press.
Pennycook, A. (1994) *The Cultural Politics of English as an International Language.* London: Longman.
Piller, I. (2001) Identity constructions in multilingual advertising. *Language and Society* 30 (2), 153–186.
Piller, I. (2003) Advertising as a site of language contact. *Annual Review of Applied Linguistics* 23, 170–183.
Reh, M. (2004) Multilingual writing: A reader-oriented typology – with examples of Lira Municipality (Uganda). *International Journal of the Sociology of Language* 170 (1), 1–41.
Robertson, R. (1992) *Globalization: Social Theory and Global Culture*. London: Sage.
Shohamy E. and Gorter, D. (2009) *Linguistic Landscapes: Expanding the Scenery.* New York: Routledge.
Stroud, C. and Mpendukana, S. (2009) Towards a material ethnography of linguistic landscape: Multilingualism, mobility and space in a South African township. *Journal of Sociolinguistics* 13 (3), 363–386.

4 (Un)Emancipatory Hybridity: Selling English in an Unequal World

Beatriz P. Lorente and T. Ruanni F. Tupas

Hybridity lulls us to sleep
Hutnyk, 2005: 95

Introduction

There are different ways of understanding hybridity (for example, Bhabha, 1994; Hall, 1996; Papastergiadis, 2005; Pieterse, 2001; Young, 1995); however, 'it is predominantly deployed as a boundary-subverting, unquestionably transgressive, critical tool' (Kompridis, 2005: 320). In other words, hybridity is essentially good. This chapter, however, argues that hybridity is a problematic concept. More specifically, it situates and examines the mix of discourses in the websites of a company that offers training in teaching English as a foreign language (EFL) to Filipinos. In looking at the mix of discourses the company uses to sell its services, this chapter hopes to shed light on how hybridity is deeply entangled with the mechanisms of capitalist globalization.

Many deployments of hybridity are highly descriptive, if not celebratory, thus silent to the reality of continuing violence wrought upon politically, economically and culturally marginalized peoples of the world, whose hybrid lives and discourses presumably are essentially transgressive. Indeed for many, 'hybridity saves' (Hutnyk, 2005: 96), but our investigation shows that hybridity as third space may be creative, but not necessarily transformative or emancipatory, especially because its use can be and has been exploited to advance specific economic agendas (Chouliaraki & Fairclough, 1999; Mitchell, 1997).

Of course hybridity does have redemptive qualities, but different contexts dictate its specific nature. For example, in Higgins' (2009) recent work on hybrid, multivocal language practices in East Africa some social contexts provide more emancipatory possibilities for some (middle-class) speakers than others, such as the schools where normative practices of teaching and assessment are firmly upheld by authorities and gatekeepers. In other words, hybridity per se should not be the cause for celebration or despair; after all, it is 'in reality ... not essentially good' (Werbner, 2001: 149). Our question, thus, should be: who and what hybridizes, for whom and for what purposes? As Chowdhury argues, 'as we recognize the liberatory potential of hybridity, we have to be circumspect about whose interests these hybrid enunciations serve' (2002); for example, why it is the political elites who draw upon hybrid identity to advance their own versions of nationhood (Yanik, 2011), why the rise of hybrid televisual content has coincided with increasing commercialization of journalism and entertainment (Wood, 2004), or why the hybridity of both diasporic intellectuals and poor migrants of the same country actually 'separates them more than unites them' (Sajed, 2010: 364). For us then, Chowdhury's admonition above is a constructive starting point to discuss the theoretical nuances of the term.

In what follows, we will trace our justification as the main concern of the chapter, starting with a quick glance at hybridity as a complex concept, continuing with brief notes on the disparate history of hybridity in linguistics and then arguing for the need for hybridity to be, borrowing the words of Hollinshead *et al.* (2009: 440), 'moderated by deep material inspections of the capitalized and globalized scaffolding' (see Bianchi, 2009). We hope to contribute to a re-evaluation of linguistics' relationship with hybridity – from one that deploys the term in order to understand linguistic and discursive phenomena to one that 'reads' these phenomena in order to contribute to a more nuanced understanding of hybridity and its (mis)uses. 'As hybridity appears in several guises', argues Hutnyk (2005: 83), 'it is important to look at what it achieves, what contexts its use might obscure, and what it leaves aside'. Indeed, our argument is that hybridity leaves aside the central role of sociopolitical and economic processes in the production of hybrid discourses and practices (Canagarajah, 1999; Chouliaraki & Fairclough, 1999; Mitchell, 1997; Spivak, 1999). The relationship between hybridity and economic gain is curiously obscured in linguistics of the hybrid.

Hybridity at a Glance

Why indeed is it important to approach hybridity in the particular way we describe above? It is because the very core of the term is, first of all, philosophically incoherent (Hutnyk, 2005: 81). The history of hybridity is perplexing and complex, leading some scholars to describe ideas surrounding the term as 'bizarre' (Papastergiadis, 2000: 169) and 'paradoxical' (Carton, 2007: 145). For example, the earlier uses of the term have been associated with positive, essentially unproblematic notions and references of biological mixing in agricultural and horticultural sciences, such as the hybrid mule that was produced from a horse and a donkey. But it was soon to be appropriated in colonial discourse to describe in pejorative and derogatory ways the mixing between the colonizer (white) and the colonized (non-white).

To recuperate the term from its colonial moorings, scholars have deployed the term to mean various positive things – as third space, agent of change, resistance and subversion, possibility of new knowledge and cultural practice, and so on. In a 'remarkable act of reappropriation', asserts Ahmad (2001: 74), postcolonial scholars of hybridity (for example, Bhabha, 1994; Gilroy, 1994; Hall, 1996) 'have dusted off the concept's epistemological origins in scientific racism and used it as a stick with which to beat the essentialisms of "pure" cultures' (Ahmad, 2001: 74). Unfortunately, many scholars of hybridity have only 'seized on the progressive theoretical potential of the term itself, and abstracted it away from the situated practices of everyday life' (Mitchell, 1997: 535), thus ironically glossing over relevant issues and problems against which hybridity has been deployed as a practice of resistance in the first place.

Moreover, people also worry about the assumption of 'purity' in the many deployments of the term (Gilroy, 1994), in particular focusing on the question of whether hybridity be used successfully without recourse to the 'original' 'purities' of discourse and life. Yet, such theoretical calisthenics seems marginal to the main issues at hand and, in fact, seems like a curious work in theoretical refinement or tightening because this really does not redress directly the many sexual, economic and cultural questions associated with the term. Lastly, the term also has different political genealogies in the study of contact zones and liminality in anthropological work, diaspora in sociology and cultural criticism, creolization in linguistics, translation in cultural studies and cyborg in science and technology (Hutnyk, 2005). Our point here is that specificities of history, geography, discipline, ideology and culture necessitate various deployments of hybridity, so it is therefore necessary to ask why particular uses of the term are deployed and not others.

The Linguistics of the Hybrid

In theoretical and applied linguistics, there is a relative absence of sustained engagement with the notion of hybridity (but see Kumaravadivelu, 2008: 118–140) in the same manner that the concept animates the rest of the humanities and social sciences, especially cultural criticism, postcolonial studies, sociology, anthropology and even political economy (for example, Bhabha, 1994; Dirlik, 1994; Lowe, 1991). It does not mean that hybridity is a foreign concept in the field – for example, linguistics of the hybrid is central to the works of Bakhtin (1991), Fairclough (Chouliaraki & Fairclough, 1999) and Kachru (1997), except that the term is essentially deployed by most scholars as a descriptive lens through which textual and discursive practices are understood and interrogated. 'Hybridity', Hinnenkamp explains (2003: 35), 'emphasizes the – some unexpected – blending of linguistic and cultural systems'. In its more applied uses, it refers to when 'students cross traditional academic boundaries of genre, media, and modality in the production of texts' (2003: 432).

Consequently, important questions concerning the impact of particular scholarly deployments of hybridity on people and institutions are rarely taken up. On the one hand, the term is essentially used as a non-evaluative concept, focusing much more on descriptions of the hybrid and much less on how and why the hybrid has come about in the first place. This is a crucial point to make because what usually lies behind the aesthetics of the hybrid is a history of unhappy or violent clashes between cultures, groups and individuals (Hutnyk, 2005). On the other hand, hybridity is deployed as an essentially cultural phenomenon, not as both cultural *and* economic phenomena which 'must be theorized in tandem' (Mitchell, 1997: 539). The resulting work – characterized by two papers to be discussed later in this section – are conceptualizations of hybridity within the limited immediate contexts of its use. Therefore, the problem with hybridity is not so much because scholars do not theorize it (for example, see Kachru, 1997) but because many people rarely locate their theorization within the interplay of cultural and economic processes which are the essential generators of pervasive inequalities in today's capitalist world (Anthias, 2001; Bush & Szeftel, 1999). In other words, while hybridity is used to describe contested textual/discursive spaces and practices, it is rarely taken up as a contested concept itself whose disparate meanings and agendas can perhaps be best understood within the tightening 'grip of global capitalism' (Hirsch, 1999: 288).

This is especially true in the study of creolized languages which emerged out of the violent conditions of colonial slavery, such as the interactions between African and European people in the Caribbean (Hutnyk, 2005: 85).

Hybridity here has a 'distinct history' but the problem is that research on these interesting language phenomena was 'often undertaken in isolation from, and even blissful neglect of, socio-political contexts' (Hutnyk, 2005: 85). More recent studies on code-switching, language contact, language varieties and professional discourse (for example, Clarke & Hiscock, 2009; Darling-Wolf, 2000; Hinnenkamp, 2003; Makoe & McKinney, 2009; Sarangi & Roberts, 1999; Spencer, 2011) can trace their methodological lineage to such textually biased descriptive research on hybridity, even if some of them do try to relate the term to larger issues of social and educational change by using the concept to problematize essentialist and totalizing notions of identity, ethnicity, hegemony, colonialism and language, among many other things (for example, Bhatt, 2008; Higgins, 2009; Gebhard, 2005; Gutiérrez *et al.*, 1999; Piller, 2002). Nevertheless, hybridity, even in these critical studies, remains a largely unproblematic and celebratory concept (but see Chouliaraki & Fairclough, 1999; Darling-Wolf, 2006); it destabilizes almost everything except itself.

Two studies on pedagogical discourse reveal the two main theoretical tendencies of hybridity in language studies. The first paper by Gutiérrez *et al.* (1999) conceptualizes hybrid discourses in English language classrooms as 'third spaces' that enable teachers and learners to explore alternative ways of engaging with content and knowledge. Based on ethnographic research in a dual immersion elementary school classroom in the US, the paper demonstrates how contending literacy practices, official and unofficial discourses and other mediating cultural practices collectively generate third spaces of language development.

The second paper by Duff (2004) also explores how hybridity and diversity promote learning. In the context of Canadian Grade 10 social studies lessons, the paper examines how the entry of pop culture discourse into formal education discourse affects classroom dynamics and content learning. Duff found that popular culture can become exclusionary in classroom contexts because intertextual cultural references and practices are not readily accessible to all. This is particularly true among English as a second language (ESL) learners who have recently migrated to Canada and have limited access to the necessary cultural resources. 'What was cultural play for some', argues Duff, 'was heavy cognitive and identity work for others and there seemed to be little common ground or third space' (2004: 253). In other words, who is included and excluded in the celebration of hybridity? This is the crucial question that separates the two papers above.

Nevertheless, the two papers together still tell us something about the nature of hybridity as an academic creation in applied linguistics. First, hybridity is not a stable concept, and much of what it means actually depends on how it is being deployed. Second, the particular theoretical lens of hybridity dictates how language data are being read and, at the same time, the nature of data also helps define what hybridity can mean. And third, and in particular reference to the papers and types of work that they represent in applied linguistics, hybridity is deployed without recourse to larger conversations about the concept. The papers reference postcolonial work on hybridity, for example through the concept of the third space in relation to hybridizing discourses and practices, but they do not directly engage with such work. What is missing then is a sustained engagement with hybridity as a concept deeply imbricated in issues of power and marginalization in society and the world. In the words of Kumaravadivelu (2008), hybridity 'fails to address certain hard realities that characterize the practice of everyday life in this era of globalization' (p. 140).

This is the missing link in linguistics' largely romanticized relationship with hybridity, and perhaps a possible explanation why recent linguistic studies for the most part have not really become a part of the greater academic conversations about the concept and the many cultural and economic issues associated with it. To some extent, linguistics has usefully (and correctly) deployed hybridity as a critical/analytical tool to unsettle unquestioned ideologies and unquestioned language phenomena, but it has not seriously engaged the term as a contested concept in the first place.

The Purpose of the Chapter

This chapter thus attempts to fill a few gaps in linguistic studies of hybridity by not only re-locating the term within critical conversations concerning its political and ideological (and thus, theoretical) viability, but more importantly, by self-reflectively interrogating our own use of the term, with the hope of gaining more nuanced understandings of an unequal world. In particular, we hope to answer the following questions:

- What sort of discursive mixing or hybridizing is happening in the selling of English language services?
- Who or what does the hybridizing, for whom and for what purpose?
- Is the third space created by such mixing or hybridity emancipatory or not? Why?

Our choice of a website where training for Filipino EFL teachers is 'sold' is particularly situated in the fact that 'the internet (now) offers a wide and virtually uncontrolled space for language learning packages' (Blommaert,

2009: 245). More broadly, the website is situated in the dynamics of the highly lucrative global English language education industry where a 'dogmatic belief in a monolingualist approach' and in the supposed innate expertise of native speakers (Pennycook, 1994: 168–176) are predominant. While the US and the UK are still the countries most preferred as destinations for learning English, 'non-traditional' countries such as Malta, South Africa (*Language Travel Magazine*, 2006), and the Philippines are now in the picture. The fact that countries where English is not the first language and where teachers are not native speakers are now destinations for learning English raises questions as to how such countries are positioned vis-à-vis the still dominant and profitable discourse that a monolingual classroom taught by an English native speaker is the ideal setting for English language learning.

Furthermore, the fact that we have chosen a website highlights the increasingly critical role of the internet in the construction of modern narratives, histories, identities, cultures and discourses about places and people due to globalization, or what is essentially referred to in the literature as 'image-making' or 'world-making' (Hollinshead *et al.*, 2009; Patil, 2011; Choi *et al.*, 2007; Fürsich & Robins, 2004). 'Hybridity', according to Chouliaraki and Fairclough (1999: 59), 'is an irreducible characteristic of complex modern discourse'. As such, there is a 'need for scholars to pay more attention to the "global, multimedia hypertexts" that are circulated via the World Wide Web' (Patil, 2011: 1005), especially because such hypertexts are positioned within a complex nexus of state and transnational networks of power, politics and co-optation (see Bianchi, 2009) in the use of the internet. Arguably, these websites are prime examples of hybrid texts, as

> home page authors engage in *bricolage* adopting and adapting borrowed material from the public domain of the Web in the process of fashioning personal and public identities. Graphics, sounds, text, and code used to generate a particular format are often copied or adapted from other people's pages. (Chandler, 2006: 305)

We will first provide a brief background of the Philippines as an EFL destination. We will then examine its general features before focusing on the mix of discourses used in the website to discursively market EFL training to Filipino teachers.[1] Our analysis 'fixes' the version of the website at a particular point in time, 6 June 2009. We first encountered the website in early 2009, while doing online searches for language schools in the Philippines that offered English language teaching (ELT) classes to South Koreans. What made the company behind the website very different was its apparent focus on providing ELT training for Filipinos rather than on providing ELT for EFL students in the Philippines. In this sense, the company was operating on a somewhat different scale: it was tapping into and profiting from the market of Filipinos who were interested in teaching EFL. In doing so, it discursively overturns endemic ideologies of monolingualism (Phillipson, 1992) and native speakerism (Holliday, 2005) while simultaneously also implicating itself discursively in corporatist pursuits of new capital, in this case through 'non-native' ELT as cheap labor.

The Philippines as an EFL Destination

While globally the Philippines is not a top destination for English language learning, it is emerging as a *niche* destination for one of the largest markets for EFL: South Korea. This phenomenon of *jogi yuhak*, that is, pre-university South Koreans migrating to English-speaking countries for a relatively short period of time (one–three years) in order to learn English is fuelled by the pursuit of 'authentic' English, which is considered to be essential and valuable capital for economic mobility and social distinction in South Korea (Shin, 2010; Song, 2010; Park & Bae, 2009). *Jogi yuhak* has become very popular among Korean middle-class families. Between 2000 and 2005, the number of students who left Korea on student visas increased from 4397 to 20,400 (Kim, cited in Shin, 2010); the increase was explosive among elementary school children whose numbers have increased almost 40 times over the past five years (Kim, cited in Park & Bae, 2009). However, it must be emphasized that these official numbers do not include the 'huge number of students who embark upon short-term forays to English speaking countries in various forms and for varying durations, not all of which necessarily require student visas' (Shin, 2010: 18). This *jogi yuhak* market constituted a US$550 million industry in the first quarter of 2004 alone (Shin, 2010).

While the preferred destinations of students on *jogi yuhak* are still Western English-speaking countries (for example, US, UK), 'the rapid increase in the number of students has led to a diversification of destinations, with many non-Western post colonial countries such as Malaysia, India, the Philippines, and Singapore emerging as new centers for studying overseas' (Park & Bae, 2009: 369). The influx of South Korean students into the Philippines must certainly be sufficiently high for it to have drawn the attention of the Philippine government in the past few years. This can be seen in, for example, how the country's Department of Tourism has started to actively market the Philippines as a 'top destination for overseas education in Asia ... particularly in learning the English language' (*Seoul Times*, 2006). As of 2008, South Korea was the top source of foreign students in the

Philippines, with approximately 100,000 South Korean students enrolled in various English courses, mainly in the cities of Metro Manila, Baguio and Cebu (Cerralbo, 2008). These figures do not reflect the Korean students who head to the Philippines to study English for very short periods of time that do not require a student visa.

It must be made clear though that the increasing influx of *jogi yuhak* in the country should not be immediately read as a sign that notions of the primacy of monolingual English classrooms and English native speaker teachers are on the decline. Instead, it appears that as the demand for English has increased across social classes in South Korea, destination countries have become positioned in different niches in the ELT market, with English being sold at different price points to Korean customers who have varying economic means (Shin, 2010).

The Philippines is favored primarily because of the affordability of English language courses and the cost of living in the country (Magno, 2010). It is also geographically nearer to South Korea, making travel between the two countries convenient and relatively inexpensive. As such, the country is emerging as a favorite destination for short, that is, less than a year, English trips (Shin, 2010) wherein Koreans head to the country to cram for English language examinations such as the Test of English as a Foreign Language (TOEFL) and International English Language Testing System (IELTS), or to review English during the school holidays.

This demand for 'affordable', 'quality' English from *jogi yuhak* is the material context in which the website, the virtual face of an ELT company, is rooted. It capitalizes on this demand by supplying 'non-native' EFL teachers from the Philippines and profiting from the 'professionalization' these teachers may seek.

The Website and Its Hybrid Discursive Marketing Strategies

How then does the website 'sell' English? In the following section we argue that the website sells English through hybrid discursive strategies, specifically by legitimizing (and liberating) 'non-native' ELT through inventive intermeshing of 'local' and 'global' elements, as well as 'professional' and 'specialist' discourses, together re-placed in the material context of *jogi yuhak* and, more generally, capitalist globalization. The hybrid in the website evacuates ELT/ Teaching English to Speakers of Other Languages (TESOL) from its monolingualist and native-speakerist moorings while perpetuating a new hierarchy of ELT destinations where the Philippines reprises its 'traditional' role in the global capitalist market as a supplier of cheap and affordable labor, and where English language learning (at least among Koreans) is stratified along class lines.

The website's economic interests

The website's name is TESOL Philippines (www.tesol.com.ph).[2] While the website's name may, at first glance, seem to be that of a professional organization, the fact that it has a .com domain (compared to a .org domain) signals its commercial character. In other words, this webpage of what appears to be a professional organization is just one of the online faces of a commercial ELT company. In the company's own words, TESOL Philippines is managed by a 'duly registered company run by former international lawyers and academics who have combined to establish business schools, law schools, second language schools or English language villages across the Asia Pacific region' (http://www.asian-esp-journal.com/business_articles_june_ttil.php, accessed 6 June 2009). Its head office is in the British Virgin Islands. The goals of the company are twofold. It aims: (1) 'to provide investors with maximum return, hand over schools that are both profitable, well established, accredited, and have attractive sales potential' and (2) 'to provide users with vast free resources that cover all subject areas promulgated by the content providers; and to reach almost 500 million academics and teachers & students – both English native speakers and speakers whose mother tongue is not English' (http://www.time-taylor.com/mission.php, accessed 6 June 2009).

Economics and discursive hybridity

These avowedly economic goals of the company embed the website's primary interest in teachers or would-be teachers of English in the Philippines. It targets this specific market of Filipino teachers through a number of discursive strategies. First, TESOL Philippines is marketed and visually made to appear as a professional organization. This can be seen in the homepage of TESOL Philippines, which draws from the conventional elements of the webpages of professional organizations: a name ('TESOL Philippines') that strongly alludes to an international organization that is well-known among English language teaching professionals, the thumbnails of various academic journals, information about membership, certification and the like, and an announcement about an upcoming conference.

Second, the website capitalizes on an interplay between 'global' and 'local' elements, giving the impression that 'global' and 'local' expertise are involved in the organization, and that the organization is recognized both 'globally' and 'locally'. This can already be seen in the name of the organization and the name of the webpage (TESOL Philippines) which combines the name of an international (and US-based) organization for ELT professionals (TESOL) with that of the specific country that is being targeted (Philippines). This can also be seen in the titles of the academic journals on the right-hand side. Here, the strategy of 'localization' by specifying countries or geographical areas is most apparent, for example, *TESOL Law Journal*, *Chinese EFL Journal*, *The Philippine ESL Journal*, and so on. Doing this suggests that the organization has 'global' academic cache by being linked to many academic journals and 'local' country or area specialization. In the 6 June 2009 version of the website, TESOL Philippines was also advertising a conference and its announcement had two headlines, namely: 'TESOL *Philippines* proudly presents (an) *international* EFL seminar' and '*World* EFL leaders are coming to *Cebu*'.

The way in which the conference was marketed again used catchphrases which combined the 'global' and the 'local'.

It is worth noting here that most if not all of the elements on the homepage of the website are 'self-referential', that is, while the various elements (the professional organization, the journals, and so on) appear to be separate and independent entities, they are all actually owned and managed by the very same company that owns and manages the website. The 'professional organization' (TESOL Philippines) is neither an affiliate nor a partner of TESOL and it is not clear who its members are or what its organizational structure, if any, may be. Clicking on the links on the left-hand column leads to certificates, courses and conferences that the company offers or organizes for would-be or current ELT teachers in and beyond the Philippines. To our knowledge, all of the journals on the right-hand column exist as online platforms, instituted and managed by the very company that owns the website, with 'local' editorial boards and contributors.

Discourses of specialization and professionalization

Let us discuss in more detail the discourses of specialization and professionalization referred to in the earlier section. As regards *specialization*, this is perhaps most apparent in the conference announcement that was a clear focus of the website at that time. This is also evident from how the announcement was, at that time, located right in the very middle of the homepage and how it occupied the most space on the page.

The theme of the conference ('the teaching roles of the EFL teacher in an ESL country') and the desired focus of the papers ('related into research and practice into EFL ESL teaching and the teaching of ESL EFL in Asian contexts or with Asian students') explicitly address the fact that the Philippines is not a monolingual English country, that the EFL teachers are non-native speakers of English and that the target students are Asian. This is further reinforced by the suggested topics for the papers which include: 'Teaching EFL students in an ESL zone', 'Cultural impact of teaching EFL students', 'Teaching English in the Philippines', 'Teaching teachers to teach EFL students', 'Teaching English grammar to Koreans and Japanese' and 'Setting standards for English language schools in the Philippines'.

This specialization in Asian EFL countries can also be seen in how the training courses for teachers were described as being: 'written by leading academics for the Asian EFL countries' and as differing 'from standard TESOL (CELTA-UK) courses due to its researched and clear focus on L2 acquisition within Asian language learning and cultures'. If located within the broad ELT academic literature, this *specialist* discourse may be seen as a hugely postcolonial assertion of the legitimacy of non-Western English language learning trajectories and practices (Kachru, 1976; Holliday, 2005; Pennycook, 1990).

On the other hand, the website also quite extensively deploys a *professional* discourse through words such as 'certificate' (for example, 'TESOL *Certificate* Course Cebu', TESOL *Certificates,* Philippines), 'accredited' (for example, 'I-TAA Accredited'), and visuals such as the thumbnails of various academic journals and links to universities. At the same time, the website also significantly highlights how these forms of professional 'capital' (which the company offers) are connected to 'institutions'. As such, it is 'TESOL Philippines' (a professional organization) that presents a 'TESOL Certificate Course Cebu' and these certificates are 'I-TAA accredited', 'run by the Asian EFL Journal' and 'supported by Anaheim University, USA'. Such professionalization is also affordable. This is best encapsulated in how 'TESOL Certificates, Philippines' are 'affordable and accredited'.[3]

Hybridity and the struggle against monolingualism and native speakerism

Professionalism and *specialization* in the website appear to diverge to a certain degree from the dominance of beliefs in the ideal of a monolingual English classroom and the primacy of the native speaker as a teacher of English.[4] In the case of the discourse of specialization, the Philippines being an 'ESL country' or an 'ESL zone', with teachers who are not native speakers, appear to be taken as givens that, if anything, are to be capitalized on. The discourse of specialization also highlights the specificity of learner backgrounds and learning settings (for example, 'teaching EFL students in an ESL zone', 'teaching English grammar to Koreans and Japanese') and by doing so, hints that norms of teaching may need to be 'localized' to better fit the particular needs of students. As mentioned earlier, such notions are relatively progressive and one may be tempted to celebrate this as an instance of a 'third space' that is producing emerging discourses and practices that resist dominant ideologies regarding native speakers and monolingualism.

Similarly, in the case of the discourse of professionalization, it would appear to some degree that offering such courses to Filipinos may signal that English teaching is no longer the exclusive domain of English native speakers. Those who wish to teach English (native speaker or not) need to learn to do so by taking courses, attending conferences and earning certificates. Teaching English is made even less exclusive by marketing the certification as being affordable, so that potentially more Filipinos can then become professional English teachers.

However, it is worth bearing in mind again that the specialization and professionalization discourses which appear in hybrid forms in the website actually demarcate the market niche of the company that manages it. The company stands to profit from training 'professional' teachers who specialize in teaching (read: Korean) students in an ESL country (the Philippines). As such, what propels the discourses is the need to capitalize on a market niche for profitable ends and not necessarily shifts in how, for example, 'English proficiency' is coming to be conceptualized or how norms in English language teaching are changing. Furthermore, these discourses echo the discourse of made-to-order labor that characterizes the promotion of migrant Filipino workers (Lorente, 2012). This time, the made-to-order Filipinos are not would-be migrant domestic workers bound for various destinations, but prospective English teachers trained especially for Korean students bound for the Philippines.

Conclusion: Hybridity and Global Capitalism

The unique configuration of discursive hybridity that characterizes the website is not accidental but, in fact, constitutive of a particularly recent nexus of economic interests and practices surrounding the selling of English training (to would-be EFL teachers) in the Philippines. ELT as a commercial enterprise deliberately pursued largely by British and American institutions, has been vigorously discussed and debated for at least two decades now (see Phillipson, 1992). However, the case of the website above points to recent twists in the marketization of English, where the increasing demand for English from South Korea intersects with the 'professionalization' and 'specialization' of the Third World labor required to teach it.

The material evidence is the short-term Korean students lured to the Philippines as an English language learning destination with cheap and affordable labor (and beautiful beaches for that matter). The Philippine government actively pursues the Korean market of English language learners because of its obvious potential for revenue generation, yet in the process is complicit with the kind of academic capitalism (Hall, 2010) in which respectable institutions are co-opted to give a certain degree of credibility to this specific ELT business enterprise. Here we see in the website archetypes of the third space where the Philippines is championed as a 'non-native' and 'norm-providing' source of 'authentic English'. Yet in the end, the discursive hybridity of the website is a trajectory from which to view the cultural and economic workings of capitalist globalization.

Indeed, the Philippines is a 'new' destination for English language learning, but in the hierarchy of marketable ELT destinations the country falls behind the US, UK, Canada, Australia and New Zealand. Philippine labor, here in the context of the teaching of English, is sought not because it teaches the most desirable variety of English, but because it is cheap and affordable. If one traces the political context of Philippine labor from the early postcolonial Philippines (1960s) to the present, this is hardly surprising. The Philippines has historically positioned itself as a producer of cheap labor, either for economic survival (for example, through remittances from Filipinos abroad which keep the economy afloat) or for political survival (for example, through the policy of labor exportation during the Marcos dictatorship to curb civil unrest against its excesses) (Schirmer & Shalom, 1987). This has led one recent scholar to brand Filipinos as 'servants of globalization' (Parreñas, 2001). Essentially, the Philippines serves, not drives, globalization.

There is no doubt that hybridity as a concept from postcolonial and cultural studies, and appropriated in various ways in linguistics, has positively worked against essentialist conceptions of identity, culture, power and the like, thus opening up new voices of struggle and hope among the many marginalized and silenced groups of people in the world. But we cannot be complacent with hybridity. From its use as a concept that destabilizes much of the world, there is likewise a need to read the world in order to destabilize the concept. Linguistics of the hybrid will be much more meaningful only if it goes beyond aestheticizing the hybrid and tears it apart to reveal the logic of its construction.

Notes

(1) Every effort was made to obtain written permission from the website's owners to use screen captures of the website in this chapter. As the authors received no responses to the requests made, a description of specific features of the 9 June 2009 version of the website is given instead, as necessary.

(2) The layout of the website at the time of writing is not significantly different from the 9 June 2009 version. The elements in the banner and the left- and right-hand

columns of the website have essentially remained the same. What have changed are the announcements in the middle column.

(3) At that time, no specific prices were given and those interested were requested to contact the organization for more information.

(4) The chief executive officer of the company that owns the website was quoted in a Philippine newspaper as saying that: '... the thinking is that only someone with English as the second language can be a true teacher because he or she can teach the complexities of learning another language. I don't have that experience, and yet that is now the trend across the globe' (*Sunstar Cebu*, 2008). His remarks were in connection to a possible chance of launching a hub for EFL teaching in Cebu.

References

Ahmad, A.N. (2001) Whose underground? *Third Text* 15 (54), 71–84.

Anthias, F. (2001) New hybridities, old concepts: The limits of 'culture'. *Ethnic and Racial Studies* 24 (4), 619–641.

Bakhtin, M. (1991) *The Dialogic Imagination: Four Essays* (M. Holquist, ed. and C. Emerson, trans.). Austin: University of Texas Press.

Bhabha, H. (1994) *The Location of Culture*. London: Routledge.

Bhatt, R. (2008) In other words: Language mixing, identity representations, and *third space*. *Journal of Sociolinguistics* 12 (2), 177–200.

Bianchi, R. (2009) The 'critical turn' in tourism studies: A radical critique. *Tourism Geographies* 11 (4), 484–504.

Blommaert, J. (2009) A market of accents. *Language Policy* 8, 243–259.

Bush, R. and Szeftel, M. (1999) Bringing imperialism back in. *Review of African Political Economy* 26 (80), 165–169.

Canagarajah, A.S. (1999) On EFL teachers, awareness, and agency. *ELT Journal* 53 (3), 207–214.

Carton, A. (2007) Historicizing hybridity and the politics of location: Three early colonial Indian narratives. *Journal of Intercultural Studies* 28 (1), 143–155.

Cerralbo, Y. (2008) Korea is no.1 in the Philippines. *The Korea Herald*, 14 April.

Chandler, D. (2006) Identities under construction. In J. Maybin and J. Swann (eds) *The Art of English: Everyday Creativity* (pp. 303–311). Houndmills and New York: Palgrave Macmillian and The Open University.

Choi, S., Lehto, X.Y. and Morrision, A.M. (2007) Destination image representation on the web: Content analysis of Macau travel related websites. *Tourism Management* 28, 118–129.

Chouliaraki, L. and Fairclough, N. (1999) *Discourse in Late Modernity: Rethinking Critical Discourse Analysis*. Edinburgh: Edinburgh University Press.

Chowdhury, K. (2002) It's all within your reach: Globalization and ideologies of postnationalism and hybridity. *Cultural Logic: An Electronic Journal of Marxist Theory* 5, accessed 12 March 2011. http://clogic.eserver.org/2002/chowdhury.html.

Clarke, S. and Hiscock, P. (2009) Hip-hop in a post-insular community: Hybridity, local language, and authenticity in an online Newfoundland rap group. *Journal of English Linguistics* 37 (3), 241–261.

Darling-Wolf, F. (2000) Texts in context: Intertextuality, hybridity, and the negotiation of cultural identity in Japan. *Journal of Communication Inquiry* 24 (2), 134–155.

Darling-Wolf, F. (2006) The men and women of non-no: Gender, race, and hybridity in two Japanese magazines. *Critical Studies in Media Communication* 23 (3), 181–199.

Dirlik, A. (1994) The postcolonial aura: Third World criticism in the age of global capitalism. *Critical Inquiry* 20, 328–356.

Duff, P. (2004) Intertextuality and hybrid discourses: The infusion of pop culture in educational discourse. *Linguistics and Education* 14, 231–276.

Fürsich, E. and Robins, M.B. (2004) Visiting Africa: Construction of nation and identity on travel websites. *Journal of Asian and African Studies* 39 (1–2), 133–152.

Gebhard, M. (2005) School reform, hybrid discourses, and second language literacies. *TESOL Quarterly* 39 (2), 187–210.

Gilroy, P. (1994) Black cultural politics: An interview with Paul Gilroy by Timmy Lott. *Found Object* 4, 46–81.

Gutiérrez, K., Baquedano-López, P. and Tejeda, C. (1999) Rethinking diversity: Hybridity and hybrid language practices in the third space. *Mind, Culture and Activity* 6, 286–303.

Hall, C. (2010) Academic capitalism, academic responsibility and tourism academics: Or, the silence of the lambs? *Tourism Recreation Research* 35 (3), 298–301.

Hall, S. (1996) When was 'the post colonial'? Thinking at the limit. In I. Chambers and L. Curti (eds) *The Post-Colonial Question* (pp. 213–220). London: Routledge.

Higgins, C. (2009) *English as a Local Language: Post-Colonial Identities and Multilingual Practices*. Bristol: Multilingual Matters.

Hinnenkamp, V. (2003) Mixed language varieties of migrant adolescents and the discourse of hybridity. In J.J. Normann (ed.) *Bilingualism and Social Change: Turkish Speakers in North Western Europe* (pp. 12–39). Clevedon: Multilingual Matters.

Hirsch, J. (1999) Globalisation, class, and the question of democracy. *Socialist Register* 35, 278–293.

Holliday, A. (2005) *The Struggle to Teach English as an International Language*. New York: Oxford University Press.

Hollinshead, K., Ateljevic, I. and Nazia, A. (2009) Worldmaking agency – Worldmaking authority: The sovereign constitutive role of tourism. *Tourism Geographies* 1 (4), 427–443.

Hutnyk, J. (2005) Hybridity. *Ethnic and Racial Studies* 28 (1), 79–102.

Kachru, B. (1976) Models of English for the Third World white man's linguistic burden or language pragmatics? *TESOL Quarterly* 10 (2), 221–239.

Kachru, B. (1997) World Englishes and English-using communities. *Annual Review of Applied Linguistics* 17, 66–87.

Kompridis, N. (2005) Normativizing hybridity/neutralizing culture. *Political Theory* 33 (3), 318–343.

Kumaravadivelu, B. (2008) *Cultural Globalization and Language Education*. New Haven and London: Yale University Press.

Language Travel Magazine (2006) The global market, accessed 21 July 2009. http://www.houthousemedia.com/ltm/ltmbackissues/nov07web/nov07specreport.htm.

Lorente, B.P. (2012) The making of 'workers of the world': Language and the labour brokerage state. In A. Duchene and M. Heller (eds) *Language in Late Capitalism: Pride and Profit*. London: Routledge.

Lowe, L. (1991) Heterogeneity, hybridity, multiplicity: Marking Asian American differences. *Diaspora: A Journal of Transnational Studies* 1 (1), 22–44.

Magno, C. (2010) Korean students' language learning strategies and years of studying English as predictors of proficiency in English. *TESOL Journal* 2, 39–61.

Makoe, P. and McKinney, C. (2009) Hybrid discursive practices in a South African multilingual classroom: A case study. *English Teaching: Practice and Critique* 8 (2), 80–95.

Mitchell, K. (1997) Different diasporas and the hype of hybridity. *Environment and Planning D: Society and Space* 15, 533–553.
Papastergiadis, N. (2000) *The Turbulence of Migration.* Cambridge: Polity Press.
Papastergiadis, N. (2005) Hybridity and ambivalence: Places and flows in contemporary art and culture. *Theory Culture Society* 22 (4), 39–64.
Park, J. and Bae, S. (2009) Language ideologies in educational migration: Korean *jogi yuhak* families in Singapore. *Linguistics and Education* 20, 66–377.
Parreñas, R.S. (2001) *Servants of Globalization: Women, Migration and Domestic Work.* Stanford, CA: Stanford University Press.
Patil, V. (2011) Narrating political history about contested space. Tourism websites of India's northeast. *Annals of Tourism Research* 38 (3), 989–1008. doi:10.1016/j.annals.2011.01.018.
Pennycook, A. (1990) Towards a critical applied linguistics for the 1990s. *Issues in Applied Linguistics* 1, 8–28.
Pennycook, A. (1994) *The Cultural Politics of English as an International Language.* Harlow: Longman.
Phillipson, R. (1992) *Linguistic Imperialism.* Oxford and New York: Oxford University Press.
Pieterse, N.J. (2001) Hybridity, so what? The anti-hybridity backlash and the riddles of recognition. *Theory, Culture & Society* 18 (2–3), 219–245.
Piller, I. (2002) *Bilingual Couples Talk: The Discursive Construction of Hybridity.* Amsterdam: John Benjamins.
Sajed, A. (2010) Postcolonial strangers in a cosmopolitan world: Hybridity and citizenship in the Franco-Maghrebian borderland. *Citizenship Studies* 14 (4), 363–380.
Sarangi, S. and Roberts, C. (1999) Introduction: Discursive hybridity in medical work. In S. Sarangi and C. Roberts (eds) *Talk, Work and Institutional Order: Discourse in Medical, Mediation and Management Settings* (pp. 61–74). Berlin and New York: Mouton de Gruyter.
Schirmer, D. and Shalom, S. (eds) (1987) *The Philippines Reader – A History of Colonialism, Neocolonialism, Dictatorship, and Resistance.* Quezon City: KEN Incorporated.
Seoul Times (2006) Philippines: Asia's top choice to learn English, accessed 6 June 2009. http://the seoultimes.com/ST/?url = /ST/db/read.php?idx = 4354.
Shin, H. (2010) 'Gireoji Gajok': Transnationalism and language learning. Unpublished doctoral dissertation. Ontario Institute for Studies in Education, University of Toronto.
Song, J. (2010) Language identity and ideology in transnational space: Globalization, migration and bilingualism among Korean families in the USA. *International Journal of Bilingual Education and Bilingualism* 13 (1), 23–42.
Spencer, A. (2011) Americans create hybrid spaces in Costa Rica: A framework for exploring cultural and linguistic integration. *Language and Intercultural Communication* 11 (1), 59–74.
Spivak, G.C. (1999) *Critique of Postcolonial Reason: Towards a History of the Vanishing Present.* Cambridge, MA: Harvard University Press.
Sunstar Cebu (2008) Filipinos 'more able' operators of ESL schools – Foreign linguist, 30 September, accessed 6 June 2009. http://www.sunstar.com.ph/static/ceb/2008/09/30/bus /filipinos.more.able.operators.of.esl.schools.foreign.linguist.html.
Werbner, P. (2001) The limits of cultural hybridity: On ritual monsters, poetic license and contested postcolonial purifications. *The Journal of the Royal Anthropological Institute* 7 (1), 133–152.
Wood, B. (2004) A world in retreat: The reconfiguration of hybridity in 20th-century New Zealand television. *Media, Culture and Society* 26 (1), 45–62.
Yanik, L. (2011) Constructing Turkish 'exceptionalism': Discourses of liminality and hybridity in post-Cold War Turkish foreign policy. *Political Geography* 30, 80–89.
Young, R. (1995) *Colonial Desire: Hybridity in Theory, Culture and Race.* London: Routledge.

5 Unremarkable Hybridities and Metrolingual Practices

Emi Otsuji and Alastair Pennycook

Hybridity as Unmarked

This chapter starts with the assumption that hybrid language use is unmarked. That is, we take hybridity as the starting point rather than viewing it as a ramification of the interaction between pre-given discrete 'languages'. This argument is a response to several different concerns with the notion of hybridity, which has been critiqued along various lines, from its botanical and colonial origins (Young, 1995), or its almost fetishistic status within some areas of postcolonial and cultural studies (Hutnyk, 2005), to the ways in which it potentially maintains the prior purities it claims to overcome (Gilroy, 1993). The notion of hybridity, as Hutnyk (2005: 80) argues 'is a usefully slippery category, purposefully contested and deployed to claim change'. All too often it assumes dichotomous relations even as it claims to supersede them, reassigning 'fixed identity into what becomes merely the jamboree of pluralism and multiplicity' (Hutnyk, 2005: 99).

Hybridity has been mobilized to oppose what are seen as essentialist accounts of culture and identity. Rather than people being assumed to adhere to ascribed identities (Indian, Singaporean, man, woman, teacher, linguist) whose characteristics are pre-given and known, hybridity has emphasized multiplicity and the diversity of mixed outcomes. This leads to the problem, however, that hybridity is always looking backwards, always invoking precisely those essential categories that it aims to supersede. As Hardt and Negri (2000) explain, the politics of postcolonial and postmodernist thinkers have been to identify the operation of power through binary oppositions, and then to oppose these through strategies of hybridization. Hybridity is thus 'a realized politics of difference, setting differences to play across boundaries'

(Hardt & Negri, 2000: 145) but these strategies 'remain fixated on attacking an old form of power and propose a strategy of liberation that could be effective only on the old terrain' (2000: 146).

One of these dichotomous pairs is the local and global, which are assumed to be juxtaposed and in need of reconciliation. In possibly the most trivializing example of this thinking, their hybridity is fixed together in the term 'glocal'. These backward-looking strategies, we are suggesting, these ways of supposedly resolving local and global relations by invoking hybrid glocality, do not give us sufficiently new ways of addressing current conditions of diversity. Our analysis of bilingual workplaces in Australia, furthermore, has led us to argue for the need to move beyond the strategy of arguing for a pluralization or hybridization of what are seen as discrete and static characterizations of linguistic and cultural practices, and instead to take these as the starting point. Put another way, it is not so much that languages, cultures, the local, or the global exist in isolation only to become hybrid when they come into contact under particular circumstances, but rather that their prior separation was always a strange artifact of particular ways of thinking. Hybridity, therefore, if we wish to use the term, needs to be seen as the unmarked starting point, the place of difference from which things emerge, rather than the endpoint towards which things converge.

In line with this questioning of linguistic categories, we consider the notions of bilingualism and multilingualism equally open to investigation since they are all too often premised on underlying assumptions about the existence of discrete mono-languages fixed in time and place that may become pluralized. Multilingualism, and versions of hybridity based on it, may therefore continue to support an understanding of non-hybrid languages. Blommaert (2010) proposes thinking in terms of the 'sociolinguistics of mobility', premised on language-in-motion rather than language-in-place. Language-in-motion provides new insights into global linguistic phenomena/practices, suggesting that we need to move away from thinking in terms of 'intrinsically defined objects' called language (Blommaert, 2010: 5). As an alternative, Blommaert argues for an understanding of linguistic resources such as styles, genres, features or registers that are constituent of the linguistic phenomenon and allow comprehensive spatiotemporal frames of linguistic movements. While largely in accord with Blommaert's proposition, we also want to emphasize that while globalization is clearly leading to changed patterns of language and mobility, we should not overlook the long history of language mobility that has always been part of the human condition. That is to say, it is not only that we need new sociolinguistics for new material conditions but that we need new sociolinguistics for all eras of language use. Put another way, we need not just to adjust our lenses because people are moving around more, but also to rethink language in more radical ways.

Our focus, therefore, is on the hybrid starting point of mixed linguistic resources, where genres, styles, practices and discourses are mobilized as part of everyday linguistic interaction. This is not to say, however, that we completely discard the idea of language boundaries. In her identity journey, migrant performance artist Guilermo writes that 'the border is no longer located at any fixed geopolitical site. I carry the border with me, and I find new borders wherever I go' (Gomez-Peña, 1996: 5). In this light, we wish to look at the creative ways in which geopolitical, geolinguistic sites produce, resist, defy and rearrange linguistic borders and practices. Like Ang's claim (2003: 141) that hybridity as mixture is more complex and entangled than multiculturalism, we argue that linguistic diversity needs to be understood not so much as convergent multilingualism but rather as emergent difference. This understanding disrupts the common perspective and views monolingualism, multilingualism, or more largely language, to emerge from hybridity: hybridity is a starting point rather than an end product.

From Multilingualism to Metrolingualism

Drawing on interviews and everyday conversations between participants in a multilingual workplace in Australia, this chapter scrutinizes a number of basic assumptions about hybrid language use and questions ways in which a focus on hybridity always implies its non-hybrid other as a possibility. Studies of contemporary language use – from new Englishes to multilingual workplaces – often invoke the notion of hybridity to capture the dynamics of language mixing that are observed. In the same way that multi-, poly- and plurilingualism focus on a plurality of entities to describe diversity, however, so hybridity also suggests the mixing of different and recognizable entities. Studies of global English(es), for example, often assume the existence of English before either pluralizing the idea (world Englishes) or focusing on language mixing (hybridity) in order to account for diversity.

By mobilizing the newly defined concept of metrolingualism (Otsuji & Pennycook, 2010), by contrast, this chapter starts with the assumption of mixing and diversity as a given, as the state from which we start the analysis, as a singularity. Metrolingualism does not start from the notion of a discrete language attached to nation and culture but rather focuses on how people produce, resist, defy and rearrange linguistic resources in and through local linguistic practices. We therefore focus on creative linguistic practices and provide a new way of understanding 'linguistic hybridity'. From this point of view, linguistic diversity is best understood not as a pluralization of languages (multilingualism), where enumerability of languages is taken as the key mode to capture diversity (Moore *et al.*, 2010), but rather through the assumption of diversity as a starting point, with the spatiality of the city (metro) as the organizer of diversity. Our argument is that hybridity is best seen as a site of emergence rather than convergence.

The following two examples shed light on this way of thinking. Excerpts 1 and 2 are naturally occurring conversations held in two separate workplaces in Australia. Participants in both conversations are from various linguistic and cultural backgrounds with extensive experience and exposure to various languages and cultures, particularly 'Japanese' and 'Australian'. Excerpt 1 is a conversation held in a commercial production company (Japaria) dealing with Japanese products in Australia. All the participants – Atsuko, Adam, Asami and Robert – are highly proficient in both English and Japanese. The following conversation in a meeting room was held during the lunch break when they finished eating take-away hamburgers from a corner shop. This is part of a conversation where Atsuko and Adam jokingly argue over whose sticky fingers resulted in the volume button on the TV remote becoming oily.

Excerpt 1 (A: Atsuko, Ad: Adam, R: Robert, As: Asami) English translation for Japanese utterances is provided in brackets in italics.

1. Ad はい? (*Yes?*)
2. A I only touched the volume button.
3. Ad Look how much is on the button.
4. A No that's your hand. You've been holding on to it. All I did was like press it like that.
5. Ad So it was me then, who did 'boogers' on it.
6. As きたないな::[1] (*It's dirty::*)
7. R Boogers?
8. Ad Boogers.
9. R Yeah.
10. A もう。(*Come on.*)
11. R だからみんな風邪引くんだよな (*That is why we all get colds.*)
12. As 本当ね (*It's true.*)
13. Ad <coughing> もういいや、気持ち悪くなってきた (*Enough already. I feel sick now.*)
14. R Look at that just in time for lunch.
15. A なにも見えないじゃん。(*Can't see anything.*)

16. Ad あとは I have to buy some wine. Where should I buy it? Just across the road? (*After this*, I have to buy[2]...)
17. A 何を？ (*Buy what?*)
18. Ad Wine.

We might approach an analysis of this conversation through the lens of bilingual code-switching, asking why the participants switch between English and Japanese, why, in effect, they produce this hybrid mix of two languages. From this perspective, however, it is hard to account for the ways in which the participants move back and forth between these languages. Atsuko uses English to blame Adam for making the volume button dirty (line 4) but she uses Japanese in the rest of the conversation (line 10, 15, 17). Robert, who is listening to Atsuko and Adam also participates in their conversation, first in English (line 7 and 9) and then in Japanese (line 11), not necessarily corresponding to the language chosen in the previous turn.

It is difficult to find a rationale based on topic, previous utterance or speaker background for the varied uses of language here. Such attempts to account for the ways in which participants apparently manipulate their two distinct codes may not be the best way to account for such data. Rather than starting with a duality of languages, and then seeking an account of their code-mixed hybridity, it may be more fruitful to work with hybridity as our starting point and thence to pursue the implications of this as the unremarkable point of departure. The following accounts of their own understandings of their language use support this interpretation. In interviews the above staff members report little awareness of using one language or the other. For example, Adam states that 'In Japaria I don't consciously speak in English or in Japanese I choose the one I feel comfortable with at the time.' Atsuko and Asami respectively report that 'I don't have any awareness that I am choosing language' and 'when I recall a particular conversation, it is often the case that I can't remember in which language it was spoken'.

Of course, the inability to recall particular language use in retrospective accounts of conversations does not in itself mean that we should reject the possibility of finding an explanation for what might still be interpreted as code switches here. Nevertheless, if we take seriously the views of the language users themselves, there is a clear indication that they are not aware of, and do not consider important, the moves they make between languages. Excerpt 2, a conversation held in a language department of a government educational institution in Australia, provides further evidence of this. There were four Japanese-speaking staff members in the Japanese language section of the department, two 'Anglo-Australians' and two ethnically Japanese. Within this group, Patricia, a female Caucasian Australian national, and

Yuri, a female Japanese national, are involved in online material development. The former was a hired project officer and the latter was a senior education official. The conversation started right after a conversation between Patricia and Sarah, the Japanese section manager, about an overcharged invoice they received and how to handle it.

Excerpt 2 (P: Patricia, Y: Yuri)

1. P I am good at advising others.
2. Y Oh, yes, you are.
3. P 私鳴ったら 'Hello Kent ( )[3]' I don't know (*I... if the phone rings* 'hello Kent ( )'...)

<Both laughing >

4. P 私が出るから、ね、電話が来たら 'OK so what's your handling thing' (*I will answer the phone. OK? If the phone rings* 'OK what is your ...)
5. Y Change the voice.

<Both laughing >

6. Y 本当ね (*It is true, isn't it.*)
7. P 'I am so disappointed I work with about 5000 people and I was going to recommend you <laugh > I still will if you'. OK.
8. Y OK はい。だから ( ) like that (OK. *Yes so* ( ) like that)
9. P 見せたいと思ったら別の質問になる。(*If you want to show this, we have to create a separate question.*)
10. Y そうね I agree (*That's right*. I agree.)
11. P 何か質問入れる? 土曜日か日曜日 (*Do you want to put some questions? About Saturday or Sunday?*)

Patricia has a reputation in the office for being good at negotiating with people. She is softly spoken and indirect but strategic in handling problems. Her set phrase in negotiation is 'I am disappointed'. Yuri on the other hand, is seen by others and herself as someone whose communication style is direct (a reversal, incidentally, of common stereotypical 'Japanese' and 'Anglo' characteristics). From lines 1 to 7, after Sarah left, Patricia jokingly demonstrates how she would negotiate with their client, Kent, with whom they are having problems.

Again observable here are frequent instances of what might be deemed to be code-switching or language choices. While it might be possible to explain the use of one language or the other in some instances, in most cases there seems little reason for the apparent change of code. In line 3, Patricia changes to Japanese from English when she leads into the demonstration of the telephone conversation: '私 鳴ったら (*I... if the phone rings*)'. This is then followed by an English phrase, 'Hello Kent' but her attempt to say something is immediately given up by saying 'I don't know'. In line 4, Patricia tries for the second time. Yuri gives her advice to change her voice and then comments in Japanese in line 6. Yuri sometimes uses Japanese and sometimes English when responding to Patricia in lines 2, 5 and 6. After the climax of Patricia's performance, by jokingly quoting her favorite phrase, 'I am disappointed', she attempts to terminate the topic with the word 'OK' in line 7. Yuri responds by saying OK and both start to discuss work matters. Here again a frequent switch between English and Japanese is observed even within one turn. What makes this example interesting is not just the almost seamless frequent 'switch' between 'Japanese' and 'English' but the difficulty in identifying the rationale behind the switch. Indeed, Patricia herself reflected on her language choice at the end of the conversation she had with Yuri at other occasions but seemed to struggle to identify the rationale behind her language choices.

Excerpt 3 (P: Patricia, Y: Yuri)

P So when I am happy I speak in Japa in English っていうこと？今？(so when I am happy I speak in Japa in English *is that what it is?? Now?*)
Y あ：： そうかな (*We::ll, could be.*)

On another occasion:
P O.K. 今日本語で話したのは日本のことだったらからですね。(*The reason why I spoke in Japanese right now is because it was about Japan, right?*)
Y そうですね。(*That's right.*)

Both Patricia and Yuri have a good command of English and Japanese and have been working in both languages comfortably. Lack of proficiency certainly does not appear to cause switches; indeed, it is the very proficiency in both languages that appears to enable this switching. In the following interview excerpts about their language choices both speakers orient towards a sense of 'feeling' as guiding language change.

Excerpt 4 (P: Patricia, Y: Yuri)

1. P 私も時々英語に変える。どうして英語に変えたいか？ 二人とも急に英変える (*I also sometimes change to English. Why do I want to change to English? We swiftly change to English.*)
2. Y パトリシアとどっちを使ってもいいということを経験したときに、自分の子供たちがどうしてこういうときには英語の単語、こういうときに日本語の単語を使って、と自分の気持ちに一番近い言葉を作ってしまっているという気持ちがわかるようになった。
(When I experienced that I can use both languages with Patricia, I started to understand the feeling why my children use an English word at a certain moment and Japanese for another. They create the language that is close to their own feelings.)

3. P 気持ちに近いってあると思いますね。面白いですね。
(I agree with the closeness to one's feeling. It is interesting.)

Like Adam's earlier claim that he chooses the language he feels comfortable with at the time, Yuri also mentions that she and her children use words that they feel are close to their feeling. What is also intriguing here, however, is Yuri's remark in line 2 that they are creating language. There is more going on here than word choice in relation to certain feelings; rather there is a creative emergence of something new.

A central question that emerges from the creative linguistic practices we observe in this data is whether notions such as bilingualism or code-switching account adequately for what is going on here. While it is tempting to see these interactions as the hybrid mixing of two languages, as code-mixing by people of different linguistic backgrounds, it gradually became clear to us that this line of thinking approaches the question from the wrong direction. Is it not possible, instead, to consider these interactions from the starting point of hybridity, to consider hybridity as the point from which difference emerges rather than the endpoint of convergent multilingualism? Rather than viewing the above interactions from the standpoint of linguistic pluralization (bilingualism) becoming hybrid (code-mixing), we want to argue that language has always been hybrid. We are interested, then, in disrupting the ontological order that non-hybrid discreteness (monolingualism, bilingualism, multilingualism) precedes hybridity (code-mixing, code-switching).

Looking for new ways of conceptualizing language to meet this challenge, the notion of metrolingualism seems to open up new avenues of thought. By challenging the tendency to interpret current multilingual phenomena as additive separate languages, we (Otsuji & Pennycook, 2010, 2011) have proposed metrolingualism as a way to shift from enumeration strategies to the already different. In doing so, language is no longer seen as a stable entity attached to ethnicity, culture, state or territory. Metrolingualism attempts to move away from ascriptions of language and identity along conventional statist correlations, and instead provides an alternative way to look at late modern urban linguistic mobility. We do not need to seek explanations for code-mixing in the above examples: They are already metrolingual.

Hybridity and Metrolingualism

Metrolingualism, then, makes the spatial context of modern urban interaction (metro) the modifier of language, rather than a pluralization of languages (multi, pluri, poly). This helps us make sense of interactions such as the following, where neither of the two speakers, Adam and Heather from Japaria, is Japanese, yet both use Japanese and English resources in their conversation:

Excerpt 5 (H: Heather, Ad: Adam)

1. Ad I've got friends coming up from Osaka.
2. H Um.
3. Ad On Saturday.
4. H Yeah.
5. Ad And they want to stay at my place.
   <H laughs >
6. Ad All five of them.
7. H Oh my god. <laugh >
8. H That's pretty きちがい isn't it (That's pretty *crazy*, isn't it.)
9. Ad すごい小さい。大丈夫 大丈夫。(*Very small. It's OK, OK.*)
10. H 'All roll now.'
11. Ad 雑魚ねするから (*They'll sleep like sardines.*)
12. H ふとん BYO ふとん (*Futon, BYO Futon.*)
13. Ad 前もやっている。(*I have done this before.*)
14. H Is it たたみ? (*Is it Tatami*?)
15. Ad No just floor.

In lines 8–14 there is an interwoven flow of Japanese and English. The pattern of the language use is very similar to excerpt 1 apart from the fact that this time the conversation was exclusively between 'non-native speakers of Japanese' (if such terminology still makes sense). It is also worth noting that it is not always evident what language some words are 'in'. The phrase BYO ふとん (line 12) (Bring your own Futon), for example, has been transcribed in *romaji* and *hiragana*[4] to denote the two languages, based on the pronunciation of 'futon'. A case might be made, however, for its transcription, when spoken by two Anglo-Australians, in roman script. If BYO, on the other hand, were to be seen as already incorporated into their Japanese, the case might be made for its transcription in katakana.

In the same way as people in Japaria did not perceive the separate use of different languages, they also seem to have loose associations between language and ethnic identities. Atsuko (excerpt 1), for example, claims 'I don't consciously think that I am a Japanese. I stop being aware of noticing people as Japanese or Australian', while according to Heather (excerpt 5) 'When I was living in Japan, I was often asked "how about in Australia?" At the beginning I was saying "generally . . ." but then, I changed my attitude and I started to say "in my opinion" . . . rather than generalizing Australia'. James and Mika, colleagues of Atsuko and Heather correspondingly said 'I stop thinking it is different because s/he is Japanese, when you acquire a language, you stop differentiating people according to their countries, don't you?' and 'nowadays, I don't differentiate between Japanese and Australians', respectively.

The same pattern was also identified in the language department of a government educational institution in Australia. Excerpt 6 occurred just before excerpt 2 above, when Sarah, the Japanese section manager, came to seek advice from Patricia about the overcharged invoice.

Excerpt 6 (S: Sarah, P: Patricia)

1. S 面白い電話がはいってきた。Xから 'I have charged you more ( )' (*I received an interesting phone call. From X* 'I have charged . . .')
2. P そういった？よかった You didn't even call them. So it was a mistake. (*Did they say that? That was good.* You didn't even . . .)
3. S It was only 60 dollars the difference is not huge but . . . I think they must be feeling guilty, because of my reaction.
4. P Yes why don't you ring back and say they overcharged you 100 dollars.
   <a few exchanges>
5. S. But I think it is really suspicious.
6. P 本当ね。(*It really is.*)
7. S If I haven't said anything.

Patricia and Yuri's desks are next to each other. When Sarah came to Patricia to report the phone conversation, Yuri was sitting next to Patricia. The conversation, however, was exclusively between Sarah and Patricia and the content of the conversation was not relevant to Yuri. And yet, it is interesting to note that Sarah started the conversation in Japanese and Patricia responded to Sarah by inserting Japanese expressions (in lines 2 and 6). One might say that the choice of Japanese by Sarah and Patricia was affected by Yuri's presence. It is, however, hard to justify this claim since Yuri and Patricia always mix English and Japanese anyway, and Yuri's level of English is proficient to the extent that she would not have felt excluded even if the conversation between Patricia and Sarah were exclusively in English. Rather than trying to account for the use of English here or the use of Japanese there, it seems to make more sense to say that if the nearby presence of Yuri had any effect on their language choice it was to reinforce the metrolinguistic practices of the workplace. And yet, as we have seen elsewhere, participants do not need the presence of a linguistic/cultural 'other' to trigger metrolingualism: This is the workplace norm.

If, as we have argued, these examples of local interactions are better understood in terms of metrolingualism rather than multilingualism, the next question we want to address is whether we should consider metrolingualism to be a form of hybridity. To make sense of this question, which will depend on how we understand hybridity, let us take a slight detour. In previous work on metrolingualism (Otsuji & Pennycook, 2010, 2011), we have discussed the relationship between metrolingualism and metrosexuality. It has been common to associate the metrosexual with a certain apparently superficial level of grooming and appearance. As Coad (2008: 197) argues, however, there are good reasons to see it as more profound than this: 'Metrosexuality tells us something about the relations between the sexes, about nonnormative sexualities, and about how gender and sexuality are used as interpretative tools to label individuals and as markers of self-identity.' Likewise, we have been arguing that the idea of metrolingualism can shed light on relations between languages and the ways in which languages are interpretative tools to label individuals and as markers of self-identity. 'Changing attitudes in these areas', Coad (2008: 197) goes on,

> is where metrosexuality has the most potential importance as a cultural phenomenon. Metrosexual males may look prettier and more beautiful than their nonmetrosexual brothers, but metrosexuality is the motor behind more decisive changes in the realm of sexual politics; it influences how heterosexual males interact with homosexual males and it is in the process of replacing traditional categories of sexual orientation.

We have argued that certain aspects of metrolingualism can be interpreted in the same way, that even when metrolingual practices are seen as playful linguistic acts – and this is certainly not, as we see from the above examples, an obvious or necessary interpretation of the term – there is also serious business afoot in the challenges to linguistic orthodoxies (retrolinguistic views of language). But is metrosexuality hybrid? In its challenges to orthodox views of how men should behave, in its realignment of sexuality, in its deployment of attributes that might be viewed as 'feminine' (though the problematic circularity of such attributions is also evident), is it therefore hybrid? In spite of the incorporation of what are assumed to be non-essential elements (the groomed, the fashionable, the sensitive) into the male persona, it does not seem useful to consider the metrosexual hybrid precisely because it is challenging the very ascription of those ideals to normative categorizations of sexual identity. To see metrosexuality as a hybrid of the masculine and feminine is to retain normative accounts of the constitution of such identities. Here, then, we return to the problem of whether the hybrid maintains or questions the categories on which the 'mixture' is based.

Metrosexuality, however mild, sweet-smelling and fashionable, seems to question the stability of categorizations rather than blend them. This is surely because it is a realignment of ways of being, doing and thinking, and to talk simultaneously of hybridity seems to reinvest in those very categories that it aims to go beyond. Likewise, then, metrolingualism: Even though we are cautious about aligning the ordinariness of everyday metrolingualism with those characteristics of superficiality, effete elitism and commercialization often attributed to metrosexuality, the comparison draws attention to the point that to see metrolingualism as a hybrid mix of languages is to reinvoke those very categories of language we hope to avoid. On these grounds, therefore, we would argue that metrolingual practices are not hybrid in the sense that they combine pre-made languages into a new mix.

This does not mean, however, that we can ignore the continued deployment of fixed categories of linguistic and cultural identity. These are still very real as part of the discursive world in which we operate, and such categories may equally be used by those who follow a metrolingual lifestyle at other times. The point, however, is that we do not see metrolingualism as the hybrid blending of such categorical entities but rather as involving the interplay between a given diversity and its static institutional and discursive nemesis. When considering metrolingualism, therefore, we are by no means blind to the fact that people also incorporate fixed modes of identities. Metrolinguists view language as emergent from complex local interactions with people moving between a fixed and fluid understanding of language. In this sense, creativity means emergent dynamism rather than convergent diversity.

This movement between fixed and fluid identities is observed in a number of cases in the data. It was not uncommon to observe that the very person who has shown resistance to essentialist views of language and people can also at other times make quite sweeping cultural generalizations. Atsuko from Japaria (excerpt 1), asserted on the one hand 'I don't have any awareness that I am choosing language' and 'I don't consciously think that I am a Japanese. I stop being aware of noticing people as Japanese or Australian.' On the other hand, fixed views of culture could also be found as naturalized assumptions. As the example below suggests, the perception of her belief is one thing, but how she displays her understandings in conversation is another.

Excerpt 7 (M: Mika, A: Atsuko)

1. M あぶない。あぶない (*That's scary, so scary*)
2. A そうよね、そこってきちんと調べられたら問題になるんじゃない？ロバートが行ったエービーロードにあるね、なんかロシアン系のジューが多いからエービーってへんなところ。
(*That's right. If the place was checked officially, I think they'd be in trouble. The place Robert went to in AB road is like, well, there are a lot of Russian Jews so, it's a strange place.*)
3. M いや：：eugh(*eu::gh*)?

The very person who seemed to show a loose association between language choice and identity here employs a fixed and apparently discriminatory position towards Russian Jews. Atsuko's statement shows her assumption of a link between the strangeness of the area and her pre-given images of Russian Jews. These views of a particular culture, again, contrast with the borderless understanding she displayed during the interview, showing the complexity and flux of the conception of culture and people as well as how borderless and bordered ideas can actively interact with each other. This also suggests that our focus should not be on people or languages as the localities of identity so much as the circulation of discourses.

Similarly, Yuri, who in the previous excerpts 2, 3 and 4 also showed an ambivalent position regarding Japanese and Australian practices, was able to show on the one hand a complex view of unbounded identity:

Y 私から見るとパトリシアさんはすごくわたしよりも日本人的ないいところを兼ね備えていると思う。例えば日本のいいところを「す、す」と取り入れている。(*I think Patricia has good quality of Japanese-ness much more than I. She adapts good things about Japan very effectively.*)

On the other hand, however, she also acknowledged that she is not able to attribute her quality to Japaneseness entirely:

Y これが日本的かどうかってなると、それはまた・・・パトリシアさんのそんなdiplomatic なところは、前マネージャーだったり、そういう仕事の経歴から得た経験から来ていると思う。(*Whether this is Japanese-like or not, that is also ... I think Patricia's diplomatic quality comes from the fact that she was a manager and the experiences she has had through her work trajectories.*)

Yuri, also commented that she was very surprised to find out how Australians and Japanese are very similar:

Y で、なんかもっとはっきり言わないといけないとか、その、なに？そのコンフリクトをものともせず自分を押さないといけないと、ミーイズムそのままみたいな、そういうのがそういうのがウェスタンの考え方っていう風に、なんとなく日本にいるときは思っているけど、オーストラリアに来て、そういう風にそういうことじゃないということに、ものすごくそうじゃないじゃないと思った。やっぱりすごく気を使うところは気を使うし。

(*And, you think things like you have to say things more clearly ... and well, you should not be scared of having conflict or being forceful and nothing but Me-ism. These are what we think ... Western ways of thinking are about when we are in Japan. But after I came to Australia I realized that it is not necessarily so. I strongly felt that. People are considerate of others.*)

The above examples show that Yuri, on the one hand, can attribute Patricia's characteristics, rather counter-intuitively, to her greater Japaneseness, thus simultaneously reinforcing notions of what it means to be Japanese and opening up the possibility that non-Japanese may be more so than Japanese. On the other hand, she also acknowledges both that supposed cultural characteristics may not in fact be as different as commonly supposed and that they may equally derive from social roles. Here again, the movement between fixity and fluidity can be observed through the presence of and the breaking of the dichotomy of A (Japan/East) and B (Australia/West).

Our understanding of metrolingualism, then, seeks to avoid the potential traps of 'hybridity-talk' (Hutnyk, 2005), where hybridity becomes the solution to preconceived difference, where a 'neither A nor B' conclusion ends in 'third spaces' or 'hybridity', where *happy hybridity* becomes an unproblematic category of cultural diversity (Allatson, 2001; Perera, 1994), where 'liberal exoticist enthusiasm' (Hutnyk, 2000: 12) endlessly seeks out forms of perceived cultural miscegenation, where 'the notion of the "hybrid" can become as fixed a category as its essentialist nemesis' (Zuberi, 2001: 239–240). As these and other critics have pointed out, the idea of hybridity, the mixture at the interface of the local and global, these third spaces of cultural and linguistic mashing, do not do enough to challenge ontologically the definitions of non-difference that they seek to go beyond. Metrolingualism, by contrast, is not constituted by 'neither A nor B', nor by a 'third' position. It does not therefore become an alternative but restabilized position of hybrid fixity. Metrolingualism, instead, is movement: the movement between fixity (familiar and fixed boundaries) and fluidity (transgression and elimination of boundaries). In this sense, although metrolingual fluidity may imply its fixed other as a possibility, this relation is different from the fixity/mixing of hybridity: Hybridity implies a notion of fixity or purity that it seeks to go beyond, whereas our understanding of metrolingualism takes difference as the starting point and sees the fixity of languages and cultures as discursively produced social facts with which metrolingual practices interact.

This epistemological identification of metrolingualism refers back to the earlier question: Is metrolingualism hybrid? This chapter is based on the assumption of mixed language as a given, as the state from which we start the analysis as a singularity that stands against retrolingual mono/multilingual dichotomies. This is akin to Higgins and Coen's (2000: 15) observation about the ordinariness of difference: 'diversity is the given reality of human social action'. The 'metro' of metrolingualism not only carries the idea of the city but also of a singular starting point (as opposed to the pluralization strategies of multi-, poly- or pluri-lingualism). This approach to diversity does not seek to account for difference by mixing or pluralizing but rather by challenging the ascriptions of language and identity along conventional lines. In this sense, this singularity *is* hybrid, implying (and accommodating) its non-hybrid other in and through the interaction between fixity and fluidity.

Derrida (1981) shows the ways in which traces are always present and we are never able to identify anything on its own terms. He claims 'neither A nor B is simultaneously either A or B' (Derrida, 1981: 43). This means that 'A nor B' exists only by identifying A and B. If so, hybridity is about identification as part of the non-hybrid other. It is the impossibility to understand itself outside the political and ideological forces that constitute the categories and binarity. Thus, instead of conceiving hybridity in terms of a new position that is merely 'neither A nor B' or 'in-between-ness space', we understand hybridity as a movement in which 'neither' can be part of 'either' or 'both' (enabled by fixity and fluidity). With the impossibility of self-identification on its own terms, we can only start from hybridity. That is, hybridity is the starting point. In this sense, metrolingualism is hybridity that accommodates complex movement between fixity and fluidity. This understanding of hybridity can in turn overcome common ways of framing language through its capacity to deal with contemporary language practices.

Conclusion: Unmarked Metrolingualism

Just as Gilroy (1994: 55) describes his move away from the terminology of hybridity on the grounds that 'Cultural production is not like mixing cocktails', so we have argued in this chapter that hybridity does not account well for metrolingual production, which is far more than just mixing drinks or languages. We have argued here that metrolingualism is characterized by the perpetual movement between fixity and fluidity. If we take seriously the argument that all language practices are local (Pennycook, 2010), then the assumed polarity between the local and global is disrupted: we cannot talk about global practices without acknowledging that everything happens locally. Likewise, if we assume that all language practices are hybrid, then the assumed polarity between the hybrid and the non-hybrid is disrupted. Following Kraidy (1999: 191), 'we have to recognise that both global and local cultural formations are inherently hybridized', that locality in itself is a complex cultural phenomenon, and the polarization between the global and local does not hold. 'Mobility is the rule', Blommaert (2010: 23) reminds us, 'but that does not preclude locality (...)'. Locality and mobility co-exist, and whenever we observe patterns of mobility we have to examine the local environments in which they occur. While we need to find better ways of understanding our multiple, hybrid and complex world, we need both to avoid turning hybridity into a fixed category of pluralization, and to find ways to acknowledge that fixed categories are also mobilized as an aspect of hybridity.

Notes

(1) Colons indicate prolongation of the immediately prior sound.
(2) The transition to non-italic shows the shift to the original English utterance.
(3) Single inverted commas indicate the utterance as quoted text. Brackets indicate untranscribable utterance.
(4) Hiragana and katakana are Japanese orthographies. Hiragana is used to write Japanese originated words while katakana is used for loan words. Romaji is the Roman script.

References

Allatson, P. (2001) Beyond the hybrid: Notes against heterophilic authoritarianism. *Genre* (22), 191–207.

Ang, I. (2003) Together-in-difference: Beyond diaspora, into hybridity. *Asian Studies Review* 27 (2), 141–154.

Blommaert, J. (2010) *The Sociolinguistics of Globalization*. Cambridge: Cambridge University Press.

Coad, D. (2008) *The Metrosexual: Gender, Sexuality, and Sport*. Albany, NY: SUNY Press.

Derrida, J. (1981) *Positions* (A. Bass, trans. and annotated). Chicago, IL: The University of Chicago Press.

Gilroy, P. (1993) *The Black Atlantic: Modernity and Double Consciousness*. London: Verso.

Gilroy, P. (1994) Black cultural politics: An interview with Paul Gilroy by Timmy Lott. *Found Object* 4, 46–81.

Gomez-Peña, G. (1996) *The New World Border*. San Francisco, CA: City Light.

Hardt, M. and Negri, A. (2000) *Empire*. Cambridge, MA: Harvard University Press.
Higgins, M. and Coen, T. (2000) *Streets, Bedrooms, and Patios: The Ordinariness of Diversity in Urban Oaxaca*. Austin: University of Texas Press.
Hutnyk, J. (2000) *Critique of Exotica: Music, Politics and the Culture Industry*. London: Pluto Press.
Hutnyk, J. (2005) Hybridity. *Ethnic and Racial Studies* 28 (1), 79–102.
Kraidy, M.M. (1999) The global, the local, and the hybrid: A native ethnography of glocalization. *Critical Studies in Mass Communication* 16 (4), 456–476.
Moore, R., Pietikäinen, S. and Blommaert, J. (2010) Counting the losses: Numbers as the language of language endangerment. *Sociolinguistic Studies* 4 (1), 1–26.
Otsuji, E. and Pennycook, A. (2010) Metrolingualism: Fixity, fluidity and language in flux. *International Journal of Multilingualism* 7 (3), 240–254.
Otsuji, E. and Pennycook, A. (2011) Social inclusion and metrolingual practices. *Journal of Bilingualism and Bilingual Education* 14 (4), 413–425.
Pennycook, A. (2010) *Language as a Local Practice*. New York: Routledge.
Perera, S. (1994) Unspeakable bodies: Representing the Aboriginal in Australian critical discourse. *Meridian* 13 (1), 15–26.
Young, R. (1995) *Colonial Desire: Hybridity in Theory, Culture and Race*. New York: Routledge.
Zuberi, N. (2001) *Sounds English: Transnational Popular Music*. Urbana: University of Illinois Press.

6 Countering the Dual: Transglossia, Dynamic Bilingualism and Translanguaging in Education

Ofelia García

What is dual about bilingualism? From the point of view of monolingual people, everything; from the perspective of bilingual people themselves, nothing is dual, nothing is simply two, or just three, or even more. And yet, as more language minorities become bilingual through immigration and increased contact with others, and as more language majorities incorporate global language practices, especially English, more educators are constraining it to a duality. This ignores the enormous linguistic variation of bilingual speakers and constrains the possibilities of constructing an education that truly reflects the fluidity of language practices and identifications in the 21st century. Increasingly, educators and scholars talk about bilingualism in a 'dual way', referring to dual language learners, dual language classrooms, dual language teachers, dual language books and even dual language programs. But what is dual about bilingualism? And what does this shift in discourse, from bilingual to dual, mean? It is precisely the exploration of this question that is the topic of this chapter.

To do so, this chapter focuses on bilingual education in the US, describing how it is that the discursive shift – from bilingual education to dual language education – has been constructed. The chapter explores reasons for the shift, and considers how this naming change has constrained equal educational opportunities for language minority students in the US.

This chapter then explores how this discursive shift has had the effect of further normalizing monoglossic ideologies within studies of bilingualism and education in additional languages. *Monoglossic ideologies* perceive bilingualism from a monolingual angle and see only the sum of two separate languages. By normalizing the 'dual' through a monolingual perspective, the language education field uses terms and concepts that have had the effect of negating the fluidity of bilingual language practices and furthering inequalities in the education of language minorities.

This chapter deconstructs the dual monoglossic concepts that have been so central in the field of language education and that may have contributed to some of the failures that can be observed today in the promotion of plurilingual practices for a global world. These concepts, named with a duality that comes from monoglossic understandings of bilingualism that were prevalent in the 20th century are (1) diglossia and (2) additive and subtractive bilingualism, with its concomitant concepts of L1/L2, mother tongue and native speaker. Data is then presented from a study of two bilingual classrooms – a kindergarten and a fifth grade classroom – to illustrate the dynamic bilingualism that is evidence of more heteroglossic language practices.

In countering the 'dual' in the language education field, this chapter argues for the use of translanguaging (García, 2009) as a bilingual pedagogy. Data from a study of a secondary school for emergent bilingual students are then presented to show how a pedagogy that builds on the fluid languaging of bilingual children holds much promise to meaningfully educate bilingual students, especially those from minority communities.

From Bilingual to Dual: The US Case

Histories and ideologies of US bilingual education

Bilingual education to educate immigrants is not new in the US, although its use has waxed and waned throughout the centuries. The contemporary bilingual education movement in the US has to be understood as a civil rights victory for the more equitable education of language minorities, and especially of Spanish-speaking Latinos. By the time the Bilingual Education Act was reauthorized in 1974, bilingual education was defined as transitional; that is, the use of the students' home languages was authorized only until the children learned English, at which time they had to be transitioned to English-only classrooms. Nevertheless, the focus was on providing these children with equal educational opportunity, as was evident in the US Supreme Court decision of *Lau* v. *Nichols* (1974). During the 1970s, bilingual education programs, mostly of the transitional type, grew in school systems with high language minority enrollment.

The prevailing ideology about bilingualism in education was then based on the distinction that the Canadian scholar William Lambert (1974) had made about two types of bilingualism – *additive bilingualism* and *subtractive bilingualism*. Lambert referred to additive bilingualism as the type fostered by bilingual education programs for majorities, based on Lambert's substantive experience in the creation and development of Canadian immersion bilingual education, in which a 'second language' was added to a 'first language', and both languages were subsequently maintained and developed. Subtractive bilingualism, however, was the type involved in the transitional bilingual education of language minorities in the US, in which the child's 'first language' was subtracted as the 'second language' was taught. US bilingual educators involved in the struggle for more educational opportunity for language minority students advocated strongly for additive bilingual programs, but programs other than transitional bilingual education programs, that is, 'developmental maintenance bilingual education programs' that were developed in the 1960s and early 1970s, started to be dismantled (for a history of bilingual education in the US, see especially Crawford, 2004).

In the midst of the growth and struggle over bilingual education programs to teach language minority children in the US, global and local shifts started to change the linguistic landscape. Responding to geopolitical as well as technological changes, there were changes in flows of information, goods and people, as well as ideologies. In the US, the nature of immigration was transformed, the consequence of a greater need for labor that was supported by changes to the Immigration and Naturalization Services Act of 1965. Quotas that restricted immigration, particularly of Latin Americans, Africans and Asians, were lifted. The result has been the greater linguistic diversity that we find in the US today, coupled with the greater resistance to bilingualism. I look at the greater linguistic diversity in the next section. I then describe the growing opposition to bilingualism and bilingual education in the US, coupled with the discursive shift that has taken place – from 'bilingual' to 'dual'. I argue that this in turn had led to decreased educational opportunities for language minorities in the US. I propose that the arguments that advocates for bilingualism in education are using to resist the opposition are old and inadequate. While the geopolitical, technological and sociolinguistic terrain has shifted, many language education scholars and teachers continue to use instruments from the 20th century – linear conceptualizations of bilingualism that affirm a duality which has little to do with the fluid discursive practices of the 21st century.

Language diversity in US classrooms

Although census figures do not tell the whole picture, or even an accurate one, I start with what we know of the categorical counts made by the US census. Although I argue against many of these categories and deconstruct them later on, census figures offer a first approach to exploring diversity.

In the 21st century the US experienced not only a marked increase in its foreign-born population, but also a new complexity in immigration. Although in 1990 the foreign-born made up 8% of the total US population, in 2009 that had increased to 17% (US Census Bureau, 1990, 2009). There are many more children who are foreign-born in US classrooms today (and parents of those children) than in 1990. The foreign-born make up almost one-fifth of the US population (and most likely more, since many of the undocumented are undercounted). But beyond the greater numbers there is also more diversity of language, racial and ancestry backgrounds than ever before. For example, Latinos, who often (although not always) speak Spanish, make up 16% of the US population, and Asians, who often speak many languages, account for 4% (US Census Bureau, 2009).

The growth of the Latino and Asian populations in the United States, coupled with the continued residential segregation of many US communities of color, means that many schools have overwhelming majorities of, for example, Spanish speakers or Chinese speakers. But even within this supposed homogeneity there is much language variation, as students come from different national and local contexts, immigrate at different times and for numerous reasons and have varied lengths of residency in the US.

This greater linguistic complexity has consequences for how language minorities are perceived and classrooms structured. Oftentimes teachers confuse nationality for language. Teachers in classrooms often only notice those children who speak English with difficulty, those that the federal government refers to as 'limited English proficient', and US educators often call 'English language learners'. And yet, many children whom teachers notice only as monolingual English speakers come from very diverse language backgrounds; and their home language practices are not solely in English.

The more complex diversity of the US in the 21st century has been met with increased opposition. As we will see in the next section, in some states bilingual education has been simply outlawed. But in others the resistance has been managed by a discursive shift – from 'bilingual' to 'dual'. It is to be noted, however, that advocates of bilingualism themselves have many times adopted this discursive shift, ignoring how this shift is enmeshed in social systems of domination and subordination of groups, relating to language, ethnicity, race and class (for more on language ideologies, see especially Irvine & Gal, 2000).

US bilingual education under attack

Xenophobic ideologies have become more prevalent as the US linguistic landscape has grown to be more multilingual. US English was founded in 1983, claiming to preserve 'the unifying role of the English language in the United States' (http://www.usenglish.org/view/3) and lobbying for a constitutional amendment to make English the official language. And although efforts to pass a constitutional amendment at the federal level to make English the official language of the US have been abandoned, by 2010 28 states had passed English-only laws (García & Kleifgen, 2010).

As children and parents became increasingly multilingual, bilingual education as a way to teach immigrant children came under attack. English-only statutes that banned bilingual education were passed in two states with large Spanish-speaking populations – California in 1998 and Arizona in 2000. In 2002, Massachusetts also passed a proposition that replaced transitional bilingual education with 'structured English immersion programs'. Bilingual educators were forced to give up the temporary 'safe spaces' (Pratt, 1991) offered to recent immigrants in transitional bilingual classrooms, and bilingual education programs were increasingly substituted with English-only spaces.

At the same time, the word 'bilingual' was struck out of every single federal education office and project name, as well as legislation. For example, the Office of Bilingual and Minority Language Affairs came to be called the Office of English Language Acquisition. Even more significant was that the Bilingual Education Act itself was substituted by Title III of the No Child Left Behind Legislation of 2002, now named Language Instruction for Limited English Proficient and Immigrant Students. The word 'bilingual' had become the 'B' word (Crawford, 2007); that is, a word not to be named.

Some educators pointed to the linguistic complexity of classrooms and claimed that bilingual education was no longer possible in neighborhoods and communities that had become highly multilingual. On the other hand, through the renewed emphasis of No Child Left Behind, the education of immigrant students and of those whose English was developing became, rightly so, everyone's concern. Bilingual students were renamed 'limited English proficient students' by the federal government, and 'English language learners' by educators and the general public. In so doing, bilingualism was further restricted because now teachers who were not bilingual were in control of the education of these children, and the bilingualism of the students could be ignored. Increasingly, bilingual teachers were substituted by English-as-a-second-language teachers.

While ceding many bilingual spaces to English-only instruction, the bilingual profession decided to accept the other discursive changes that were taking place. In an effort to rescue part of the bilingual education enterprise, they promoted the use of 'dual language' education, and favored it over what they learned to call 'bilingual education', that is, transitional bilingual education, something that had to be outlawed in some states because it was transitional, subtractive and simply 'bad'.

In the beginning, the term 'dual language' referred to two-way bilingual education programs in which immigrant language minority children who were developing English were taught alongside children who spoke only English, with all becoming bilingual through education (Lessow-Hurley, 2005). But this type of bilingual education also became enmeshed in the flows of globalization, for it became no longer always possible to delineate one language group, or one 'speech community', from the other. For example, the Latino group, as we said before, had become highly heterogeneous, with many speaking English only or being bilingual. Thus, those who spoke English were now often Latinos, Asians and other immigrants whose home languages were not English. In some neighborhoods these 'dual language' programs became nothing more than developmental bilingual education programs in disguise, a way to provide the only means possible for Latino children with different bilingual proficiencies to be educated in both English and Spanish. And yet, as bilingual educators adapted to the discursive change that was being proposed in an effort to hold on to some bilingual instruction, bilingual education programs continued to be dismantled. Mostly abandoned, the ideologies, programs and pedagogies of bilingualism that remained were rooted in another era that had little to do with the complex language practices of the 21st century.

The Promise of 'Dual Language' Unfulfilled

As a way to survive, bilingual educators put all their eggs in the 'dual language' basket, and turned their backs on transitional bilingual education programs and on developmental maintenance bilingual programs. But as Guadalupe Valdés (1997) warned early on and many others have repeated (García, 2006), the dual language basket of two-way bilingual programs had a hole, and thus its promise remains unfulfilled. The intent of 'dual language' was to promote bilingualism among all children, language majorities and language minorities. But in the growing anti-bilingual, xenophobic climate, only a few enlightened parents recognized its potential.

'Dual language' also became associated with a particular type of bilingual education where, regardless of language profile, students were instructed, at least 50% of the time, in the language other than English. Additionally, 'dual language' also meant that bilingual education could continue beyond the time in which a child was declared English proficient, usually through elementary school. But again, in the growing anti-bilingual education climate, few 'dual language' programs of any kind were developed.

Eventually, 'dual language' began to mean a type of bilingual education that led to bilingualism, whereas 'bilingual education' began to mean transition to English-only monolingualism. Study after study declared the supremacy and effectiveness of 'dual language' over transitional bilingual education programs (Collier, 1995; Ramírez, 1992; Thomas & Collier, 2002). In the way that it was not named, bilingual education was silenced. How could all parents be convinced of the value of bilingualism when even advocates declared that 'dual language' was good and 'bilingual' was bad? Little by little, transitional bilingual education lost ground, but these programs were replaced not by 'dual language' programs, but by English-only programs. Whereas at the elementary level some efforts were made to develop these 'dual language' programs, at the secondary level they remain mostly nonexistent, leaving adolescent immigrant students with only one option – English-only. For example, in New York City in 2010–2011 these 'dual language' programs represented only 3.8% of the programs used to teach immigrant children who were developing English (New York City Department of Education, 2011), and there was only one 'dual language' education program at the secondary level. In this way, bilingual students have been increasingly robbed of the opportunity to use their bilingualism to construct meaning and to acquire deep understandings and knowledge.

Transgressing the Duality of Diglossia and Additive/Subtractive Bilingualism: The Power of Transglossia and Dynamic Bilingualism

Throughout the 20th century the concept of *diglossia* dominated the ways in which we viewed the bilingualism of groups. Diglossia, according to Fishman (1967), who extends Ferguson's original 1959 definition, refers to the idea that the stable bilingualism of societal groups could only respond to the functional allocation of languages, with one language (a 'High' language) used for specific purposes in a certain domain of more prestige, and the other one (a 'Low' language) used for others. Diglossia was developed when a 'speech community' was understood as stable and homogeneous and when power was not distinctly explored as a sociolinguistic dimension.

Diglossia paved the way for our understanding of individual bilingualism as linear, with languages added. The norm described was either monolingualism or a monoglossic bilingualism with a High and a Low language functionally distributed. Thus, bilingualism could not be anything but a 'second language' added to a 'first language' (additive bilingualism), or, in language minority situations, a 'first language' subtracted and replaced by a 'second language' (subtractive bilingualism).

The normalization of the power differentials of the languages involved in societal diglossia, combined with the conceptualization of emergent bilinguals as simply learners of a 'second language', and having a 'first language', a 'native language', a 'mother tongue', has meant that a more flexible bilingualism in itself has not been recognized. One could be a 'language learner', but one could not be a 'bilingual' with a complex linguistic repertoire that has features that cannot be simply assigned to one language or another. By reifying the concept of a 'second language', the language education field has negated the idea that it is possible to be simply bilingual, and that we are all emergent bilinguals (for more on the concept of emergent bilingualism, see García, 2009; García & Kleifgen, 2010). In schools in the US, for example, teachers are well aware of 'English language learners' for whom English is a 'second language'. And teachers are equally ignorant of the fact that by developing language practices that are seen as English, students are becoming bilingual. Once they pass an examination that declares them 'English fluent', their bilingualism is completely ignored.

On the other hand, by reifying the concept of a 'High', 'first' or 'native language', privilege or exclusion is assigned. For example, 'native' English speakers are often sought-after in Asian countries as English teachers, often meaning monolingual Americans, English and Australians, preferably white, with other bilinguals excluded.

Speaking of 'mother tongue', Skutnabb-Kangas (1981) points out that depending on the criteria used, the term could mean different things for any bilingual person. It could mean, as with 'first language', first learned. But even order of acquisition is problematic for bilinguals, since many bilinguals grow up with complex language practices that cannot be easily assigned to a 'first' or 'second language'; that is, there is bilingual first language acquisition (BFLA) (for more on this topic, see Genesee, 2003; see also De Houwer, 2009). According to Skutnabb-Kangas (1981), a mother tongue could also be, as with 'first language', the language one uses most, or the language one knows best, or the language with which one identifies, or the language with which others identify the speaker. But for bilinguals, all of these different criteria could result in a different answer or in no answer at all, since it is often impossible for bilinguals to view their language practices according to monoglossic views of autonomous languages. Regardless of the complexity of criteria, the problem with all of these terms is that they insist on shaping bilingualism according to monolingual monoglossic classifications of one or another autonomous language, when bilingual practices are a lot more complex and interrelated, especially in the globalized world of the 21st century.

In the 21st century, the concept of diglossia has been called into question, as more situations of stable societal multilingualism without functional allocation are described, and as critical sociolinguistics has explored aspects of power. Many have used the case of the complex and stable multilingualism of India and many African countries to question diglossic arrangements as the only way to achieve stable social bilingualism (see, for example, Makoni & Pennycook, 2007; Mohanty, 2006). In the European Union, the promotion of *plurilingualism* has posited that it is possible for citizens to acquire and use different language practices to varying degrees and for specific purposes (Council of Europe, 2000: 168), even if within the same space and for the same function, and without threatening home language practices. The spread of English throughout a globalized world has also meant that more groups of people use English without giving up their language practices, and most often use English language practices and other language practices in interrelationship, as the multimodalities made possible through advanced technology present us with different language practices simultaneously.

The greater movement of peoples and communication in the 21st century has also made us realize that the concept of a homogenous speech community tied to a national territory is flawed. Instead of 'speech communities' what we have are 'communities of practices', groups of people who interact and communicate regularly.

I have argued elsewhere (García, 2009) that a societal stable, and yet *dynamic*, communicative network in the 21st century, with many languages in functional interrelationship, might be better called '*transglossia*'. *Transglossia* has the potential to release ways of speaking of subaltern groups that have been previously fixed within static language identities and hierarchical language arrangements and that are constrained by the modern/colonial world system. Transglossia can develop what Mignolo (2000: 249) calls 'an other tongue', 'the necessary condition for "an other thinking" and for the possibility of moving beyond the defense of national languages and national ideologies ...'. Whereas diglossia was said to rely on static language patterns in different domains to achieve stability and preservation of group bilingual practices, transglossia refers to the fluid, yet stable, language practices of bilingual and multilingual societies that question traditional descriptions built on national ideologies, and that also interrogate the notion of bilinguals possessing two autonomous systems of languages (for a critique of the autonomous position of language, see Makoni & Pennycook, 2007).

The language practices of today's bilinguals are not additive, and do not respond to an additive or a subtractive model of bilingualism. In today's flows, language practices are multiple and ever adjusting to the multilingual multimodal terrain of the communicative act. I have referred to this type of bilingualism as *dynamic*.

A dynamic conceptualization of bilingualism (García, 2009) goes beyond the notion of two autonomous languages, of a first and a second language, and of additive or subtractive bilingualism. Instead, dynamic bilingualism suggests that the language practices of *all* bilinguals are complex and interrelated; they do not emerge in a linear way. As García (2009) has said, they do not result in either the balanced wheels of two bicycles (as in additive bilingualism) or in a unicycle (as in subtractive bilingualism), but instead bilingualism is the all-terrain vehicle that results when individuals adapt their language practices to both the ridges and craters of communication in uneven terrains (see also, García & Kleifgen, 2010). Dynamic bilingualism sees languages not as monolithic systems made up of discreet sets of skills, but as a series of social practices that are embedded in a web of social relations (for a similar view on literacy practices, see Pennycook, 2010; Street, 1984).

Within a dynamic conceptualization of bilingualism, bilinguals are valued for their differing multi-competence (Cook, 2008) because their lives, minds and actions are different from those of monolinguals. As Herdina and Jessner (2002) have pointed out, the interactions of bilinguals' interdependent language systems create new structures that are not found in monolingual systems. Learning is then not just the 'taking in' of linguistic forms by learners, but 'the constant adaptation of their linguistic resources in the service of meaning-making in response to the affordances that emerge in the communicative situation, which is, in turn, affected by learners' adaptability' (Larsen-Freeman & Cameron, 2008: 135). We turn now to exploring the more transglossic relationship of Spanish and English among US Latinos, and their dynamic bilingualism. To do so, we focus on a kindergarten class where young five-year-old Latinos are becoming bilingual; and on a fifth grade class where bilingual Latinos speak out about their own bilingualism.

Transglossia and dynamic bilingualism in a kindergarten[1]

In this bilingual kindergarten, of the type known as 'dual language', all five-year-olds are emergent bilinguals; half of the children are learning Spanish, whereas the other half are learning English. The program supposedly compartmentalizes the use of the two languages by having a 'side-by-side' arrangement in which one teacher teaches only in Spanish, while the other teacher teaches only in English and vice versa. The sociolinguistic reality of student language use in the classroom is very different.

On one occasion, Maia Starcevic, the English teacher, has taken the children who are new to English outside, for a lesson on comparisons. The children are sitting in a circle and I'm sitting next to a girl, Angélica, who is mumbling under her breath. The teacher is asking the students to repeat: 'This tree is bigger. That tree is smaller.' Angélica is trying out under her breath what she knows. 'This tree is…', and then she stops, and grins to herself as she says: *'grander'* (Observation, 23 September 2007). Angélica draws 'grande' from her home language practices to make sense of the new language practices that she is confronting in school. She does not keep the 'grande' at home, and she does not attach 'er' to words she learns in school, but draws on her entire linguistic repertoire to appropriate and integrate into her life the new words and sounds she is hearing at school for the first time.

That the bilingualism that these young children display is dynamic, and not simply additive or subtractive, is evidenced by a conversation between young children who are more bilingual with those who are less so. One day, Eric, who is bilingual, is helping Enrique in an art project. Enrique is a talented artist who is learning English. I reproduce below the dialogue in which they were engaged:

Eric: *¿Quieres deste así?*
[Do you want this one this way?]
Enrique: OK
Eric: *Cortando algo ... Pa pegar ... Ahí.*
[Cutting something … To glue … There!]
And now we're going to put a line.
Quieres así éste, pero ¿a lot?
[Do you want this one this way, but, a lot?]
Teacher: Enrique, are you writing your name?
Eric: *Tu nombre. Así Enrique* … [Writes Enrique's name across the paper] *Mira.*
This way.
[Your name. This way Enrique …, look …]
Miss x, where should he write his name?
Enrique: Ohhhhh.
Eric: *¿Quieres más ...?*
[Asking Ofelia as he searches for the word for 'glue'.]
How do you say in Spanish [pointing to the bottle of glue]?

Enrique: *Cola.*
Eric: *Ah, mira, now we got to just color.* (Observation, 23 September 2007)

Clearly Eric displays a dynamic bilingualism that allows him to use his entire linguistic repertoire flexibly to make sure that Enrique, as well as the teacher, understands him. He uses an entire semiotic system meaningfully and competently, knowing when what he is saying has to be said in one or the other language, and understanding that if accompanied by an action or gesture, Enrique will understand. For example, as he draws a line he uses English to tell Enrique: 'And now we're going to put a line.' And as he starts to color he adds: 'now we got to just color'. For Eric, Spanish and English do not exist in different worlds, or even domains, they function as part of an entire linguistic repertoire, in interrelationship, to make meaning.

Transglossia and dynamic bilingualism in a fifth grade classroom

In a fifth grade bilingual classroom, Rodolfo is telling me about his bilingualism, as he explains his complex language use:

> *Yo tengo una vida muy loca porque yo sé cómo rezar en español pero no en inglés, pero sé como más de inglés que español.* [...] For me it's easier in English, well because I feel more comfortable in English, but when I talk to my parents I speak in Spanish. And sometimes I only speak in Spanish, then Spanish and a little bit of English. (Interview, 5 November 2007)
> [I have a crazy life because I know how to pray in Spanish but not in English, but I know, like, more English than Spanish.]

Rodolfo knows that his bilingualism must respond to the many situations in which he finds himself, with features from Spanish and English in interrelationship because his bilingualism must address the complex social worlds of Latinos in the US.

But it is perhaps what his classmate Antonio tells me that most explicitly explains the dynamic bilingualism that characterizes the language use of these US Latino bilingual students: 'Even though Spanish runs through my heart, English rules my veins' (Interview, 22 October 2007). Clearly it is English that rules, but Spanish is what keeps life going, the motor that pumps the English. Without either, life for these bilingual students would stop.

A model of societal transglossia and of individual dynamic bilingualism needs a different pedagogy. In the next section we develop what we consider to be the key to an effective bilingual pedagogy – translanguaging as pedagogy.

Countering the Duality of L1/L2 Pedagogies: Translanguaging as Pedagogy

Learning another language cannot be the result of a simple transmission of knowledge from teacher to students, but of collaborative social practices in which students try out ideas and actions (Lave & Wenger, 1991), and thus socially construct their learning and language practices (Vygotsky, 1978). A constructivist bilingual pedagogy by which students socially negotiate their learning in interaction with others, while teachers facilitate it, must rely on bilingual strategies.

Jim Cummins' interdependence hypothesis posits that 'to the extent that instruction in Lx is effective in promoting proficiency in Lx, transfer of this proficiency to Ly will occur provided there is adequate exposure to Ly' (Cummins, 2000: 38). Resting on the interdependence of the languages of bilinguals, Cummins has moved away from discussing an L1/L2 dichotomy, characterizing the way in which languages had been conceptualized in Canadian immersion bilingual classrooms in the 20th century as 'two solitudes' (Cummins, 2007), and calling for bilingual instructional strategies in the classroom as a way of promoting 'identities of competence among language learners from socially marginalized groups, thereby enabling them to engage more confidently with literacy and other academic work in both languages' (Cummins, 2007: 238).

García (2009), extending Williams (cited in Baker, 2001), takes up *translanguaging* as a constructivist pedagogy, referring to the ways in which bilingual students and teachers engage in complex discursive practices that include, at times, the home language practices of students in order to 'make sense' of teaching and learning, to communicate and appropriate subject knowledge, and to develop academic language practices. In conceptualization, translanguaging differs from code-switching in that it refers not simply to a shift between two languages, but to the use of complex discursive practices that cannot be assigned to one or another code. Bilingual students use these complex and fluid discursive practices to perform their learning – reading, writing, listening, discussing, taking notes, writing reports and essays, taking exams – by drawing on their entire linguistic repertoire (for more on the use of translanguaging, see especially, Blackledge & Creese, 2010; and Creese & Blackledge, 2010).

Translanguaging as a pedagogy refers then to the use of bilingual students' language practices *flexibly* in order to develop new understandings and new language practices, including academic language practices. Translanguaging pedagogies are particularly important for immigrant students who are emergent bilinguals because they build on students' strengths. They also reduce the risk of alienation at school by incorporating languaging and cultural references familiar to immigrant students.

Translanguaging in the bilingual classroom is precisely a way of working in the gap between, on the one hand, the global designs of nation states and their education systems that set up bilingual programs with strict compartmentalization between languages, and on the other, the local histories of peoples who language differently, especially in bilingual situations. Translanguaging in US classrooms shows the tensions between the global design of the US in educating immigrants and language minorities and the local histories of those students. In their design, classrooms separate languages and are sometimes supposed to exclude the minority language. In reality, students and teachers violate these compartmentalizations, acting on the new meanings of what it is to be an American bilingual.

Translanguaging as pedagogy in secondary schools

To contextualize a translanguaging pedagogy, we draw from one example of a high school in a study on Latino emergent bilinguals in New York City high schools (García, forthcoming; García *et al.*, 2012). This is a high school for Spanish-speaking newcomer immigrants, part of a network of high schools for newcomers in New York City known as International High Schools (for more on these schools, see García & Sylvan, 2011).

Camila Leiva is a teacher of 'English'. On this particular Monday, Camila is working on the theme of literary conflicts. First she plays for the students the rap *'Sí se Puede'*, by El Chivo of Quinto Sol. *'Sí se Puede'* communicates the idea that *'Yes, we can'*, as issues of racism and discrimination against immigrants are identified. Camila provides the students with a worksheet where they are asked to translate the lyrics, which are printed in Spanish, into English, as well as to identify key words, the type of conflict there is and the reasons for the conflict. After an extensive discussion with the students, she then plays the rap 'Mosh' by Eminem. Again, she provides the students with the lyrics, this time in English and asks them to translate them into Spanish.

The transcript that follows is from the classroom dialogue after the listening of *'Sí se Puede'* (C stands for Camila, S for students):

C: Four million US citizens are being separated from their fathers and mothers because their parents are being deported.
S1: *Que los niños nacieron aquí. Legalmente son ciudadanos. Pero los padres no.*
S2: *Entonces esta es la preocupación de que los separen ...*

C: It's a very worrying situation. So, because we don't have that much time and I want to get to the Eminem video . . . What are four keywords? *Las palabras importantes, palabras claves?*
S3: *Deportar.*
S4: Families together.
S5: Protection.
S6: Discrimination.
C: I love how even though the song is in Spanish, we're choosing words in English. Quinto Sol grew up in the US but they do hip-hop in Spanish, and we're doing the same.
C: What problem do you see in the song?
S7: That many white people don't like Spanish people.
S8: It's the voice of the people.
C: The chivo, the rapper, says that some people don't like Latinos but . . .
S1: *No sé cómo decirlo en inglés, pero ... que los latinos tenemos que pagar lo que otras personas ...*
Ss: . . .
C: Don't shoot her down. We're respecting each other's opinions. What else do we see?
S1: *Que las familias*, this guy, every time he has problem. Taking care something. It's a Latino that help. [. . .]
C: The custodian is a Latino person. And who takes care of his daughter?
Ss: Latinos!
S2: *Miss, ¿yo puedo poner que muchas familias están separadas?*
C: *A causa de qué?*
S2: *Deportan los inmigrantes.*
C: How did you start the answer?
S2: They want the Latinos to get out of America.
C: What do you think the problem is? What is the type of literary conflict?
Ss: Me, me, me . . .
C: I like the enthusiasm. What type do you think it is?
S3: I have three. Because he has a problem with other people, and *cuando fueron reparar el carro; no es, pero que tiene un problema, pues así*, character vs. character.
C: What else can he say? Good . . . new hands. People who haven't spoken.
S4: *Porque tiene un problema consigo mismo: character vs. himself.*
S5: *Porque los Latinos es una sociedad, y él es un character.*
C: Why do you think . . .
S5: *que lo quieren matar?*

C: *Ramón, cuéntanos en español.*
C: Latinos, are we the majority or the minority?
Ss: Majority!/minority!// *Somos mayoría en números!// No minoría!*
C: They call us a minority, even though we're a majority in many places. I'm going to give you some time before you finish. *Si ya terminaron, avancen a la segunda parte a la canción de Eminem ...* (Observation, 28 February 2011)

Camila translanguages to involve students, to extend what she is saying, to clarify, to ask questions, to reinforce what has been said, and to advance the pace of the lesson. But beyond the discourse functions enabled by translanguaging, this pedagogy makes possible a social criticality that is important for immigrant students. For example, Camila uses translanguaging as a way to implement a social justice curriculum. Through translanguaging she gives voice to those who do not speak, she problematizes social situations, and she works through the tension that exists between minority and majority society. Translanguaging also enables her to construct her students' fluid identifications, as she encourages the students to use their entire linguistic repertoires. She explicitly tells them: 'Even though the song is in Spanish, we're choosing words in English. Quinto Sol grew up in the US but they do hip-hop in Spanish, and we're doing the same.' Camila encourages these 'crossings' (Rampton, 1995) as ways of building a US Latino group pan-ethnicity, for she tells the students: 'Los Latinos es una sociedad.' And for this US Latino society to develop, a tranglossic interfunctionality that draws from the entire linguistic repertoire of their dynamic bilingualism is most important.

Translanguaging as a pedagogy thus offers the alternative of developing dynamic bilinguals. For US Latinos this means the possibility that they will be released from the constraints of both an 'Anglophobic' ideology that demands English monolingualism for US citizens, and a 'Hispanophobic' ideology that blames US Latinos for speaking 'Spanglish' (Otheguy & Stern, 2010), or for their 'incomplete acquisition' of their 'heritage' language. Translanguaging as a pedagogy holds the promise of developing US Latinos who use their dynamic bilingualism in ways that develop a transglossic repertoire, able to meet the global, national and social needs of a multilingual future.

Conclusion

This chapter has considered how theoretical frameworks that have been used to study bilingualism in the past may be responsible for the misunderstandings and misconstructions of bilingualism that are prevalent throughout the world today, and most especially in the United States. By countering the dual in bilingualism, this chapter offers possibilities of different theoretical lenses to study the complex discursive practices of bilinguals, especially in schools – transglossia, dynamic bilingualism and translanguaging.

The chapter suggests that the global designs of nation states and their education systems have much to do with social systems of domination and subordination of groups relating to language, ethnicity, race and class. By focusing on the local positionality of bilingual speakers, and especially of emergent bilingual students, it is possible to break out of the duality that strictly separates the dominant language of the state, and especially the academic standard language, from the language practices of people and students. It is by encouraging the use of the complex discursive practices of bilingual citizens; that is, their translanguaging, that linguistic repertoires will be extended to also encompass the standard languages that states often require for the full participation of its citizens.

Especially in classrooms of language minorities, and particularly in those where students are emergent bilinguals, translanguaging as a pedagogy offers the possibility of producing integrated knowledge, deep understandings and coherent identifications. To do so, schools must build transglossic spaces where students' multiple language practices are acknowledged and used. These transglossic spaces will no doubt often exist alongside the diglossic curricular language arrangements of many bilingual education programs. But until we design classroom spaces where bilingual students' complex discursive practices are at the center of instruction, the promise of bilingual education to empower all students, and especially language minorities, will remain unfulfilled.

Note

(1) This data comes from a study of this kindergarten class which was reported in García (2011).

References

Baker, C. (2001) *Foundations of Bilingual Education and Bilingualism* (3rd edn). Clevedon: Multilingual Matters.

Blackledge, A. and Creese, A. (2010) *Multilingualism.* London: Continuum.

Collier, V. (1995) Acquiring a second language for schools. *Directions in Language and Education*, 1 (4), 1–12.

Cook, V. (2008) *Second Language Learning and Language Teaching* (4th edn). London: Hodder Educational.

Council of Europe (2000) *Common European Framework of Reference for Languages: Learning, Teaching, Assessment.* Strasbourg: Language Policy Division.

Crawford, J. (2004) *Educating English Learners: Language Diversity in Classrooms* (5th edn). Washington, DC: Bilingual Education Services.

Crawford, J. (2007) The decline of bilingual education in the USA: How to reverse a troubling trend? *International Multilingual Research Journal* 1 (1), 33–37.

Creese, A. and Blackledge, A. (2010) Translanguaging in the bilingual classroom: A pedagogy for learning and teaching? *Modern Language Journal* 94 (i), 103–115.

Cummins, J. (2000) *Language, Power, & Pedagogy: Bilingual Children Caught in the Cross-Fire.* Clevedon: Multilingual Matters.

Cummins, J. (2007) Rethinking monolingual instructional strategies in multilingual classrooms. *The Canadian Journal of Applied Linguistics* 10 (2), 221–240.

De Houwer, A. (2009) *Bilingual First Language Acquisition.* Bristol: Multilingual Matters.

Ferguson, C. (1959) Diglossia. *Word* 15, 325–340.

Fishman, J.A. (1967) Bilingualism with and without diglossia: Diglossia with and without bilingualism. *Journal of Social Issues* 23 (2), 29–38.

García, O. (2006) Lost in transculturation: The case of bilingual education in New York City. In M. Putz, J.A. Fishman and N.V. Aertselaer (eds) *Along the Routes to Power: Exploration of the Empowerment Through Language* (pp. 157–178). Berlin: Mouton de Gruyter.

García, O. (2009) *Bilingual Education in the 21st Century: A Global Perspective.* Malden, MA: Wiley/Blackwell

García, O. (forthcoming)Theorizing and enacting translanguaging for social justice. In A. Creese and A. Blackledge (eds) *Heteroglossia as Practice and Pedagogy.* New York: Springer.

García, O. and Kleifgen, J.A. (2010) *Educating Emergent Bilinguals: Policies, Programs and Practices for English Language Learners.* New York: Teachers College Press.

García, O. and Sylvan, C. (2011) Pedagogies and practices in multilingual classrooms. Singularities in pluralities. *Modern Language Journal* 95 (iii): 385–400.

García, O. (with Makar, C., Starcevic, M. and Terry, A.) (2011) Translanguaging of Latino kindergarteners. In K. Potowski and J. Rothman (eds) *Bilingual Youth: Spanish in English Speaking* Societies (pp. 33–55). Amsterdam and Philadelphia: John Benjamins.

García, O., Flores, N. and Woodley, H.H. (2012) Transgressing monolingualism and bilingual dualities: Translanguaging pedagogies. In A. Yiakoumetti (ed.) *Harnessing Linguistic Variation for Better Education* (pp. 45–76). Bern: Peter Lang.

Genesee, F. (2003) Rethinking bilingual acquisition. In J-M. Dewaele (ed.) *Bilingualism: Challenges and Directions for Future Research* (pp. 204–228). Clevedon: Multilingual Matters.

Herdina, P. and Jessner, U. (2002) *A Dynamic Model of Multilingualism.* Clevedon: Multilingual Matters.

Irvine, J. and Gal, S. (2000) Language ideology and linguistic differentiation. In P. Kroskrity (ed.) *Regimes of Language Ideologies, Politics and Identities* (pp. 34–84). Santa Fe, NM: School of American Research Press.

Lambert, W.E. (1974) Culture and language as factors in learning and education. In F.E. Aboud and R.D. Meade (eds) *Cultural Factors in Learning and Education* (pp. 91–122). Bellingham, WA: Western Washington State College.

Larsen-Freeman, D. and Cameron, L. (2008) *Complex Systems and Applied Linguistics.* Oxford: Oxford University Press.

Lave, J. and Wenger, E. (1991) *Situated Learning: Legitimate Peripheral Participation.* Cambridge: Cambridge University Press.

Lessow-Hurley, J. (2005) *The Foundations of Dual Language Instruction* (4th edn). Boston, MA: Pearson.
Makoni, S. and Pennycook, A. (2007) *Disinventing and Reconstituting Languages.* Clevedon: Multilingual Matters.
Mignolo, W. (2000) *Local Histories/Global Designs. Coloniality, Subaltern Knowledges, and Border Thinking.* Princeton, NJ: Princeton University Press.
Mohanty, A.K. (2006) Multilingualism of the unequals and predicaments of education in India: Mother tongue or other tongue? In O. García, T. Skutnabb-Kangas and M. Torres-Guzmán (eds) *Imagining Multilingual Schools: Languages in Education and Glocalization* (pp. 262–283). Clevedon: Multilingual Matters.
New York City Department of Education (2011) *The 2010–11 Demographics of NYC's English Language Learners.* New York City: Office of English Language Learners, Spring, 2011.
Otheguy, R. and Stern, N. (2010) On so-called 'Spanglish'. *International Journal of Bilingualism* 15 (1), 85–100.
Pennycook, A. (2010) *Language as a Local Practice.* London: Routledge.
Pratt, M.L. (1991) Arts of the contact zone. *Profession. Association of Departments of English Bulletin* 91, 33–40.
Ramírez, J.D. (1992) Executive summary, final report: Longitudinal study of structured English immersion strategy, early-exit and late-exit transitional bilingual education programs for language-minority children. *Bilingual Research Journal,* 16 (1–2), 1–62.
Rampton, B. (1995) *Crossing: Language and Identity among Adolescents.* London and New York: Longman.
Skutnabb-Kangas, T. (1981) *Bilingualism or Not: The Education of Minorities.* Clevedon: Multilingual Matters.
Street, B. (1984) *Literacy in Theory and Practice.* Cambridge: Cambridge University Press.
Thomas, W. and Collier, V.P. (2002) *A National Study of School Effectiveness for Language Minority Students' Long Term Academic Achievement.* Santa Cruz, CA: Center for Research on Education, Diversity and Excellence, University of California-Santa Cruz, accessed 3 October 2011. http://escholarship.org/uc/item/65j213pt.
US Census Bureau (1990) *Decennial Census, 1990.* Washington, DC: US Government Printing Office.
US Census Bureau (2009) *American Community Survey (ACS), 2008.* Washington, DC: US Government Printing Office.
Valdés, G. (1997) Dual-language immersion programs: A cautionary note concerning the education of language-minority students. *Harvard Educational Review* 67, 391–429.
Vygotsky, L.S. (1978) *Mind and Society.* Cambridge, MA: Harvard University Press.

Part 2

Hybridized Discourses of Identity in the Media

7 Reading Gender in Indian Newspapers: Global, Local or Liminal?

Rakesh M. Bhatt

To write in different ways is to live in different ways. It is also to be read in different ways, in different relations, and often by different people.
Williams, 1997: 205

Introduction

This chapter offers linguistic evidence to present a theoretical argument that gender identity in the postmodern Indian context can be properly understood in the inter-animation of the old-local-traditional and the new-global-modern; particularly, at the threshold, the liminal spaces between the old – which may no longer work—and the new/other – which is not clear. The tension between the old and the new becomes most visible in the linguistic choices that index emergent moments of gender identification, which are, arguably, in a process of transformation.

The particular theoretical focus of gendered linguistic choices in this chapter is code-switching: a strategic mobilization of two indexical codes that disturbs, and in certain cases subverts, the established and entrenched representation of gender in India; questioning its discursive authenticity by textually fusing two distinct – English and Hindi – sociolinguistic consciousnesses within the limits of a single utterance, or even a single ('mainstream') discourse. Accordingly, the theoretical argument of this chapter is that code-switching enables a hybridity of both form and meaning, adding new polysemic nuances of gendered representations that are neither wholly traditional-local nor exclusively modern-global: they are both, in more-or-less terms, often resulting in interpretive ambiguity and ambivalence.

As such, the empirical focus of this chapter is on code-switching as a linguistic strategy that is creatively used to negotiate polarizations without being caught within the binary representations of old and new, local and global, sacred and profane. Specifically, I will show that the use of Hindi in Indian English newspapers is arguably strategic: it allows for a juxtaposition of old and new identities (*cf.* Hall, 1997) – creating in the negotiation between the old and the new a third, *liminal*, space (Bhatt, 2008) that enables a concatenation of the two. It is in this new, ideological space where the two worlds converge and get renegotiated – articulating a dynamic tension between traditional practices and modernity.

Theoretical Background

I adopt the critical discourse-theoretic perspective (Fairclough, 1995; Lazar, 2005; van Dijk, 1998; Wodak, 1996) to analyze the data, mainly because I am interested in exploring gendered representations within the broader framework of linguistic mechanisms of oppression (Hill, 1993; Lippi-Green, 1997). As such, I begin with a few standard assumptions: (i) that language politics of feminism, not unlike racism, has an emancipatory aim (hooks, 1984; Lazar, 2005; Talbot, 2010); (ii) gender identity is not static, fixed or invariant: it is dynamic, variable, socially constructed, performed, contested, negotiated and emergent (Bucholtz & Hall, 2004; Butler, 1999; Cameron, 2006; Lazar, 2005; Talbot, 2010); and, specific to this chapter, (iii) text provides a meaning *potential*, the specific derivation of meaning depends at least minimally on (a) the discursive position of the reader (or hearer), and (b) the inter-textual (sociohistorical) relations that hold between texts (Bakhtin, 1981; Halliday, 1978; Fairclough, 1995; Foucault, 1972).

Further, following Bhatt (2008), I assume code-switching as a discursive practice which involves two ideological systems (here, of identity representations) to come into direct contact with each other, leading to representational synergies that produce meaning located in the liminal spaces between the two – referring simultaneously to aspects of both – language ideological systems. In the specific context of the study of linguistic representation of *gendered* identities, code-switching provides a productive site to study gender ideologies within the largely contested space of cultural ideologies in the global world of late modernity. In India, where the linguistic indexicalities of English (elite, modern, global) and Hindi (non-elite, traditional, local) are relatively transparent and stable, code-switching between them allows for gendered representations to be read 'in-between' local-traditional practices and a global-modern identity, as more or less of one or the other at any discursive moment. Given the various contested subject positions of women in India, I argue that a close reading of the patterns of code-switching between English and Hindi in Indian English newspapers reveals how certain subject positions emerge or efface as the modern middle-class women grapple with the old-traditional and the new-modern identities.

Data and Research Context

The data presented in this chapter were collected from two Indian English newspapers over a period of five years, 2001–2004, 2006, of one-month-long visits. Out of a total of 1627 tokens of code-switching that were collected, 83 tokens dealt specifically with gender issues. The switches constituted single-word switches, phrases and sentences.

The sociopolitical context of data collection needs some discussion to fully appreciate the various complexes of nuances of the contemporary politics of gender-identity representations in India. In the early 1990s, two important transformations took place in India: economic and political. The economic transformation dealt with a move to a liberal, market-economy that led to rapid economic growth, accumulation of wealth and integration with other systems of global economy. Soon after the economic liberalization, India went through a phase of political transformation that began with the emergence of the Bhartiya Janta Party (BJP), elected to government on the promise, and later successful implementation, of promoting nationalist ideologies, commonly known as *Hindutva*. *Hindutva* is an ensemble of doctrines, social movements and political formations of Hindu supremacy, emphasizing *a return to the past*: Sanskritization and Brahminical values. The political form of this ideology ('*Hindutva*') is closely intertwined with its cultural expression: Hindi-language/Hindu-religion (*cf.* Chand, 2002). The Hindu cultural nationalism agenda of the BJP reached its peak in the years 2001–2002, when governance appeared to be taking a backseat to the promotion of *Hindutva*, as the headline of *The Times of India* in example 1 indicates.

Example 1
The Sunday Times

> Has the BJP's aggressive Hindutva put governance on the back-burner?
> Source: *The Sunday Times of India* (12 May 2002).

In sum, during the years of my data collection, the political narrative of India presented a 'tension between the baldly religious political ideology of *Hindutva* in the face of the rapidly globalizing, secularizing society. The linguistic politics of these two trajectories has created conditions that simultaneously favor economic globalization and modernity, via English, and cultural nationalism and traditional practices, via Sanskritized Hindi, as a path for the country's progress and transformation into a modern nation.

And, finally, a quick note on the choice of newspaper data: code-switching in the 'sphere' – dedicated interactional zone (Habermas, 1991) – of newspaper journalism presents the theoretical possibility of a new socio-ideological consciousness, a new way of meaning-making, of dialogic play of verbal intentions. It offers one of the ways in which cultural texts participate in the construction of wider cultural values and ideologies (*cf.* Bhatt, 2008). As such, I claim that newspapers are legitimate sites of investigation of competing ideologies, expressed in code-switching.

Data Analysis

What is striking about contemporary representations of women in news media, at least in newspapers, is that authority and status for them is portrayed in terms of decorative displays of traditional gender practices; code-switching allows modern women to subvert their own positions in traditional spaces by constructing social identities and patterns of alignment that conform to the roles assigned to them in those spaces – this critical awareness of different subject positions enables the modern identity to coexist with the traditional.

Consider, first, example 2, taken from another article in *The Sunday Times of India*. The switch to Hindi [The young women – always overdressed – will typically say, *'Mummyjee, aap rahne deejeye, Chai mein bana ke laungi, mujhe apne kartavyon ka ehsas hai'* ('mom, please leave it to me, I will make tea and bring it over, I am aware of my (traditional) responsibilities')], presented in the 'character voice', corresponds to the local cultural etiquette: it recalls a particular ritual-cultural practice that cannot be adequately translated into English without engendering cultural-semantic dispossession.

Repudiating the anachronistic representation of women in contemporary TV soaps, it becomes communicatively economical for the author to move her narrative from a 'modern' public [narrative] voice (of English) to a distinctive 'ethnic/traditional' [character] voice in Hindi, embedded within quotation marks, to animate the identity struggles that the modern Indian woman must manage in her daily interactional encounters. The last part of the quoted text, 'I am aware of my (traditional) responsibilities', recalls historical practices and local-traditional gendered scripts and embeds them skillfully in contemporary discourses of social engagements by switching into Hindi. Code-switching thus enables the modern Indian woman to be read as simultaneously displaying two, seemingly contradictory, identities: the modern identity, carried through English, and the traditional-local identity, recruited through the use of (code-switching to) Hindi. The 'double standards' in the title, however, do not do justice to the different subject positions that modern Indian women must symbolically negotiate in order to creatively manage the cultural requirements of gendered interactions. What becomes clear is that the modern Indian woman does not speak in one voice, much less with one voice. The multivocality, engineered through code-switching, speaks to both modern and traditional roles that Indian women routinely perform in their daily rituals.

Example 2

The double standards in today's serials reflect real life

> The young women – always overdressed – will typically say, *'Mummyjee, aap rahne deejeye, Chai mein bana ke laungi, mujhe apne kartavyon ka ehsas hai.'*
> Source: *The Sunday Times of India* (12 May 2002).

Example 3 similarly reports the traditional media representation of women, although the woman in question is Sonia Gandhi, the Italian-born wife of the late former prime minister of India. Sonia's rise to power, as the leader of the Congress Party, was challenged by the then nationalist government of BJP that spared no effort to call into question her ability to lead the country, discrediting her as a foreigner. In this example, the semantics of the switched items *layak bahu* ('competent daughter-in-law') is socioculturally grounded, its explication offered in the English relative clause that follows the Hindi noun *bahu*: one who stands by her husband (in a supporting role), raises children and carries on the family tradition. This local interpretation of gender roles is vital in (a) constructing ideological distinctions – native/local, non-native/foreign, (b) presenting iconic images of what counts as authentic, and (c) erasing other roles that modern Indian women assume outside of the home domain.

Example 3

Support for Sonia

I really don't like the way our ministers in Parliament treat Mrs Sonia Gandhi. What wrong has she done? Is she to blame for having fallen in love with an Indian and married him? Honestly, how can anyone be so unfair as to blame someone for having done that. We have all experienced love in one form or the other and we all know how beautiful it makes us feel. How enriching it is. I think we should respect her for fact that she did not leave this country along with her children after her husband's assassination. What's more we should respect her for being a *layak* Indian *bahu* who stayed on to do her duty by her husband's family. She reared her children and instilled in them the best Indian values, she took care of her mother-in-law and husband's legacy – the Congress Party. So, let us not descend to targeting a poor defenseless woman.

Ambreen Zaidi, via email

Source: *Times of India* (20 May 2002).

As such, the switch from English to Hindi presents a 'foreigner' as entrenched in indigenous discursive practices (men-women roles), authenticating her as (one of) 'us', through the use of an indigenous language. The bilingual code-switched mode thus serves several interpretive functions: (i) it authentically expresses the sociohistorical experiences of the Hindi-English bilingual population, (ii) it captures the local cultural-semantics of the utterance; specifically, the different roles that a woman is summoned to successfully perform in order to be recognized as legitimately belonging to the local-indigenous ethos, and (iii) it reflects a hybrid identity, which mobilizes aspects of both local and non-local indexicalities. Most importantly, it appears that even contemporary gendered roles must reference traditional gender ideologies, made possible, of course, most authentically in the local language, and hence the switch to Hindi.

The practice of authenticating traditional gendered practices in India by code-switching to Hindi appears in different genres of the Indian English newspaper register. The text in example 4 is taken from a jewelry advertisement that is accompanied by the visual image of a popular Indian movie star, targeting the celebration of international women's day.

Example 4

Have you discovered the shakti within?

Source: *Times of India* (8 March 2006).

The lexical insertion of *shakti*, meaning 'power/energy', in the context of this English advertisement is strategic given its indexical biography, its circulation mainly in religious discourses where its use refers to the divine female energy force capable of destroying demonic forces and restoring balance. It is through this inter-textual reference that the English-Hindi text in the advertisement makes available the ambiguity of Indian femininity: a modern woman engaged in material pleasures, yet grounded in the spiritual narratives of the local-traditional universe. To the bilingual English-Hindi readership, the traditional meaning of *shakti* becomes culturally salient, readily available, when embedded in an English text within the context of 'Celebrating International Women's Day'. As such, the medium, English-Hindi code-switching, capably indexes the local message, that the two femininities – modern-traditional – can co-exist.

Finally, the switch to Hindi in example 5 illustrates another important paradigm of reading gender in Indian English newspapers. In this example, the Hindi word is put in single quotation marks to guide its reading as a re-cited, and recycled, piece of historical text – lifted from the epic Hindu narrative, Mahabharata, familiar to the readership – and inserted in the new, re-located synchronic space of newspaper reporting. The quoted Hindi text in the title of the news story frames the 'preferred reading' of the text: Draupadi, a princess, is married, by sheer accident of fate, to the five Pandava brothers. Despite the difficulties of living a polyandrous, and a polygamous life, Draupadi emerged as one of the most respected women in the epic story.

Example 5

Unwilling 'Draupadi' pays with her life

Source: *Times of India* (7 March 2006).

The entextualization (Silverstein & Urban, 1996) in the news story, the replication of the traditional gendered roles in contemporary context, is not only contested and firmly opposed but, in fact, refused as a synchronic possibility. The news narrative that follows the title tells the tragic story of a woman who is murdered for her refusal to be shared by the brothers. The framing of rejection of traditional gendered practices is enabled by the clever use of a switch to Hindi that, in the embedding of the past (Hindi) in the present (English), allows the readers to reinterpret what the acceptable gendered practices ought to be in a contemporary civil society: a break from traditionally entrenched gendered roles, of servility and sacrifice. The patterns of switches as in example 5 thus open up a possibility for creating a new 'archive' (Foucault, 1972; Blommaert, 2005) – the transformation that can serve as a new foundation – in which the modern voice of the Indian woman gains interpretive force over, in textual juxtaposition with, historical-traditional voices.

While the English-Hindi code-switching activates a politics of nostalgia – *return to the past* – in gender-identity representation, as shown in the data above, it is not always uncontested. Predictably, we find ample evidence of English-Hindi code-switching used as a form of discursive resistance, representing struggle for a space where the old/traditional is re-contextualized, as shown in the title of a guest column in example 6.

Example 6

GUEST COLUMN ***Whose ghar ki kahani is this, anyway?***
SAGARIKA GHOSE
Source: *The Sunday Times of India* (11 November 2001).

The text in example 6, authored by Sagarika Ghose, a middle-class, middle-aged woman, 'voices' a modern feminist concern over (and a critique of) the production of gender ideologies in local (Hindi) soap operas that she finds, basically, anachronistic and outdated. The context of the text is the daytime soap operas producing images of women as homemakers following old traditional rituals and Hindu symbolism. The use of a Hindi noun phrase with a prepositional phrase complement [$_{NP}$ *ghar* [$_{PP}$ *ki* kahaani]] ('story of household') frames the established, traditional, social (gendered) practices that are negatively evaluated in the text, and transformed in recontextualization by embedding it in the matrix language frame, English.

The letter to the editor (example 7) from Ashish, a high school senior, appears with a title that is all in Hindi, flagging the inter-textual connection between his response and the main article (example 6). Here, the author, presumably representing urban youth, not only acknowledges the merits of the critique of Ghose (in example 6), but also urges the readership (and the soap opera viewers) to dispense with the traditional family values and practices. This political stance, as evidenced in examples 6 and 7, actively disturbs the normative (re-)production of feminism, creating discursive spaces where a shift in regimes of gender representation become possible – licensing apparent transgressions and transformations. The collection of such transformations opens a space for a new archive where the new-modern gender identities can coexist with the old-traditional ones.

Example 7

LETTERS ***Kis ghar ki kahani?***
Source: *The Sunday Times of India* (18 November 2001: 16).

The 'resistance' discourse, such as shown in examples 6 and 7, aims at disrupting any attempts to re-install traditional gendered practices (and stereotypes) in mainstream media, opposing the dominant political discourse of *Hindutva*: *return to the past*. There are several instances where local journalists have voiced their concerns in local newspapers over the anachronistic representation of Indian women in soap operas. For instance, writing for the Indian English newspaper, *The Times of India*, Dhawan (2006: 1) notes (see example 8), '[A]lmost without realizing it, today's advertisers and soap script-writers have transformed the intrepid woman of the 1990s, and taken her back to where she was in the 50s – the kitchen'. In this article, while tacitly acknowledging and critiquing the influence of the dominant political discourse (of *Hindutva*) of gendered representation in mainstream media, the author attempts to engage the local representations with a global neoliberal discourse of postfeminism: women as assertive, assured and autonomous.

Example 8

Spunky salesgirl gives in to family values
Source: *Times of India* (25 February 2006).

I close this section by pointing out that the overt form of 'resistance' in code-switching data, examples 6 and 7, does not oppose the 'compliance' use discussed earlier in examples 2–5. These contradictions are not unexpected as modern Indian women routinely appear in different subject positions: wife, mother and full-time wage earner. These different roles are managed rather skillfully, especially in contexts where the two identities – traditional and modern – come into conflict. These conflicts are strategically resolved in middle-class India, as most aptly described to me by a 53-year-old middle-class Indian woman, given in example 9 [I: Interviewer; R: Respondent; *Italics*: switches to English; **Bolded**: switches to Hindi]:

Example 9

I: to kyaa expectations haiN?
R: (1) yahii ki ab ham ghar bhii calaayeN aur bahar jaa kar kamaayeN bhii [pause]
(2) *I don't want to come across as, y'know, typical western woman but I refuse to be a sati Savitri.*
(3) Ab jaise Papajiki ko dekho, 'R zaraa yeh banaa do, R zaraa kehve pine ka dil hai'.
I: Why do you think voh siidhaa S se nahiiN kehte
R: (1) *He could ask S,* lekin nahiiN, voh mujhe kehte hain.

(2) *I ask S to do all that* to voh bhii khush rahte haiN. Mujhe bhi koi farak nahiN paRhtaa
(3) Maybe he thinks [slight pause] **Yeh auratoN ka kaam hai na**.
(4) But I work all day, **mujhse yeh kitchen ka kaam nahi hota**, unless there is a special occasion.

Translation

I: So, what are the (societal) expectations (of women in India)?
R: (1) That we are supposed to run the household and go out and earn as well . . .
(2) I don't want to come across as, y'know, typical western woman but I refuse to be a sati Savitri (the iconic woman [modest, chaste, determined to stay by the side of her husband] appearing in one of the Hindu religio-cultural narrative).
(3) Now look at Papaji (R's father-in-law), (as he would ask) 'R can you make this', 'R, I would like to have kehva (Kashmiri tea)'.
I: Why do you think he doesn't ask S (the house-maid) straightaway?
R: (1) He could ask S, but no, he asks me.
(2) I ask S to do all that so that he is also happy. And it makes no difference to me.
(3) Maybe he thinks this is a woman's job, y'know (how it is).
(4) But I work all day, I can't deal with the kitchen work, unless there is a special occasion.

In example 9, this middle-class modern Indian woman refuses to be identified within the traditional roles of domesticity. In line (2) of her first turn, she switches to English to present explicitly her gender identity as neither 'typically' Western nor strictly (aligned to Savitri) traditional. In line (2) of her second turn, she does not confront the traditional roles that are assigned to her (by her father-in-law), she manages to delegate those roles to her housemaid without causing any generational friction in her household. In line (3) of this turn, she returns to answering my question directly, switching to Hindi, almost a quoted text, voicing the indexical order of gendered interaction. The Hindi switch presents a meta-linguistic commentary on what the traditional gender roles are in her societal context. However, in line (4) she quickly returns to offering her personal identity as a modern, working woman who can also take her place in the kitchen if the situation warrants so, at her own choosing. This excerpt shows rather insightfully how gendered interactions play out in urban domestic settings of India, which is where the traditional structures of societal complexes come into conflict with elements of late modernity: acceptance of traditional roles does not undermine projections of modernity and agency. The apparent compliance with traditional roles in these settings is a 'face-saving' behavior, reflecting positive politeness (*cf*; second turn, line (2) of R in example 9), as building solidarity, group integrity, is valued highly in Indian interactional settings.

As such, I leave it as a hypothesis, for further exploration, that the apparent 'compliance' with traditional values of the modern middle-class woman has a subversive meaning – of creative, non-overt resistance (*cf.* Mertz, 1989; Reed-Danahay, 1993; Bhatt, 2008). The willingness to accept dominant traditional values is arguably a bid to not lose solidarity/intimacy with the local, as the modern woman assumes power/authority in her new contemporary roles. The price of power/authority, modern Indian women realize, is the loss of intimacy and solidarity, and they work to avoid this loss – the alternative is to find a space, the *third space*, where this struggle, between power and solidarity, is reconciled. The linguistic indexing of this discursive space is flagged by code-switching.

Conclusion

In conclusion, I have presented code-switched English-Hindi data as evidence to claim that the local-traditional and global-modern gender identity positions are in the process of constant negotiation, read mainly as an ambiguous interpretive stance between the old sociohistorical structure and a new discursive-transformative agency. The data show that code-switching is used both as a rhetorical authentication of indigenous gendered practices AND as a form of discursive resistance to such traditional practices and values; representing a struggle for a space – between power and solidarity – where new, potentially hybrid, identities emerge. These new identities that are forged in the inter-animation of old-traditional and new-modern display a creative alchemy where both identities coexist in the changing sociolinguistic landscape of India.

References

Bakhtin, M. (1981) *The Dialogic Imagination* (M. Holquist, ed. and C. Emerson, trans). Austin: University of Texas Press.

Bhatt, R.M. (2008) In other words: Language mixing, identity representations, and *third space*. *Journal of Sociolinguistics* 12 (2), 177–200.

Blommaert, J. (2005) *Discourse*. Cambridge: Cambridge University Press.

Bucholtz, M. and Hall, K. (2004) Theorizing identity in language and sexuality research. *Language in Society* 33 (4), 469–515.

Butler, J. (1999) *Gender Trouble: Feminism and the Subversion of Identity*. New York: Routledge.

Cameron, D. (2006) *On Language and Sexual Politics*. London: Routledge.
Chand, S. (2002) *Saffron Fascism*. Delhi, India: Hemkunt Publishers.
Dhawan, H. (2006) Spunky salesgirl gives in to family values. *The Times of India*, 25 February, 1.
Fairclough, N. (1995) *Critical Discourse Analysis*. London: Longman.
Foucault, M. (1972) *The Archeology of Knowledge*. London: Routledge.
Habermas, J. (1991) The public sphere. In C. Mukherji and M. Schudson (eds) *Rethinking Popular Culture: Contemporary Perspectives in Cultural Studies* (pp. 398–404). Berkeley: University of California Press.
Hall, S. (1997) Old and new identities: Old and new ethnicities. In A.D. King (ed.) *Culture, Globalization and the World-System: Contemporary Conditions for the Representation of Identity* (pp. 19–40). Minneapolis, MN: University of Minnesota Press.
Halliday, M. (1978) *Language as Social Semiotic: The Social Interpretation of Language and Meaning*. Baltimore, MD: University Park Press.
Hill, J. (1993) Hasta la vista, baby: Anglo Spanish in the American southwest. *Critique of Anthropology* 13 (2), 145–176.
hooks, b. (1984) *Feminist Theory: From Margin to Center*. Boston, MA: South End Press.
Lazar, M. (ed.) (2005) *Feminist Critical Discourse Analysis: Gender, Power, and Ideology in Discourse*. London: Palgrave MacMillan.
Lippi-Green, R. (1997) *English with an Accent: Language, Ideology, and Discrimination in the United States*. London: Routledge.
Mertz, E. (1989) Sociolinguistic creativity: Cape Breton Gaelic's linguistic 'tip'. In N. Dorian (ed.) *Investigating Obsolescence* (pp. 103–115). London: Cambridge University Press.
Reed-Danahay, D. (1993) Talk about resistance: Ethnography and theory in rural France. *Anthropological Quarterly* 66, 221–229.
Silverstein, M. and Urban, G. (1996) The natural history of discourse. In M. Silverstein and G. Urban (eds) *Natural Histories of Discourse* (pp. 1–17). Chicago, IL: University of Chicago Press.
Talbot, M. (2010) *Language and Gender*. Cambridge: Polity Press.
van Dijk, T. (1998) *Ideology: A Multidisciplinary Approach*. London: Sage.
Williams, R. (1997) *Marxism and Literature*. Oxford: Oxford University Press.
Wodak, R. (1996) *Disorders of Discourse*. London: Longman.

8 Linguistic and Cultural Hybridity in French Web Advertising

Elizabeth Martin

Introduction

Expanding on our existing knowledge of identity construction and multilingual advertising (for example, Kelly-Holmes, 2005; Piller, 2003), this study examines cultural mixing and linguistic hybridity in web advertising designed for French consumers. By focusing solely on corporate websites designed for French companies that address French-speaking audiences, this research sheds light on how English not only serves as a global language of communication in advertising, but also the creative aspects of French-English mixing developing in marketing directed at French consumers. As these examples illustrate, corporate advertising websites for French companies are used simultaneously as both a transnational and intra-national form of communication, exploiting the global reach of the internet (including links to social networking sites, international music videos and other media in their French-language web content) while disseminating brand messages designed to specifically appeal to local markets. French visitors to these websites navigate seamlessly between local and global representations of the brand, experiencing a blending of cultures and identities, presumably designed to enhance their online experience and create brand loyalty. These 'glocal' dimensions of web advertising are evident in visual, textual and auditory strategies utilized by advertising agencies taking full advantage of the multimodal features of internet discourse.

Patterns of linguistic and cultural hybridization in commercial advertising have been documented in various regions around the globe, including

Asia, Africa, Europe, North America and South America. Many of those investigating this phenomenon have noted the predominant role of English as a pair-language in advertisements as well as the cultural effects of globalization on advertising discourse. The research literature on this topic has primarily focused on print and television advertising (for example, Baumgardner, 2006, 2008; Bhatia, 1987, 1992; Griffin, 1997; Hsu, 2008; Kamwangamalu, 2008; Martin, 2002, 2006, 2008; Masavisut *et al.*, 1986; Meraj, 1993; Piller, 2001; Takashi, 1990; Ustinova & Bhatia, 2005). There have been, however, some efforts to document other media, including radio (Pavlou, 2002; Smakman *et al.*, 2009) and non-traditional media (Bhatia, 2000). Language-mixing in public signage, such as shop signs, billboard advertisements and other elements of urban linguistic landscapes, is another burgeoning field of inquiry (Backhaus, 2007; Dumont, 1998; Rosendal, 2009; Thonus, 1991). Although a few recent studies have shed light on multilingual strategies used in web advertising (for example, Lee, 2010; Wu *et al.*, 2007), culture-mixing and linguistic hybridity in this discourse domain remains largely unexplored from a sociolinguistic perspective.

From the standpoint of international marketing and advertising practitioners, however, any discussion on linguistic or cultural hybridity is generally couched in terms of standardization versus localization (Mooij, 1998; Mueller, 1996). Although most advertising executives agree that the advantages of adapting global campaigns to regional and local markets outweigh the disadvantages (Kanso & Nelson, 2002), advertising agencies must also consider time and resource constraints, knowing that any localization strategy will involve higher costs due to the duplication of efforts in multiple countries. In response to the growing trend towards localization, country-specific variations in advertising strategy have received considerable attention in the international marketing literature in recent years, with studies aimed at increasing the effectiveness of localized advertising campaigns. Market researchers have examined, for instance, culture-specific communication preferences in terms of advertising appeals, information content and cross-cultural differences in color perception, as well as cultural variability in web interface design (for example, Ju-Pak, 1999; Madden *et al.*, 2000; Singh & Pereira, 2005; Tsao & Chang, 2002; Yunker, 2003; Zhou & Belk, 2004).

Theoretical Approaches to Hybridity

Drawing on Appadurai's (1996) theory of cultural hybridity and globalization, the world Englishes paradigm (Kachru, 1982, 1986) and the notion of 'glocalization' with respect to advertising (Bhatia, 2000, 2001; Bhatia &

Ritchie, 2008), this study aims to investigate the global and local fusion of identities and multimodal bilingual creativity emerging in French web advertising discourse, providing further insights into the role of media disseminated images, languages and music in constructing the hybrid identity of today's online consumer.

Mediascapes and cultural hybridity

Borrowing global theorist Arjun Appadurai's (1996) concept of 'mediascapes', this study underscores the transnational cultural flows occurring in advertising, where 'imagined worlds' and representations of the Other created by media are widely used to sell products. Appadurai (1996: 35) describes this concept as follows:

> Mediascapes [. . .] tend to be image-centered, narrative-based accounts of strips of reality, and what they offer to those who experience and transform them is a series of elements (such as characters, plots, and textual forms) out of which scripts can be formed of imagined lives, their own as well as those of others living in other places.

Operating as attention-getters, these multicultural fantasies sometimes combine global imagery from the most unlikely sources. Consider, for example, a Bedouin couple seated outside their tent in the middle of the desert downloading the American film classic *Singin' in the Rain* on computer-equipped sunglasses in a French TV commercial for VISA (Martin, 2005). Advertising agencies also use a variety of optical illusions, shooting commercials in more affordable foreign locations that resemble the target audience's country (Pinard, 2004), for instance, or inserting stock images in print campaigns as a cost-saving measure (Kattleman, 2003), such as the Colorado mountain imagery used in magazine advertisements for the Swiss bedding manufacturer Robusta (Martin, 2006: 74). Foreign languages may also be used as attention-getters in these imaginary landscapes (Martin, 2006: 32–38; see also Myers, 1994: 92–96).

As Appadurai (1996: 35) notes in the following comment, the boundaries between sociopolitical issues and corporate branding may also be blurred in this particular realm of communication:

> What is most important about these mediascapes is that they provide (especially in their television, film, and cassette forms) large and complex repertoires of images, narratives, and ethnoscapes to viewers throughout the world, in which the world of commodities and the world of news and politics are profoundly mixed.

This ambiguity is evident, for instance, in the sports and cultural events, fair trade and labor practices and environmental initiatives highlighted in advertising campaigns for major corporations. Some multinationals must also compete with the agenda of cyber activists trying to destroy their brand image, the anti-McDonald's website McSpotlight (mcspotlight.org) being a classic example (Kelly-Holmes, 2005: 81; Klein, 2000: 394).

Hybridity and creativity in world Englishes

This study also draws inspiration from the world Englishes paradigm introduced by Braj Kachru (1982, 1986), a concept that highlights 'the pluricentricity of the language and its cross-cultural reincarnations' (Kachru, 2006: 447). Central to this model is the notion that English, while operating as a lingua franca in diverse intra- and international contexts, has also developed into indigenized varieties, each with a unique range of functions and distinctive linguistic features. The multiple identities associated with these different varieties are characterized by a number of phonological and grammatical processes as well as culture-specific messages. Kachru's (2006: 451) conceptualization of English as a 'culturally pluralistic world language' is particularly useful in analyzing web discourse, where the traditional boundaries associated with English no longer apply. From a world Englishes perspective, the hybridity characterized by the French-English mixing in advertising directed at the French exemplifies both English as a global access language and the creativity and vitality of local uses of English. As Braj Kachru (2006: 452) so eloquently put it, 'English is used effectively for "thinking globally", and used, by choice, "to live locally" – thus establishing a pragmatic link between the two identities – global and local'.

In the case of advertising directed at consumers in Outer and Expanding Circle countries (the latter of which includes France), innovative uses of English appearing in advertisements designed for local audiences are seamlessly blended with English used as an international language in global advertising campaigns, forming a hybrid discourse that joins the 'best of both worlds' (Martin, 2006: 73–76). From a marketing perspective, combining 'global' English with localized forms of English enables corporations to project a unified global brand identity in their advertising while adapting advertising messages to local markets for greater appeal (Bhatia & Ritchie, 2008). In French advertisements, local adaptations of English may include hybridized product names (for example, French automaker Renault's *Avantime*, connoting that this particular model is 'before its time'), bilingual puns (for example, *HOT couture* ['high fashion'] for Givenchy perfume), code-mixed translations combining English with French (for example, *Que du hit sur NRJ* for a French radio station's slogan *NRJ, hit music only*), and various forms of multimodal mixing used for special effect (Martin, 2006: 196–202). English used as a pair language in advertising may also produce culturally specific humor (Vizcaíno, 2011) or evoke ethnic or national stereotypes associated with users of English from the Inner Circle (Martin, 2006). Local uses of English may also include product names that are perfectly acceptable in Outer or Expanding Circle regions but would likely offend English-speaking consumers of the Inner Circle, such as the *Calpis Water* and *Pocari Sweat* beverages sold in Japan (Bhatia, 2006: 614; see Goddard, 2002: 62; and Martin, 2006: 38–40, for additional examples). The same applies to English obscenities appearing in advertising in non-Anglophone countries, as documented, for instance, in France (Martin, 1998: 124) and Germany (Myers, 1994: 95).

As one of the functional domains of English across the Three Circles (Kachru, 2006: 453), advertising also exploits some of the symbolic values of English proposed by Kachru (1986), creating, in this particular context, positive associations to convey a brand message. In this regard, English in advertising designed for Outer and Expanding Circle countries indexes, for example, superior technology when used to sell products such as electronics, automobiles or kitchen appliances (see Kelly-Holmes, 2005; Martin, 2006; Vesterhus, 1991) and often serves as a linguistic expression of modernity (Haarmann, 1984; Lee, 2006; Piller, 2001; Takashi, 1990; Wu *et al.*, 2007). In French advertisements for cosmetic face creams, pseudo-scientific jargon in English (for example, the *Vascular Endothelial Growth Factor* embedded in French advertising copy for Chanel's *Précision Eclat Original*) reassures consumers that the product has been tested in the best-equipped research labs and has been 'scientifically proven' to reduce wrinkles (Martin, 2007: 178–179). It may also operate as an access code, as seen, for instance, in the English headline 'MADE IN FRENCH ALPS' used to market Evian mineral water (a French brand) in Japan (Mueller, 1996: 32), where French is not likely to be understood by the general population. Here, English is also being used to accentuate the country origin of the brand (in this case, France). Bhatia and Ritchie (2008: 10) refer to the symbolic value of English in advertising as the 'mystic factor' and argue that 'language mixture in advertising adds new semantic and affective features which single language advertising is incapable of rendering'. The hybridization of linguistic forms exhibited in French web advertising provides additional evidence to support this claim.

'Glocal' narratives in advertising

Research has shown that cross-fertilization of English with other languages, as well as local adaptations of English specifically designed for marketing purposes, are becoming increasingly prevalent in advertising across the globe, producing culture-specific meanings that resonate with local audiences (Baumgardner, 2006; Lee, 2006; Bhatia & Ritchie, 2008; Hsu, 2008; Martin, 2010; Ustinova, 2008). When code-mixed advertising messages of this nature are coupled with visual and/or auditory effects that reflect globalization juxtaposed with local cultural references, English is performing both global and local functions in a process that Bhatia (2001: 214) refers to as 'glocalization':

> In its role as the language of global advertising, not only is English leading to the homogenization of the advertising discourse worldwide, it is also diversifying itself in a number of ways. Taking in account the two main aspects of global advertising discourse, namely unification and diversification, the role played by English can best be characterized as *glocal*. The glocalization of English has lead to an ever-growing appetite for English in advertising worldwide, which has changed and continues to change the quantitative and qualitative patterns of English usage in advertising around the world.

In designing their web advertising, French corporations have also adopted this 'glocal' approach, addressing their French customers as both global and local consumers. As a global means of communication, English, likely to be intelligible to world audiences, appears in signature lines, webpage navigation buttons, video product demos and other online material. At the same time, a more localized, 'Frenglish' discourse is used to specifically appeal to the French. This 'glocal' web environment reflects the global and local realities that French audiences associate with English, creating new meanings through linguistic and cultural hybridity. Although language-mixing is evident in all areas of French advertising copy, this hybridity manifests itself most vividly in product names and slogans where linguistic innovations and experimentation play a vital role.

Methodology

Twenty French corporations were randomly selected from the 2009 Fortune Global 500 list for inclusion in the study. These companies represent a variety of sectors, ranging from oil, banking and electricity to retail, luxury goods and food (see Table 8.1).

In order to access web marketing specifically aimed at French consumers, data were collected from French-language customer sites (typically designated

Table 8.1 French corporations included in the study (by country/global ranking)

Country ranking	*Company*	*Global ranking*	*Sector*
(1)	Total	6	Oil and petroleum
(2)	BNP Paribas	24	Banking
(3)	Carrefour	25	Retail
(4)	Société Générale	43	Banking
(7)	Electricité de France	57	Electricity
(9)	Peugeot	75	Automotive
(10)	France Télécom	77	Telecommunications
(11)	Saint-Gobain	102	Construction materials
(13)	Auchan Group	126	Retail
(14)	Renault	130	Automotive
(17)	Bouygues	156	Telecommunications
(21)	Vivendi	207	Entertainment
(22)	SNCF	209	French National Railway Company
(23)	Air France-KLM Group	240	Airline
(26)	Lafarge	322	Construction materials
(27)	Schneider Electric	330	Electricity
(29)	Christian Dior	338	Luxury goods
(30)	L'Oréal	346	Cosmetics
(32)	Michelin	376	Automotive tires
(33)	Danone Group	413	Food

Source: money.cnn.com.

in French as *espace client, service client* or *particuliers*) as opposed to global corporate sites designed for investors.

Data collection (March–May 2010) involved identifying links on each company's French-language homepage that led consumers to product or service information and noting any use of English as well as all textual, visual and auditory references to global and/or local culture (for example, recording artists, athletes, actors, urban and rural landscapes, references to cultural beliefs or practices, and so on). Due to the multiple layers of information retrieval possible in websites of this nature, the examples of linguistic and cultural hybridity documented are by no means exhaustive. The data do, however, provide clear evidence that web advertising aimed at language-specific markets is, in fact, an intricate blend of global and local interpretations. These 'glocal' meanings are both entertaining and purposeful, enabling audiences to engage meaningfully with the company while building brand loyalty.

Results and Discussion

A content analysis of the webpages designed for each of the 20 corporations included in the study reveals the multimodal bilingual creativity and blend of global and local cultural references prevalent in French web marketing, demonstrating how the boundaries of hybrid cultures are negotiated in this particular environment through text, imagery and music.

Blending cultures in web advertising

The mixing of global and local cultures to create hybrid 'mediascapes' (Appadurai, 1996) is a prominent strategy used in designing web advertising for French corporations. Indeed, the French companies included in this study are positioning their French-speaking audiences as part of a global community while simultaneously providing web content that is carefully designed for French consumers. The French cosmetics company L'Oréal, for instance, juxtaposes their French TV commercial download featuring the quintessentially French football player Eric Cantona with beauty tips delivered in streaming video by an international panel of dermatologists and makeup artists (speaking a combination of French and English). Accompanying these images are L'Oréal spokesmodels from a variety of different countries, further enhancing their global brand image.[1]

As a public relations ploy, the French oil company Total has included in their web content a short film documentary on ocean conservation efforts worldwide, counteracting negative publicity surrounding the BP oil disaster in the Gulf of Mexico. This 'global' imagery is juxtaposed with more 'localized' content, such as the company's iPhone application offering local weather forecasts and traffic reports. French tire manufacturer Michelin is promoting local tourism by selling travel guides and maps for different regions of France while making ample use of English for product names and services for both their local and global markets (such as the Michelin OnWay roadside assistance package and Michelin Junior Bike event for children, promoting helmets and other safety precautions).

As the above examples indicate, the 'glocalized' approach used in French web marketing, where global references are blended with localized content, extends across all product categories. These 'global cultural flows' (Appadurai, 1996) enable French consumers to self-identify as global citizens while reinforcing their perceptions of the brand from a local perspective through cultural references that are specific to France (for example, French celebrities, TV stations, tourism, and so on). Web material for Total also provides evidence that major corporations sometimes embed ideological discourse in their advertising to disassociate the brand from controversial current events, illustrating the mixing of commodities, news and politics in media described by Appadurai (1996: 35).

Hybridity, identity and global music

The role of English in the construction of identity is a recurrent theme in the literature on advertising distributed in non-Anglophone countries (for example, Kelly-Holmes, 2005; Lee, 2010; Piller, 2001, 2003; Ustinova, 2008). Piller (2001), for instance, argues that Germans targeted by advertisements containing English are addressed as 'transnational' consumers, noting that 'English is portrayed as the language of a certain segment of German society, namely the young, cosmopolitan business elite' (Piller, 2001: 180). In her study of English in Korean television commercials, Lee (2006: 65) also examines how language mixing relates to identity construction, describing Korean-English bilingual creativity as a linguistic expression of modernity:

> The innovative use of English in Korean ads is not merely an ad hoc attention-getter. It is used to express Korean-English bilinguals' engagement with modernity. For these bilinguals, English is not an alien language but part of their socially active verbal repertoire. These bilinguals are not passive consumers of so-called canonical Standard English varieties, but active interlocutors and participants in the process of creating localized uses of English.

The present findings point to a similar symbolic use of English in French advertising where creative, localized forms of English are emerging. At the same time, consumer identities and modes of interaction have become more fluid and multidimensional. With the multimedia capacity of the web, the hybrid discursive practices used to lure consumers are growing increasingly complex, involving video clips, virtual tours and 3D animation, links to radio, television and digital media, social networking, custom product demonstrations and other interactive features. Through web technologies, corporations can easily showcase their global brand identity via powerful imagery, rhetoric and symbolism while taking into account local cultural identities, immersing their online audiences in a world where local and global discourses are seamlessly interwoven.

These 'glocal' narratives are often accentuated through music, with English serving as both a marker of globalization and a mood enhancer (Martin, 2006: 167–169). Copywriters interviewed in Paris (see Martin, 2006: 33–36), for example, indicated that the 'feeling' created by English music soundtracks in French TV advertisements is often more important than the lyrics. So much so, in fact, that French advertising agencies sometimes record 'gibberish lyrics' that are designed to imitate English for their campaigns aimed at French audiences. In the present study, one notes the predominant use of English soundtrack lyrics for online product videos. A much awaited sequel to an Evian commercial featuring babies performing a synchronized swimming routine (created in 1998 by French advertising agency Euro RSCG) appears on Danone's website. In the latest TV advertisement, Evian-sipping babies roller skate to a rap music soundtrack, a perfect accompaniment to the Danone Group's flagship water brand slogan, *Evian*: *Live Young*:

> *Rock rock yall, throw it on the floor.*
> *I'm gonna freak ya here I'm gonna freak ya there.*
> *I'm gonna move ya outta this atmosphere ...*

Under the 'Live Young Training' link, web users can request a personalized exercise program demonstrated online by babies seen in the commercial. Interactive features such as these illustrate how corporations are blurring the lines between different media, exploiting the multimodal potential of web advertising to draw audiences into their campaigns while building brand loyalty. In this case, Evian is capitalizing on youth trends and the communication patterns of online consumers, one of which is posting and viewing TV commercials on video-sharing sites. The fact that the (2009) Evian Roller Babies commercial quickly became a YouTube sensation, breaking the world record for online views for any advertisement in history, likely influenced the company's decision to make it an integral part of their web advertising (Button, 2009).

Vivendi's Universal Music France link offers French and English music videos featuring an eclectic mix of recording artists (including Senegalese-born French rap artist MC Solaar, Belgian pop/rock group Absynthe Minded, French reggae singer from Guadeloupe Edalam, and Canadian R&B/hip hop star Justin Bieber) along with a video clip featuring the 2010 Eurovision Song Contest winner (a German recording artist singing in English). Although it could be argued that Vivendi is a multinational label that is simply representing the global popular music industry, their web advertising is a classic example of the transnational cultural flows generated by media (Appadurai, 1996) and the musical hybridity to which today's audiences have grown accustomed. In his analysis of world music, Feld (2000: 145) aptly describes the ethno-cultural hybridity characteristic of global pop music in recent years:

> Music's deep connection to social identities has been distinctively intensified by globalization. This intensification is due to the ways cultural

> separation and social exchange are mutually accelerated by transnational flows of technology, media, and popular culture. The result is that musical identities and styles are more visibly transient, more audibly in states of constant fission and fusion than ever before.

The use of global music soundtracks is one of the many persuasive strategies used by web advertisers to seduce their audiences, creating contemporary imagined worlds while drawing attention to the brand. In doing so, these corporations are recognizing the fact that today's consumers – through exposure to 'global cultural flows' and the various 'mediascapes' (Appadurai, 1996) available to them – are constructing fluid identities that extend well beyond national borders.

Linguistic hybridity in French advertising

As the previous examples illustrate, the virtual world of web advertising offers unique opportunities for identity construction and newer forms of expression, with interactive features having become a staple of online advertising for major corporations. Indeed, surfing a company's website for product information is now a fully immersive multimedia experience, complete with online videos, self-directed quizzes, interactive chat rooms and discussion forums, electronic 'advergames' promoting the brand, digital avatars, 3D flash-based page turning online brochures and catalogues, and other virtual gadgetry. In many cases, the discourse accompanying the characteristic textual, visual and auditory features of interactive web design is heavily influenced by English. It is evident from the data that French corporations and the advertising agencies who design their web marketing have developed increasingly sophisticated communication strategies, and that English continues to play an important role when addressing French consumers.

In some respects, English operates as a lingua franca affording global access to company information. As is customary for multinational corporations, the official global website for many of these French brands, for instance, is presented entirely in English, with links to country sites in different languages. English has also been 'repackaged' for French consumers, however, becoming a truly localized, hybrid variety, as seen in 'Frenglish' product names, bilingual puns and code-mixed multimodal messages specifically designed for advertising. This 'mixed' discourse, with its morphosyntactic and phonological features mirroring the structural characteristics of the French language, is both appealing and intelligible to French audiences for whom English in this context has a number of positive associations. The 'glocal' representations and functioning of English in this environment clearly illustrate the 'pluricentricity' of English depicted by Kachru (2006), whose 'world Englishes' model has been applied to code-mixed advertising in many Outer and Expanding Circle countries (for example, Bhatia, 2001; Hsu, 2008; Masavisut *et al.*, 1986; Jung, 2001; Martin, 2006; Takashi, 1990; Ustinova & Bhatia, 2005, among others).

'Frenglish' product names

The use of English in product names around the globe has been widely discussed in the literature (for example, Haarmann, 1984; Friedrich, 2002; Wilkerson, 1997). Earlier studies on French advertising have highlighted a number of linguistic innovations observed in product names involving French-English hybrids (for example, Grunig, 1990; Martin, 2002, 2006). The present study provides evidence that this trend is continuing despite the French government's efforts to dissuade French companies from using English in their product names and advertising (Martin, 2006: 215–217). Indeed, both newer borrowings and foreign cultural concepts are now being introduced, resulting in a truly global and local fusion of identities in French advertising discourse. Note the following example drawn from recent web advertising for the French retailer Carrefour:

> *Midibag*

Used to denote one of their take-home lunch specials, this bilingual creation combines the French term for 'noon' (*midi*) with the English element 'bag' presumably inspired by the quintessentially American 'doggie bag' concept encountered by French tourists traveling in the US. The English word order (adjective + noun, rather than the reverse order as seen in the French expression *repas de midi*, or 'lunch') only adds to its appeal.

Adopting a similar approach, major French retailer Auchan is advertising its pre-packaged salad using another concept that the French typically associate with American culture:

> *Le Salad'Bar est ouvert! -10% sur les salades composées.*
> [The salad bar is open! 10% reduction on all mixed salads.]

The English possessive marker arbitrarily punctuating the term *Salad'Bar* appearing in this slogan is commonly seen in English elements borrowed into French, the earliest manifestations of which were most likely *pin's* (used as both a singular and plural noun in French to refer to collectable label pins) and *jean's* (also a singular and plural noun with no possessive quality in French).[2] The ubiquitous English-inspired apostrophe reappears in Auchan's

Class'Croute service, consisting of gourmet box lunches delivered to a person's office or workplace (another concept that is foreign to the French). This Frenglish hybrid uses the English word 'Class' (borrowed into French with its 'classy' connotation) and a truncated version of the French expression *casse-croûte*, meaning 'lunch' or 'snack', minus the circumflex accent mark normally required in French.

Another relatively newer English borrowing appearing in French company product names is the word 'box' which now accompanies its more assimilated cousin 'pack'.[3]

A few examples from the present corpus include the following:

Bbox Junior <Bouygues Telecom>
Neufbox TV <SFR>
Smartbox <Lafarge>
L'Oreal Cherrypack <L'Oréal>
Pack de Gervais Mon Yaourt Rigolo <Danone>
Pack Jeunes <Société Générale>
Packéco <EDF>
Packs Guide Vert + Carte <Michelin>

Morphosyntactic innovations

New technological advances have also inspired French neologisms, such as those that incorporate the lowercase prefixes /e-/ or /i-/ from the English term 'email' (borrowed in the 1990s) and Apple Computers' portable music digital player the 'iPod' (introduced in 2001). The following are a sampling of lexical innovations of this nature appearing in the data (underlining added):

e-billet <SNCF>
e-boutique <Total>
e-brochure <Renault>
e-card <Christian Dior>
e-catalogue <Schneider Electric>
e-culture <Carrefour>
e-guide <Renault>
e-magazine <Carrefour>
e-marchands <BNP Paribas>
e-recrutement <SNCF>
e-travaux <Lafarge>

Station iPig Rose pour iPod, iPhone <France Télécom>
[France Télécom's Pink iPig docking station for Apple iPod or iPhone.]

Tarif iDTGV <SNCF>
[SNCF's iD ticket price for their high-speed train TGV.]

A number of English borrowings have also been assimilated into the morphological and syntactic rules of French in the data, acquiring French verb and noun endings, gender and plural markers and other structural characteristics of the host language. Note the following examples (underlining added):

Avec les bébés Evian, laissez-vous coacher pour cultiver and entretenir votre jeunesse! <Evian>
Les blogueurs BD font leur festival! <SNCF>
Le podcasting, comment ça marche? <SNCF>
Internet prêt-à-partir: Connectez – surfez – rechargez *<Bouygues Telecom>*

Even the French government, notorious for legally restricting the use of English in French media discourse (Martin, 2006: 212–241), acquiesced regarding the 'surf' borrowing, creating a website dubbed *'Surfez intelligent'* whose link appears on the Bouygues Telecom homepage:

www.surfez-intelligent.gouv.fr

The government's mission reads as follows (underlining added):

Le Secrétariat d'Etat en charge de la Prospective et du Développement de l'économie numérique vous propose quelques repères et bonnes pratiques indispensables pour 'surfez' en toute sérénité.

[The French Secretary of State for Strategic Studies and the Development of the Digital Economy offers you a number of useful tips for surfing the web safely.]

Although there exists a widely accepted French translation for 'surfing' (*naviguer sur le Web*), the decision on the part of Bouygues Telecom to use the localized English borrowing *surfez* was likely motivated by the desire to produce punchier and more succinct advertising copy (as using one 'Frenglish' word – as opposed to its four-word French equivalent – creates symmetry between the advertising slogan and URL). English in French advertisements for this product category also has a powerful symbolic value – or 'mystic factor' to borrow Bhatia and Ritchie's (2008) terminology – connoting that Bouygues Telecom customers are hip, friendly, tech savvy, intelligent, professional, and so on.

Other loanwords, such as 'chat' or 'chat room', exhibit adaptations that are motivated both phonetically and orthographically. In this case, in order to imitate, in French, the English consonant cluster /ch/ (presumably to avoid any confusion with the French term *chat* meaning 'cat'), web designers for French companies are now widely using the three-consonant cluster /tch/. In their web advertising, France Télécom displays this combination with a capitalized /C/ and an eliding apostrophe, producing terms such as *t'Chat*, *t'Chatter* and *t'Chatteur* (underlining added).

> *Réservez votre pseudo t'Chat Orange gratuitement. Vous pourrez t'Chatter et utiliser les forums avec votre pseudo Gratis de manière illimitée. [. . .] Dialoguez avec des t'Chatteurs qui vous ressemblent.*
> [Register your Orange chat room pseudonym free of charge. You'll be able to freely chat and use the forums with your pseudonym [. . .] Converse with other chat users with similar interests.]

Semantic borrowing

Several processes of semantic borrowing also emerge from the data. The Auchan group, for instance, is marketing their *Little Extra* collection in their French-language webpages, attributing the English meaning of this expression to a French product line of elegant household items. Whereas the term *extra* in French advertising has often been used as a truncated version of *extraordinaire* ('extraordinary'), here, the original English meaning is the one used as a marketing ploy, denoting 'a little something extra'.[4] To French audiences, however, the English adjective *Little* also infers 'inexpensive', having been modeled after the French expression *petits prix*, or 'little prices'. This nuance is highlighted in both a video presentation of the product line and a letter to Auchan customers appearing on the website (signed *Littlement votre* as a bilingual pun evoking *Cordialement vôtre*, or 'Sincerely Yours'). The *Little Extra* brand features the following collections: *Little cuisine* ('Little kitchen'), *Little bain* ('Little bathroom'), *Little intérieur* ('Little interior'), *Little bureau* ('Little office'), and for the 'little ones' (in other words, their children's collection), *Little Little*!

Several cases of semantic shift were also noted in the data, one example being that of the English acronym VIP which retained its original meaning ('Very Important Person') when first borrowed into French for use in advertising campaigns. In recent years, however, French copywriters have been offering additional connotations for VIP, one of which is reported in Martin (2007: 183):

> *Match TV: V.I.P. ou very important poitrine?*
> [Match TV: V.I.P. or very large breasts?]

The visual accompanying the slogan depicts a close-up of a rather buxom woman wearing a VIP badge attempting to gain access to movie stars attending the Cannes Film Festival. The code-mixed version (*very important poitrine*) was added for humorous effect. In the present corpus, however, the term VIP has a more prestigious connotation, having been adopted by Carrefour for their loyalty program. As the slogan implies, membership privileges include early-bird discounts through their e-catalogue and other online promotions.

> *V.I.P.: Ventes Internet Privilèges*
> [V.I.P.: Online Sales Promotions]

These examples provide further evidence of the fusion and hybridization of linguistic forms emerging in advertising as a result of globalization (Bhatia & Ritchie, 2008) and 'the multi-identities English has created across cultures' (Kachru, 2006: 447). Two types of English are represented here: an 'International' English functioning as a lingua franca (experienced in pop-up videos, links to social networking sites and other features) and a more localized version of English blended with French, seen in product names, product descriptions and advertising slogans created specifically for the purposes of advertising. In addition to viewing, and hearing, a wide variety of 'Frenglish' mixing online, visitors to the French-language webpages of these French corporations are also experiencing a kaleidoscopic representation of cultures. The global branding and references to corporate global initiatives (for example, Total's ocean conservation efforts, Lafarge's operations in China), foreign concepts (for example, Japanese bento boxes and the US-inspired 'doggie bag' used to market Danone products) and global music soundtracks (as used by SNCF, Renault, Danone, Evian and others) surfacing in the data are indicative of the global imagery used for persuasive purposes in advertising. At the same time, these brands are tailoring their French-language advertising for French audiences, infusing their messages with local culture references and humor. Web consumers have grown accustomed to receiving a 'glocal' mix of cultures and languages in advertising designed for multinational corporations, hybrid visual/verbal interpretations that are often enhanced with multimodal features, and the French are no exception. This interactive virtual environment increases one's exposure to global and local discourses, a fact that has not gone unnoticed by corporations marketing their products via the web using a seductive, interactive blend of cultures and languages in their efforts to increase brand awareness.

Conclusion

Virtual marketing has become a fertile breeding ground for cultural and linguistic hybridity. In this environment, English is functioning as both a global access language symbolizing modernity, global interconnectivity and professional mobility, and a pair language for locally meaningful code-mixing, satisfying the creative and innovative needs of advertising, and illustrating the 'multiple identities' English has created across cultures (Kachru, 2006: 447). The contact-induced structural innovations featured in product names and advertising slogans provide further evidence that French e-marketers are blending English and French in highly creative ways, producing new localized forms of English and hybrid expressions with meanings that resonate with French consumers. Through 'Frenglish' mixes such as *midibag, Class'Croute* and *Littlement votre*, they infuse their advertising messages with humor, sophistication and other positive associations while communicating both global and local concepts familiar to French audiences. These hybrid textual features are woven into a 'glocal' tapestry of visual stimuli and music, creating 'mediascapes' consisting of 'image-centered, narrative-based accounts of strips of reality' (Appadurai, 1996: 35) used to draw the audience's attention.

This complex negotiation of cultural identity between French brands and online customers is facilitated through interactive web design. Whether it be Renault associating its latest sedan with the jazzy world of bebop, or Danone combining Japanese references with French TV programming to sell yoghurt, web advertisements project audiences into an 'imaginary world' where global and local cultures collide. Encouraging website visitors to share their brand messages on Facebook, YouTube, Twitter and other social networking sites conveniently embedded in the advertising material, French corporations are embracing the idea that 'hybrid marketing' fusing traditional and social media marketing strategies has now become the norm while increasing their visibility exponentially. This intermingling of local and global discourses in web advertising is helping to shape the hybrid cultural identities and linguistic practices of today's online consumers and is a vital component of the 'glocal' approach to marketing. The fact that French corporations are using these strategies to communicate with French audiences provides compelling evidence that cultural and linguistic hybridity has become an integral part of the global landscape of advertising.

Notes

(1) Spokesmodels for L'Oréal featured in their French-language web advertising include Laetitia Casta (France), Eva Longoria (USA), Doutzen Kroes (the Netherlands) and Claudia Schiffer (Germany).

(2) A comprehensive review of English neologisms borrowed into French is provided by Picone (1996).
(3) Characterized as 'Advertising English' in earlier studies on French advertising (Martin, 2007, 2008), similar product-related borrowings (for example, *pack*, *twist*, *spray*) have also been documented in Mexican advertisements (See Baumgardner, 2006).
(4) See Martin (2006: 193–195) for additional examples of 'extra' in French television and print advertising.

References

Appadurai, A. (1996) *Modernity at Large: Cultural Dimensions of Globalization*. Minneapolis: University of Minnesota Press.

Backhaus, P. (2007) *Linguistic Landscapes: A Comparative Study of Urban Multilingualism in Tokyo*. Clevedon: Multilingual Matters.

Baumgardner, R. (2006) The appeal of English in Mexican commerce. *World Englishes* 25 (2), 251–266.

Baumgardner, R. (2008) The use of English in advertising in Mexican print media. *Journal of Creative Communications* 3 (1), 23–48.

Bhatia, T.K. (1987) English in advertising: Multiple mixing and media. *World Englishes* 6 (1), 33–48.

Bhatia, T.K. (1992) Discourse functions and pragmatics of mixing: Advertising across cultures. *World Englishes* 11 (2–3), 195–215.

Bhatia, T.K. (2000) *Advertising in Rural India: Language, Marketing Communication, and Consumerism*. ILCAA Study of Languages and Cultures of Asia and Africa Monograph Series, No. 36, Tokyo University of Foreign Studies, Tokyo, Japan.

Bhatia, T.K. (2001) Language mixing in global advertising. In E. Thumboo (ed.) *The Three Circles of English* (pp. 195–216). Singapore: UniPress.

Bhatia, T.K. (2006) World Englishes in global advertising. In B.B. Kachru, Y. Kachru and C.L. Nelson (eds) *The Handbook of World Englishes* (pp. 601–619). Oxford: Blackwell Publishing.

Bhatia, T.K. and Ritchie, W.C. (2008) The bilingual mind and linguistic creativity. *Journal of Creative Communications* 3 (1), 5–21.

Button, S. (2009) Evian – Roller babies. *Unruly Media*, 9 November 2009, accessed 13 May 2010. http://www.unrulymedia.com.

Dumont, M. (1998) *Les Enseignes de Dakar: Un Essai de Sociolinguistique Africaine*. Paris: L'Harmattan.

Feld, S. (2000) A sweet lullaby for world music. *Public Culture* 12 (1), 145–171.

Friedrich, P. (2002) English in advertising and brand naming: Sociolinguistic considerations and the case of Brazil. *English Today* 18 (3), 21–28.

Goddard, A. (2002) *The Language of Advertising*. London: Routledge.

Griffin, J. (1997) Global English invades Poland. An analysis of the use of English in Polish magazine advertisements. *English Today* 13 (2), 34–41.

Grunig, B. (1990) *Les Mots de la Publicité: L'Architecture du Slogan*. Paris: Centre National de Recherche Scientifique (CNRS).

Haarmann, H. (1984) The role of ethnocultural stereotypes and foreign languages in Japanese commercials. *International Journal of the Sociology of Language* 50, 101–102.

Hsu, J-L. (2008) Glocalization and English mixing in advertising in Taiwan. *Journal of Creative Communications* 3 (2), 155–183.

Ju-Pak, K-H. (1999) Content dimensions of web advertising: A cross-national comparison. *International Journal of Advertising* 18 (2), 207–231.

Jung, K. (2001) The genre of advertising in Korean: Strategies and 'mixing'. In E. Thumboo (ed.) *The Three Circles of English* (pp. 257–275). Singapore: UniPress.

Kachru, B. (1982) *The Other Tongue: English across Cultures*. Urbana, IL: University of Illinois Press.

Kachru, B. (1986) *The Alchemy of English: The Spread, Functions and Models of Non-Native Englishes*. Oxford: Pergamon Press.

Kachru, B. (2006) World Englishes and culture wars. In B.B. Kachru, Y. Kachru and C.L. Nelson (eds) *The Handbook of World Englishes* (pp. 446–471). Oxford: Blackwell Publishing.

Kamwangamalu, N.M. (2008) From linguistic apartheid to linguistic co-habitation: Codeswitching in print advertising in post-apartheid South Africa. *Journal of Creative Communications* 3 (1), 99–113.

Kanso, A. and Nelson, R.A. (2002) Advertising localization overshadows standardization. *Journal of Advertising Research*, January/February, 79–89.

Kattleman, T. (2003) When travel's not an option: Stock in action: Two campaigns for BMW motorcyles. *Creativity* (September), 54.

Kelly-Holmes, H. (2005) *Advertising as Multilingual Communication*. London: Palgrave Macmillan.

Klein, N. (2000) *No Logo*. London: Flamingo.

Lee, J.S. (2006) Linguistic constructions of modernity: English mixing in Korean television commercials. *Language in Society* 35, 59–91.

Lee, J.S. (2010) Commodified English in East Asian internet advertising. In H. Kelly-Holmes and G. Mautner (eds) *Language and the Market* (pp. 109–120). London: Palgrave Macmillan.

Madden, T.J., Hewett, K. and Roth, M.S. (2000) Managing images in different cultures: A cross-national study of colour meanings and preferences. *Journal of International Marketing* 8 (4), 90–107.

Martin, E. (1998) Code-mixing and imaging of America in France: The genre of advertising. PhD thesis, University of Illinois at Urbana-Champaign.

Martin, E. (2002) Cultural images and different varieties of English in French television commercials. *English Today* 18 (4), 8–20.

Martin, E. (2005) Global advertising à la française: Designing ads that 'speak' to French consumers. *The Journal of Language for International Business* 16 (1), 76–95.

Martin, E. (2006) *Marketing Identities through Language: English and Global Imagery in French Advertising*. London: Palgrave Macmillan.

Martin, E. (2007) 'Frenglish' for sale: Multilingual discourses for addressing today's global consumer. *World Englishes* 26 (2), 170–188.

Martin, E. (2008) Language-mixing in French print advertising. *Journal of Creative Communications*. London: Sage.

Martin, E. (2010) Language policy and multilingual advertising in France. In H. Kelly-Holmes and G. Mautner (eds) *Language and the Market* (pp. 83–95). London: Palgrave Macmillan.

Masavisut, N., Sukwiwat, M. and Wongmontha, S. (1986) The power of the English language in Thai media. *World Englishes* 5 (2–3), 197–207.

Meraj, S. (1993) The use of English in Urdu advertising in Pakistan. In R.J. Baumgardner (ed.) *The English Language in Pakistan* (pp. 221–252). Karachi: Oxford University Press.

Mooij, de M. (1998) *Global Marketing and Advertising: Understanding Cultural Paradoxes*. London: Sage Publications.
Mueller, B. (1996) *International Advertising: Communicating Across Cultures*. Belmont, CA: Wadsworth Publishing Co.
Myers, G. (1994) *Words in Ads*. London: Edward Arnold.
Pavlou, P. (2002) The use of dialectal and foreign language elements in radio commercials in Cyprus. Paper presented at the 13th World Congress of Applied Linguistics, 16–21 December, Singapore.
Picone, M.D. (1996) *Anglicisms, Neologisms and Dynamic French*. Philadelphia: John Benjamins.
Piller, I. (2001) Identity constructions in multilingual advertising. *Language in Society* 30, 153–186.
Piller, I. (2003) Advertising as a site of language contact. *Annual Review of Applied Linguistics* 23, 170–183.
Pinard, R. (2004) Ailleurs, P.Q. *Infopresse* 20 (1), 37.
Rosendal, T. (2009) Linguistic markets in Rwanda: Language use in advertisements and on signs. *Journal of Multilingual & Multicultural Development* 30 (1), 19–39.
Singh, N. and Pereira, A. (2005) *The Culturally Customized Web Site: Customizing Web Sites for the Global Marketplace*. Oxford: Elsevier.
Smakman, D., Korzilius, H., van Meurs, F. and van Neerven, E. (2009) English words and phrases in radio commercials in the Netherlands: Their use and effects. *ESP Across Cultures* 6, 109–128.
Takashi, K. (1990) A sociolinguistic analysis of English borrowings in Japanese advertising text. *World Englishes* 9 (3), 327–341.
Thonus, T. (1991) Englishization of business names in Brazil. *World Englishes* 10 (1), 65–74.
Tsao, J.C. and Chang, C. (2002) Communication strategy in Taiwanese and US corporate web pages: A cross-cultural comparison. *Asian Journal of Communication* 12 (2), 1–29.
Ustinova, I. (2008) English and American culture appeal in Russian advertising. *Journal of Creative Communication* 3 (1), 77–98.
Ustinova, I. and Bhatia, T.K. (2005) Convergence of English in Russian TV commercials. *World Englishes* 24 (4), 495–508.
Vesterhus, S.A. (1991) Anglicisms in German car documents. *Language International* 3 (3), 10–15.
Vizcaíno, M.J.G. (2011) Humor in code-mixed airline advertising. *Pragmatics* 21 (1), 145–170.
Wilkerson, K.T. (1997) Japanese bilingual brand names. *English Today* 13, 12–16.
Wu, D., Feng, J. and Chan, C.Y. (2007) Glocalization and hybridization of languages in Chinese web advertising. *China Media Research* 3 (2), 1–8.
Yunker, J. (2003) *Beyond Borders: Web Globalization Strategies*. Berkeley, CA: New Riders.
Zhou, N. and Belk, R.W. (2004) Chinese consumer readings of global and local advertising appeals. *Journal of Advertising* 33 (3), 63–76.

9 What's Punjabi Doing in an English Film? Bollywood's New Transnational Tribes

Anjali Gera Roy

There's been a history of seeing difference, in terms of culture ... as problematic. For me, difference is celebratory.
Gurinder Chadha in Hornaday, 1994

Today, Delhi is a strange 'globalized' world where tradition butts heads with modernity at every turn. Gucci and Prada exist side by side with power cuts and traffic jams, and the spoken language is colorful and inventive, crisscrossing easily between English, Hindi, and Punjabi.
Mira Nair in Taylor, 2002

Contemporary Indian Film Industry: Local and Global

Anupama Chopra, in her article 'Bye-bye Bharat' (1997), asserts that the 'the funky, straight-out-of-Manhattan loft' of film director Yash Chopra's *Dil to Pagal Hai* (1997) and 'the carefully constructed slice of America' in Karan Johar's *Kuch Kuch Hota Hai* (1998) could be viewed as 'a sign of Bollywood's fascination with westernized, city centric storytelling' that heralded the arrival of the urban Bollywood film.[1] If the 1990s ignored 'the heartland' and made films for 'A class centres'[2] and NRI markets, the new millennium signaled both the return of the 'rural' film and the birth of the 'crossover' film. Crossover is

> a film or production that is made for one audience, but may easily 'cross-over' to another unexpected audience; it also refers to a film,

actor, or production that appeals to different demographic groups or age groups and can move between two or more distinct franchises. (Film Terms Glossary)

Marks (2000: 6) prefers the term 'intercultural' to crossover, hybrid, transnational, postcolonial or Third World to define a work that 'is not the property of any single culture, but mediates in at least two directions'. Pointing out the limitations of Gilles Deleuze's binary of the *sayable* and *seeable*, Marks states that intercultural cinema, expressing the disjuncture between orders of knowledge, reveals 'the new combination of words and things that cannot be read in terms of the existing languages of sound and image but calls for new, as yet unformulated languages' (2000: 3) and suggests that meaning must be found not in what is there but in the gaps. Interpreting language in a broad sense, Marks argues that to overcome the limits of Western visual, auditory and other languages in articulating the experience of other worlds, particularly its 'nonvisual sense memory', the intercultural filmmaker evolves new idioms to translate cultural difference through which intercultural cinema develops 'non-audio visual' ways of seeing. Marks proposes the notion of 'haptic visuality' to critique the Western privileging of the visual through embodied ways of experiencing and shows that the understanding of the sayable as dialogue is equally limiting because the soundtrack contains more than words, including symbolic sounds, extradiscursive sounds and images that appear as noise or 'spice'. Viewing the intercultural or 'crossover' film from a postcolonial Indian/Punjabi position, this chapter foregrounds the 'untranslatability' of cultural difference that compels the filmmaker to evolve other languages to produce the 'sensuous geographies' of other places in this sense. In addition to slipping into 'foreign' Hindi and Punjabi, the filmmakers turn to the Bollywood vocabulary of song and dance, visual images, haptic visuality and 'memory images' to articulate the *unsayable* that eludes the sayable in Standard English.

Crossover *Punjabiyat*: A Look at Three Crossover Films and the Hybrid Use of Language

The mid-1990s witnessed a pronounced shift in Bollywood's spectator positioning from the idealized national subject of post-independence Hindi cinema to the ethnolinguistic subject, which partially occurred as a result of Bollywood's transnationalization. Bollywood's new market segmentation (in which the diaspora is clearly factored into its financial economy), constructs the subject as Punjabi in deference to the Punjabi domination of the diaspora whose body consequently becomes the site for the play of tradition and modernity. The valorization of Punjabi peasant values as 'ours' over those of other ethnolinguistic groups could also be attributed to Bollywood's pandering to diasporic techno-nostalgia. The association of Punjabis with agricultural prosperity in India and the diasporas results in the diasporic nostalgia for the non-technologized homeland with its exoticized traditions mapped onto a specifically Punjabi rural imaginary.[3] The text that set the trend for valorizing an essentialized *Punjabiyat* as rusticity, namely *Dilwale Dulhania Le Jayenge,* is often cited to establish the nexus between NRI capital, the location of the director, Bollywood culture industry and the imagined spectator.[4] With every second film being peppered with Punjabi since *Dilwale Dulhania Le Jayenge,*[5] Bollywood's 'Punjabification', as Anupama Chopra calls it (cited in Viswanathan, 2009), culminated in *Singh is Kingg* (2007) featuring a Sikh protagonist for the first time in the history of Hindi cinema. With nearly half its dialogue in Punjabi, the film set a trend that continued in *Love Aaj Kal* (2009) and *Dil Bole Hadippa* (2009). The change in their address makes the celebration of *Punjabiyat* or Punjabi-ness in the 1990s in Bollywood films quite different from the comic portrayal of ethnic stereotypes in Hindi cinema of the 1950s and 1960s. The naturalization of Punjabi words like *munda* (boy), *makhna* (handsome), *soni* (beautiful), *rab* (God), *kudi* (girl), *mauja* (fun), *tussi* (you), *puttar* (son), *praah* (brother) and *oye* (an exclamation) in the Bollywood vocabulary has truly 'Punjabified' the Bollywood audience. While the Punjabi in Hindi films, as Deepa Gahlot (2005) points out, is a simplified hybrid closer to Hindi, it has invited the wrath of non-Punjabi audiences such as Nandini Ramnath who says, 'I suggest that producers start subtitling the Punjabi bits, both in the main film and in the songs' (cited in Viswanathan, 2009). Notwithstanding Ramnath's objections, the Punjabi overdose of the Punjabi-Hindi or Punjabi-English film has not posed a barrier to its crossover either into the Indian or Euro-American mainstream.[6]

In addition to Bollywood films, three crossover films, *Monsoon Wedding* (2001), *Bend it Like Beckham* (2002) and *Bollywood Hollywood* (2002), identify the Indian diaspora in the United States, United Kingdom and Canada, respectively, as unmistakably Punjabi and specify Indian family values as Punjabi Hindu or Sikh, thereby connecting Punjab with the Punjabi diasporas in global Delhi, Southall and Toronto. These crossover films, *Monsoon Wedding, Bend it Like Beckham* and *Bollywood Hollywood,* included in the category of 'global appeal' (Bellman, 2010) in Indian trade journals and magazines, produce regional 'localities' in global cities and may be viewed as postmodernist translations of 'critical regionalism' (Frampton, 1983).[7] The films in this category have been directed by filmmakers of Indian origin who have been raised and live in different parts of the world but have more in common than gender. Although the filmmakers grew up in different parts of India and the world and have 'no fixed address' as they frequently shuttle between the US, the UK, Canada, South Africa and India, they have a distinct ethnolinguistic location, Mira Nair's Hindu Punjabi and Gurinder Chadha's Sikh Punjabi.[8] Indian American Hindu Punjabi Nair's 'love song' to her 'home city' Delhi, *Monsoon Wedding*, was an international co-production between India, the US, Italy, France and Germany. *Monsoon Wedding* won not only the British Independent Film Award for the Best Foreign Language Film, the Canberra International Film Festival-Audience Award, the Venice Film Festival Golden Lion and the Venice Film Festival Laterna Magica Prize but also earned over $20 million at the box office.[9] 'Twice migrant' Sikh Punjabi British Asian director Gurinder Chadha's *Bend it Like Beckham* picked up a host of awards even as it topped the box office charts. Though Chadha herself positioned it as a British film set in Hounslow, its universal theme enabled it to be enjoyed simultaneously as a 'soccer', 'teen coming-of-age' or 'girl power' movie dealing with the clash of traditional Indian values with British ones.

Despite their global address (all three being English language films by directors of Indian origin residing in the diaspora), these films retain liberal helpings of the local Hindi/Punjabi vernacular with no attempt at semantic glossing as their characters switch between English, Hindi and Punjabi with consummate ease. The films' code-switching could be alternately seen as an authentic reproduction of contemporary urban Indian speech, as Nair (cited in Taylor, 2002) maintains, or as the filmmakers' playful implementation of the Indian nation state's three-language formula. But the films do more than add local flavor or fulfill the authenticity requirement by retaining Hindi and Punjabi vernacular idiom. While such dialogue might appear to serve no purpose other than inscribing 'foreignness' in the films' global marketing, the films' refusal to translate Hindi/Punjabi colloquial speech problematizes cultural incommensurability. Cultural difference is enunciated in the films at the precise moment of Hindi or Punjabi language slippage as their non-Hindi, non-Punjabi viewers grapple with their verbal semantics. Code-switching becomes the key to the films' translation of postcolonial difference into a language that is not the filmmakers' own. The filmmakers' strategy is to use the gap between the colonial language and the colonized world to enunciate cultural difference. This gap between the colonial sign and the colonized experience alters the sign's significatory function as it signifies meaning as absence.

The Punjabi *Unsayable*

In his analysis of *Bend it Like Beckham* in a pedagogical context, Sharma (2006: 211) argues that 'the possibility of alterity emerging from a counter-hegemonic representational politics offering an alternative discourse of South Asianness outside of Orientalism is unlikely'. He proposes that 'a more immediate, though no less difficult practice may be considered, by first rethinking what is *un/knowable* about the other'. The *un/knowable* about the Other appears to be locked in the unfathomability of her language.

Parciack's (2008: 234) use of Fiske's notion of the 'uncodable' 'as a signifier that seemingly remains obstructed and unattainable', along with Dyer's concept of polysemy to understand the way Hindi music is 'encoded' as the 'uncodable' in the Israeli consciousness, offers an interesting parallel to the encoding of Punjabi phrases as uncodable in the English language films. Punjabi signifies as either an exoticized foreignness to non-Punjabi viewers in the West or a stereotyped *Punjabiyat* to those in India. Confronted with the challenge of communicating 'the intoxicating zest for life' (Nair, 2002) of the Punjab culture in languages in which Punjabi is burdened with colonial and postcolonial significations, the filmmaker deconstructs the meanings signified by the sign Punjabi through the sayable and the seeable but also the *sensible*. Instead of reversing its significations in the imperial or postcolonial imaginary, the filmmakers play upon these to tease out meanings produced in the gap between English, Hindi and Punjabi. While watching *Monsoon Wedding*, Iyer (2009) observed that 'several languages were mingling in every sentence, so that even a two-word curse was sometimes polylingual – "bloody *feranghi*" (dutifully translated in the subtitles as "bloody foreigner")', and connected it to 'the laughing chaos, the delighted jostle of a country'. However, the oscillation between English, Hindi and Punjabi observed in *Monsoon Wedding*, for those who can decipher its hidden codes, is more finely nuanced than Iyer's Rushdiesque reading of India and of Nair's film. Unlike Iyer (2009) and Sharpe (2005), who trace Nair's new aesthetic style back to a homogenized Indian culture, other Western reviewers have exhibited greater sensitivity to the film's specifically Punjabi milieu and the particular inflections of the Punjabi wedding.

Nair's play on different varieties of English in *Monsoon Wedding* foregrounds aspects of the Other's lives that are unsayable in the English language. 'Come on come on', Lalit Verma, the father of the bride, effusively greets his soon-to-be son-in-law, 'we are soon to be in the family way', inviting a contemptuous smirk from the groom's aristocratic parents, the Rai couple. Verma's erroneous repetition of the colonial sign calls forth the absence rather than the presence of the signified and defers meaning through its difference. Later, at the dance performed at the musical evening preceding the wedding, Verma's switching from English to Punjabi as he introduces a close relative to Mr Rai accentuates the failure of the colonial language to express the relations of obligation that bind partitioned Punjabi families to one another: *Batware de baad asi ethe aye/sada koi agga piccha naheen si/Tej bhraji hor ainande tabbar ne sadi dekhbhal kiti si/sanu paraha likhaya apne pairan te khada kita* (After partition we came here with nothing/Nowhere to go, no future/Brother Tej and his family looked after us/He educated us made us stand on our feet). Nair plays on the multiple meanings of family by switching between Punjabi, Hindi and English in the family benefactor Tej Puri's embarrassed response: *Hisab naheen hota family men/ab to aap bhi hamari family mein hain* (There are no accounts between families/Now you are part of the family). Puri's choice of formal Hindi over intimate Punjabi reflects not just the glottophobia of Punjabi by Hindi but also kinship relations radically altered after partition.

These intimate rituals of bonding articulated in pure Punjabi are framed against an evening of dance and entertainment, which is itself a modified version of the *sangeet* (musical soiree) performed at modern Punjabi weddings, compered by C.L. Chadha, the bride's uncle. His curious mix of Indian English with elite Urdu elicits derisive laughter from the sophisticated Mrs Rai, whose perfect enunciation of Urdu poetry matches her flawless English diction. 'Who is that clown?', she inquires with a contemptuous smile. Yet Nair casts an affectionate look at the Chadha couple's in-the-face *Punjabiyat* through investing their speech and bodily gestures with the lust for life and warmth conventionally mapped on the Punjabi body in the Indian imaginary. It is the Chadha couple who appear to be more comfortable in their Punjabi skin than any other member of the extended Verma family. It is they who have the final word in the film when they break into pure Punjabi to greet their son Umang and unselfconsciously ensconce him in a bear hug: *Oh Umang aagya ji zara dekho te sahi kaun aya hai/oh mera puttar, Umang mera beta*! (Oh Umang is here! Look who is here! Oh my son, Umang, my darling son!). Unlike the Chadhas, Pimmi Verma, like her husband Lalit, shifts between languages. Yet, Punjabi signposts, even for the Verma couple, affection and intimacy as in the scene where Pimmi teases her son about making sure that he changes his underwear or when she steals a dirty joke with her sister-in-law Shashi Chadha during the singing of the wedding song *madhorama*. Similarly, Lalit Verma's agonized plea to Pimmi '*mannu sambhal lai*' (Help me pull myself together) when they retire to their bedroom after Ria's unmasking of the pedophile elder Puri demonstrates that the unsayable can be expressed only in Punjabi. Punjabi, in *Monsoon Wedding*, as in other crossover films, is the language of intimacy that family members of a certain generation retreat into in moments of stress, affection and humour.[10]

Unlike *Monsoon Wedding*, Gurinder Chadha's film *Bend it Like Beckham* switches between different varieties of English instead of three languages but also slips into Punjabi in moments of anger, distress and intimacy. The film opens with a dream sequence of Jesse's mother, Mrs Bhamra, hurling abuses at her in pure Punjabi. As expletives in any language problematize the untranslatability of languages, the English translation of the expletive *khasmanoonkhani* (which roughly means 'the one who ate up her mate') used by Mrs Bhamra, not only elides its multiple significations – of extreme anger or passion – but fails to convey the embarrassment that a Sikh girl's exposed legs can cause to her family. Punjabi returns in Titu's parents' outrage when they report Jesse's alleged kissing of a white boy to her parents: *Bachche ma piyo di chawan honde ne* (Children are a reflection of their parents). Similarly, a one-liner by Jesse's father *'rajma chowl baneye ne'* ('have you cooked beans and rice?') is telling in its indication that Punjabi continues to be the home language. Instead of switching between Hindi, English and Punjabi, Chadha plays with different varieties of English to produce meanings at the margins of Standard English. Since accent is a passport to belonging, senior Punjabis' thickly accented Punjabi English and Mr Bhamra's Indian English excludes them from the wholeness of Standard English and positions them at the margin of the British nation. However, while their accented English might lend them easily to comic caricatures, Chadha suggests that their unproblematic inhabitation of Punjabi makes them more rooted compared to the second generation while underscoring the unknowability of the Other. If the filmmakers' retention of Punjabi is one way of articulating the unknowable, song and dance is another.

Singing and Dancing the *Unsayable*

Scholars have commented on the 'understandings of the function of song and dance sequences (such as the spaces of fantasy and the imaginary disrupting the limitations of the narrative)' (Desai & Dudrah, 2008: 11) and their enabling and incorporation of multiple forms of performance and viewing within the Bollywood film. While the song and dance, the Bollywood grammar for articulating the unsayable, conventionally performs the unsayable through the mixing of the aural with the visual and kinesthetic, they are reinscribed to underline the limits of the sayable in the colonial language in the crossover film. Consciously aware of the failure of the colonial language to embody the experience of the Other, the filmmaker resorts to the aural and the visual to reproduce experiences that lie at the edge of language. It is in the crossover film that song and dance becomes the prime instrument for producing embodied knowledge that Marks (2000) speaks of through its manipulation of sound and image to produce affect. Rather than using dialogue, both Chadha and Nair resort to the song and dance idiom of Bollywood cinema to articulate the unknowable and to provide interiority to characters that dwell ill at ease in English. It is the Punjabi song – the women's songs, the Bhangra numbers and remixes, and original scores expressing a whole range of emotions from conviviality to nostalgia – through which Punjabi difference is articulated and Punjabi is recovered from 'the half-life, half-light of foreign tongues' (Bhabha, 1994: 199). The polysemy of the songs and dances emerges from the isolation of the verbal from the aural. The meanings hidden in the Punjabi lyrics are reiterated by the mood, the melody and the visual images. Both the wedding songs and dance music, largely consisting of nonsense formulae, invite repetition by both insiders and outsiders while effectively shutting out outsiders from ritual re-enactments of collective Punjabi memory through the performance of traditional songs. Even Sukhwinder Singh's original score in *aj mera jee karda ai* with its formulaic simplicity displays Punjabi music's capacity to produce a pensive mood as effectively as joy. While both films exploit their targeted audience's familiarity with Bhangra for encoding conviviality, their inclusion of songs of separation extends Punjabi's expressive range by disengaging it from its stereotyped associations with *balle balle* exuberance. Malkit Singh's warning in the *jind mahi* number in *Bend it Like Beckham* about never forgetting one's roots or language strongly resonates with those who can decode the song's lyrics. But Chadha uses the aural sense to produce affect in those who cannot.[11] The polysemy of the song and dance that enables the inscription of universal emotions on culturally specific kinemes contributes to the universality that Western reviewers have perceived in the films. It must be noted that the Indian *rasa* theory underpinning Indian music, dance and other arts is essentially a theory of affect with the object of art or that of music being experiential rather than representational. Not only the sound score, connoting meanings beyond the sayable, but also the song and dance offer the filmmaker an affective medium that more than covers the gap between the sayable and seeable and that between languages.

Marks' (2000) point about the different sensoriums the audience bring to the intercultural film that interact with those embodied in the film is particularly true of the songs and dances. Yet the songs and dances are inscribed with an intertextuality and interreferencing through which meanings are multicoded for Punjabi and Indian listeners predicated on their familiarity with the original scores. For example, the first song in *Monsoon Wedding*, a

Mohammad Rafi number from the 1970s film *Loafer*, is heard playing on a transistor as P.K. Dubey and his assistants prepare the marquee for the wedding celebrations and Dubey and the housekeeper Alice set their eyes on each other. If the song lyrics *'aaj mausam bada baiman hai/aane wala koi tufan hai'* ('The weather is wicked today/It is the beginning of a storm') speak to the vocabulary of the 1970s Hindi film romance, the wistful and longing tone, reverberating with Nair's nostalgic look at the Delhi of the 1970s, signposts the trope of romance. The familiarity of the nonsense verses of the women's song *madhorama* by the renowned folk performer Madan Bala Sidhu or the parting lament invests them with a strong interactivity through which Punjabi memories may be collectively performed. Even the Punjabi pop numbers by Malkit Singh (*jind mahi* in *Bend it Like Beckham* and *gud nal ishq mitha* in *Monsoon Wedding*) and Hans Raj Hans (*aaja nach lai* in *Monsoon Wedding*), while inviting global recognition through their generic classification as *bhangra*, are reinscribed with new meanings through their reincorporation in ritual settings. If Chadha glides between different genres of Punjabi and English songs in *Bend it Like Beckham*, Nair explores the affective range of Bollywood song, ghazal, sufiana, hindustani classical, Punjabi bhangra and *virahgit* (a song of separation) to evolve an aural language to embody experience that lies at the edge of the verbal. The two filmmakers complement the aural and visual kinesics of song and dance with a manipulation of the entire sensorium to underline the limits of the sayable.

Haptic Visuality Conveying *Punjabiyat*

Punjabi dialogue and lyrics express the filmmakers' frustration with the sayable in English as well as a desire to lock meaning as difference through 'the visual and aural overload of Indian culture to create a new aesthetic style' that Sharpe (2005: 59) has observed in *Monsoon Wedding*. This new visual and aesthetic style has been attributed to the hand-held cameras of *Monsoon Wedding* and *Bend it Like Beckham* and their appropriateness in producing certain affects.[12] Given Marks' view of the 'sensorium as the only place where cultural memories are preserved' (Marks, 2000: 195), the choice of the hand-held camera is determined by the filmmakers' skepticism about the ability of standard cinematic apparatus to represent their audio-visual as well as sensory knowledges. The films' lingering on the images of things falls into place in view of things embodying cultural memory that remains at the edge of consciousness.

Reviews of *Monsoon Wedding* invariably begin by paying homage to 'its captivating visual style and loose, off-the-cuff verve' (Hornaday, 2002) and end with a gushing tribute to the riot of color, movement and sound produced through 'a traditional wedding arch of marigolds, and richly colored, elegant silk fabrics juxtaposed to the grimy, chaotic and polluted streets of Delhi, India' (Wilkins, 2010). Nair (cited in Alam, 2008) believes that 'cinematic language does not need verbal language, sometimes' – the reason why she has very few dialogues in her films – and describes her films as 'more visual than verbal'. Marks (2000: 195) attributes this shift in the intercultural film to the loss of language and asserts that 'when language cannot record memories, we often look to images'. While the visual is the dominant mode, the reviews create a sense of the multisensory experience that the film produces through a combination of visual, auditory, tactile and kinesthetic images that Marks (2000) has described as haptic visuality. However, contradicting her (2000) view that the intercultural filmmaker turns to non-visual sensory images to interrogate the imperialism of the visual, Nair harnesses a multisensory language to underline the limits of the visual in producing the sensuous geographies of other places.

In privileging the visual, Nair could be accused of reproducing neo-orientalist constructions of the South, as Marks (2000) alleges in her reading of *Kama Sutra,* particularly in capturing the sumptuous visual feast that a Punjabi wedding, with its rich array of silks, brocades and jewelry, presents. Nair's dexterous play on color to encode meanings in a spectroscopic idiom reiterates the imperialist image only to expose its limited focus. Verma's rage at the wedding planner P.K. Dubey's choice of funereal white for the wedding *shamiana* (marquee) educates the viewer in the traditional palette of *lal, peela, hara* (red, yellow, green) that encodes auspicious meanings in traditional Hindu weddings. Nair's reproduction of the *haldi* (turmeric) yellow naturalized in wedding invitations in the title sequence spills over to the harvest of marigolds in the canopy and garlands. Yellow is balanced with rich shades of red – crimson, maroon and rust in the saris and other ethnic outfits worn by female characters and set off with the ceremonial pink of the turbans sported by males. Like Eskimos who can differentiate between different shades of white in snow, Nair's Hindu *dristi* (gaze), programmed to distinguish between the rich bridal red sari, the muted maroon worn by the bride's mother, and the vibrant burgundy, crimson and vermilion hues sported by her cousins reinscribes the orientalist gaze with intimate meanings. Through her choice of ceremonial reds, yellows and pinks, jasmines and marigolds, Nair creates a semiotics of color to reproduce visual images of the Punjabi Delhi of the 1960s and 1970s. The images in her 'ode to Delhi', as she calls *Monsoon Wedding,* are split between *actual images* and *virtual images* and are supplemented by *recollection images* – that is, the memory of the shooting of the film – to produce a complex of all sense impressions that Delhi conveyed to Nair. Her affectionate recovery of her remembered Delhi must begin by engaging with the dominant discourses of the imperial photograph and the tourist brochure through which the capital is conventionally represented. While Atkinson (2002) has described *Monsoon Wedding* as 'an air-conditioned bus tour of Punjabi ritual', it must be pointed out that Nair's memory guides the viewer neither into Lutyens' planned imperial Delhi nor into the Lonely Planet's colorful chaos. Instead, it lovingly leads them through the forgotten by-lanes of refugee Punjabi Delhi in Karol Bagh that lead spatially and chronologically to the palatial farmhouse in post-liberalization Delhi. Despite the unmistakable influence of the photographer Raghu Rai, whose work Nair admires, in the long framing shots of the city, Nair stops to gaze at the remembered sights of Punjabi Delhi.

Nair glides from the foreignness of Punjabi words to a specifically Punjabi visual semiotics in articulating the violent knowledge of altered relations through the family elder Tej Puri's desecration of Punjabi kinship codes that cannot be expressed in modern psychoanalytic jargon. Reaffirming Marks' (2000) point about the *sensible* as complementing the sayable and seeable in intercultural cinema, Nair uses a particularly evocative visual image of ritual pink turbans, exclusively worn by male family members at Punjabi weddings, to encode an unpardonable transgression of filial relations. As Lalit Verma enters the Puja room to seek his deceased elder brother's blessings, a grainy close-up of a large palm against a glass window is followed by that of the pedophile relative's face. Like the silk sari in *Seeing is Believing* that Marks (2000) cites as an example of haptic visuality that produces a tactile image, Nair uses the outline of the large palm against the window to produce an eerily tactile experience of Puri's molestation of the young Ria. The close-up of Puri's turbaned head and the ritual removal of the ceremonial turban as Verma finally musters the courage to confront the patriarch but pleads, still addressing him as *bhaisaab* (brother), that he leave the wedding, signifies the rupture of a complex Punjabi kinship structure through 'the poisonous knowledge' of altered relations after partition.

The echoes of Nair's visual aesthetic in *Monsoon Wedding* found in Chadha's *Bend it Like Beckham*, particularly in the wedding sequences, produce a specifically Punjabi visual semiotics. Red continues to be the dominant color in *Bend it Like Beckham's* Sikh wedding in England with a similar distribution of shades of red worn by the bride, her sister and other family members. However, while framing the wedding scenes with shots of the park, streets and football field in a British neighborhood as well as the juxtaposition of Punjabi/Asian figures, Chadha engages with visual regimes in which a racialized Asianness is also made to signify Otherness by a new visual grammar in which brown, despite its shocking contrast with white, is made to inhabit the British space.

Fetish Objects: Embodying Cultural Memories

The objects that the celebrated hand-held camera of the two films gropes are not only the rich silks that catch Western reviewers' attention but other remembered objects in private and public spaces that embody cultural memories. Opaque recollection images of *aloo gobhi* in a tilted pan, of *salwar kameezes* hanging on the washing line in Jesse's courtyard, double-decker buses on London's streets and carts, autorickshaws and scooters on those of Delhi are recollection objects and transnational objects used as part of the *mis en scène* that connects them to memory to translate into a kind of affect. The filmmakers speak to the fetishization of food in Punjabi cultural practices and find values in them unrecognized in the colonial and postcolonial context to make objects encode meaning both metaphorically and materially. Close-up shots of *aloo-gobhi* in a frying pan, of *jalebis* in a *kadai* in Southall, or the marriage hall in Delhi, and *samosas* being served to the wedding guests are models of fetish objects 'that can encode knowledges that become buried in the process of temporal or geographic displacement but are volatile when activated by memory' (Marks, 2000: 87). Considering the displaced histories of the first-generation migrant Nair and 'the twice migrant Chadha', their encoding of the cultural geographies of the lost Punjabi homeland in fetish objects recovers transnational objects from the global economy of the circulation of capital and signs and re-endows even the humblest of objects with history. Migrant Sikh Punjabis' loss of homeland, and partitioned Punjabi Hindus' loss of homeland and language, makes their memories constitute home in recollection objects of which humble objects like *roti* or *jalebis* often remain the last archive. Chadha (quoted in Fisher, 2003) when asked about why food figures so large in all her films, stated, 'I think because food is a really great codifier of culture. It is a, it's a great way of expressing cultural things, you know, what you eat tells who you are.' In a sense, both the films are excavations of memories erased in public histories that survive in the domestic archive of food, music, dance, attire, rituals and everyday practices.

'Fossil' and 'fetish' objects of Punjab for the twice-displaced filmmakers, embedded in *recollection images* of Delhi and London, are formed in interaction with other cultural objects. Punjabi fetish objects compete with recollection objects of London's parks, streets and underground or with the Hindi/ Urdu or Hinglish mishmash of Old and New Delhi, respectively. While redeeming fetishized objects by finding values in them that are unrecognized or denigrated in the colonial or postcolonial context, the filmmakers also play with their traditional significations to interrogate essentialized narratives of identity or culture. Nair's reinscription of yellow in *Monsoon Wedding* through the displacement of images of the mustard fields that have now become mandatory in Bollywood films and Punjabi music videos with those of cut marigold flowers interweaves the sensuous geographies of the remembered Punjabi village that partition survivors carried with them with those of the rehabilitated capital city. But she also identifies the partitioned Punjabi memory as Hindu rather than Sikh. In Chadha's film, the image of the Sikh guru in her Hounslow home and the *salwar kameez*, competing with iconic images of Britain such as football and Beckham, on the other hand, carry the trace of the century-old undocumented history of Sikh migration. Like Nair, Chadha also activates new meanings of fossil objects by encoding both 'the discursive shifts and the material conditions of displacement' (Marks, 2000: 79). She plays with the meanings of *sikhi* (Sikh identity) in the tragic-comic image of Jesse kneeling before the image of the Sikh guru to pray for success in football even as her family thanks Babaji or Guru Nanak for her excellent academic performance.

The synthasesia of sound, touch, color, smell and sight that Marks' (2000) haptic visuality connotes is epitomized in the shots of the rain in which the film transcends its optical visuality by making us not only see but hear, feel, smell and touch the rain. The shots of Delhi bathed in torrents of rain that contributed to the splashy, noisy feel of the film were taken in real rain as well as 'insurance paid rain', as Nair calls it (2002). Nair plays on the familiar Bollywood rain trope to inter-reference it with mystery, romance and benediction as in Bollywood films, but rematerializes the fetishized rain scene of Bollywood *masala* films to inscribe the desire and longing for the forgotten home. In the rain sequence, Nair, recognizing the limits of the visual medium in reproducing the sensuous memory of rain in Delhi, has her camera make us hear the rain on Delhi's streets, feel raindrops fall on the drenched bodies of the lovers Alice and Dubey, walk through the squelch with the bride and her sisters and even smell it on the parched earth. The cathartic effect of the Punjabi song by Sukhwinder Singh, noted by many of the film's reviewers, a prayer to the Lord to bring rain, sounds like a benediction when mixed with the women's song that is heard playing in the background.

Conclusion

Speaking the language of the Other, the Punjabi self always sounds like a caricature, particularly when its command of the Other's language is barely functional. However, the two diasporic filmmakers, while functioning within the comic genre that presents them a strong temptation to slip into British popular cultural or Bollywoodized caricatures of Punjabis and Sikhs, accomplish the astounding task of capturing interiority in languages rooted in orientalist or national histories of representation.[13] They do so by liberally peppering Standard English with Indian English, Hindi and pure Punjabi. But, in addition to the playful mixing of Indian English, immortalized in the 24-hour Indian music channel Channel V's signature line 'we are like that only', they also offer 'perverse pleasures of discovering a hidden code there at the edge of the text' (Stoneman, 2002). This code is produced through the familiar Bollywood song and dance grammar and a complex visual, aural and tactile vocabulary that enables them to articulate the unsayable, unseeable and the *unknowable*. However, in order to discover these hidden codes deployed by the filmmakers, the spectator must be equipped with a double, or multiple, vision.

Notes

(1) Although the term Bollywood has a specific historical and generic connotation, it is now loosely used to refer to any film with an Indian connection and includes, in addition to Hindi popular cinema, Indian commercial cinema as well as films made by filmmakers of Indian origin. Madhava Prasad (2003) in 'This Thing Called Bollywood' refers to 'the naturalisation of "Bollywood" as the designation for what was previously known as Hindi cinema, Bombay cinema, Indian popular cinema, etc'. Ashish Rajadhyaksha (2003) prefers a more diachronic reading and uses Bollywood to refer not only to films but an entire Bollywood-centered culture industry targeted at a Non-Resident Indian (NRI) viewer since the mid-1990s.

(2) This corroborates Chopra's point about 'a distinct market segmentation' dictated by 'Bollywood economics' that splits the Bollywood audience (1997).

(3) 'Years of association and usage of the farmlands of Punjab and the stereotype opulent Punjabi farmer may have been instrumental in this region, symbolising the archetypical rural India. Just as much as, unfortunately, Dharavi and poverty have come to symbolise urban India', states Rafeeq Gangjee, Vice President, Marketing and Communications Yash Raj Films. While filmmaker Imtiaz Ali attributes the Hindi film's Punjabi overdose to a large part of the film industry hailing from Punjab, trade analyst Vinod Mirani cites Punjabi's closeness to Hindi as the primary reason for the elision of Hindi and Punjabi particularly in the Punjabi-Hindi film (as quoted in Viswanathan, 2009).

(4) The positioning of the Bollywood subject as ethnolinguistic rather than national in the NRI film is carried over in films intended for home consumption, which also borrow *Punjabiyat* to signify family values. The 'Hindu Family Values' film, of which *Dilwale Dulhania Le Jayenge* (DDLJ) (1995) is the prime example, begins the synecdochic mapping of Punjabi bodies and sites onto a national imaginary. As a result, the 'feel good' aspect of 'our culture' that Ashish Rajadhyaksha views as being exported (2003) comes to be suspiciously close to the *apna* or 'our' culture that Gurinder Chadha (in Hornaday, 1994) speaks of. The *apna* that Gurinder's films sketch is specifically Punjabi Sikh but it could be one entered through any other

Indian locality. The unabashed celebration of *Punjabiyat* as family values since the 1990s unleashed the repressed *Punjabiyat* of Hindi cinema, traces of which might have been visible earlier. After DDLJ, *Punjabiyat* returned home in *Dillagi* (1999), *Dhai Akshar Prem ke* (2000), *Mujhse Dosti Karoge* (2002), and became firmly entrenched by the time *Kabhi Khushi Kabhie Gham* (K3G) (2001) was released.

(5) Bollywood's 'Punjabification' continues in films like *Veera Zaara* (2004), *Rang De Basanti* (2006), *Apne* (2007), *Jab We Met* (2007), *Rab Ne Bana di Jodi* (2008) and *Dev. D* (2009).

(6) Wilmington (2002) says, 'And since much of the dialogue is in English (as it would be in India), with occasional dashes of Punjabi and Hindi, "Monsoon Wedding" is highly accessible to American audiences – who will be bewildered, if at all, only by its unusual richness and density of character and plot.'

(7) 'Critical regionalism' is a concept coined by Kenneth Frampton (1983) to refer to postmodern architecture's incorporation of regional vernacular elements in modernist structures to recover a sense of place.

(8) 'We are all trying to make crossover films; (instead) we should just try to make good films. What is *Crouching Tiger* ... it is a folktale; *Monsoon Wedding* or *Bend it Like Beckham* are good Punjabi stories', points out Yash Chopra, promoter of Yash Raj Films (in Kohli-Khandekar, 2009).

(9) The film was directed by Oscar-nominated filmmaker Mira Nair (*Salaam Bombay!* (2008), *Mississippi Masala* (1997), *My Own Country* (1998), *Kama Sutra* (1996)) and written by first-time screenwriter Sabrina Dhawan, who graduated from Columbia University's graduate film program. It was produced by Caroline Baron, who co-produced *Kama Sutra* as well as Joel Schumacher's *Flawless* and Nicholas Hytner's *Center Stage*. The cinematographer was the internationally acclaimed Declan Quinn (*Leaving Las Vegas*, *Kama Sutra*, *Vanya On 42nd Street* and *One True Thing*). Mychael Danna, the award-winning composer of Atom Egoyan's films, Nair's *Kama Sutra* and Ang Lee's *The Ice Storm*, scored the film, collaborating on an original song with one of India's leading pop musicians, Sukhwinder Singh.

(10) In *Namastey London* (2007), London born Katrina Kaif points out that her father, played by Rishi Kapoor, slips into Punjabi when he is enraged, to which Kapoor's character corrects her by saying that he does so whenever he gets *jazbati* or emotional.

(11) As Malkit Singh put it, '[i]n "Bend it Like Beckham", they took a traditional meaningful Punjabi song' (www.cityonlinemag.co.uk/arts/articles/malkitsingh.html). Nagra (in Morales 2003) says, '[i]t's a soundtrack to Jess' journey. I think it's really powerful. I love the Indian music that Gurinder has put in. There's a scene where I'm scrubbing my kicks and I'm crying, there that's Indian song. It's a Punjabi song, which means "Never forget your roots" and "Never forget who you are". It's such a powerful song.'

(12) According to Donawan (2009), 'Nair and Quinn use a mostly handheld camera in the way that was the intended effect, to create a wonderful intimacy within the chaos.' According to Cater (2003) 'Danna elevates Nair's naturalistic hand-held camera narrative to a transcendent spiritual plane. The mystical "Fuse Box" almost single-handedly accomplishes the task of transforming the clownish wedding planner P.K. Dubey from a hilarious marigold-eating Indian version of Martin Short's *Father of the Bride* character to a thoroughly credible and even charming romantic lead.'

(13) According to Nair (in Dupont, 2001), '[We] Punjabis are the butt of many jokes, for we are an aggressive, loud people, peasant people, known for our lusty appetite for

life. The Punjabis are to India what the Italians are to Europe. The film is an homage to major vulgarity.' Iyer (2009) points out that in *Monsoon Wedding* Nair 'shows us a bewildered and beholden older man [Lalit Verma] whom we take to be a comic character and lets him turn the film around with an act of courage that can bring tears to the eyes'.

References

Alam, P. (2008) Mira Nair interview. *India-EU Film Initiative*, accessed 31 May 2010. http://www.iefilmi.eu/204.html

Atkinson, M. (2002) Prosaic nations. *The Village Voice: Movies*, accessed 31 May 2010. http://www.villagevoice.com/2002-02-19/film/prosaic-nations/1

Bellman, E. (2010) India journal: In praise of Bollywood's global appeal. *The Wall Street Journal*, accessed 1 July 2010. http://blogs.wsj.com/indiarealtime/2010/06/07/india-journal-in-praise-of-bollywoods-global-appeal/

Bhabha, H. (1994) *The Location of Culture*. London: Routledge.

Cater, E. (2003) All music guide, 1 January, accessed 31 May 2010. http://www.answers.com/topic/monsoon-wedding

Chopra, A. (1997) Bye-bye Bharat. *India Today*, 1 December, accessed 11 September 2009. http://www. india-today.com/itoday/01121997/cinema.html

Desai, J. and Dudrah, R. (2008) The essential Bollywood. In J. Desai and R. Dudrah (eds) *The Bollywood Reader* (pp. 1–17). Maidenhead: Open University Press.

Donawan, E. (2009) Monsoon Wedding (Criterion). *GreenCine's Official DVD Review Blog*, accessed 3 May 2010. http://guru.greencine.com/archives/2009/10/monsoon_wedding_1.html

Dupont, J. (2001) Mira Nair peels back layers of Punjabi society. *International Herald Tribune*, 21 September, accessed 31 May 2010. http://mirabaifilms.com/wordpress/?page_id = 32

Film Terms Glossary. Accessed 8 January 2011. http://www.filmsite.org/filmterms7.html

Fischer, P. (2003) Gurinder Chadha – Success at Last as *Beckham* Finally Hits US. March 13. Accessed on 30 May 2010. http://www.filmmonthly.com/Profiles/Articles/GChadha/GChadha.html

Frampton, K. (1983) Towards a critical regionalism: Six points for an architecture of resistance. In H. Foster (ed.) *The Anti-Aesthetic: Essays on Postmodern Culture* (pp. 16–30). Port Townsend: Bay Press

Gahlot, D. (2005) In 'global fit'. *Business World*, accessed 11 September 2009. http://www.businessworld.in/index.php/Global-Fit.html

Hornaday, A. (1994) 'Bhaji on the Beach', feminism meets the diaspora. *The New York Times*, 22 May

Hornaday, A. (2002) 'Monsoon Wedding': From India a flood of wonderments. *The Washington Post*, 8 March, accessed 31 May 2010. http://www.indianembassy.org/.../washingtonpost_com%20'Monsoon%20Wedding'%20From%20India

Iyer, P. (2009) Monsoon Wedding: A marigold tapestry. *The Criterion Collection*, 19 October, accessed 31 May 2010. http://www.criterion.com/current/posts/1266-monsoon-wedding-a-marigold-tapestry.

Kohli-Khandekar V. (2005) Global fit. *Business World*, accessed 11 September 2009. http://www. businessworld.in/index.php/Global-Fit.html.

Malkit Singh. Interview, accessed 31 January 2006. http://www.cityonlinemag.co.uk/arts/articles/malkitsingh.html.

Marks, L.U. (2000) *The Skin of the Film: Intercultural Cinema, Embodiment, and the Senses.* Durham: Duke University Press.

Morales, W. (2003) Bend it Like Beckham: An interview with Parminder Nagra. *BlackFilm.com*, accessed 31 May 2010. http://www.blackfilm.com/20030509/index.shtml?

Nair, M. (2002) Interview, May 2002, accessed 8 January 2011. http://www.countingdown.com/features?feature_id = 716479.

Parciack, R. (2008) Approaching the uncodable: Hindi song and dance sequences in Israeli state promotional commercials. In S. Gopal and S. Moorti (eds) *Global Bollywood: Travels of Hindi Song and Dance* (pp. 221–240). Minneapolis: University of Minnesota Press.

Prasad, M.M. (2003) This thing called Bollywood. *Seminar 525*, May, accessed 31 May 2010. http://www.india-seminar.com/2003/525/525%.

Rajadhyaksha, A. (2003) The Bollywoodization of Indian cinema: Cultural nationalism in a global arena. *Inter-Asia Cultural Studies* 4 (1), 25–39.

Sharma, S. (2006) Teaching diversity – Im/possible pedagogy. *Policy Futures in Education* 4 (2), 203–216.

Sharpe, J. (2005) Gender, nation, and globalization in 'Monsoon Wedding' and 'Dilwale Dulhania Le Jayenge'. *Meridians: Feminism, Race, Transnationalism* 6 (1), 58–81.

Stoneman, R. (2002) Between Monsoon Wedding and Behind Enemy Lines. *Kinema: A Journal for Film and Audiovisual Media* (18), 23–28, accessed 31 May 2010. http://www.kinema.uwaterloo.ca/article.php?id = 140&feature.

Taylor, C. (2002) Monsoon Wedding. *Salon*, accessed 11 September 2009. http://www.salon.com/entertainment /movies/review/2002/02/.../monsoon.

Viswanathan, J. (2009) When will Bollywood's Punjabi obsession end? *Sunday Mid-Day*, accessed 11 September 2009. http://www.mid-day.com/.../020809-Bollywood-Punjabi-culture-Rab-Ne-Bana-Di-Jodi-Dev-D-Singh-is-Kinng-Jab-We-Met-Play.htm.

Wilkins. F. (2010) Movie review, 'Monsoon Wedding'. *Reel Reviews*, accessed 31 May 2010. http://www.franksreelreviews.com/reviews/monsoonwedding.htm.

Wilmington, M. (2002) Movie review, 'Monsoon Wedding'. *Metromix Chicago*, accessed 31 May 2010. http://chicago.metromix.com/movies/review/movie-review-monsoon-wedding/158420/content.

10 Hybridizing Medialect and Entertaining TV: Changing Korean Reality

Jamie Shinhee Lee

This chapter examines hybridized *medialect* (Hjarvard, 2004) on Korean TV. As the pressure to be proficient in English, reinforced by the Korean globalization drive called *segyehwa* (Lee, 2011), is mounting, the increasing presence of English expressions is observed in the entertainment media. Linguistic hybridization is a manifestation of both global consciousness and local sensibility. It concurrently manifests linguistic creativity and linguistic anxiety, both serving and challenging performers and viewers alike. Korean 'entertainers' use linguistic hybridization in their performance, euphemizing and mitigating potentially offensive and vulgar discourses, representing fresh concepts that recently emerged, repackaging old concepts in a new light, and marking both self and others' identities. Linguistic hybridization is often used in creating a comic relief and eliciting laughter from panelists and studio audiences. TV functions as a cultural medium reflecting and reproducing hybridized linguistic practices, both real and imagined, and Korean celebrities utilize hybridized medialect to fulfill their roles as entertainers.

Changing Linguistic Reality on Korean TV

Korean TV viewers went wild when the Korean soccer team defeated the Japanese team two to zero at Saitama Stadium, Japan, on 25 May 2010. *Netizens* praised *Chaminator's* aggressive play, which was undoubtedly instrumental in Korea's victory. Enthusiastic viewer support is not limited to sports events aired on TV. Korean teenage girls attending a rock concert as a live audience in a TV studio scream and cry when *cimsungdols* sing, dance and tear their shirts on stage revealing their *chocolatepokkun*. Korean talk show hosts tease *motaysolo* guests on the panel while female panelists make goo goo eyes at *vitengs*. These scenes were viewed on different channels but on the same day.

Netizen (internet + citizen) refers to a computer user frequently surfing the internet. *Chaminator* (Cha 'Korean last name' + terminator) is an affectionate nickname for a famous Korean soccer player named Cha Du Ri for his powerful, destructive offense, like that of the main character in the movie *Terminator*. *Cimsungdol* (cimsung 'animal' + idol) is a new breed of young media personalities widely known as *idols*. The term *idol* was once used to refer to young and cute female bubblegum pop singers in Korea. Now its gender exclusive usage is not in fashion anymore, although the age restriction of the term is still valid, referring mostly to teen or 20-something singers. What is equally noteworthy in its current usage is the addition of the Korean word *cimsung* to highlight masculine sexual energy, not represented in past idols, but often viewed as a desired quality these days. This new hybridized term is reserved only for male idols exuding sex appeal. These *cimsungdols* gladly show their six-pack abs, which are often dubbed *chocolatepokkun* (chocolate + pokkun 'abdominal muscles') based on their physical resemblance to the well-defined lines of a chocolate bar. *Motaysolo* (motay 'in the womb' + solo) indicates an individual with absolutely no relationship or dating experience. It is worth mentioning that the English word *solo* in contemporary Korea refers to a single man or woman. *Motaysolo* is not a flattering title because it implies that the person is physically so unattractive that he or she has never been romantically involved with anyone. In fact, a comedienne named Oh Na Mi is often called *motaysolo* because of her homely appearance. In contrast, *viteng* (visual + tengeli 'mass') literally means a visually exceptional object, and only exceptionally attractive people are 'honored' with this title.

These examples are all representative types of linguistic hybridization available on TV in contemporary Korea. The most predominant pattern seems to be the clipping and blending of English and Korean words. Some of these hybridized lexical items offer new ideas and concepts. *Chimsungdol* is a good example of this type; it is a new concept that was not articulated before but the new word is now in good use. Others, on the other hand, touch on old concepts but are repackaged; these ideas existed before and required a somewhat lengthy description or explanation, but now can be expressed in just one word. *Viteng* is a good example of this type of hybridization – a new word for a concept that is not necessarily new. I argue that linguistic hybridization, among other things, maximizes what I would call linguistic economy, allowing speakers to use one word to convey the same meaning, which would normally require multiple words, phrases or sometimes sentences.

The text above and its accompanying explanation are a glimpse of the changing linguistic reality on Korean TV where these linguistic hybridities have recently become quite common.

The verbal creativity of many Korean *yenyeyins* ('entertainer') is showcased through linguistic hybridization (Lee, 2007a, 2007c). When bilingual creativity is discussed in relation to English, mostly literary texts and written communication are used as data. Bilingual creativity in everyday language use in spoken communication is not generally discussed. Furthermore, the idea of 'creativity' is not always clearly defined and often perfunctorily equated with any formal innovation in language mixing. However, Jones (2010) stresses the need to produce more function-based and discourse-oriented analysis of linguistic hybridity. Citing Boden's (1990) 'the new and the valuable', Sternberg's (1990) 'the novel and the appropriate' and Pope's (2005) 'the original and the fitting', Jones (2010: 471) emphasizes the 'pragmatic value' of linguistic creativity. He further elaborates:

> Instead, what may be 'creative' may have more to do with the strategic way language is *used*, and what may be 'created' may not be an inventive linguistic product, but rather a new way of dealing with a situation or a new set of social relationships. (Jones, 2010: 472)

The TV programs analyzed in the present study show that Korean entertainers using linguistic hybridization have functional competence in Korean as well as English. They recognize the synergetic, entertaining potential of fusing the two codes to create something both Korean and English at the same time but neither strictly Korean nor English. This type of hybridizing practice is performed not only linguistically but also culturally; not just linguistic features but concepts, values, images and identities are also hybridized. Seemingly contrastive and incongruent ideas are blended to produce something new and yet pragmatically appropriate and contextually pertinent. Concepts normally perceived as divergent are not represented separately but converged as one. For instance, traditional and modern, old and new, Korean and Western, and local and global are all present in one semiotic package, which I have called 'global-local syncretism' elsewhere (Lee, 2010b). These polarities (in concepts, values, images, identities, and so on) are embedded, but neither can be distinctively extracted because they are merged. Each element in linguistic hybridization needs to be there. Without each other and, more importantly, without their linguistic and cultural synergy, the hybrid ceases to mean what it is intended to mean.

Linguistic hybridization is also pertinent to the concept of identity. Bakhtin's (1981) *simultaneity* and Woolard's (1999: 3) *bivalency* are particularly helpful for us to discuss bilingual and multilingual speakers' 'simultaneous claims to more than one social identity': not 'a mere wavering between two mutually exclusive possibilities' (Bakhtin, 1981: 281) but 'a real simultaneity of contrasting elements in tension' (Woolard, 1999: 4).

In an empirical study discussing linguistic hybridization and its implication for identity marking, Bhatt analyzes language mixing in Indian newspapers and argues that linguistic hybridity 'reflects a new way to negotiate and navigate between a global identity and local practices' and 'offers a new linguistic diacritic for class-based expressions of cultural identity' (2008: 196). Although his analysis focuses mainly on the print media in an 'Outer Circle' English country, it is also relevant to the broadcast media in an 'Expanding Circle' English country. In the present study, I discuss a hybridized spoken medialect effectively serving as a language of entertainment that allows Korean TV personalities to perform various pragmatic functions and project certain entertainer identities. This study supplements earlier research on the coexistence of English and Korean in song lyrics (Lee, 2004, 2007b, 2010b) and advertising (Lee, 2006, 2010a) by expanding the empirical scope to TV variety shows and dramas.

Globalization, English and TV Celebrities

Television is an affordable and popular entertainment medium readily available in modern societies, but it does more than entertain viewers. Newcomb and Hirsch (2000) treat television as 'a cultural forum' (p. 564) that enables us to see 'the collective cultural view of the social construction and negotiation of reality' (p. 563). The concept of entertainment is often perceived as a mere pleasure-seeking activity, but Mendelsohn and Spetnagel (1980: 13) view it as 'a sociological enterprise', occurring 'within a context of complex interactions that involve institutions, social norms, group behaviors, and traditions'.

In Korea this is true for the sociolinguistics of English, whose importance is emphasized in educational and professional domains and reinforced by the concept of *segyehwa* (Korea's drive towards globalization) through government policies and public discourses in the media, particularly on TV (Lee, 2011). Similarly, Kim (2000: 2) notes that *segyehwa* 'has been touted as no longer a matter of choice but one of necessity'. As English is recognized as a language essential for *segyehwa*, the push for speaking better English has led to its increasing use in several domains of Korean society, including the entertainment media. In this light, the media, particularly the entertainment media, shows creative adaptations of global English by those who react positively to and participate in this innovative process but also struggling attempts by those who are pressured to participate but do not feel comfortable with it.

On Korean TV English is now deployed not only as a topic but also as a means of communication for creating a comic effect. Lee (2007c: 299) notes that Korean comics, actors and TV show hosts use English to 'establish themselves as humorous and linguistically adaptable entertainers'. Humorous discourses *about* and *through* English in Korean dramas and variety shows require sustained comprehension efforts from audiences. As society puts more emphasis on English, Korean TV features more English in advertising (Lee, 2006, 2010a), song lyrics (Lee, 2004, 2007b, 2010b), dramas (Lee, 2007c), sketch comedies (Lee, 2007a), reality shows and talk shows (Lee, in press). As a result, Korean viewers have more opportunities to hear celebrities use English. Korean celebrities use English to project their linguistically versatile and humorous 'entertainer' identity (Lee, 2007c).

Discussion

Hybridized medialect on Korean TV tends to create humor. Some hybridities are more calculated than others and some are somewhat fortuitous. Lee (2007a) analyzes how humor is achieved through a deliberate hybridization of Korean and English in sketch comedies. Lee's notion of *code-approximation* refers to a process involving 'a search for the closest sounding meaningful unit matching a target item in another code' (2007a: 147). Citing Moody and Matsumoto's (2003) concept of *codeambiguation*, Lee explains why code-approximation better explains Korean-English humor:

> Its purpose is not to make two codes ambiguous at all, since it is unequivocally known to the addressee that two distinctive codes are involved and they provide different pieces of information for the entire utterance; one code is designated to provide phonological input, and the other code yields semantic output as a consequence. (2007a: 147)

One of the examples Lee (2007a) discusses is the expression *tonnwe*, which is the Korean phonological approximation of 'don't know'. This code-approximated expression means 'to put money down' or 'to deposit', which semantically has nothing to do with 'lacking knowledge' (Lee, 2007a: 149). Viewers can understand the humor intended in this expression only if they understand 'the discrepancy between the original meaning in English and the contrived and distorted meaning of the same sentence in Korean' (Lee, 2007a: 149).

This study shifts the focus from carefully calculated and scripted linguistic hybridization to a more spontaneous and adlib variety. The examples are from TV dramas, talk shows and reality shows that are ranked high in ratings and popularity on the internet and in the local newspapers. These shows have been viewed by the researcher for the past 12 months on a regular basis, generally once a week. A detailed observation log regarding English use or comments on English use has been kept, revealing the range in the predominant patterns and types of hybridization. Linguistic hybridization occurs almost exclusively in the form of English mixing and normally blending and clipping are involved. The reasons why linguistic hybridities are utilized do not present a unified profile, but predominant functions are euphemizing, representing new concepts, repackaging old concepts, enhancing expressivity while economizing linguistic efforts and marking identity.

Euphemizing

Potentially offensive discourses or vulgar expressions are euphemized through hybridization. Excerpt (1) shows an interesting discourse about a hybrid lexical item featured on the show *Nolewa* ('Come and Visit'). A comedienne named Kim Hyo Jin tells a story about a guest on her radio show.

(1)

Hyojin: Ceyka radio halttay guest-lo hamkkey nawa kaciko cheumey hanpen sokaylul haytalako kulayssteni 'celul sokayhacamyen hanmatilo hal swu issupnita. Cenun **double s. a. n. g.sulepsupnita**'.
'When he appeared on my radio show as a guest for the first time, I asked him to introduce himself to the listeners. Then he said "I can introduce myself with just one word. I am double s. a. n. g."'

Jaesuk: S. S. A. N. G. suleptaniyo? (Spelling it out one by one)
'S. S. A. N. G., what does that mean?'

Hyojin: Hanmatilo ssangsuleptanun kecyo.
'In short, it means that he is *ssangsulepta* (vulgar, indecent, or unsophisticated).'

Wonhee: Ettehkey pomyen sangtanghi caychiissnunkeko.
'In a sense, that is pretty clever.'

Jongwan: Kim Hyojin-ssi mannase cey aney issnun SSANG-ul cal palkyen hanunkes kathayo.
'I feel like I have found *ssang* within me thanks to Hyojin.'
(*Nolewa* 'Come and Visit' aired on 8 March 2010)

The Korean expression *sangsulepta* is phonologically fortified as *ssangsulepta* to emphasize uncouthness or vulgarity, but it is orthographically represented as an English acronym, SSANG, to mitigate the offensiveness of its Korean connotation and add modern sophistication. In so doing, being coarse in manners is not necessarily portrayed as a character flaw but as a refreshing quality showing unpretentious, defiant spirit. Jongwan's creative Korean and English hybrid was positively evaluated as a linguistically creative move by a show host. The word *ssang* in Korean is often used either alone as a swear word or as a prefix to the curse words such as *nom* (masculine curse word 'asshole') and *nyen* (feminine curse word 'bitch') to intensify vulgarity. However, the English orthographic representation of the same word and its corresponding phonological production of the word help Jongwan successfully transform the originally offensive word into a neutral lexical item. Also, connotation wise, the word undergoes amelioration, indicating a positive unassuming quality, not indecency. Jongwan's positive perspective on *ssang* is made clear in the last line as he frames it as an inner quality he did not know he had but that has been cultivated ever since he met Hyojin.

Another interesting example of hybridization as a euphemism is featured on a talk show called *Sungsungcangku* ('Win Win'). Ahn Naesang, an actor, discusses his family's financial struggle when he was a child. Having lived in a slum in Seoul after his father's once successful textile business had gone bankrupt, he explains how shocked he was to see for the first time the unsanitary living conditions, particularly poor water quality and sewage system. As a former spoiled rich kid who did not understand what it was like to be without money, this experience was quite traumatic.

(2a)

Naesang: Motun ssuleyki omwulul tapelinun keeyyo. Kulayse wancenhi pyenmwuli toysscyo. Pyenmwul.
'All the garbage and dirty things were dumped. That made the nearby stream completely contaminated by human feces. Feces water.'
(*Sungsungcangkwu* 'Win Win' aired on 31 May 2011)

When he tells a story, a caption appears on the TV screen, summarizing his comment. The caption reads as follows:

(2b)

Pyenwater yessten chengkyeychen phancachon.

The hybridized word *pyenwater* sums up the water condition in one word: pyen ('feces') + water. This is normally expressed by the word *ttongmwul*, which literally means 'shit water'. Thus, Ahn Naesang's use of *pyenmwul* is a euphemistic innovation. I suspect that he created this particular word to sound less offensive on national TV and for humor. His attempt was successful since both the panel and the studio audience were laughing hysterically. What is further noteworthy is that the show writer's edited summary on the TV screen was even more euphemistic than Ahn's. The Korean word *mwul* ('water'), which was originally used by Ahn, was replaced with the English word *water*. The combination of a formal register *pyen* ('feces') in place of its slang equivalent *ttong* ('shit') and *water* instead of *mwul* significantly reduces the vulgarity of the word.

Although it is not as drastic a euphemism as the previous two examples, excerpt (3) below also shows that hybridization adds a positive connotation. In a dramedy called *Tonganminye* ('The Youthful Looking Beauty'), the male lead character's family background is being discussed among his colleagues. They are impressed that Jinwook himself is so unassuming and down to earth when his family is very wealthy.

(3)

Manager Jang:	Ceyneycip buildingi myeskayntey. Caki Wangsilcokpal alci? 'His family owns several buildings. You have heard of the restaurant chain called *Wangsilcokpal* ('Royal Pig Knuckles'), haven't you?'
Female designer:	Yes.
Manager Jang:	Jinwooki cey nalum princeya. **Prince of cokpal** ('pig knuckles')! 'Although it doesn't look obvious, he is a prince. He is the prince of pig knuckles.'
Female designer:	Eme! (In an admiring tone) 'Wow!' (*Tonganminye* 'The Youthful Looking Beauty' aired on 30 May 2011)

While the colleagues are at a workshop, Jinwook's mother, without telling Jinwook, has delicious pig knuckles delivered as a late night snack. Pig knuckles are not an upscale sophisticated delicacy but a popular dish in Korea especially among middle and working-class families. A female designer in the company, who is materialistic and snobbish, expresses her contempt for pig knuckles, and then Manager Jang reveals that Jinwook's father is the president of the successful franchise *Wangsilcokpal* and a wealthy businessman and hence Jinwook deserves the honorable title 'prince' and needs to be treated as a royal family. His status as an heir to a successful business is linguistically defended in the form of hybridization. The word *cokpal* is a food name but is also often used to refer to unattractive female legs in a degrading manner. Thus, *cokpal* as a word, in general, does not possess any redeeming qualities. However, in the excerpt above, with the help of the English word *prince*, it demands respect.

Representing new concepts

It is not uncommon to use linguistic hybridization to express new ideas, concepts and images on Korean TV. The following text is from a popular variety talk show called *Happy Together*, which often features TV actors promoting their upcoming shows. In this particular episode, the main show host Jaysuk offers a flattering comment to a female cast member of the dramedy called *Romance Town*. Jaysuk's use of the hybridized term *baglnye* is not understood by two male panelists who are in their forties. At first, both males pretend to know the term, but soon admit that they do not know the exact meaning when questioned by Jaysuk.

(4)

Jaesuk: Min Hyorinssi mal kutaylo **baglnye**-eyyo!
'Miss Min Hyorin, you are truly a baglnye!'

Misun: Mwenci alcyo? **Baglnye** mwenci alayo? (Looking at Myungsu)
'You know it, don't you? Do you know what **baglnye** means?'

Myungsu: Alcyo!
'(Of course) I know!'

Misun: Mweeyyo? (Not convinced)
'What is it?'

Myungsu: Yey. (Hesitating)
'Yes.'

Jaesuk: Mwenteyyo? (Staring at Myungsu)
'What do you think it is?'

Myungsu: Moluntako kulayyo. (Laughing and looking embarrassed)
'I admit I don't know.'

Jaesuk: Son Byunghossi **baglnye** aseyyo? (Looking at Son Byungho)
'Mr. Son Byungho, do you know what baglnye means?'

Byungho: Kulenika babylul salanghanun . . .
'Well, loving babies . . .'

Jaesuk: Baby face-ey
'The one who has a baby face.'
Bongsun: Glamour mommay.
'But with a glamorous body.'
(*Happy Together* aired on 5 May 2011)

The hybridized term *baglnye* in the text above is composed of two clipped English lexical items, *baby* and *glamour* and the Korean feminine marking morpheme *-nye*, referring to a young, innocent looking woman with a sexy body. The word *glamour* in Korea is semantically deviant from the English counterpart; it indexes a voluptuous physique, which is perceived to be rare among Asian females. Thus *baglnye* captures one modern version of a beauty in Korea, one possessing both Asian innocence and Western sexiness. The old idea of an Asian beauty as a delicate flower with an innocent face in a petite physique is not admired as much as previously. What is interesting is the idea that nothing purely Asian or nothing strictly Western is desired in a woman; a balanced combination is considered praiseworthy. This balance between East and West is achieved linguistically through hybridization.

A hybridized term is used not only to describe a newly emerging group of females but also a new breed of males who project images different from the usual male TV characters. In excerpt (5), Misun interviews Minjun for his role in an upcoming drama. In comparing his character with another lead male character, who is dubbed *chatonam*, an abbreviation of **cha**kawun **to**siuy **nam**ca ('a cold-hearted city man'), Minjun suggests a new hybrid term to describe his own character in a similar abbreviated manner. However, unlike his friend's, Minjun's nickname consists of an English word and a clipped Korean word.

(5)
Misun: Pwucascip atul?
'(Do you play) a son of a rich family?'
Minjun: Ani, atul anieyyo. Mwe pwuca aniyessnuntey halapeci apenim tolakasiko nase.
'No, it's not a son. Well, my character is not originally from a rich family but after his grandfather and father passed away (he becomes rich).'
Misun: Ung.
'Uh uh.'
Minjun: Chatonamey (pointing to his co-star, Giuwoon) cenun **chicleng** (pointing to himself). 'Gyuwoon

	plays chatonam (a cold-hearted city boy) and I play chicleng.'
Misun & Bongsun:	**Chicleng**? (Asking at the same time) '(What do you mean) chicleng?'
Minjun:	Chic-han nungkwulengi. 'Chic smooth talker or player.'
Misun & Bongsun:	(Laughing) (*Happy Together* aired on 5 May 2011)

Minjun's coinage, *chicleng* (chic + leng), however, is not readily understood by the two show hosts. Feeling a strong urge to reveal the meaning of the word, Minjun explains that it is a combination of *chic* and *nungkwulengi* ('smooth talker'). The two show hosts are taken by Minjun's creativity and humor. The word *nungkwulengi* literally means a yellow-spotted serpent and figuratively refers to an insidious, sly person. However, in this context, combined with the English word *chic*, its original venomous image softens. The English word *chic* also suggests that he plays a fashion conscious metrosexual, no longer a rarity among young Korean heterosexual males.

Another newly innovated hybridization in excerpt (6) is from the same episode. Yuri, the lead female character of the same show, confesses to fasting after 6 o'clock in the evening because she fears that her face may appear puffy on camera if she eats dinner too late. Two female show hosts, Bongsun and Misun, comfort Yuri with humor, claiming that eating late night snacks is effective for reducing wrinkles because puffy faces will not show as many crow's feet.

(6)

Bongsun:	Swuceypi mekko cwumwusimyen swutox. 'If you go straight to bed after eating *swuceypi* (wheat gnocchi), then it's called ***swutox***.'
Misun:	Lamyen mekumyen ***latox***. 'If you eat *lamyen* (instant noodles) instead, then it becomes *latox*.' (*Happy Together* aired on 5 May 2011)

Bongsun and Misun lightheartedly state that the impact is analogous to receiving a Botox treatment. Botox, foreclipped to *tox*, is combined with popular Korean comfort food such as *swuceypi* ('wheat gnocchi') and *lamyen* ('instant noodles'), hindclipped to *swu* and *la* respectively. The subsequent blending results in the newly hybridized lexical items eliciting hysterical laughter from the panelists.

Repackaging old concepts

Some may argue that creating new lexical items for fresh concepts is not so novel. On the other hand, creating new hybridized terms to refer to already available concepts and ideas is intriguing. In a popular survival/travel reality show called *Ilpakiil* ('One Night Two Days'), Korean celebrities travel to a location, which is not revealed in advance, and need to figure out clues on the way, competing in mental and physical games to win food and lodging. Those who win can cook dinner using the ingredients they receive as a reward and stay in a decent motel room, whereas those who lose have no choice but to starve, camp outside without sleeping bags, and sometimes must jump into a cold river as a punishment. In a supporting actors' special, Sung Dongil gets hungry on the bus and eats one of the eggs his team won. Since cooking is not allowed on the bus, he eats a raw egg and then has a few more later in the show. Eating raw eggs is not unusual in Korea, especially for those who wish to improve their voice and throat condition before a music performance. Eating several raw eggs, however, is not frequently done. On a survival game show like this, eating that many raw eggs can be perceived as a skill that deserves some type of recognition. Because of his fast, superb egg-eating skills, Sung Dongil is named as follows:

(7)
Naltalkyaldrinking (naltalkyal 'a raw egg' + drink + king)
(*Ilpakiil* 'One Night and Two Days' aired on 12 June 2011)

This hybridized lexical item is a combination of the Korean word *naltalkyal* ('a raw egg') and the two English words, *drink* and *king*, indicating that he is the champion of eating raw eggs. Because raw eggs have a runny texture or consistency, they are more suitable for drinking than for eating, hence, *drinking*, not *eatking*.

Similarly, the show *Namcauy Cakyek* ('Men's Bucket List') features a group of Korean celebrities completing a task, often called a 'mission', each week. In an episode where the members of the show went camping in a remote area, Lee Kyungkyu complained about Jun Hyunmu's snore. In excerpt (8a), Lee Kyungkyu complains on the morning after, using humor. He views Jun's snore as exceptionally noisy and notes that one can achieve that level of 'mastery' only by practicing diligently while enrolled in an intensive snoring program.

(8a)
Lee Kyungkyu: Hakwenul taninkes kathay. Paywesse.
'He must have taken classes at a private institute.'

Lee Kyungkyu neither prefaces his complaints nor explains what his complaints are about since he does not directly mention Jun's snoring. Jun Hyunmu walks into a tent after washing his face and looks at Kyungkyu clueless when Kyungkyu makes the comment above. The caption on the TV screen sums up the situation as follows:

(8b)
Seyswulul machin **khokoliterrorist**.
'The snore terrorist with a freshly washed face.'
(*Namcauy Cakeyk* 'Men's Bucket List' aired on 19 June 2011)

The hybrid word *khokoliterrorist* is a combination of the Korean word for snore, *khokoli* and the English word *terrorist*. As the strong word *terrorist* indicates, Jun Hyunmu's snore was so aggressive and vicious that Lee Kyungkyu felt that he was under attack. The idea that snoring can be disruptive to others is not new, but by repackaging it in a newly hybridized word, the sense of disruption is intensified.

Another example of repackaging an old concept is contributed by a rocker named Park Jihun on the show *Star Pwu Pwu Show* ('Star Couples Show'). He reminisces about his struggling days as an artist and recalls having lived in a tiny basement apartment and survived on a can of vegetables with rice for a week because he had no income. He claims that he was not miserable at the time and explains why that was the case in the excerpt below.

(9)
Park Jihun: Kukel culkyeyo. Kukey mesilako calangul hayyo. Rocker-uy sangcing **hungrycengsin** (hungry + cengsin 'spirit')
'I enjoyed it (struggle/poverty). I thought that was charming. I used to brag about it. That (struggle/poverty) is the symbol of a rocker. The hungry spirit.'

Park Jihun states that when it comes to an artist, poverty is not something shameful; rather, he thinks that there is something beautiful about a struggling artist. He later argues that struggle and pain can help artists create beautiful music. The idea that a strong will and determination can overcome financial struggles is summed up in the hybrid word *hungrycengsin*, consisting of the English word *hungry* and the Korean word for spirit, *cengsin*.

Identity marking nicknames

Another function of linguistic hybridization has to do with identity marking. Nicknames are often hybridized. A recent popular drama called

Choykouy salang ('The Most Wonderful Love') featured a star couple struggling to keep their romance under the radar. The top movie star character Dokgo Jin and the former bubble gum pop singer character Ku Aejung argue in excerpt (10). Dokgo Jin urges Ku Aejung to discontinue her appearance on a particular show because he is afraid that she may unintentionally share details of his private life and consequently jeopardize his reputation and career. When Dokgo Jin offers unsolicited advice in a threatening manner, asking her to quit, Ku Aejung strongly protests. Their verbal sparring includes a few creative linguistic hybridizations.

(10)

Dokgo Jin: Pihokamulo isscimalko clear-hakey outhay
'Don't appear desperate and remain unpopular. Get out. Clear and simple.'
[...] (A few turns deleted)

Ku Aejung: Mwe? Clear-hakey outhalako?
'What? Completely out?'
[...]

Dokgo Jin: Michyess kuna ne!
'You are out of your mind!'

Ku Aejung: Anici yenge moshayse kkayessci cham. Mwe clear-hakey out cohahako issney.
Kuttan yenge hayssunika nika kkainkeya yala?
'Oh, that's right. You got fired because you spoke poor English. What is this nonsense with clear-hakey out? Because you spoke that kind of English, you got sacked. You know that?'

Dokgo Jin: Ne cikum mwelanun keya?
'What the heck are you talking about?'

Ku Aejung: You ***kingssakaci***! Um! (showing her thumb to indicate that he is the number one jerk in a scornful tone). Very much ***dirtyccang***!
'You kingssakaci (the king of jerks). Very much number one *dirtyccang* (epitome or king of dirtiness).'

Dokgo Jin: (Looking at her shocked and speechless)
(*Choikoui Sarang* 'The Most Wonderful Love' aired on 5 May 2011)

Dokgo Jin is an extremely successful actor with a huge ego and Ku Aejung is, on the other hand, a former celebrity 'on a D list'. Dokgo Jin arrogantly threatens her dying career by telling her to quit, as expressed in the hybridized expression 'clear-hakey out', suggesting that she should go cold turkey instead of desperately attempting to revive her pathetic non-existent career. Aejung, a fighter and survivor at heart, does not take his verbal abuse; she fights back by verbally retaliating against him. She reminds him of his broken movie deal and contends that it has something to do with his awful and pretentious English. She verbally attacks him by using hybridized insulting nicknames, that is, *kingssakaci* (king + ssakaci 'jerk') and *dirtyccang* (dirty + ccang 'number one, best'), meaning that he is the most manipulative man. Dokgo Jin uses hybridization to show off his sophistication, and Ku Aejung uses hybridization to mock his pseudo-sophistication. At least in the interaction above, hybridization enables Ku Aejung to be Dokgo Jin's equal, which is not normally the case outside of this conversation. The use of hybridized unflattering labels for her arrogant boyfriend empowers her and gives her the much-needed upper hand in the relationship.

Self-labeling or self-identity marking is also achieved through hybridization. In a special episode titled 'elkwulepsnun kaswu' ('faceless singers'), the show *Nolewa* ('Come and Visit'), invited singers to start their music careers without revealing their faces because they were not as attractive as many other singers active in the music industry. Even their album jacket covers were created without artists' images or with a partial photo so that fans and consumers would not know what they looked like. According to an interview given by Kim Bumsu, this was done deliberately and for commercial purposes because their 'visual' was not as strong as their vocal. The same artist recently revealed his face on a very popular show *Nanun Kaswuta* ('I am a Singer'), which is a survival game for professional singers. They perform a different song each week, which should not be one of their own hits, and TV viewers vote who will advance to the next round. Since this show focuses solely on the artist's voice, it provides a favorable platform for singers such as Kim Bumsu. In fact, according to the entries on the blog of the show, the viewers were pleasantly surprised to see that Kim Bumsu was not as unattractive as the media portrayed him. Kim Bumsu has gained some confidence since the show aired. He discusses what his experience has been like with the hosts of the show *Nolewa* below.

(11)

Kim Bumsu: **Visualkaswu**-lo ketupnancika twutalyeintey.
'It's been two months since I was reborn as a visual singer.'
(*Nolewa* 'Come and Visit' aired on 13 June 2011)

Kim Bumsu made an appearance with two other singers in the episode. When the show hosts reveal that this particular episode is titled 'faceless singers', Kim expresses his discomfort by stating that he cannot be grouped together with these two artists because he believes that he is physically more attractive than they are. He protests that he is now a 'visual' singer, meaning that he is a good-looking singer. His hybridized term ends in the Korean word for a singer, *kaswu*.

This type of self-identification through hybridization occurs not only with the so-called *yenyeyin* ('entertainer') but also non-*yenyeyin*. The morning talk show, *Yeyumanman* ('Relaxed and Composed'), featured mothers of a few celebrities to discuss ways in which they helped their children become successful celebrities. In excerpt (12), Okjung, singer Haha's mother, is interviewed by the show co-host, Cho Youngku, who is aware of Okjung's penchant for cotton velvet dresses.

(12)

Youngku: Cipeyseto mayil ilen dresslul ipko kyeysinkayo?
'Do you wear a dress like that at home every day?'

Okjung: Keuy ipnun phyenicyo. Ney, yungdulanun pyelchingun ceyka phyengsangsiey yungdu osul cohahanuntey e **yungduOkjung**.
'Almost every day. Yes, my nickname *yungdu* is given precisely because I like velvet dresses. Uh, it's yungduOkjung.'

Audience: (Laughing)
(*Yeyumanman* 'Relaxed and Composed' aired on 12 June 2011)

Haha revealed his mother's unusual liking for cotton velvet dresses in another program, which the co-host Cho Youngku knew about. Her nickname consists of *yung* ('cotton velvet'), *dress*, and her name *Okjung*. The English word *dress* is hindclipped and appears between the two Korean words, that is, *yung* and *Okjung*.

A similar strategy of combining an English word and a Korean name was adopted on the show *Namcauy Cakyek* ('Men's Bucket List') by Chun Hyunmu, who recently joined the group on the show's 10-day backpacking tour to see Australian wildlife. When they signed up for the 'off-road' journey to Bungle Bungle, they had to drive through water puddles and streams, which posed great challenges for them. Their car got stuck in the mud a few times and the production of the show almost came to a complete halt. After completing several obstacle courses, they became confident enough to enjoy the experience towards the end of the show. In excerpt (13), their newly gained confidence is expressed through hybrid lexical items. The conversation below occurs in a car among three Korean men who drove a few thousand miles together. A caption on the TV screen, which normally summarizes what is shown concurrently, reads, 'Welcome to macho off road!'

(13)

Hyungbin: **Global-yasayng**. **Off-Jun**! (Looking at Jun Hyunmu who is driving).
'Global wildlife. Off-Jun!'

Jun Hyunmu: Mwul baby!
'Water baby!'
(*Namcauy Cakeyk* 'Men's Bucket List' aired on 26 June 2011)

In contrast to the beginning of the show, Jun Hyunmu is now neither timid nor afraid. When faced with rather deep water puddles he screams for joy and speeds up, successfully passing through them. The hybrid word *Off-Jun* is composed of the hindclipped English word *off-road* and his last name *Jun*, suggesting that he is now a skilled off-road driver. This 'honorable' title is given by his traveling companion, Hyungbin. Jun Hyunmu himself expresses his excitement by yelling 'water', indicating that he is no longer going to shy away from water puddles.

Conclusion

Korean global ambition, both personal and national, fosters more hybridized linguistic practices which accommodate both the global and the local. Koreans seem to reconcile the difference between the pressure to be proficient in English and the desire to fully and freely express themselves in Korean through linguistic hybridization. TV functions as a cultural medium reflecting and reproducing hybridized linguistic practices, both real and imagined, and is a site where Korean celebrities utilize hybridized medialect to fulfill their roles as entertainers.

The linguistic hybridization in the study is predominantly performed through blending and clipping of English and Korean lexical items. Through linguistic hybridization, Korean TV personalities neutralize and euphemize offensiveness and vulgarity of their narratives, represent new concepts that were not available before, repackage already established ideas and images and project their self-identity and mark others' identities. Linguistic hybridization often produces a comic effect, eliciting laughter from the participants in the programs.

This study mainly focuses on creative uses of linguistic hybridization with a textual and discursive focus. What is not discussed in the study and needs to be addressed further in the future is the impact of this increasingly hybridized medialect on Korean viewers. As English, promoted by *segyehwa*

(Korean globalization drive), appears more often across different domains of Korean society, both the advantage of knowing and using English and the disadvantage of not knowing and using English in contemporary Korea now affect one's employability and academic success as well as the mundane activity of TV viewing. Lee (2007a: 146) observes that English 'is arguably the most revered and the most feared language in Korea'. Although its importance in modern Korea is hardly questioned, English is rarely associated with pleasure; rather, it is often framed as a language causing stress and anxiety, particularly in pedagogical and professional settings (Lee, 2012). TV poses sociolinguistic challenges for certain subpopulations in Korea due to its growing hybrid linguistic practices, which often strengthen identity marking within an English-knowing group but can easily exclude monolingual Korean groups that do not have a hybrid verbal repertoire. Exclusively locally-bound practices (for example, profession, education, travel, consumer culture, and so on), including language, are perceived as anachronisms, going against the flow of 'global Korea', a phrase that encapsulates the Lee Myung-bak administration's pragmatic globalism (Kim & Kang, 2008).

English is a social stratification variable in Korea, making a distinction between bilinguals and monolinguals – the English knowing and the English unknowing. Although Ramanathan (2006) discusses the 'English-vernacular divide' in postcolonial territories such as India, English-related social dichotomies are also observed in Korea. Increasingly hybridized linguistic practices on Korean TV provide wonderful career opportunities for bilingual entertainers and viewing pleasure for bilingual viewers. At the same time, the same hybridized linguistic practices may further isolate monolingual performers and viewers. The specific ways in which they are impacted by hybridized medialect are beyond the scope of the current project and need to be empirically investigated in the future.

References

Bakhtin, M. (1981) *The Dialogic Imagination: Four Essays* (M. Holquist, ed. and C. Emerson and M. Holquist, trans). Austin: University of Texas Press.

Bhatt, R. (2008) In other words: Language mixing, identity representations, and *third space*. *Journal of Sociolinguistics* 12, 177–200.

Boden, M.A. (1990) *The Creative Mind: Myths and Mechanisms*. London: Routledge.

Hjarvard, S. (2004) The globalization of language: How the media contribute to the spread of English and the emergence of medialects. *Nordicom Review* 1–2, 75–97.

Jones, R.H. (2010) Creativity and discourse. *World Englishes* 29, 467–480.

Kim, S.S. (2000) Korea and globalization (segyehwa): A framework for analysis. In S.S. Kim (ed.) *Korea's Globalization* (pp. 1–28). Cambridge: Cambridge University Press.

Kim, Y. and Kang, H. (2008) Conservatism, pragmatism, globalism sweeping Korea. *The Korea Times*, 30 January.
Lee, J.S. (2004) Linguistic hybridization in K-pop: Self-assertion and resistance. *World Englishes* 23, 429–450.
Lee, J.S. (2006) Linguistic constructions of modernity: Korean-English mixing in TV commercials. *Language in Society* 35, 59–91.
Lee, J.S. (2007a) Don't know = put some money down = save!: Mock English in Korean comedy. In *Proceedings of the 8th ISKS International Conference on Korean Studies* (Vol. 1). *Language/Linguistics, Literature, Society/Education* (pp. 144–154). London: Center of Korean Studies; School of Oriental and African Studies; University of London.
Lee, J.S. (2007b) *I'm the illest fucka*: An analysis of African American English in South Korean hip hop. *English Today* 23 (2), 54–60.
Lee, J.S. (2007c) Language and identity: Entertainers in South Korean pop culture. In M. Mantero (ed.) *Identity and Second Language Learning* (pp. 283–303). Charlotte, NC: Information Age Publishing.
Lee, J.S. (2010a) Commodified English in east Asian internet advertising. In H. Kelly-Holmes and G. Mautner (eds) *Language and the Market* (pp. 109–120). Basingstoke: Palgrave-Macmillan.
Lee, J.S. (2010b) Glocalizing *keepin' it real*: South Korean hip hop playas. In M. Terkourafi (ed.) *The Languages of Global Hip Hop* (pp. 139–161). New York: Continuum.
Lee, J.S. (2011) Globalization and language education: *English Village* in South Korea. *Language Research* 47 (1), 123–149.
Lee, J.S. (2012) *Please Teach Me English*: English and metalinguistic discourse in South Korean film. In J.S. Lee and A. Moody (eds) *English in Asian Popular Culture* (pp. 127–149). Hong Kong: Hong Kong University Press.
Lee, J.S. (in press) Language anxiety and humor: polarizing representations of English on Korean television. *World Englishes*.
Mendelsohn, H. and Spetnagel, H.T. (1980) Entertainment as a sociological enterprise. In P.H. Tannenbaum (ed.) *The Entertainment Functions of Television* (pp. 13–30). Hillsdale, NJ: Lawrence Erlbaum Associates, Inc.
Moody, A. and Matsumoto, Y. (2003) Don't touch my moustache: Language blending and code ambiguation by two J-pop artists. *Asian Englishes* 6 (1), 4–33.
Newcomb, H. and Hirsch, P.M. (2000) [1983]. Television as a cultural forum. In H. Newcomb (ed.) *Television: The Critical View* (pp. 561–573). New York: Oxford University Press.
Pope, R. (2005) *Creativity: Theory, History, Practice*. London: Routledge.
Ramanathan, V. (2006) The vernacularization of English: Crossing global currents to re-dress West-based TESOL. *Critical Inquiry in Language Studies* 3 (2–3), 131–146.
Sternberg, R.J. (1990) Wisdom and its relations to intelligence and creativity. In R.J. Sternberg (ed.) *Wisdom: Its Nature, Origins, and Development* (pp. 142–159). New York: Cambridge University Press.
Woolard, K.A. (1999) Simultaneity and bivalency as strategies in bilingualism. *Journal of Linguistic Anthropology* 8, 3–29.

Part 3

Multilingual Diaspora and the Internet

11 The Language of Malaysian and Indonesian Users of Social Networks: Practice vs System

Mario Saraceni

Setting the Theoretical Scene

The word *hybrid* signifies something that is the result of the combination of two or more different entities, from which it takes its salient characteristics. According to this basic definition, the constituents of a hybrid – its 'parents' – and their features are well identifiable. The term, originating from biology, is used in a wide range of domains. A *hybrid bicycle*, for example, combines the features of a *mountain bike* (number of gears, width of tires) and those of a *road bike* (size of wheels, shape of handlebars). Also, generally speaking, a hybrid is 'sterile', in the sense that its characteristics do not mix further with those of another cognate entity. This reflects a biological law, according to which hybrids, such as mules for example, are not normally capable of reproduction. Intended in this way, hybridity is a fairly straightforward concept.

The linguistic phenomena that come closest to the notion of hybridity defined above are those of code-switching/mixing and creoles/pidgins. The former can be defined as the use of more than one language in the same piece of discourse, which can then be considered 'hybrid'. The latter is a process whereby two or more languages come into contact thereby causing the emergence of a new language which takes on features from the 'parent' languages and enables their speakers to communicate with one another. Both of these definitions involve mixing languages and match quite closely the notion of hybridity as given above. However, this apparent conceptual symmetry needs to be probed a little further before any serious analysis can be undertaken.

The very concept of language mix takes it as a given that languages are discrete identifiable entities. However, this quasi-commonsensical assumption has been questioned in linguistics for some time. Indeed, there has been no conclusively satisfactory answer to the very question of what it is that constitutes a language X and distinguishes it from language Y. As Sydney Lamb (2004: 413) points out, 'There is no generally applicable way to make the distinction between one language and another. Languages are neither discrete objects nor are they uniform across speakers.' He is unequivocal about the issue: 'There is no such thing as a language. There is such a thing as Language, but it is a mass noun' (Lamb, 2004: 218). Similarly, Hudson (1996: 36) states that 'the search for language boundaries is a waste of time' and rejects the possibility that mutual intelligibility (or the lack of it) can be a valid measure of distinction between languages. As he contends, '[m]utual intelligibility is a matter of degrees' and, ultimately, it is not really a fixed property of languages but depends on the willingness and/or ability of individual speakers to negotiate meaning and understand each other.

If the distinctions between discrete languages cannot be established scientifically, how should entities such as 'Malay', 'English', 'Tamil', and so on, be understood? In this respect, Bolton (2006: 308) has noted that there is 'a tension between what are seen as the organic qualities of dialects and varieties as the "natural" expression of vital linguistic systems, and the view of languages and language varieties as social and political constructs'. Joseph (2006: 27), for example, claims that 'the question of what is or isn't a language is always finally a *political* question. The linguist cannot answer it objectively by measuring degrees of structural differences or mutual comprehensibility.' Thus, in other words, even if individual languages are not satisfactorily describable at the linguistic level, their ontology should nevertheless not be discounted but sought elsewhere, that is, at the sociopolitical level.

The political dimension of languages becomes particularly evident if one considers, for example, the context of 19th-century Europe, when the postulation of the existence of national languages and their codification were part of the establishment of the nexus language-people-territory, which, in turn, was cardinal in the narratives that were articulated at the time for the formation of the various nation states (Wright, 2000). Significantly, as the construct *nation state* has come under pressure by both sub- (for example, separatist and independentist movements) and supra-national (for example, the European Union (EU)) forces, so has the (more or less official) recognition of languages. Catalan, in post-Franco Spain, for example, has been elevated to the status of a language in parallel with the increased wealth, power and sense of identity of the people of Catalonia. In northern Italy, independentist movements predicate the existence of a distinct *Padan* language as part of their narrative about a *Padan* nation, separate from the Italian. The ways in which the nomenclature of languages is reconfigured in accordance with political events has been most evident in the context of the former Yugoslavia, where the post-Socialism disintegration of the nation has been accompanied by the separation of languages which were once considered unitary. What used to be called Serbo-Croat is now split into three separate languages: Serbian, Croatian and Bosnian. And, indeed, linguists' efforts to classify languages are not only fruitless but also inconsequential for the wider community:

> what does it matter if a few thousand linguists are convinced that Serbian and Croatian are the same language, or that Chinese is a family of distinct languages, when umpteen millions believe the opposite, and it's on their lives that the question has a direct impact? (Joseph, 2006: 26)

So, the reality of languages resides within the decisions of policy-makers but also, crucially, within people's mindsets: '[s]o long as people *believe* that their way of speaking constitutes a language in its own right, there is a real sense in which it *is* a real language' (Joseph, 2006: 27). Pennycook is even more explicit in this regard, as he observes that 'languages exist only to the extent that speakers perceive them to do so' (2007: 95). The adverb 'only' may sound somewhat reductive here, but what this means is that the existence of languages is not rejected in any way, but problematized and relocated from the plane of objective, primordial reality to that of the sociopolitical persuasion, both collective and individual.

This constructionist conceptualization of discrete languages has profound implications for the notion of hybridity. If distinctions among languages are fundamentally the products of sociopolitical constructs, in what sense can one talk of combining 'different' languages together? What are the substances in the mix? As Makoni (2011: 683) observes, 'the notion of hybridization does not resolve the problematic of a coded, discrete entity, because it is predicated on an assumption that there exist two distinct codes or separate entities which are combined'. With regard to code-switching and mixing, for example, an anti-essentialist view of language is uncomfortable with the idea that certain words belong to language X and others to language Y. As Pennycook (2010: 129) observes, 'languages are always mixed, hybrid and drawing on multiple resources'. Hybridity, that is, is in the very essence of language, it is part of its texture, and should not be described as a peculiar act of merging two otherwise pure entities. In addition, Makoni *et al.* (2007: 43) question the validity of the term 'hybrid' by noting how it 'may lead to misconstrue the sociolinguistic situation' since different speakers 'may differ considerably in the nature of their linguistic repertoire'.

This seems to be consonant with the recent shift of focus in sociolinguistics from the global to the local (see, among others, Canagarajah, 2005; Higgins, 2009; Mufwene, 2008; Pennycook, 2010) and, at the same time, from language as 'system' to 'language as *practice* (constantly in flux)' (Mufwene, 2008: 32, emphasis in the original). Significantly, in his theory of language evolution, Mufwene makes the point that

> All causes of change in any language [lie] in the communicative acts of speakers, such as the accommodations that speakers make to each other in order to be (better) understood and in the explanations they make of old materials to convey new ideas. (2008: 31–32)

Thus, Mufwene clearly foregrounds the role of speakers as *actors*, rather than mere users, of language. In essence, this is very similar to Canagarajah's conceptualization of what he calls 'lingua franca English' (LFE):

> Because of the diversity at the heart of this communicative medium, LFE is intersubjectively constructed in each specific context of interaction. The form of this English is negotiated by each set of speakers for their purposes. The speakers are able to monitor each other's language proficiency to determine mutually the appropriate grammar, phonology, lexical range, and pragmatic conventions that would ensure intelligibility. Therefore, it is difficult to describe this language a priori. (Canagarajah, 2007: 925)

But LFE need not be made a special case in this sense. Canagarajah's observations can be applicable to language communication in general, especially if we do not lose sight of the pervasively and inherently hybrid nature of language.

The investigation of language hybridity, therefore, cannot yield entirely satisfactory results if it indulges too long in the corridors of conventional linguistic description, limited by the imposed fixity of its parameters, which would be at odds with the dynamic constructions and re-constructions of language that continually take place in each instance of communication. Within a speaker-centered approach, investigative questions need to extend their reach beyond the level of detached language description and directly involve the *doers* of language hybridity. Of course, given the theoretical framework that I have delineated here, the resulting apparent paradox inherent in the very expression 'language hybridity' must be dealt with. In this chapter I have chosen to do so by adopting a two-phase approach. In the first instance, I shall present and discuss samples of textual data collected from internet-based discourse displaying characteristics which would traditionally be identified as occurrences of language hybridity. Second, I shall consider the opinions and perceptions of the people who produced those pieces of discourse. In doing so, my aim is not so much to provide a feature-focused description of samples of hybrid language (*cf.* for example, Hassan & Hashim, 2009), but to try and go a little deeper and use those samples as initial prompts for some reflection on the language practice that takes place in online social networks and, to some extent, language communication in general.

Textual Data

For the purpose of this chapter, all textual data come from online communication by eight Malaysian and six Indonesian users of the online social network site Facebook. All users are university students, with the exception of two of the Indonesian users, who are university lecturers. All of them are in the English department of their institution. The choice of this particular geographical region was dictated by the multilingual character of its society, with which I am reasonably familiar, and also by the fact that in the traditional Kachruvian three-circle model, the two countries belong to different 'circles' – Malaysia in the Outer Circle and Indonesia in the Expanding Circle, the latter not having been colonized by Britain. Given the multilingual base of the two countries, internet constitutes a trans- and supranational locus which potentially multiplies the possibilities of language (re) construction, but also a place where local and global meet and intermingle in ways which make the distinction between the two almost entirely superfluous, as I will discuss later.

The first example I wish to present is a snippet from a conversation between two Malaysian users, simply referred to as A_{Mal} and B_{Mal}:

1 A_{Mal}: merlin?
2 B_{Mal}: wut?

3 A_{Mal}: u said that the magical story . . . i guess it is merlin
4 B_{Mal}: no la . . . harry potter . . . = P
5 A_{Mal}: ooo . . . so many wizard and witch craft movies
6 B_{Mal}: saje nk bg hangpa pikiaq!!haha
7 A_{Mal}: ooo . . . kat sini laa bermulanya warcraft . . . defence of the ancient

Here we notice features which could be described as fairly universal in online communication, such as the absence of capitalization and of syntactic punctuation, the phonetic representation of words such as 'what' (*wut* in line 2) and 'you' (*u* in line 3), and the use of emoticons (= *P* in line 4). From the point of view of language hybridity, this is a classic case of code-switching, whereby speakers switch from one language to another at a particular point (line 6) in the conversation. The use of the particle *la* (line 4) – often spelled *lah* – is very common in Malaysia, but also in Singapore and Hong Kong. Its status is significant in a discussion about hybridity, since there is no agreement as to which language it should rightfully belong to, whether Chinese languages (for example, Hokkien, Cantonese), Malay (where it is an inflectional suffix) or English. Interestingly, in the Oxford English Dictionary it is classified as part of Singaporean English, although its ubiquitous presence in Malaysians' speech makes that geographical identification far too restrictive. Indeed, *lah* is so common among Malaysians that they consider it a marker of shared identity, even though, at the same time, many see it negatively as an indicator of the impurity of English in their country (Saraceni, 2010: 122–123). These preoccupations about the use of *lah* are indicative of the fact that sometimes 'the most minor differences will be invested with the ideological value' (Joseph, 2004: 144) needed to mark the distinction between a language or variety from another. At the same time, the particle is so widely used that it would be mistaken to locate it within one particular language. More accurately, it can be said to be part of the rich linguistic repertoire which many people (especially from urban areas) in Southeast Asia draw from as they carry out their day-to-day activities.

The following is a very short extract from a conversation between three other Malaysian users, here referred to as C_{Mal}, D_{Mal}, and E_{Mal}:

1 C_{Mal}: nice~ waaaa
2 D_{Mal}: dialah di hati . . . siti 4ever . . . i really like this song . . . try 2 sing this song unfortunately sore x sampai . . . =,
3 E_{Mal}: try hard ika!! i'm sure you can . . . hehe thanks 2 those yg memuji . . . hehe

Again, common 'online' features can be observed here, such as the use of abbreviations and the representation of words, or parts of words, by means of digits that are phonologically equivalent. Interestingly, while the emotional expression *hehe* enjoys global currency, the elongated *wa* in the first line is an orthographic representation of an exclamation of emphasis/surprise commonly used in Southeast Asia. Also, the emoticon =, is not as universally understood as others. From the point of view of language hybridity, this could be classified as code-mixing, whereby Malay and English are used together in the same turns. However, we can already see emerging how the terms *code-switching* and *code-mixing* seem to be incapable of grasping the full make-up of the type of language practice under scrutiny. What happens here is more than just the combination of different languages.

First and foremost, these are examples of an increasingly common language practice: friends communicating on an online social network. This kind of conversation is typically characterized by varying degrees of asynchronicity, given that lag between turns can be of a few seconds but also of a few days. Also, anybody who belongs to a user's list of 'friends' can participate in any conversation initiated by that user, whose first turn acts as a general prompt not normally directed at anybody in particular. The participants can be physically very near one another (even, theoretically, in the same room) or very far (for example, in different continents). So, the switching and mixing is not just one of conventionally recognized languages (for example, English and Malay), but also involves different points in time, different physical locations and different participants, who can shift in and out of a conversation as they wish. In addition, and very importantly, this kind of communication is also multimodal, as digital photographs and videos are often integral components in the exchanges.

The following text is a snippet of a conversation between three other Malaysian users, F_{Mal}, G_{Mal}, and H_{Mal}:

1	F_{Mal}:	Darling! Slamat hari raye:) jgn nangis okay raye anak rantau;)
2	G_{Mal}:	trimaz..i'll try my best not to NANGES!!!! huhuhu..
3	H_{Mal}:	..miss you =)
4	G_{Mal}:	..miss ya tooo..nnti jumpa kat mesia keyh . . . ak pi sleep over kat umah hg . . .
5	H_{Mal}:	boleh2 . . . =)

Here, Malay and English are even more seamlessly amalgamated, so that the boundaries between them are even fuzzier. And, indeed, the solidity of other boundaries also comes under pressure here. One more aspect of hybridity observable in these conversations could be said to be the combination of 'global' and 'local', given by the simultaneous utilization of elements that are of localized diffusion and others that are more universally available, such as, above all, the Malay language and the English language, but also, more particularly, different emoticons belonging to one and the other category. The potentially great or very small geographical distances between participants is a further dimension of the global-local blend inherent in social network communication. However, the dichotomy between *global* and *local* may be a false one and the terms unsuitable to describe what really goes on here, since every act of communication takes place in, and is anchored to, its own locality which, in turn, is situated and, at the same time, transcends physical space. The act of someone in Malaysia conversing on Facebook with a friend in England constitutes an act of local language practice, where the adjective *local* refers not so much to geography but, more significantly, to the specific participants involved, their purposes and the modes of communication employed. It is, in other words, what is often referred to as context of situation, of which language practice is an integral component. Firmly embedded in its own locality, then, language can only be seen as hybrid by a third party, an external observer (such as a linguist). By contrast, the participants, themselves embedded in their locality, make use of the linguistic resources that are available in the shared context of situation, without much regard to the 'official' designation of individual words, grammatical patterns of syntactic structures.

It is for this reason that the texts seen so far should not be considered exceptional or acts of particular linguistic creativity. On the contrary, they constitute the norm insofar as they illustrate how speakers make use of the language resources available. And it is in this sense that Canagarajah's definition of LFE seen above can actually be applicable to all instances of language-based communication: all speakers intersubjectively determine their shared linguistic repertoire and, drawing from it, construct their language in each specific context of interaction. In online communication this is particularly evident because, as Canagarajah himself observes, 'the new media of communication, such as the Internet, encourage greater hybridity and fluidity' (2005: xxiv).

The following short extracts were taken from three different conversations among a total of six Indonesian Facebook users. A_{Ind} and D_{Ind} are lecturers, while the others are students, all in the same university.

1	A_{Ind}:	Hari ini salah forward email dan kasi uang ... What's wrong with me? Maybe I need some enlightenment :)
2		:D=))°°°°°°≈HåHåHå°°°°°°≈°=))
3	B_{Ind}:	pergi berlibur ^__^
4	A_{Ind}:	º"º†Hªηk'sº"º.. Great idea :p

5	A_{Ind}:	In between 'Harmoni' and 'Cellular' ... Stunning and thrilling la ... la ... la :)
6	C_{Ind}:	Kenapa ci?? Lagi senengg yah??
7	A_{Ind}:	yup, bisa lihat a good movie and fantastic concert di TV :)
8	C_{Ind}:	Oooo konserr apaan ci??

9	D_{Ind}:	speak your mind, guys, even if your voice shakes.
10	E_{Ind}:	Apa gak sebaiknya dilakukan?
11	D_{Ind}:	Maksudnya, Pak?
12	F_{Ind}:	sore throat ??

Apart from the very creative use of typography in lines 1 and 2, the linguistic features observable here are very similar to those found in the previous extracts with Malaysian users. One interesting difference, however, is the fact that although English and Bahasa Indonesia seem to be just as amalgamated as English and Malay in the previous extracts, here the portions of language that can be labeled 'English' display greater conformity to what could be regarded as 'written standard'. Namely, no abbreviations of phonological substitutions are found, while line 9 even shows full use of syntactic punctuation. This could be due to the fact that English has become an integral part of the Indonesian linguistic wealth relatively recently in comparison to Malaysia and, as a consequence, people's sense of 'ownership' of the language may still not be strong enough for them to feel entitled to re-forge it in the same way in which they mold the shape of Bahasa Indonesia according to their communicative needs and wishes. To some extent, therefore, the difference between Outer and Expanding Circles[1] would seem to be valid insofar as one considers the historical dimension of the 'circles'.

Interview Data

In this section of the chapter I shall discuss the perceptions expressed by my informants about the language practice that they are actors of. All of my informants agreed that mixing languages is very common in their social environment. As A_{Mal} noted, in Malaysia it is often referred to as *bahasa rojak*, where 'bahasa' means 'language' and 'rojak' is a dish made up of the combination of many different ingredients together. C_{Mal} explained that it is 'a mixture of Malay, English, Chinese, and Tamil' but that the proportion of each may vary according to the ethnic/cultural background of the participants:

> Usually, for me, I'm speaking three or four languages, but it depends who I'm speaking to. English and Malay are always there. And if I'm speaking to a Chinese friend, you might know some Chinese words and you might use them. The Malays, some of them know certain words in Tamil, or certain words in Chinese.

A_{Mal} said that Malaysians use *bahasa rojak* 'most of the time' because they 'share common knowledge but in different languages'. The commonality of knowledge and experiences that can be expressed in different but coexisting and partially shared languages is, according to my informants, the essence of language hybridity. Interestingly, when I asked them to be more specific as to what reasons they had for using words from different languages, they tended to reply that such words acted as replacements when they 'could not think of the exact word' (A_{Mal}) in one language. As B_{Mal} stated: 'sometimes when I speak in English, I can't figure out the words I want to use, so I'll mix it up with Malay'. This was echoed by D_{Mal}:

> Sometimes you don't know a word in English or Malay, you just use the Chinese word. For example, 'hey, you so ma fan!' Ma fan in Mandarin means troublesome. So let's say if 'troublesome' doesn't pop up, you just say 'hey you ma fan, lah'. That kind of thing.

E_{Mal} added that it may be more suitable and/or natural to use certain words than their equivalents in other languages, and cited 'let's go to pasar malam' as an example where 'night market' would sound 'weird and awkward'. Conversely, but following the same principle, A_{Ind} said that 'there are some expressions better stated in English ... "eating out", for example: the equivalent words in [Bahasa] Indonesia are too long for this short phrase'. However, besides these observations, which seem to underline an awareness of the diverse linguistic components within the *rojak*, my informants also preponderantly expressed the idea that language hybridity was something that came to them naturally and without conscious effort. A_{Mal}, for example, noted that 'it just comes naturally, I guess', echoed by E_{Mal} and F_{Mal}, according to whom the mixing of languages takes place especially in casual conversation and 'comes so naturally that we don't realize'. Similarly, for B_{Mal}, 'mostly people just do it out of no reason, it's like a norm already, just because everyone's doing it, maybe'. The same notion was expressed by A_{Ind}:

> [language mixing] comes naturally. The words just come out naturally as I usually do with my twin sister. I mix [Bahasa] Indonesia, English, Javanese, Chinese-Javanese dialects, Thai, Japanese, but I don't speak them equally proficient. In Indonesia at least we speak two languages, [Bahasa] Indonesia and Javanese. In an English department like ours, it becomes three even four since many of us are Chinese Indonesian. Especially in informal contexts, we tend to switch and mix a lot ... it even sounds unnatural to stick to one language.

This last sentence is particularly significant, as it reinforces the idea that language hybridity is the norm, rather than an exception. Indeed, there was a perceptible common pattern during the interviews, like a thought trajectory from an initial description of language hybridity as a collection of discrete languages to one, as the discussion proceeded, where linguistic boundaries began to fade. Referring to the use of the expression 'ma fan', D_{Mal} commented that 'we don't learn it, we *acquire* it when Chinese people are speaking', which again points to the fact that language hybridity is not a peculiar act of lexical borrowing, but, as C_{Mal} put it, 'it is part of our speech' or, in B_{Mal}'s words, *bahasa rojak* has 'become a culture'.

Another word mentioned during the interviews was 'macha', which my informants identified as a Tamil word, a friendly form of address roughly equivalent to 'buddy' or 'mate' (but more literally meaning 'brother'). My two Malaysian Indian informants pointed out that despite its Indian 'origin', the word is routinely used by the other ethnic groups in Malaysia, for example, in 'hey macha, apa khabar?' When I queried non-Indian respondents about the same word, they confirmed that they use it and, interestingly, one of them noted that 'it doesn't feel like Tamil anymore'. However, D_{Mal}, one of my Malaysian Indian informants, felt uneasy about the fact that this word seemed to be losing its Tamil 'roots': 'some people might think that the word "macha" is from Malay ... We don't want that, because "macha" is a Tamil written word', while C_{Mal}, the other Malaysian Indian, added:

> That's what's happening to the Malay language now – they've been taking words from different languages for many many years and now they claim these words are theirs. So in that way the Malay language has become not authentic any more.

D_{Mal} reiterated that this was something that was 'worrying', since 'language is like food for the soul – you are supposed to know where it derives from'. Even though it contrasts with the idea of language hybridity as a borderless linguistic amalgam, this is a sentiment that needs to be taken seriously. Despite the fact that individual speakers may seem to have somewhat contradicting perceptions of language hybridity, the idea of distinct languages, and of their symbolic power (Bourdieu, 1991) is not at all weakened. If the notion of hybridity dissolves in actual language practice, it nonetheless remains very clear when the actors of such practice are invited to reflect upon certain aspects of it.

Attitudes towards language hybridity are, themselves, mixed. On the one hand, *bahasa rojak* is seen as a useful strategy for effective communication as well as a marker of identity. E_{Mal} and F_{Mal} were of the opinion that 'it's good because it helps to communicate what you're trying to say ... with almost everyone', while both C_{Mal} and D_{Mal} agreed that it was 'part of our Malaysian identity – it's one way for us to show that we're Malaysian and we're speaking the same language'. On the other hand, however, my informants also expressed negative attitudes towards language mixing, maintaining that it is only appropriate in informal situations. Referring to Malaysian school children, A_{Mal} noted that they 'use it to convey their meanings but eventually they will learn that it can only be used as informal language, not in exam'. D_{Mal} highlighted negative effects of *bahasa rojak*:

> because in time the younger Malaysians will feel that it *is* a language by itself, so the formality of Malay, Mandarin, Tamil will not be there when they write. We don't want that. I don't mind that style shifting when you go to the store, I don't mind you talking like that, but when it comes to academic language and things like that I think it is better to know the formality of the language. Bahasa rojak is not formal.

F_{Mal} felt that 'mixing up languages can be confusing if I'm trying to learn proper English, like, using proper grammar, proper sentences'. This clearly suggests that there was a strong sense of the distinctness of individual languages and a perception that mixing them was detrimental to their correctness and formality. This confirmed the findings in Tan (2005) and Saraceni (2010) that showed predominantly negative attitudes in the Malaysian press towards the idea of English as a 'Malaysianized' language. Another point that was made with specific reference to English was that both in Malaysia and in Indonesia it tended to be part of the mix mainly in urban areas. A_{Mal}, for example, said that in the area where she was from 'it just seems weird to mix [the local variety of Malay] with English', while A_{Ind} reported that in rural areas people 'will just switch and mix their local languages and Bahasa Indonesia [and] some people might have negative opinions when I mix the language because they think I'm trying to show off my English to them'.

Conclusions

A discussion on linguistic hybridity requires reflections that go deep to the very heart of the concept of language. Depending on the orientation of such reflections, hybridity can assume one of the two following senses: (a) a particular form of language combining items from two or more different languages; (b) a linguistic amalgam used in language practice where speakers negotiate and draw from a shared repertoire. While recent trends in sociolinguistics would tend to favor the latter conceptualization, the former remains nonetheless significant in terms of the representational power of languages. Indeed, both understandings of hybridity emerged from the discussion of the data presented in this chapter. Online social networks are loci where various dimensions of hybridity intersect and the language practice that goes on therein lends itself particularly well to being described according to the second sense of hybridity mentioned above. The actors of such a language practice, that is, the participants in online conversations, on their part, seem to express both understandings of hybridity. On the one hand, they describe language hybridity as normal, natural, requiring no conscious act of any particular creativity, while, on the other hand, they remain very conscious of certain discrete ingredients of language mixing and particularly sensitive to their symbolic, cultural and identity significance. This suggests that even if, from a modern sociolinguistic point of view, it would be more accurate to think of language as practice rather than as system, the contrasting perceptions of the speakers cannot be discounted, as they are part of the local practice just as much as, and even prior to, the language they produce.

Note

(1) Kachru's three-circle model has been criticized by a number of scholars (for example, Bruthiaux, 2003; Jenkins, 2003/2009; Pennycook, 2009; Saraceni, 2010; Yano, 2009) for its rigidity and over-simplified representation of English in the world.

References

Bolton, K. (2006) Varieties of world Englishes. In B.B. Kachru, Y. Kachru and C.L. Nelson (eds) *The Handbook of World Englishes* (pp. 289–312). Oxford: Blackwell.
Bourdieu, P. (1991) *Language and Symbolic Power.* Cambridge: Polity Press.
Bruthiaux, P. (2003) Squaring the circles: Issues in modeling English worldwide. *International Journal of Applied Linguistics* 13 (2), 159–178.
Canagarajah, S. (2005) Reconstructing local knowledge, reconfiguring language studies. In S. Canagarajah (ed.) *Reclaiming the Local in Language Policy and Practice* (pp. 3–24). Mahwah, NJ: Lawrence Erlbaum Associates.
Canagarajah, S. (2007) Lingua franca English, multilingual communities, and language acquisition. *The Modern Language Journal* 91 (5), 923–939.
Hassan, N. and Hashim, A. (2009) Electronic English in Malaysia: Features and language in use. *English Today* 25 (4), 39–46.
Higgins, C. (2009) *English as a Local Language*. Bristol: Multilingual Matters.
Hudson, R.A. (1996) *Sociolinguistics* (2nd edn). Cambridge: Cambridge University Press.
Jenkins, J. (2003/2009) *World Englishes*. London: Routledge.
Joseph, J. (2004) *Language and Identity: National, Ethnic, Religious*. Basingstoke: Palgrave.
Joseph, J. (2006) *Language and Politics*. Edinburgh: Edinburgh University Press.
Lamb, S.M. (2004) *Language and Reality*. London: Continuum.

Makoni, S. (2011) Sociolinguistics, colonial and postcolonial: An integrationist perspective. *Language Sciences* 33 (4), 680–688.

Makoni, S., Brutt-Griffler, J. and Mashiri, P. (2007) The use of 'indigenous' and urban vernaculars in Zimbabwe. *Language in Society* 36 (1), 25–49.

Mufwene, S. (2008) *Language Evolution: Contact, Competition and Change*. London: Continuum.

Pennycook, A. (2007) The myth of English as an international language. In S. Makoni and A. Pennycook (eds) *Disinventing and Reconstituting Languages* (pp. 90–115). Clevedon: Multilingual Matters.

Pennycook, A. (2009) Plurilithic Englishes: Towards a 3D model. In K. Murata and J. Jenkins (eds) *Global Englishes in Asian Contexts: Current and Future Debates* (pp. 194–207). Basingstoke: Palgrave Macmillan.

Pennycook, A. (2010) *Language as a Local Practice*. London: Routledge.

Saraceni, M. (2010) *The Relocation of English: Shifting Paradigms in a Global Era*. Basingstoke: Palgrave Macmillan.

Tan, P.K.W. (2005) The medium-of-instruction debate in Malaysia: English as a Malaysian language? *Language Problems & Language Planning* 29 (1), 47–66.

Wright, S. (2000) *Community and Communication: The Role of Language in Nation State Building and European Integration*. Clevedon: Multilingual Matters.

Yano, Y. (2009) The future of English: Beyond the Kachruvian three circle model? In K. Murata and J. Jenkins (eds) *Global Englishes in Asian Contexts: Current and Future Debates* (pp. 208–225). Basingstoke: Palgrave Macmillan.

12 Constructing Local and Global in the E-Borderland

Tope Omoniyi

Clearly the Net blurs the boundaries between 'reality' and 'virtuality', but rather than reveling in the idea of ratiocination, we suggest that ontogeny recapitulates phylogeny: on the Net one may try to do things differently, but too often we end up plugging in the same old attitudes.
Interrogate the Internet Group, 1996: 126

Explanations for cross-cultural and cross-linguistic literacy practices on the Internet and social attitudes toward CMD practices often reference local identities, leading to the construction of hybrid postmodern identities.
Koutsogiannis and Mitsikopoulou, 2007: 143

Introduction

This chapter is premised upon two crucially significant global events that occurred in 2011: the WikiLeaks affair and the first ever e-G8 Forum. On 25 April 2011, WikiLeaks, a non-profit media organization 'dedicated to bringing important information to the public' (http://wikileaks.org/About.html) carried out a mass internet dissemination of information that had hitherto been classified by various territorially defined national governments around the world. This unilateral declassifying action made the information available globally but the responses and repercussions of it have had local, international, institutional and personal ramifications all at once. The event marks a turn in the way we conceptualize the management and control of information and its dissemination and access.

The WikiLeaks affair has, arguably more than any other event, forced the concept of boundaries and spaces of authority of nations in a deterritorialized post-nation era, and perhaps what Heller (2011: 28) has referred to as 'the challenges of doing a post-national sociolinguistics'. Even though the latter had a francophone Canada focus, it had a similar challenge to that discussed by Heller in the relative role of English in the transformation process. The language of dissemination was English but this was most probably because the official language of the source nations of the original e-documents was English. However, the discussions around the subject, judging by media coverage around the world, have taken place in many more languages in different countries.

The second event, as if to confirm the arrival of the post-nation era and the role of the internet in its mapping, the e-G8 Forum, took place on 24–25 May 2011, preceding the conventional G8 Summit (26–27 May 2011) in Deauville, France. The former was the meeting of the chief executive officers (CEOs) of the world's major global internet players ahead of the conventional G8 meeting of the stewards of the leading economies of the world, which are bound to the notion of nation. The corporations over which the former are governors are global in reach with local constructions and impact. For example, the Google Corporation is a global company with national (local) chapters, such as Google Singapore, Google China and so on. But equally important is the fact that, as legal bodies, each of the CEOs has a declared citizenship in a particular country by whose laws their businesses are primarily bound. But these CEOs also have a supervisory remit over global virtual teams so that in their daily negotiations the borderlands are determined based on specific issues and moments (*cf.* Omoniyi, 2006) and how they concern or affect corporate identity in the physical locations in which the corporation operates.

In this chapter I want to explore the indexing of local and global in language use practices involving English in what I call *e-borderland* contexts. Elsewhere (see Omoniyi, 2004) I have discussed language politics and identity in a conventional borderland. Patricia Hodgson remarks in her foreword to Steven Barnett *et al.*'s (2000: 1) volume *e-britannia: the communications revolution* that 'the *convergence* of telecoms, IT, the internet and broadcast media is creating a communications revolution. It is a revolution every bit as significant for our economy, society and culture as the Industrial Revolution'. She notes the American domination of internet economies and posts the question 'is Europe simply a colonial *outpost* of a new American *imperium*? In an ironic reversal of roles, are we simply a market for AOL/Time Warner or AT&T/TCL, those East India or Hudson Bay companies of the 21st Century?' (emphasis added).

In the BBC's *Handy Guide to the Gurus of Management Programme 7* (http://downloads.bbc.co.uk/worldservice/learningenglish/handy/ohmae.

pdf.), Kenichi Ohmae describes the new Invisible Continent in which globalization operates in consonance with his earlier (1994) notion of a 'borderless world'. The contradiction here is in the semantics of 'continent' and our conventional association with a specific territory until now. According to Ohmae, e-commerce knows no boundaries. But we do know that policies and practices which facilitate its operations are also subject to some nation state laws and these are crafted in specific languages using the framework of specific literacy cultures. Thus we can assume that in the diversity of practices amongst participants in e-commerce and other cyber activities is an implicit awareness of some notion of boundaries and resulting third spaces and the unexplained 'middle'. It is the discursive operationalization of these and what an e-borderland might look like in language use practice that is our focus here. How do outposts and imperia signal the need for a redefinition of spaces of discourse and identity? And more specifically then for this volume,

- How are the constructs of 'the local' and 'the global' realized linguistically?
- How does the construction of local and global cultures relate to hybrid language practices?

Defining the E-Borderland

What is *e-borderland*? The idea of the borderland is a hybrid in the sense that it is a subset of two contiguous states. Thus it derives its integrity from that of the states from which it is constituted. By extrapolation therefore, the integrity of the e-borderland must derive from that of the units constituted by defined spaces, spheres or nuclei of authority in online interactions. This will become clearer as we proceed.

Countries have assigned internet identities conveyed through country domain names, such as '.uk' for the UK, '.es' for Spain and '.de' for Germany. It is within this framework that respective national governments exercise control over virtual space and digital technology operations. For instance, the restrictions that the Chinese government allegedly placed over the operations of Google China do not extend to Google UK. However, there are non-country-specific or what we may call universal domains like .com. Ironically this domain is often associated with institutions territorially based in the US, a point that explains the idea of the imperium of the digital era referred to earlier. But Google.com, the 'universal', may be incapacitated or blocked within a nation's virtual space, in other words rendered inaccessible. This is the paradigm within which countries can take steps to secure virtual territories – meaning all their online transactions.[1] My contention is that any discussion of local and global language practices in the e-borderland must be framed by these structures of control.

I draw our attention to Sibley *et al.*'s (2005: 153) remark concerning the treatment of boundaries by geographers in the mid-20th century as an 'unproblematic aspect of taxonomy'. They note that,

> The inadequacy of such binary classification had already been recognised elsewhere in the social sciences, particularly in social anthropology, where transitional and ambiguous states were seen as one key to understanding other cultures. Questions of liminality, spaces of uncertainty that resist binary classification, have now become an important focus of cultural geography . . .

The creation of new 'borderlands', new zones of contact and hybridity are expected consequences of previously non-existent dynamics of social mixing in which the cultural properties introduced into the mix derive from several traditional cultural quarters. In other words, they are normative rather than unusual or abnormal social processes. Let us proffer a *working* definition for e-borderland. First and foremost, as with all other 'e-' prefixed concepts and activities – e-mail, e-commerce, e-'xyz' – it is a virtual and digital environment that is characterized by 'rapid and disturbing social change where conventional social formations and institutions are being deconstructed' (Hawisher & Selfe, 2000: 279). Following from Omoniyi (2004), an e-borderland may be defined as a zone of contact between contiguous group or community networks in what Ohmae described as the 'New Continent'. It is a social space that is potentially global, imagined inasmuch as it has no identifiable geographic location, in which local individuals, groups and/or institutions with citizenships spread across more than one conventional nation state or territory, constitute a virtual community and, as stakeholders, interact wholly or partially in online networks.

The discourse generated in the groups and communities must reflect a society made up of a variety of codes and dialects of one or more languages, a fact that immediately supports the recent critique of canonical distribution of language speakers based on essentialist conceptualizations of identity. Sociolinguistic scholarship is increasingly looking at language as social practice, which in reality involves repertoires that cannot be accounted for fully within a singular linguistic system, especially in the metropolitan areas. The emergence of metrolingualism (Otsuji & Pennycook, 2010) is indicative of this development.

In relation to the above, the idea of the e-borderland allows us to see the elusiveness and multiple interpretations of local within the constitutive networks. If we take the example of medical data outsourcing between the US and the Philippines, the discourse community (medical professionals) and the business (health care industry) belong to a continuous social *system* that straddles the two countries involved (Omoniyi, 2007). The transactions are perceivable as a *discourse stream* flowing between these countries and segments of the community of practice and arguably constituting a form of e-borderland and the site of language brokering and globalization of genre practices. My purpose is to explore language use practices in an online social network or *discourse community* in an attempt to establish the transformative and hybrid nature of those practices. The transnational and/or global nature of the transactions is bound to entail cross-cultural dimensions.

The epigraphs call our attention to reconfigured social, cultural and economic communities. But the Industrial Revolution is responsible ultimately for the reconfiguration of societies that comprised former colonial empires around the world through the expeditions it engendered and the necessity it created for cheaper sources of raw materials for expanding European industries as well as for new markets for their products. The consequence of reconfiguration was the emergence of new physical boundaries and new borderlands. These had local and global realities and came under two separate regimes of managerial authority; on the one hand, the everyday lived lives of indigenes and, on the other, the international networks. The latter impacted the cultural landscape of the former to varying extents. Arguably, online communities represent a brand of community contact situations established in sociolinguistics with the accompanying possibility of hybridization and hybridity.

Conceptualizing Local and Global in E-Borderlands

Local and global as reference frames are troubled articulations in contemporary scholarship in social and cultural geography. They are spatial delimiters that provide a perspective on inclusion, exclusion, membership, involvement, application and interpretation of norms, practices and values, and international politics and relations. The local has been indexical of immediacy both in time and space, events of the here and now, or those capable of impacting the here and now. They also involve, and impact, a relatively small population and space. In contrast, the global is less (de)limited, relatively distant, more widespread in its sphere of influence or impact. It is metropolitan and arguably it has a contemporary and/or scientific appeal. But these parameters of differentiation are unquestionably problematic or in fact flawed as multidirectional culture flows (*cf.* Pennycook, 2007), performativity, construction and negotiation of membership and identity all indicate the insertion of features of these categories in one another to varying degrees.

Based on the sets of principles above, we can assemble some characteristic features of e-borderlands. They are fluid, momentary, event/incident-determined, individual/group or institution-defined and, perhaps most importantly, anchored to some positions in the conventional world. The first three are interrelated. These features are in a sense captured in what Rosowsky (2011: 11) refers to when he says:

> This is, therefore, not only a theoretical distinction between a modernity view of 'language', or 'nation-state', or 'ethnicity', as intact, integrated, holistic, unitary categories, tightly defined and bonded, and a post-modern view of fluid and flowing sociolinguistic practices and processes enacting identity and performance-constituting selves and relationships, applied to any time or to any place.

This constructionist fluidity propels the spirit behind Creese and Blackledge's (2011: 1206) young people

> . . . using linguistic resources from a wide range of sources including those associated with religious texts, the 'homeland' national heritage, diverse popular cultural forms, coarse, vernacular insults, academic English, non-standard English, and many more. Their complex linguistic repertoires bear the traces of past times and present times, of lives lived locally and globally.

To take print illustrations of the futility of a binarization of local and global engendered by the fluidity that we are describing, I shall mention the appropriation of the TuPac[2] brand in naming *2Pac Store*, the dry goods retailer in Kigogo, Dar es Salaam that is the cover image of Christina Higgins' (2009) book *English as a Local Language*. Also, sports attire, like jerseys with the names of European league footballers or NBA (National Basketball Association) stars inscribed on them worn as oversized t-shirts, a form of light dressing by youths in response to humidity and heat on the streets of Lagos, Nigeria, and elsewhere around the world, exemplify the senselessness of separating local and global into discrete and unrelated categories. It is this realization that scholars have attempted to capture with concepts such as glocalization and transcultural flows that are indexical of hybridity.

Swyngedouw, following Harvey (1996), notes that 'social life is process-based, in a state of perpetual change, transformation and reconfiguration'. He goes on to contend that

> Starting analysis from a given geographical scale, such as the local, region, the national or the global, seems to me, therefore, to be deeply antagonistic to apprehending the world in a dynamic, process-based manner. This has profound implications for the significance of spatial scale. I conceive scalar configurations as the outcome of socio-spatial processes that regulate and organise social power relations. As a geographical construction, scales become arenas around which socio-spatial power choreographies are enacted and performed. (Swyngedouw, 2004: 4)

Thus, sociolinguistic scales (see Blommaert, 2007) which take into consideration the dimensions of space and time and the processes through which we negotiate complex networks of relationships potentially provide a framework for conceptualizing hybridity and constructing local and global realities. Let us turn our attention then to the question of what hybridity is.

Hybridity

In its non-critical sense, hybridity had hitherto been associated with Creole studies in sociolinguistics in the description of contact phenomena among which number various forms of language mixing. Studies have been largely descriptive and researchers have attempted to re-present the nature of the mix. Zuckermann (2009: 41) observes, for instance, that 'whereas most forms of Israeli are Semitic, many of its patterns are European', thus making Israeli a hybrid language of sorts.

However, there is a critical dimension to hybridity in which the consequences of contact such as code-switching and code-mixing are analyzed at an interpretive level. For instance, as a function of globalization, we can view hybridity as part of the process of localization even though local homogeneity is displaced and replaced with global diversity. This is aptly illustrated by Waters' (2001: 228) account of McDonald's announcement of a subsequent plan to set up three new restaurants in Jerusalem that were kosher following the widespread localizing reaction to its first restaurant which was not kosher. Hybridity here lies in the introduction of menus that are not traditionally Jewish but which are prepared with sensitivity to Jewish cultural and religious kosher practices. In this latter sense, we have invoked the treatment of hybridity in cultural studies for adaptation in a paradigm befitting critical sociolinguistics.

Stuart Hall (2003), in claiming that it was possible to rethink the positioning and repositioning of Caribbean cultural identities, borrowed Aimé Césaire and Léopold Senghor's metaphor *Présence Africaine, Présence Européene* in creating his *'Présence Américaine'*. He described the latter as the New World, the 'juncture-point where the many cultural tributaries meet' (Hall, 2003: 234). The New World of Hall's theorization has transformed from the territorial to the virtual. The notion of boundary is accommodated in the latter, so that with the transformation and shift to the virtual environment the boundary lines are constituted into the spine of an e-borderland. This is a Third Space (*cf.* Bhabha, 1994) marked by the mixed practices that are neither of one nor of the other community per se on both sides of the divide.

According to the cultural theorist Homi Bhabha, hybridity represents the 'in-between'. He notes that when the natives make intercultural, hybrid demands such as the clamor for an 'Indianized Gospel' they are 'both challenging the boundaries of discourse and subtly changing its terms by setting up another specifically colonial space of the negotiations of cultural authority' (1994: 119). By way of analogy, the e-borderland is an example of what we may call the post-national space of the negotiation of cultural authority. I shall turn next to a discussion of English in the new space.

E-Borderlands and the English Language

When participants in a communicative event are invariably multiply located and interconnected in their historical bodies (Blommaert & Huang, 2009; Scollon, 2001), the spaces encountered in the trajectories to the moments of the interactional encounters are strewn with virtual boundaries, some of which are interpolations of physical boundaries of nation states which define the stakeholders. The entire body of scholarship on English as a lingua franca (ELF) and English as an international language (EIL) is located in that context (see Jenkins, 2002 and Seidlhofer, 2003). Some of my data emanate from a BBC2 documentary, *Welcome to Lagos*, which was broadcast in three parts on 15, 22 and 29 April 2010 (http://www.bbc.co.uk/programmes/b00s3vdm/episodes/guide, accessed 8 October 2011). Although the BBC World Service has a more or less global audience, the latter are delimited by proficiency in English. In other words, those who watch the BBC are people who are competent in the language and can follow the discourse of the programs aired. One is aware of the additional opportunities of program spread made possible by subtitling, but I shall exclude this category because they constitute passive rather than active users of the English language. In other words, my focus is on those who watch a program, process it in all its ramifications and then generate feedback on a forum in the medium of English.

Pluricentrism as an ideology is the idea that global appropriation of English has occurred and that recognized varieties of English have emerged around the world which are not subordinate forms to native speaker varieties of the language. For us in this discussion, the situation is made slightly more complex because such discrete units are problematic, first because of the enduring debate about what constitutes a language or variety of a language. Second, it is indeed a luxury if we consider the potentially open-border nature of online discussion fora. In the specific instance, we found amongst the 289 comments on the *Welcome to Lagos* program a mix of varieties ranging from British Standard English, Non-standard British English, Nigerian Standard English, Nigerian Pidgin and Non-standard Nigerian English. There is a further category I shall describe as 'Others' which contains elements that do not belong to the identified varietal categories. The e-borderland accommodates all.

In effect, the e-borderland is much less determinate than the conventional physical borderland, but an equally fertile ground for hybridity. Today, the shift from nationality and ethnicity to communities such as internet discussion forums has made the latter a legitimate site for challenging the status quo by promoting fluid hybrid language forms. Hybridity is arguably a strategy of creative and resistive divergence from the essentialism of an institutionally recognized International English. These forums may be said to constitute zones of continuity or confluence of linguistic flows (Alim *et al.*, 2009; Omoniyi, 2007; Pennycook, 2007), an e-borderland marked by hybridity and multiple language regimes and scales (Blommaert, 2007). I shall explore interactions in a selection of cyber-based communities whose terrestrial extraction fall under Kachru's Outer Circle or their diaspora and argue that these communities constitute e-borderlands in which the language varieties in use represent co-constructions of the senders and recipients. For instance, in email frauds the senders determine the destinations of their fraud mail and the recipients determine the integrity of such mails. The recipients also include not only the specified mailbox owner but also the institutional representatives to whom such cases may be reported.

The Data

My discussion is based on a mini-corpus comprising three illustrative data sets extracted from YouTube and the accompanying commentary/

discussion forums. The first consisted of media data from online publications on the WikiLeaks affair that I referred to in my introduction. My interest lies in the manner in which virtual locations and resources are negotiated and deployed by different stakeholders such as nation state governments, pressure groups and individuals. The second data set consisted of 8990 comments (as of 17 March 2012) in response to the African Remix version of Chris and T-Pain's *Kiss Kiss* music video produced by Naija Boyz Radio (http://www.youtube.com/watch?v=dLfT5uwkFxE, accessed 13 March 2012). The video had attracted about 4.8 million viewings. The number of hits may not necessarily translate into full-blown viewing, but it certainly indicates some degree of popularity. The centrality of identity is flagged up by the fact that the dominant subject of the commentaries is identity – the nationality and race of the lead female actor. Both of these variables are significant in traditional identity scholarship. The fact then that we have a prolonged online debate on whether an actor is Ethiopian or Somali or just black and African arguably says something about uncertainty in online communities and identity ascription. What is interesting here is the recourse to the traditional and more conventional variables of nationality and ethnicity even though this is an e-interaction, that is, an online interaction. The third data set is similar to the second and consists of 310 comments (as of 11 March 2011) in response to the BBC2 documentary *Welcome to Lagos*, broadcast as a three-part series on 15, 22 and 29 April 2010 respectively. This video had over 8000 hits (http://www.bbc.co.uk/programmes/b00s3bmx).

I have chosen these three data sets particularly because of their association with established global cultural nexuses or points of reference, the UK and the US.

Constructing the Local

Locality may be constructed in a variety of ways in the e-borderland. One way is by reference to specific actors and actions associated with pre-existing spatio-temporal values in the conventional society. Our analysis must incorporate both form and content. By form I mean the language and by content I refer to the message encoded. For instance, in the media coverage of WikiLeak revelations and their repercussions, we find references to stakeholders – global, institutional and individual bodies – in real-time locations. The latter are constructed as local by implicitly marking their e-borderland status through the involvement of at least two nations, as we find in this extract from *The Guardian* Online (http://www.guardian.co.uk/media/2011/sep/15/wikileaks-named-ethiopian-reporter-flees). Joel Simon, the New York-based Committee to Protect Journalists' (CPJ) executive director, said:

> The threat we sought to avert through redactions of initial WikiLeaks cables has now become real. A citation in one of these cables can easily provide repressive governments with the perfect opportunity to persecute or punish journalists and activists.
>
> WikiLeaks must take responsibility for its actions and do whatever it can to reduce the risk to journalists named in its cables. It must put in place systems to ensure that such disclosures do not reoccur.

In the excerpt above, 'Joel Simon', 'New York', 'CPJ', 'WikiLeaks', 'repressive governments', 'journalists' and 'activists' represent the bodies. They are discursively constructed as local within an operational sphere that comprises numerous networks and layers of relationships monitored and impacted by and from multiple cultural and political centers. For instance, China, is described below as a 'promising place to look' as a reference to the government of the Peoples' Republic of China. In the next extract, the operational sphere of the institutional body WikiLeaks is specified as 'the web' (space) in relation to a specific time 'last month'. Arguably, the web is opaque both as a location and as an agent, but the assignment of time to the action by WikiLeaks bestows concreteness and helps to anchor the former to a specific community on the web:

> WikiLeaks put the cables on the web last month with evident relish, and ever since I have been wondering who would be its first incontrovertible victim. China appeared a promising place to look. The authorities and pro-regime newspapers are going through the names of hundreds of dissidents and activists from ethnic minorities. To date, there have been no arrests, although in China, as elsewhere, the chilling effect WikiLeaks has spread has caused critics of the communists to bite their tongues.

If the bodies and their actions localize, ironically they also hold the clue to hybrid identities. WikiLeaks and WikiLeaks.org are more or less one and the same entity; a site, a media organization, a watchdog, and so on. The extract below goes one step further to suggest that Julian Assange, the WikiLeaks CEO, and the institution he heads are one legal body. This is what facilitates the swing from the global and institutional above to the very individual and personal that we observe in the excerpt below from Nick Cohen's article

'The Treachery of Julian Assange' which was originally published in *The Observer* (18 September 2011; http://www.guardian.co.uk/commentisfree/2011/sep/18/julian-assange-wikileaks-nick-cohen?INTCMP=SRCH):

> Assange represents a new breed, which technology has enabled: the nark as show-off. The web made Assange famous. It allows him to monitor his celebrity – I am told that even the smallest blogpost about him rarely escapes his attention. When he sees that the audience is tiring, the web provides him with the means to publish new secrets and generate new headlines. Under the cover of holding power to account, Assange can revel in the power the web gives to put lives in danger and ensure he can be what he always wanted: the centre of attention.

Perhaps more than all other levels, the individual level is where the local is most glaringly identifiable. Hence, the eventual arrest of Julian Assange in London on a European warrant at the instigation of Sweden for charges of sexual assault and rape allegedly committed in August 2010 are a string of localized activities involving a variety of social and political actors (stakeholders) including national and global institutions such as the US State Department and Interpol.

In the transcript of Naija Boyz Radio, the opening of the YouTube video (http://www.youtube.com/watch?v = dLfT5uwkFxE, accessed 9 January 2011) contains form and content markers which help us to locate the actors and actions culturally:

Extract 1

> Yo, this is Naija Boyz Radio live with your boys O and Teju xxx inaudible
> Ah we love African music
> Listen we get this one caller line 1, caller wetin be da problem?
>
> I don't have a problem man, it's all you being Nigerians,
> if you're not doing 419 scams, you're??? with other people's music???
> Honestly, it's bad for Africa

By doing the elicitation in Nigerian Pidgin, the audience for which the text is designed (Bell, 1984) is identifiable as a particular demographic: informal and Nigerian. Arguably, that choice is also potentially exclusionary because additional effort, constructed by the language choice, is required in order for outsiders to access the form. The interesting point though is that the message is not wholly in Nigerian Pidgin, so it may be argued that the actors may not have intended total exclusion but that through their choice of a hybrid form they open up participation and increase their audience size. Since this is a telephone conversation, both parts of the interaction need to be looked at to see what their co-occurrence suggests. In the above extract, the caller speaks with a distinctly American accent, sets up boundaries between him and 'all you being Nigerians', and evaluates what they do as 'bad for Africa'. The program is thus constituted into an e-borderland in facilitating the meeting of the different groups identified. These claims are reinforced in Extract 2.

Extract 2

You're so fine fine fine fine
You think if you're not?
I go waste my time time time time
No do shakara/gloss: don't intimidate/grandstand
I no get time for wahala/gloss: I don't have time to waste
You're de brown sugar for my gari aka cassava

Yeah
I get different accent
Yeah
I no be current
Yeah
But if you want
I can make it less apparent (affected)
It's easy, believe me
I'm a Naija boy

Nigerian Pidgin is evident in the strings – 'No do shakara/I no get time for wahala/You're de brown sugar for my gari aka cassava' (aka: also known as). Language choice is used for negotiation as we find in the revelation that the Naija boy has 'different accents' and is capable of making his Nigerianness less apparent. In other words, he can easily affect his speech and consequently blur the boundary between his identity options.

Hybridity takes another form in Extract 3, taken from the *Welcome to Lagos* documentary transcript, a different source from Extracts 1 and 2. It is different from an individual's mixed language choice because they have a multilingual repertoire. I refer to the identification of a chunk of discourse such as the follow-up commentary to online news stories as our unit of analysis.

Extract 3

> misssherryta
> 2 weeks ago 2
>
> @vocalslender Abeg, Oga Slender.... You see as God has blessed you! Thank and Praise him, also, please help that guy you had a fight with... go and pray with the family. And dont forget your ppl at the dump....i Prayed for you then...and Im still praying for you...BEST OF LUCK!!!

In this extract, switching between Nigerian Pidgin and Standard Nigerian English as a discursive practice imposes certain modes of interpretation on the text. 'Abeg, Oga Slender' may be glossed as the nominative, 'please, Mr. Slender' or 'I beg you Boss Slender'. In the second sense, it conveys deference in the word 'Oga', which means boss. The commentary invokes the sense of an in-group that includes the protagonist in the phrase 'your ppl' (your people). The mixing of varieties is extended to traditions of writing as we find in some of the texts containing Nigerian Pidgin spellings mixed with Black British English forms like 'broda' or 'brudda' versus 'bruv' for brother with reference to the hero of the BBC2 documentary *Welcome to Lagos*, Vocal Slender/Slenda.

Also from the same data transcript, the references to Vocal Slender, the dump, BBC, Lagos, and so on, construct and locate several local and international audiences of the program. Consider Extract 4 (http://www.nigeriafilms.com/news/7819/22/vocal-slender-was-used-by-cokobar-music-festival-p.html):

Extract 4

> Vocal Slender was added to the line up of acts for the CokoBar Music Festival with the publicity for the event built round his presence.

The phrase, 'the line up of acts' implicitly refers to a specific number of artists and the CokoBar Music Festival is a specific cultural event that is tagged based on reference to the location. The construction of Vocal Slender's subjectivity at the core of the event is also a strategy of localization. The creation of heroes by the media who then become rallying points or foci of local life and emergent social narratives illustrates the potential subjects of entextualization; the reinserted and re-narrativized subjects.

Similarly, in Extract 5 from the WikiLeaks official website (http://wikileaks.org/About.html), the nominalizations 'Pentagon Papers' and 'the US Supreme Court' have localized subjectivities capable of being tracked to particular locations where they are recognized and reified and can thus be contrasted with say 'conference papers' and 'UK courts'.

Extract 5

> Scrutiny requires information. Historically, information has been costly in terms of human life, human rights and economics. As a result of technical advances particularly the internet and cryptography – the risks of conveying important information can be lowered. In its landmark ruling on the Pentagon Papers, the US Supreme Court ruled that 'only a free and unrestrained press can effectively expose deception in government'. We agree.
>
> We believe that it is not only the people of one country that keep their own government honest, but also the people of other countries who are watching that government through the media.

The fact that the online media opens up national governments to transnational scrutiny in online forums arguably relocates governance, its evaluation and global politics to the e-borderland where authority and control are nowhere as regulated as in the conventional nation states. The case of Julian Assange, who was eventually arrested in Britain for rape, a crime he allegedly committed in Sweden, illustrates this point. The online publisher guardian.co.uk at 21.30 GMT (Greenwich Mean Time) on Saturday 11 December 2010 (http://www.guardian.co.uk/media/2010/dec/11/wikileaks-backlash-cyber-war) carried the headline

WikiLeaks backlash: The first global cyber war has begun, claim hackers

As Julian Assange is held in solitary confinement at Wandsworth prison, the anonymous community of hacktivists takes to the cyber battlefields.

The attribution for the story showed it was the result of an international collaborative effort between Mark Townsend and Paul Harris in New York, Alex Duval Smith in Johannesburg and Dan Sabbagh and Josh Halliday at guardian.co.uk. This and the fact that Assange's arrest took place in the legal jurisdiction of the British nation state based on UK provisions for extraditions under international cooperation, represent the global dimensions of the incident. But implicit in that are the local dimensions too – specific conventional spatial locations policed by known legal and judicial institutions and actors who are juridical subjects. The online version also included an 'article history' which indicated that a 'version appeared on p. 23 of the Main section section of the Observer on Sunday 12 December 2010'.

The next instance I want to mention is the metaphoric extension of kinship to an addressee in order to establish closeness or in fact oneness. The following are instances of such extension from the *Welcome to Lagos* transcript that convey this idea.

Extract 6

Eh Slenda! doing up big tingz broda! Keep it up son

Extract 7

bendj89
1 week ago
Watch the documentary…am very glad you made it..
Hard work & Determination is the answer to the future…
Are you still working at the dump mate?
I am gonna be playing your song in the Clubs.
Big up Respect
DJ Ben (from London, Leicester Square)

Extract 8

apanhwer
2 months ago
I'm a simple girl from Africa/African joy, the kind of girl/you bring home to your mum

Extract 9

januarythird
1 week ago
Nuff respect to ma naija brudda.
From the slums to the big stage in ma hometown London..
Crnt wait to see u man….
U chased ur dream and have succeeded in catching it

In Extracts 6, 7, 8 and 9 we find references to broda/brudda (brother), son, mate, home and your mum, all of which mark forms of close social relationships. This kind of extension of kinship is traditionally non-Western.

However, 'mate' as an address term and 'Big up Respect' are drawn from London's informal English repertoire and thus mark the hybrid nature of urban talk.

Extract 10

akinslarry
1 week ago
you are the man oooo, we are expecting jo.... owo ti yapa man

This is a response to Black British 'Who de man?' in the assertion of masculinity, rendered in Nigerian Pidgin and complemented by the code-mixed sentence 'We are hopeful jo/please.' This Yoruba-borrowing urban discourse marker has been de-ethicized. Urban street talk is definitely Third Space and involves some negotiations between sociocultural systems and language use practices. The Yoruba borrowing 'jo' (please) followed by the title of Slender's song is used ambiguously as an assertion of the presumed fact that his wealth is established. 'Man' functions in a similar way to man/men in African American urban street language use practice.

Constructing the Global

The global is unhinged and requires the introduction of a specific context for its interpretation. As a reference, it has a more universal scope. In the analysis of discursive practices, that which is not said assumes equal significance to that which is said. If we take the events presented in this chapter, the casualties are verifiably local but the discourses and consequences they have generated have been global. In the BBC program, the local details are glossed over with the effect that the local languages in which they are conducted are unmentioned. In the online forums, composition of the membership plays a significant role in defining the media.

The global is multilayered and complex and so too the language dimensions of it, beyond what may be reckoned by simple reference to individual languages. The trajectories of certain discourses may entail language practices that may in fact no longer be obvious. Let us consider the next examples of these also from the *Welcome to Lagos* transcript.

Extract 11

oniazuma5
3 weeks ago

> All African people should move to my country, Japan. They should replace all the Chinese, Koreans, and other Asians that come to work here. Africans are so much better than asians! We love Africans! Africans should immigrate here and intermarry and become Japanese! I'm going to buy your CD!

In Oniazuma5's comment in Extract 11, a universal or global premise is established via a racial comparison and proposition that are both arguably locatable within a historical paradigm. The replacement recommended is informed by histories of Japan's engagement with China, Korea and other Asian countries. Such engagement explains the status of the Japanese in post-war Korea for example, and partially constitutes the context into which Global English is inserted in the country today. The proposition in the commentary is concluded with a commissive and localizer in which the commentator promises 'I'm going to buy your CD'.

However, in Extract 12, which is itself a response to the above comment, the commentator confines their comment to the global by issuing an implicit criticism of the historical paradigm borne out by the use of the cohesive anaphora 'that', time allocator (400 years ago) and event (slavery).

Extract 12

> fish666sublime
> 3 weeks ago
> the british already did that 400 years ago, it's called slavery!

Looking at both Extracts 11 and 12 what comes across is that the BBC documentary which served as the trigger for the online commentaries in its global reach creates an e-borderland that facilitates the discussion of global politics and the articulation of humanity and the human experience as an extensive and continuous reality. There is an implicit separator in the nominal 'the british' [sic], which also establishes cohesion with the references to Chinese and Koreans in the preceding commentary. Our link to hybridity is in the proposition to 'immigrate here and intermarry' in Extract 11, one that is equally undermined by the commentator's presumed consequence of the social process of intermarriage, 'become Japanese'; assimilation and homogeneity.

Conclusion

To conclude, it makes sense to return to the two global events I cited at the beginning of this chapter as well as the two questions I posed in my introduction on the linguistic realization of local and global and hybridity. Using the e-borderland framework to discuss the construction of local versus global we realize that it may be a futile exercise to attempt to treat the concepts as though they were completely separate and discrete. In reality, negotiations and constructions are complex and anchored to histories which we may require in order to successfully unravel some contemporary language practices.

In the old continent, actors and spaces of action may have been associated with specific languages, in this case, English; at least the version that we have access to for the purposes of our analysis. The diversity engendered by the internet in the new continent forces a review of our analytical tools. There are no parallel discourse universes around the same events, rather they are all interconnected and therefore, whether implicitly or explicitly, mutually impacting. The application of hybridity theory to this must be done within a broader reconceptualization beyond language choice, to incorporate a variety of media cultures and practices and so on.

Notes

(1) Channel NewsAsia published Singapore's setting up of a National Cyber Security Centre (21 September 2011), accessed 6 May 2012. http://www.channelnewsasia.com/stories/singaporelocalnews/view/1154632/1/.html.

(2) TuPac Shakur is an African American rap legend and actor who was assassinated in 1996 in the East Coast versus West Coast conflict.

References

Alim, H.S., Ibrahim, A. and Pennycook, A. (eds) (2009) *Global Linguistic Flows: Hip Hop Cultures, Youth Identities, and the Politics of Language*. Mahwah, NJ: Erlbaum.

Barnett, S., Bottomly, V., Cave, M. and Graham, A. (2000) *e-britannia: the communications revolution*. Luton: The University of Luton Press.

Bell, A. (1984) Language style as audience design. *Language in Society* 13 (2), 145–204.

Bhabha, H. (1994) *The Location of Culture*. London: Routledge.

Blommaert, J. (2007) Sociolinguistic scales. *Intercultural Pragmatics* 4, 1–19.

Blommaert, J. and Huang, A. (2009) Historical bodies and historical space. *Journal of Applied Linguistics* 6 (3), 267–282.

Creese, A. and Blackledge, A. (2011) Separate and flexible bilingualism in complementary schools: Multiple language practices in interrelationship. *Journal of Pragmatics* 43 (5), 1196–1208.

Hall, S. (2003) Cultural identity and diaspora. In J. Evans and A.M. Braziel (eds) *Theorising Diaspora: A Reader* (pp. 233–246). Oxford: Wiley-Blackwell.

Harvey, D. (1996) *Justice, Nature and the Geography of Difference*. Oxford: Blackwell.

Hawisher, G.E. and Selfe, C.L. (2000) Conclusion: Inventing postmodern identities: Hybrid and transgressive literacy practices on the web. In G.E. Hawisher and C.L. Selfe (eds) *Global Literacies and the World-Wide Web* (pp. 277–289). London: Routledge.

Heller, M. (2011) *Paths to Post-Nationalism: A Critical Ethnography of Language and Identity*. Oxford: Oxford University Press.
Higgins, C. (2009) *English as a Local Language: Postcolonial Identities and Multilingual Practices*. Bristol: Multilingual Matters.
Interrogate the Internet Group (1996) Contradictions in cyberspace: Collective response. In R. Shields (ed.) *Cultures of Internet: Virtual Spaces, Real Histories, Living Bodies* (pp. 125–132). London: Sage.
Jenkins, J. (2002) A sociolinguistically based, empirically researched pronunciation syllabus for English as an international language. *Applied Linguistics* 23 (1), 83–103.
Koutsogiannis, D. and Mitsikopoulou, B. (2007) Greeklish and Greekness: Trends and discourses of 'glocalness'. In B. Danet and S. Herring (eds) *The Multilingual Internet: Language, Culture and Communication Online* (pp. 142–160). Oxford: Oxford University Press.
Ohmae, K. (1994) *The Borderless World: Power and Strategy in the Interlinked Economy*. London and New York: Harper & Row.
Omoniyi, T. (2004) *The Sociolinguistics of Borderlands: One People, Two Nations*. Trenton: AWP.
Omoniyi, T. (2006) Hierarchy of identities. In T. Omoniyi and G. White (eds) *Sociolinguistics of Identity* (pp. 11–31). London: Continuum Books.
Omoniyi, T. (2007) Outsourcing and migrational anxieties in discourse perspectives. In S. Gupta and T. Omoniyi (eds) *Cultures of Economic Migration: International Perspectives* (pp. 37–51). London: Ashgate.
Otsuji, E. and Pennycook, A. (2010) Metrolingualism: Fixity, fluidity and language in flux. *International Journal of Multilingualism* 7 (3), 240–254.
Pennycook, A. (2007) *Global Englishes and Transcultural Flows*. London and New York: Routledge.
Rosowsky, A. (2011) Performance and flow: The religious classical in translocal and transnational linguistic repertoires. Unpublished manuscript.
Scollon, R. (2001) *Mediated Discourse Analysis: The Nexus of Practice*. London: Routledge.
Seidlhofer, B. (2003) Closing a conceptual gap in English as a lingua franca. *International Journal of Applied Linguistics* 11 (2), 133–158.
Sibley, D., Atkinson, D. and Jackson, P. (eds) (2005) *Cultural Geography: A Critical Dictionary of Key Ideas*. London: I.B. Tauris, accessed 9 July 2011. http://site.ebrary.com/lib/roehampton/Doc?id = 10132965&ppg = 171.
Swyngedouw, E. (2004) Globalisation or 'glocalisation'? Networks, territories and rescaling. *Cambridge Review of International Affairs* 17 (1), 25–48.
Waters, M. (2001) *Globalization* (2nd edn). London and New York: Routledge.
Zuckermann, G. (2009) Hybridity versus revivability: Multiple causation, forms and patterns. *Journal of Language Contact – VARIA 2*, accessed 27 November 2010. http://www.jlc-journal.org.

13 Facebook, Linguistic Identity and Hybridity in Singapore

Vincent B.Y. Ooi and Peter K.W. Tan

Introduction and Theoretical Overview

Arguably similar to the term 'postcolonial studies' (Talib 2012), 'hybridity' has a somewhat 'unexplained aura'. While applied linguists will take the term to involve primarily code-mixing/switching, cultural theorists such as Hutnyk (2005: 79) see hybridity as 'descriptively' and 'realistically' used nowadays to mean 'cultural mixture'. For Hutnyk, hybridity is 'an evocative term for the formation of identity' among the new migrants in their assimilation and integration in the new society. In this chapter, we take the term to involve language choices that inform such 'cultural mixture' and projections of (personal) identity. The juxtaposition of 'Facebook', 'linguistic identity' and 'hybridity' as the title of this chapter is exemplified by the case of Singapore, which is a prime example of this 'cultural mixture' in which the early diaspora of migrants mingled and formed an evolving national and linguistic identity through English. Thus, the current residents of Singapore who comprise Chinese, Malays, Indians, Eurasians, Peranakans ('Straits-born') and other ethnicities are linked together culturally by English, which has evolved in the society to both blend and contrast local and international norms and cultures.

Where does Facebook come in then? As the largest social media/networking platform of over 960 million users at the time of writing, Facebook represents the re-formulation of the concept of 'speech community' online. Facebook at once expresses hybridity at its best: friendships can be formed with so many different permutations of 'Facebook friends' in a globalized world. Although first developed in the US for primarily English-speaking users, Facebook has grown enormously to cater to diverse cultures and languages (including German, Turkish, Tagalog, Vietnamese and Arabic). The combinations of friends can therefore be dazzling, as the platform allows the Facebook user to have friends from various ages (from 13-year-olds upwards), genders, ethnicities, and from all parts of the world (excluding, say, China, which currently bans this platform). In the case of English, the Facebook user who has friends from all over the world will probably encounter not only global English but also different varieties of English at play every day.

In this chapter we seek to understand hybridity better by examining various 'styles' of online discourse that reify aspects of the English used in the multilingual/cultural setting of Singapore. By 'styles', we refer to Coupland's (2007) characterization of the ways in which speakers use the resource of language variation to make meaning in social encounters. Adapting Coupland, this 'meaning-making' resource can include the following: (1) the use of Standard English as a globalized discourse; (2) computer-mediated communication as a hybrid discourse and (3) Singapore(an) English as localized and hybrid discourse.

Teubert (2010: 2) tells us that the 'reality that counts is the reality we find constructed in the discourse, in this entirety of texts that have been exchanged and shared between the people who make up society'. While this may well be the case, it is certainly true that the construction of reality has, following the well-known linguist Kenneth Pike, both emic (insider's) and etic (outsider's) perspectives. As analysts, our perspectives are necessarily etic in nature, but if we participate in the discourse as an insider or have an intimate knowledge of the discourse practices in that community we have a richer characterization and understanding of what that discourse entails. Therefore, of all the types of discourse found within the Facebook pages available to a typical user, this chapter will be limited to the 'Comments' section which is discoursal in terms of a group of friends (that can include the Facebook user) responding to a topic initiated by that Facebook user.

In analyzing the discourse, we will see how speakers project different social identities and create different social relationships through their style choices. Coupland (2007) sees style as the wide range of strategic actions and performances that speakers engage in, to construct themselves and their social lives. He posits a series of identity contextualization processes that are originally used for understanding speech within a conventional community/society and which we will adapt for our understanding of the 'new' community that Facebook engenders. Coupland's 'Identity Contextualization Processes' model (ICP) of person-centered stylistic constructions focuses on the ways in which individual speakers perform 'acts of identity' whose formations are evocative of hybridity (Hutnyk, 2005: 79). At the same time, these speakers collectively operate within their linguistic repertoires that range from highly localized norms to internationally acceptable ones. We therefore propose the utilization of Ooi's (2001a, 2001b) Concentric Circles Model (CCM) that not only characterizes the range of linguistic repertoires in Singapore(an) English but also relates the variety to global norms (operationally taken to mean Standard British/American English). When combined, the ICP-CCM model will prove to be beneficial to the analysis of the Facebook data in this chapter.

Networked Sociality and (Linguistic) Hybridity

This new online community that embraces the various permutations of 'friends' from the various places that each Facebook user belongs may arguably be better described as a 'networked sociality' (Wittel, 2001; Papacharissi & Yuan, 2011). We will first use this notion in order to frame our discussion in terms of the overarching community space on the internet among groups of users of English (primarily) from Singapore.

Wittel's (2001) notion of 'network sociality' which, in turn, is adapted from Castells' (2000) 'network society', is based on the observation that there is a tendency in society to build on networks and foster social bonds, instead of relying on the more permanent notion of 'community'. Building on Wittel, Papacharissi and Yuan (2011: 97) see 'networked sociality' (with an '-ed') as a 'social expression of liquid modernity', in which 'social relations are not narrational but informational ... fleeting and transient, yet iterative ... of ephemeral but intense encounters ... and characterized by a combination of work and play'. As a 'contrast' to the traditional notion of 'community', networked sociality 'describes emerging social uses of technology that are a combination of "sociability" and "experimentation"' (Papacharissi & Yuan, 2011: 97).

In relation to 'networked sociality', Papacharassi and Yuan postulate that English, as the dominant language of the internet, has to accommodate this replacement for the traditional understanding of community by developing a 'hybrid vernacular', one that has to reconcile the following dichotomies that encourage the development of this vernacular 'transculturally': individual vs social, public vs private, and east vs west (Papacharissi & Yuan, 2011: 92). Their observations on the hybrid vernacular underpinning the notion of networked sociality may be reformulated in another manner. In Kraidy's (2002) appropriate explication of the term, hybridity is a 'master trope' used in a variety of discourses which range from postcolonial theory to cultural globalization. While we are cognizant of the attendant debates regarding the potential vacuity of the term because 'all cultures are (essentially) hybrid', and taking into account Derrida's well-known comment of it being an 'undecidable' (see Kraidy, 2002: 332), hybridity is still a useful concept that shows the mix of two (or more) recognizably discrete systems and the disturbance in those systems to form a third that not only inherits the characteristics of the original two systems but demonstrably shows its own inherent distinctive characteristics. Operationalizing this in language, this third system is evinced by processes such as code-mixing and code-switching but can go beyond them (since code-switching still preserves the discreteness of the two attendant original languages). Let us see how this applies to Singapore(an) English.

Singapore(an) English

As in Ooi (2010), Singapore(an) English (or SgE) may be characterized as a new variety of English (or NVE) such as Philippine English, Indian English and Malaysian English (see, for instance, Lim *et al.*, 2010). Unlike older varieties of English (or OVEs) such as British English, Australian English or US English, NVEs historically emerged primarily through the classroom (rather than the home), unabashedly incorporated the attendant cultures of a multiracial population and complemented the other languages of the country in terms of functions and roles.

SgE very much displays NVE characteristics. According to the 2010 Census of Population (http://www.singstat.gov.sg/pubn/popn/c2010sr1/cop2010sr1.pdf), English is the most frequently spoken language at home for only 32.3% of both residents and citizens alike. Despite this, English is the predominant language of instruction in learning institutions and can be considered the de facto national language (which constitutionally, and so *de jure*, is Malay). English is the leading language of administration, education, public signage and everyday interaction. English is the link language for its 3.77 million residents, which comprise 74.1% Chinese, 13.4% Malay, 9.2% Indians and 3.3% others. Many Singaporeans are bilingual or trilingual, and the linguistic repertoire of a local Chinese resident can include a knowledge of English, Mandarin Chinese and one of the Chinese dialects (typically Hokkien Chinese).

English as a linguistic entity in the country may be divided into three parts: Standard English (which usually means standard British/US English), SgE-H (educated, 'standard' Singaporean English), and SgE-L (Colloquial Singapore English, also popularly known as 'Singlish'). Standard English is the benchmark set in grammar books, dictionaries, classroom texts, official media and print materials. SgE-H may be considered the local H(igh)-variety used and comprises acceptable linguistic expressions and hybrid meaning systems that are a cross between Standard English and a local language or dialect. SgE-L, as the L(ow) variety, is used in more domestic situations and is the popular colloquial variety found in (among others) casual conversations, television humor programs, online personal blogs, chatrooms and discussion forums.

SgE-H includes such terms as *handphone* (or mobile phone), *killer litter* (heavy material thrown from a high-story building that can seriously injure passers-by below) and *airflown* (food that is freshly imported, of high quality, and so must cost more). For many expressions, the influence from a local language or dialect is obvious. An example is *sleep late.* In OVEs a song title such as *I like to sleep late in the morning* makes it clear that one gets up late in the morning; in SgE-H it would be much more common to refer to staying up late at night. Thus, a sentence such as *I like to sleep late at 3am* would have its corresponding meaning in either Malay (*'tidur lewat'*) or Chinese (*'wǎn shuì'*).

SgE-L terms include *kiasu* (from Hokkien, to mean 'afraid to lose out'), *cut* (verb) [=to overtake: *His car cut mine*] and *blur* (adj) [=to describe a person as dazed]. SgE-L is mainly influenced by Mandarin, Cantonese or Hokkien Chinese and Malay grammar structures and words. SgE-L is popularly characterized by discourse particles such as *lah, leh, lor* and *meh* that occur at the end of a sentence; their various intonations express different attitudinal meanings on the part of the speaker. For instance, the expression *Referee kayu meh*? contains the Malay term *'kayu'* (for 'wood') which metaphorically means 'block-headed/dim-witted' and the Chinese dialect particle *meh* (with a rising intonation) which is found only in questions to indicate surprise or skepticism. Thus the sentence loosely translates as follows: 'I can't believe that the referee is as stupid/dim-witted as you say he is'. In online discourse, the computer keyboard also mediates discourse (see Ooi, 2009) to reformulate Singlish in terms of such re-spellings as *lols, lolx, lolz, liaoz, mehs*, and so on.

There is the common view (see Lim *et al.*, 2010; Alsagoff, 2010a, 2010b) that Standard English represents a globalized and discrete system which does not get the 'hybridity' label, whereas SgE-H and SgE-L would be regarded as hybrid systems. Adapting Pakir (2009: 85), 'Singapore offers an example of a (tropical) country where spontaneous daily interaction among speakers of several languages over a long period of time has led to (various linguistic) innovation processes' and semantic shifts that differ from the conventional Western discourses that we tend to associate Standard English with. Thus, 'while Australians might find the description of "windy" for homes as a negative feature in the (real estate) "for sale" advertisements, Singaporeans consider "windy" as "breezy" and therefore a positive feature' (Pakir, 2009: 96). In a not dissimilar manner, Bruthiaux (2010: 103) calls Singlish (which we have termed SgE-L) a 'localized hybrid' that 'many Singaporeans – including teachers – cheerfully admit adequately meets every one of [their] social and emotional needs'.

The Identity Contextualization Processes – Concentric Circles Model

The literature on language, discourse and identity for conventional socio/ethnolinguistic investigation is rich and varied (for instance Sarangi & Coulthard, 2000; de Fina *et al.*, 2006). In recent years, research on the discourse of online communities has grown alongside the literature for conventional discourse (for instance, Scollon & Scollon, 2004; Stern, 2007; Vie, 2007). As mediated through the keyboard, online communication is in itself a hybrid of conventional speech and writing (for instance Herring, 1996; Ooi, 2009). And, in a multilingual and multicultural country such as Singapore, online English has the added dimension of being a (re-)formulation of its conventional linguistic ecology, that is, Singapore(an) English (see Lim *et al.*, 2010).

There is a growing body of work on Facebook discourse and identity in various contexts. For instance, Sharma (2012) investigates how online social networking has influenced Nepali college youth in their use of English and other semiotic resources to index local and cosmopolitan identities. He finds that these youth use Facebook to 'redefine the role of English in relation to their existing social relationships, innovatively mixing English and Nepali in order to construct their bilingual identities, and embedding English with other texts to recontextualize both local and global media content'. In another country-related context, Seargeant *et al.* (2012) analyse the Facebook wall interactions between one Thai national, known as 'Dream', and her Thai Facebook friends. They find that the participants of these exchanges use a combination of English and Thai language systems towards the 'expression of a distinct group identity'...[and] 'indexing a shared cultural space' (Seargeant *et al.*, 2012: 528). However, it is difficult to identify a direct relationship between the choice of code and the particular aspects of the community's identity that are being indexed.

Besides country-related foci, other studies focus on the effects of in-built Facebook features. Bolander and Locher (2010) examine language use on personal profiles and status updates to identity construction strategies used on Facebook. They find that identity claims tend to be mediated implicitly rather than explicitly, which may be related to the nature of Facebook friendships being pre-established offline. Social and situational factors such as asynchronicity, participant structure and message format are also found to affect their language use. In another study on Facebook status updates, Lee (2011) examines how they are used to mediate online identity. She discovers that genre is not a unitary notion, but is more of 'a hybrid of genre features' of different text types, in which its users fluidly read and compose a variety of multimodal and multimedia material (Lee, 2011: 123). Thus, Lee finds that Facebook users meaningfully and creatively embed their online and offline identities in their status updates (Lee, 2011: 118). Apart from status updates, Facebook comments are also another productive area to study. Pérez-Sabater (2012) analyzes a corpus of Facebook comments posted on official Facebook sites of universities to determine if comment posting on Facebook is conventionalized sufficiently: the Facebook comments show stylistic variations in both form and substance.

The approaches and methods that we have so far sketched for the analysis of (Facebook) discourse tend to be 'manual' in nature, that is, they characterize what we call a 'pen-and-paper' approach in which the human analyst does the bulk (if not all) of the analysis. However, this so-called 'pen-and-paper' approach, in the hands of the right analyst, may be seen as mirroring the workings of language in a probabilistic manner. Ideally, the qualitative approach should be complemented with a quantitative one in which a corpus is gathered and subjected to computational methods of analysis (see Ooi *et al.*, 2007). For the present chapter, however, we would sketch a largely qualitative model that adapts Coupland (2007) and Ooi (2001a, 2001b). We call this the ICP–CCM approach and outline the reasons.

Analyzing styles in conventional speech and ways of speaking, Coupland (2007: 111–115) seeks to 'introduce more precision into the account of how a projective act of identity engages with personhood', that is, the ways in which people construct identities in social interaction. He argues in favor of the idea of 'community of practice' rather than 'speech community', since what links people sociolinguistically is not so much the idea of structural 'being' but more so social 'doing' (Coupland, 2007: 40). In this regard, 'social doing' is not dissimilar to the idea of networked sociality. Adapting Coupland, certain linguistic forms are preferred over others as 'indexical markers' of social and cultural identification; their frequencies of usage or linguistic 'priming' distinguish members of a 'community of practice' from other groups. For instance, in a Facebook corpus of some 70,000 words collected by a student of ours (Nurulhuda Borhan Said), the terms *text(ing)* and *SMS* occur five and 14 times respectively; there is a zero occurrence of *text messaging* (associated more as the preferred form for the US).

Coupland suggests a few processes of social doing that are adapted here. The first process, *targeting*, involves shaping the persona of a particular participant who is typically the speaker or the listener. For our purposes, the identity of the Facebook (FB) speaker/user is projected or 'targeted' immediately in terms of contextual information on him/her (by friends), the stated profile information (under the 'Info' section), his/her postings and the responses from friends that give an overall view of the FB user. Facebook allows, though, the setting of certain 'privacy' options to layer information to different groups of friends, and one can never be certain of being given the full set of information about the user. In this regard, Coupland (2007: 112) is right to say that 'our personal identities are in many respects collages of different social category characteristics, complete or fragmentary'.

The second process, *framing*, would cover the following salient identity markers: gender, sexuality, age, ethnicity, more/less powerful, and may be constrained by the genre of talk (for example, conversation versus set-piece performance, business talk or informal chat).

The third process, *voicing*, refers to how an FB speaker can 'quote or reconstruct the words of other people, and in so doing they can inflect those source voices in various ways, giving them particular identity traits and qualities' (Coupland, 2007: 114).

The fourth process, *keying/loading*, relates to whether the tone/voicing is mocking, serious, bantering, playful, malicious, ironic or teasing. Keying allows us to 'infer – sometimes more guesswork than inference – a speaker's communicative motivation' (Coupland, 2007: 114). In the banter genre, for instance, there is often the playful projection of identities directed at recipients. In relation to the third process, voicings can be 'playful or malicious, acts of teasing or put-downs' (Coupland, 2007: 114). Coupland also says that irony as a device is a 'quagmire for reading acts of identity, because "as if" identities can wholly subvert the apparent meaning of a projection' (2007: 114). Loading is an extension of keying, and refers to the speaker's investment in an identity being negotiated: in an extreme case, one could appropriate another group's entire code and take possession of that code.

The processes of eliciting linguistic identity in a community such as Singapore tend to mirror the (often) hybrid linguistic choices adopted in the discourse. Consonant with Coupland's overarching term of 'styling' as a synergistic term for these processes, the CCM (Ooi, 2001a, 2001b) can be applied to the Singaporean FB user in order to show another side of the 'styling' that also at once captures the following dimensions that characterize Singapore(an) English discourse: (1) 'standard' (vs 'non-standard'); (2) 'formal' (vs 'informal'); (3) 'spoken' (vs 'written'); (4) loans from the attendant local languages; and (5) semantic shifts from conventional Western discourses (as sketched by Pakir, 2009).

Circle 1 represents the inner circle that comprises 'core/standard English' linguistic expressions that may or may not be traditionally Germanic/French/Latin in origin. Non-Anglo expressions that are codified and standardized in dictionaries nowadays include *kungfu*, *sari* and *lychee*. Circle 1 items are 'unmarked' and deemed acceptable in international settings.

Circle 2 (SgE-H) is the next outer circle containing linguistic expressions from English that are acceptable for a variety of local formal situations (including writing in the classroom), but which go beyond their conventional understanding in Western discourse. For instance, *killer litter* is a hybrid of two intriguing and yet unlikely juxtapositions in Western discourse, that is, the seriousness of 'killers' and the social irresponsibility of throwing harmless garbage on the ground. In Singaporean discourse, though, this productive neologism is needed in a densely populated society of high-story buildings. Other examples include *red packet* (money placed in a red/pink envelope and given on auspicious occasions such as Chinese New Year) and *retrench* (as a transitive verb meaning 'lay off'; in both Standard British and American English, this term is codified in dictionaries as an intransitive verb that means 'downsize').

Circle 3 (SgE-H) is the next outer circle containing linguistic expressions that are also acceptable in formal local situations and go beyond their conventional understanding in Western discourse. However, unlike those in Circle 2, the items in this circle include loanwords and expressions from other local languages (principally Chinese and Malay). There are no English equivalents without missing local associations. Examples include *silat* ('Malay kungfu'), *songkok* ('Malay hat'), *laksa* ('a popular curry dish') and *ice kachang* ('a dessert of shaved ice with various flavors and toppings' that can include *kachang*, a Malay word for 'peanuts').

Circle 4 (SgE-L) is the next outer circle of English-derived expressions that are deemed suitable for local colloquial/informal situations only. In this circle, structures from colloquial Chinese or Malay are 'filled by' English words. Thus, the expression *I follow Mother to the market* does not mean that the interlocutor walks behind but instead accompanies the mother. In casual conversations, *blur* is also used as an adjective, instead of 'confused/dazed'.

Circle 5 (Sg E-L) represents the outermost circle of least transparency (to 'core English') in having terms of non-English origin that are primed for local colloquial situations only. *Makan* is the Malay word for 'to eat', *paktor* is the Cantonese Chinese word for 'dating' and *kiasu* is a Hokkien borrowing that means 'afraid to lose out'.

Both Circles 2 and 3 would be primed for use in 'respectable' situations, for example, classroom report, newspaper editorial and broadcast news. However, both Circles 4 and 5 would be primed for colloquial or highly informal situations only (usually speech) and contain terms that are popularly known as 'Singapore Colloquial English' or 'Singlish'.

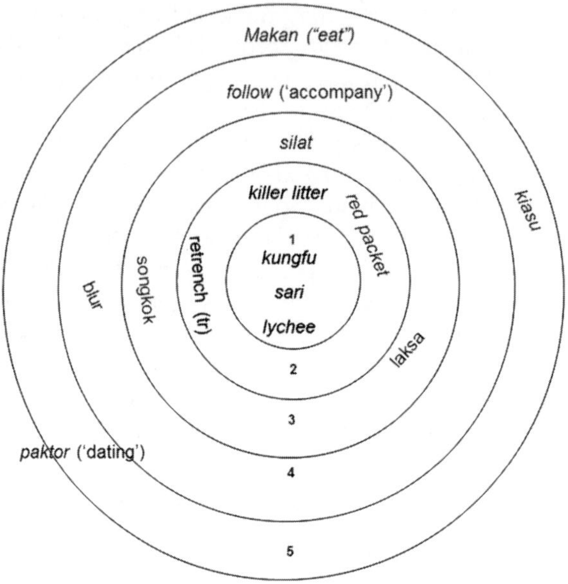

Figure 13.1 Concentric circles of Singaporean English
Source: Adapted from Ooi (2001a, 2001b)

The model has been tested on various local speakers in order to capture the 'stylized' continuum of English use in the minds of Singapore(an) English speakers (see Ooi, 2001a, 2001b). We can diagrammatically represent this model (see Figure 13.1, adapted from Ooi, 2001a, 2001b).

When combined, the ICP-CCM is a model that shows both micro and macro variationist perspectives in a variety of English. Of course, in applying the model, we should also be mindful of the emic/etic distinction (see Headland *et al.*, 1990). Coined first by Pike (1954), these useful terms are still relevant in today's context. An 'emic' description of the discourse can be obtained by the analyst or some insider who is 'in the know' (as it were) about the participants and the event. An 'etic' account of the discourse is done by the analyst or external observer who picks up on the linguistic cues.

Data Examples

Facebook allows the FB user to communicate synchronously (using the 'Chat' feature) or asynchronously. In terms of asynchronous communication, the FB user has a personal 'Wall' to write on and share with friends.

Such postings or 'status messages' are either for personal musings, directed at a specific target/friend, or meant for the wider community of friends (who can range from a few to thousands). If the writing on the Wall, as it were, resonates with a particular group of friends, it gets written comments or gets 'liked' in terms of a thumbs-up. Each posting can range from being as short as a text message (a maximum of 160 characters) but certainly less than a long blog posting: the maximum length is currently 420 characters. In Facebook the number of friends can range from anywhere between 25 and a mind boggling 4000 or so (the latter figure begging the question of how plausible it is to sustain reasonably deep online conversational chats or dinner conversations with such a large number). Instead, the FB user keeps up with the whole range of friends through not only the Comments section but also 'updates' (posted by their friends) that include their everyday likes and dislikes, photos, thoughts on life, and so on.

In the following excerpts we have removed the profile pictures and abbreviated names of users in order in order to maintain privacy and anonymity. Of course, if privacy is not a main concern, the study of Western (globalist) and ethnic Asian (localist) forms of address would certainly constitute an important pragmatic feature (see Alsagoff, 2010a: 117). And, of course, the interaction between profile pictures, video, audio and text would be the subject of multimodality that is generally beyond the remit of this chapter.

The first three excerpts (which, for convenience, have been categorized as Figures 13.2–13.4 because of their length) show a long Comments section by a group of Peranakan (commonly known as 'Baba' or Straits-born) Chinese, of which one is an FB friend (thus, we have a partial emic perspective). While these speakers have been assimilated into the Chinese community, with Chinese names, we can see that they code-mix/code-switch differently from other Chinese speakers.

In Figure 13.2, FB users LL, TK and TS generally use Standard English structures and lexical items. Exceptions include the SgE-H word *Peranakan* ('Straits-born') and the code-switched word *maaf* ('apologies', which is recognizable in both standard Malay and the vernacular Peranakan/Baba Malay). In terms of Coupland's targeting, all three speakers come across as educated and informational speakers of Standard English. FB user TS is listed in her FB page as being born in 1959. It is therefore surprising to find that she uses the spelling *noe* (which teenagers tend to spell 'know'): we may speculate that TS wants to project a younger identity ('keying'/'loading'). This younger identity projection is also seen in the dropping of capitalization (a Facebook convention among younger users) by TS and LL. In terms of framing, all three speakers are mature Chinese women. In terms of CCM notation, these FB users tend to keep to Circles 1, 2 and 3. An example of Circle

LL:	Peranakans who are Christian and worship in Peranakan language are finding fewer and fewer preachers and materials in Peranakan but more Indonesian preachers and materials especially in Singapore. Am I correct in this observation?
TK:	Yes, very few only because most of the younger generation are patois illiterate (no offence). My mum used to attend the service in Pentecost Methodist. Even Rev **ST** could speak Baba Patois. She has the hymnal too. So not only fewer preachers and materials but also fewer members. I think they still have the Peranakan service in Paya Lebar MC on Sat.
CH:	Due to our education system and the emphasis on English and Mandarin, all other "dialects" are hardly spoken or heard. Even Hokkien, the pasar and hawker centre lingua franca, is also dying a natural death with the many mainland Chinese running these stalls…
TA:	Gosh! I didn't even know there is such thing!
TS:	can i add a friend who is a penang baba, now living in singapore?
TS:	i noe above wrong thread – maaf!
LL:	no problem…

Figure 13.2 Excerpt from comments on the topic introduced by Peranakan FB user 'LL'

2 usage is *hawker centre.* Examples of Circle 3 usage include *Peranakan* and *Baba* (that interchangeably refer to 'Straits-born' people). Perhaps the only instances of Circle 4 usage are the deliberate use of *noe* and the lack of capitalization for TS (as contrasted with TA who uses the conventional spelling *know*). For Circle 5 usage, we can see a couple of instances of casual borrowing from (Baba) Malay, that is, *pasar* ('market') and *maaf* ('apologies').

Additional evidence that FB user TS would like to project a younger identity is seen in the use of the computer-mediated marker 'u' (for 'you'). A very different behavior also emerges here. There is a deliberate code-switch/mix to the vernacular such as the Baba Malay phrase *gua suka banyak* ('I like (it) a lot') and the SgE-L term *pai seh* ('embarrassing', borrowed from Hokkien Chinese). For FB user LL, who uses Standard English structures in Figure 13.2, there is also a switch to the lower status and yet more intimate structures of bazaar Malay (*lu eh blog link tahlok ah*?, in which *lu* is the indexical bazaar Malay form of 'you' and *tahlok* is the variant of the standard Malay term *taruh* or 'place'). In addition to Bazaar Malay, Peranakan/Baba Malay borrows both from Hokkien Chinese and standard Malay. So, the phrase *chik choon tak ada kerja* is a combination of Hokkien (*chit chun* = 'now') and standard Malay (*tak ada kerja* = 'no work/not working'). This hybrid structure *chit chun tak ada kerja,* mixed with the lexical item *angst* taken from existential discourse, gives the impression that the process of voicing is taking

TS:	**TK** - u give me ideas to write.. gua suka banyak.
LL:	**TS** , lu eh blog link tahlok ah?
TS:	personal blog, chik choon tak ada kerja, so write for fun, and sometimes out of angst.
LL:	kamsiah chuay chuay, **TS** Woman of Wisdom!
TS:	pai seh!!
HO:	i will also like to attend the peranakan service at PLMC at least once must.

Figure 13.3 Continuation of the comments on the topic in Figure 13.2, with a focus on FB users 'TS' and 'LL'

place: a blend of highly educated and common folk identities. Similarly, the L- form, the Hokkien phrase *kamsiah chuay chuay* ('Thanks very much'), is placed alongside the more formal and H- phrase 'Woman of Wisdom' to create the process of keying, one of bantering. In terms of CCM notation, Circle 5 structures include *gua suka banyak* (in which *gua*, meaning 'I', is highly indexical for bazaar Malay), *tahlok*, and *paiseh* ('embarrassed', from Hokkien). Circle 4 structures include the lack of capitalization, CMC spelling *u* ('you'), and casual English syntax.

As a continuation of this piece of discourse, let us turn to Figure 13.4 which shows the projection of identity by speaker TK. Recall that, in Figure 13.2, FB user TK uses Standard English grammatical structures. Here, she chooses to use a Baba Malay syntactic structure and fills it partially with English words such as *church* and *Pentecost Methodist Church.* Similar to speakers LL and TS, it is very interesting that TK also switches to Baba Malay (for example, *Dulu gua punya church* = literally 'Previously my own church' = 'Previously I attended that church'). The central point to make about all these three speakers is that they deem it *de rigueur* to switch from colloquial or Standard English (deemed the non-hybridized version) to their hybridized version of SgE-L, which at once utilizes aspects of Peranakan

TK:	**WE** - itu church ka Pasir Ris is Pentecost Methodist Church. Used to be smua orang Peranakan. Dulu gua punya church. Lu pi attend lah.
WE:	Oh ya… That's the one. Any idea of service time?
TK:	**WE** , gua pi telephone charik service time for you. Lu mo bawa mak Lu attend ah?

Figure 13.4 Continuation of the comments on the topic in Figure 13.2, with a focus on FB user 'TK'

AN:	Malaysia scored another one!!!!! Nbcb!:@ it's gonna be a draw! Wtfffffff!:@@@
EL:	Nooooo!! GG Singapore!!
AN:	Singapore better winnnnnn!:@@@@
CR:	Singapore 4-3 now, think should be can. 15 mins cnt hold one lead they can go fly kite liao lol
EL:	Suck ah.

Figure 13.5 Status update by FB user 'AN', and comments

Malay, Hokkien Chinese and Bazaar Malay for the purposes of bantering and familiarity. Notice that, in Figure 13.4, FB user WE understands TK's use of Baba Malay but responds in colloquial and Standard English. And, instead of replying in the same manner as speaker WE, speaker TK continues to use a mix of the L-version of Baba Malay (with a smattering of English words) in her final response (that is, *pi* = *pergi* = 'go'; *lu* = 'you'; *charik* = 'find'; *bawa* = 'take'; *mak* = 'mother', all Circle 5 structures in CCM notation).

Let us now turn to Figure 13.5 which shows a status update by FB user AN, a 15-year-old Chinese Singaporean girl, who is commenting on an exciting football match between Malaysia and Singapore. We can only analyze this profile from an etic perspective, since AN is not our FB friend but whose profile can be viewed through our friend's FB.

Speaker AN's projection of identity includes both localized (*Nbcb*) and globalized (*Wtf*) computer-mediated expletives as well as expressive punctuation markers (said to be more typical of online younger female users since they would like to project the 'cuteness' factor). Her male friends EL (a local Indian, also 15 years of age) and CR (a local Eurasian) are less expressive than her in this regard. CR uses the popular SgE-L expression *go fly kite* (transliteration from Hokkien Chinese, meaning 'get lost') with the localized pragmatic marker *liao* (from Hokkien Chinese, meaning 'already'). As a Eurasian, CR does not think twice about using these localist markers next to each other within an utterance that also contains the computer-mediated *lol* (Laugh-Out-Loud) emoticon. A check with the online version of *The Oxford English Dictionary* indicates that *lol* has made it into this supreme authority of the English language; *lol* is therefore globalist in perspective and can be relegated to Circle 1. CR more unusually uses three auxiliary verbs in the expression *should be can*. A google search on this expression from pages from Singapore shows possible local collocates of pragmatic particles (for example, *lah/bah/de luh/mah*) or lexical verbs (for example, *complain*). The type of Singlish, or SgE-L (Circle 4), used in Figure 13.5 is not dissimilar to that used by Chinese speakers in Figure 13.6.

LO:	LOL gary your the best luh. jessie was indirectly solding van just now for facebooking during office hours LOL
CH:	SERIOUS. how jessie know?! omg van are you sad. what did jessie say!
TA:	With please. U know she is not scolding me can. Most prob you la, sit so near still use fb. I use from my iPhone.
	LO: she mentioned 'EVEN IF THOSE USING PHONE FACEBOOK, DO NOT DO IT DURING PRODUCTIVE HOURS.'
LO:	obviously saying you can?! HAHA
CH:	wl van its confirm you lo! even those using iphone. IPHONE LEH. luke ji tao use the com one, so cannot be luke! tsk tsk its YOU la dont deny pls vanessa.
TA:	Yeah right, I'm discreet can? She sit so far as if she can see my phone la. Plus everyone else also using can, I saw many times. Including her.
LO:	haha see even gary say so! van don't deny leh. deny somemore i tmr ask Jessie see this wall :D

Figure 13.6 Asynchronous chat by FB user 'LO' and his friends

Figure 13.6 shows the keying of banter between LO and his friends regarding the boss' disapproval regarding the use of FB in the office. Hybrid syntax (Chinese structures filled in with English words) indicate the preferred shape of SgE-L here. In addition, it gives some evidence of the online re-spelling of Singlish (for example, the pragmatic particle spellings of *luh* for *lah*, and *lo* for *lor*). When interviewed on why he uses this spelling of *luh*, LO says that he follows the convention used by his group of friends: this indicates that within a 'community of practice' such as Singapore, there are in turn sub-communities of practice having their own memes (or preferred social forms). In addition, Figure 13.5 indicates an absence of the -ed marker for past tense forms, and verbs such as *sit* and *say* are uninflected for the singular pronoun. A central feature of this type of Singlish is the influence of predominantly local Chinese or Malay syntax structures filled in with English words, for example, *Sit so near still use fb* (meaning 'Can you not use Facebook when you sit so near (the boss)?'). In CCM notation, Circle 1 will have to include globalist computer-mediated markers such as *omg* ('Oh my God') and *haha*. While we can say that these markers belong to Circle 1 (since, like *lol*, they are also found in *The Oxford English Dictionary*), the use of any computer-mediated marker in the language classroom still scares the living daylights out of the language teacher in the classroom – as do Circle 4 (*Sit so near still use fb*) and Circle 5 (for example, *luh* and *la*) structures here. In addition, a central feature in Figure 13.6 is the use of chunks consisting

ZO:	‘ ahhhhhhhhhhhhhhhhhh. i am such a loser :(
GA:	; no you’re not (:
ZO:	awwwwwwwwwwwwww so sweet :b
GA:	; hahahahahah :D
AB:	Hey babe, how can you call yourself a loser. You’re Awesome to me :B

Figure 13.7 Status update by Malay FB user ‘ZO’, and comments

entirely of upper case that indicate a playful shouting match between the participants.

Teens tend to use the feature of voicing, keying and loading quite a bit in purporting not only to banter but also to vent their frustrations. Figure 13.7 thus shows speaker ZO, a Malay female teen (also not our friend directly, but a friend of a university student who is our FB friend – thus we have only an etic perspective) who uses long punctuation markers and emoticons which produce the required effect of drawing sympathy and assurances from her friends. These expressive and cute computer-mediated markers tend to get less frequent after the teenage years.

Let us now continue to demonstrate another case that can be characterized by the ICP-CCM in Figures 13.8 and 13.9. Using the process of targeting, Figure 13.8 shows that speaker YI writes no differently from a typical teenager writing in a global context. YI uses conventional written language, and there is little evidence (if at all) of code-mixing/code-switching. There are some computer-mediated markers such as *idk* (‘I don’t know’), *anw* (‘anyway’)

YI:	3-0 for manutd. could have been idk… 8-8. anyway good win :D
MC:	I’m still like… so excited, even though we lost. Good Game, gotta hand it to ManU’s counter attacking play~
YI:	I think Chelsea played equally better if not better. But winning 3-1 cant be lucky righhhttt :D hehe.
MC:	I didn’t say they were lucky, did I? Hahah! This is the Champions way! Although first goal seemed offside. Hahah! Cannot blame linesman also! How to see?!
YI:	its just my thoughts dumbass! bcs after the 1st goal, seems to be lucky to be ahead.. anw i think 1st goal is offside.
MC:	Hahah! Chelsea playing a very high line whatt. That’s why~ Yeah, looks like it’s an offside!

Figure 13.8 Comments on a football match involving Manchester United, with a focus on Malay FB user ‘YI’

HA:	Yo man, congrats :)
YI:	ahha thanks dude ^^ you too,ade anak sdare baru. heh. skg kt hospital pe?
HA:	haha thanks. going later on. you?
YI:	ahha wt coincidence boleh opp ea other. mm, i dontt thhink so uh. they all dah nak dismissed soon also i think?
HA:	haha yea man. shocking. alright. hope ur mom and the baby's well.
YI:	ameen. thankyou ^^ see u ard babeh.

Figure 13.9 Comments on the birth of his brother, with a focus on Malay FB user 'YI'

and *:D* ('big grin'/laughing emoticon). We have both emic and etic perspectives of YI who is one of our FB friends. In terms of targeting, YI does not hide the fact that he has 997 FB friends in his profile. In terms of framing, he is 18 years of age, ethnically Malay and studying engineering in a tertiary institution. In this excerpt, YI projects an identity in which he has a good command of Standard English (the H-variety) but also uses the L-variety by mixing it at times with computer-mediated communication which is a hybrid form of conventional writing and speech.

Despite this mixing, YI's linguistic behavior contrasts markedly with his discourse in Figure 13.9.

In Figure 13.9, YI not only projects his identity by using shorter colloquial sentences in English but code-mixes more in Malay (*anak sdare* = *anak saudara* = 'nephew/niece') and uses computer-mediated markers (such as the manga/anime inspired smiley ^ ^ in order to make his discourse graphically cuter). This gives the impression that YI's speech is more SgE-L, although it is strictly more a case of code-switching/mixing in Malay. In contrast, speaker HA's use of Circle 1 English only makes his speech more standard and H-like than YI's.

Finally, let us turn to Figure 13.10 to focus on VI, a local Indian speaker, and his friends. VI, a 25-year-old undergraduate, is a FB friend (thus our emic perspective on him) who has 1021 friends, mainly of Indian origin. However, in the excerpt LE is actually a Chinese girl who somehow knows some Tamil or has used Google Translate to generate the topic sentence that roughly translates as follows: *How are you? They are so difficult! And today I go to Chennai.*

Similar to the earlier speakers in this section, LE uses both Standard English structures, as evidenced by her first sentence in English, and her conscious switch to SgE-L (that is, *Somebody practice with me leh...Why u no reply*). In other words, LE 'projects' the identity of being an educated person (by using the H-form) but also evokes the process of 'voicing' to reconstruct a (Chinese)

LE: எப்படி இருக்கீங்க? தமிழ ரொம்ப கஷ்டம்!
இன்னிக்கி நான் சென்னை போங்க

LE: god, sorry, i didn't realize the font was so miniscule. apologies for bad spelling/grammar!

MU: hahah.. impressed!
VI: Haha… Impressive.. How long will you be there? And **MU** , you know Tamil?.. That would be impressive too
MU: I'm half tamil da dei… for the first time in ages i actually understood what I was reading.. Go **LE** ! hahha..
LE: Somebody practice with me leh **VI** why u no reply
VI: Haha…. I'm just seeing my wall!
HA: ahhahahahahahahahahahaha romba cute

Figure 13.10 Comments between a Tamil speaker and his friends

Singlish identity trait (the L-form) and so 'keys' in a playful tone of voice. The point is that such other Singlish structures are understood by local Tamil speakers such as MU and VI. In addition, MU, another friend, deliberately 'voices' in Tamil by using the phrase *da dei* (meaning 'dude'). The most common other hybrid form is the computer-mediated marker *haha* which is lengthened and spelt in slightly different ways for the amusement effect.

Conclusion

The glocalization of English use in Singapore on Facebook is a genuine attempt by local users to connect with their respective 'communities of practice' or networked sociality, that is, the many friends that they regard as part of their circle or community.

We trust that we have shown the productive application of ICP-CCM to the analysis of Facebook (particularly the 'Comments' section) as online discourse. Our use of the term 'style' is not intended to be restrictive in usage; instead, the term (following Coupland, 2007) is multidimensional (instead of being a single dimension such as 'formal' vs 'informal') in its coverage of various micro and macro variationist perspectives. The range of styles in turn indicates the hybrid ways in which disparate ideologies are negotiated and expressed through the medium of English in Singapore: fixed and variable identity (for example, role-playing), formal and informal, Asian and Western perspectives, conventional and computer-mediated language, local and global discourse.

While the age ranges that have been surveyed in this chapter range from mid-teens to adulthood, they are by no means completely representative of their respective cohorts. We suggest that complementary research should engage in large-scale corpus-building which would be useful for educators, linguists and students alike. In the meantime, educators of course have a duty to ensure that teenage students differentiate clearly between the discourses engendered within Facebook and those for classrooms and examinations.

Facebook is a phenomenal social networking platform that can connect users of all ages, nationalities and temperaments together under the innocent rubric of 'Friends'. It is perhaps the largest 'melting pot' of online cultural globalization in new ways not seen before. In the context of Singapore, Facebook users continue to perform various identity projections using a wide range of linguistic resources at their disposal and perhaps show the operationalization of the global-local interface most clearly.

References

Alsagoff, L. (2010a) English in Singapore: Culture, capital and identity in linguistic variation. *World Englishes* 29 (3), 336–348.

Alsagoff, L. (2010b) Hybridity in ways of speaking: The glocalization of English in Singapore. In L. Lim, A. Pakir and L. Wee (eds) *English in Singapore: Modernity and Management* (pp. 109–130). Hong Kong and Singapore: Hong Kong University Press and NUS Press.

Bolander, B. and Locher, M. (2010) Constructing identity on Facebook: Report on a pilot study. In K. Junod and D. Maillat (eds) *Performing the Self* (pp. 165–187). Swiss Papers in English Language and Literature 24, Tubingen, accessed 1 March 2013. http://dx.doi.org/10.5169/seals-131305.

Bruthiaux, P. (2010) The Speak Good English Movement: A web-user's perspective. In L. Lim, A. Pakir and L. Wee (eds) *English in Singapore: Modernity and Management* (pp. 91–108). Hong Kong and Singapore: Hong Kong University Press and NUS Press.

Castells, M. (2000) *The Information Age: Economy, Society and Culture: The Rise of the Network Society* (2nd edn). Oxford: Blackwell.

Coupland, N. (2007) *Style: Language Variation and Identity*. Cambridge: Cambridge University Press.

De Fina, A., Schiffrin, D. and Bamberg, M. (eds) (2006) *Discourse and Identity*. Cambridge: Cambridge University Press.

Headland, T.N., Pike, K.L. and Harris, M. (eds) (1990) *Emics and Etics: The Insider/Outsider Debate*. London: Sage.

Herring, S.C. (ed.) (1996) *Computer-Mediated Communication: Linguistic, Social and Cross-Cultural Perspectives.* Amsterdam: John Benjamins.

Hutnyk, J. (2005) Hybridity. *Ethnic and Racial Studies* 28 (1), 79–102.

Kraidy, M. (2002) Hybridity in cultural globalization. *Communication Theory* 12 (3), 316–339.

Lee, C.K.M. (2011) *Micro-blogging* and *status updates* on Facebook: Texts and practices. In C. Thurlow and K. and Mroczek (eds) *Digital Discourse: Language in the New Media* (pp. 110–128). Oxford: Oxford University Press.

Lim, L., Pakir, A. and Wee, L. (eds) (2010) *English in Singapore: Modernity and Management.* Hong Kong and Singapore: Hong Kong University Press and NUS Press.
Ooi, V.B.Y. (2001a) Globalising Singaporean-Malaysian English in an inclusive learner's dictionary. In B. Moore (ed.) *Who's Centric Now? The State of Postcolonial Englishes* (pp. 95–101). Oxford: Oxford University Press.
Ooi, V.B.Y. (2001b) Upholding standards or passively observing language: Corpus evidence and the Concentric Circles Model. In V.B.Y. Ooi (ed.) *Evolving Identities: The English Language in Singapore and Malaysia* (pp. 168–183). Singapore: Times Academic Press.
Ooi, V.B.Y. (2009) Computer-mediated language and corpus linguistics. In Y. Kawaguchi, M. Minegishi and J. Durand (eds) *Corpus Analysis and Variation in Linguistics* (pp. 103–120). Amsterdam: John Benjamins.
Ooi, V.B.Y. (2010) (Entry on) Singaporean English. In *Collins Dictionary of the English Language* (p. 221). Glasgow: Collins Language/HarperCollins.
Ooi, V.B.Y., Tan, P. and Chiang, A. (2007) Analyzing personal weblogs in Singapore English: The wmatrix approach. *eVariEng* (Journal of the Research Unit for Variation, Contacts and Change in English) Vol. 2: *Towards Multimedia in Corpus Studies*. Finland: University of Helsinki, accessed 1 March 2013. http://www.helsinki.fi /varieng/journal volumes/02/ooi_et_al/.
Pakir, A. (2009) Lexical variations in 'Singapore English': Linguistic description and language education. In Y. Kawaguchi, M. Minegishi and J. Durand (eds) *Corpus Analysis and Variation in Linguistics* (pp. 83–100). Amsterdam: John Benjamins.
Papacharissi, Z. and Yuan, E.J. (2011) What if the internet did not speak English?: New and old language for studying newer media technologies. In D.W. Park, N.W. Jankowski and S. Jones (eds) *The Long History of New Media: Technology, Historiography, and Contextualizing Newness* (pp. 89–107). New York: Peter Lang.
Pérez-Sabater, C. (2012) The linguistics of social networking: A study of writing conventions on Facebook. *Linguistik Online* 56, accessed 1 March 2013. http://www.linguistik-online.de/56_12/perez-sabater.html.
Pike, K.L. (1954) *Language in Relation to a Unified Theory of the Structure of Human Behavior.* The Hague: Mouton.
Sarangi, S. and Coulthard, M. (eds) (2000) *Discourse and Social Life*. Harlow: Pearson Education.
Scollon, R. and Scollon, S.W. (2004) *Nexus Analysis: Discourse and the Emerging Internet.* London and New York: Routledge.
Seargeant, P., Tagg, C. and Ngampramuan, W. (2012) Language choice and addressivity strategies in Thai-English social network interactions. *Journal of Sociolinguistics* 16 (4), 510–531.
Sharma, B.L. (2012) Beyond social networking: Performing global Englishes in Facebook by college youth in Nepal. *Journal of Sociolinguistics* 16 (4), 483–509.
Stern, S.T. (2007) *Instant Identity: Adolescent Girls and the World of Instant Messaging*. New York: Peter Lang.
Talib, I.S. (2012) Postcolonial studies. In C.A. Chapelle (ed.) *The Encyclopedia of Applied Linguistics* (pp. 4485–4490). Oxford: Wiley-Blackwell.
Teubert, W. (2010) *Meaning, Discourse and Society.* Cambridge: Cambridge University Press.
Vie, S. (2007) Engaging others in online social networking sites: Rhetorical practices in MySpace and Facebook. PhD thesis, University of Arizona.
Wittel, A. (2001) Toward a network sociality. *Theory, Culture & Society* 18 (6), 51–76.

Part 4

Performing Hybrid Cultural Identities

14 Contested and Celebrated Glocal Hybrid Identities of Mixed-Ethnic Girls in Japan

Laurel D. Kamada

This chapter examines contested and celebrated linguistic and ethnic 'hybrid' identities of six adolescent girls in Japan of Japanese and 'white/foreign' mixed parentage who assume a 'third' ethnic identity differing from either of their parents. These mixed-ethnic girls, themselves born/raised in Japan, all have one Japanese parent and one English-speaking parent who was born/raised outside of Japan, allowing them access to a world larger than Japan which few of their Japanese peers can claim. They also have Japanese relatives, Japanese (dual) nationality and they use Japanese as their first – or one of their first – languages. Nevertheless, they are still often marginalized as 'half' or 'foreign outsiders' on the local level. This study looks at how they draw on their intercultural and global knowledge and experiences in order to empower themselves in their homeland, Japan. They do this through a number of discursive strategies in their conversations together in order to contest marginalization and racialization. One strategy is to construct various forms of cultural and linguistic capital, often performed through their 'Englishing' (Joseph, 2004) or 'doing English' (Pennycook, 2007). Also examined here is their language choice along with the discursive construction or rejection of their identities as 'English-knowing bilinguals' (Higgins, 2009; Pakir, 1991) or English experts.

Chouliaraki and Fairclough (1999) conceptualized how social life in late-modernity can be explained in terms of five themes: hybridity, globalization, identity, reflexivity and commodification. This chapter illustrates aspects of these five themes through the voices of the participants, particularly focusing on hybridity, globalization and identity, as well as the added theme of glocalization. I use the concept of glocalization in this chapter to refer to the particular localizing effects of indigenous conditions and conventions on universalized globalized practices and concepts. While I refer to how the individual participants (of Japanese and non-Japanese mixed parentage) of this study expressed their particular *glocal hybrid identities* within the context of Japan, the ways in which the same individuals constructed their identity when relocated to a different local environment outside of Japan (such as American) often revealed very different formulations of identity for them based on their local experiences within different social rules. One participant, Naomi, revealing a sort of chameleon nature, constructed herself within multi-memberships, 'I'm two people and I'm one of them in Japan, the other one in America ... I become the people that I meet there, I become like the people in that place.'

Global-Local Interface: Linguistic Capital and Hybrid Identities

In spite of the tremendous impact of globalization on Japan in recent years, one of the most dominant and persistent ideologies of ethnicity in Japan continues to be a commonsensically accepted 'discourse of homogeneity' which denies (and at the same time conflicts with) the concept of ethnic diversity in Japan. While being challenged in recent years, this discourse conflates 'Japaneseness' with nationality, race, ethnicity, language and 'looking Japanese'. Someone who does not 'look' Japanese must then be a foreigner, an outsider, including these mixed-ethnic girls who struggle with their 'hybrid identities'. Bhabha (1994) describes this ambiguous identity as a fragmented 'in-between' third space. In conceptualizing the fixed notion of the *stereotype*, the threat of differences of race, color and culture constitutes the outsider in terms of a 'negative difference'. Bhabha states:

> My contention is splendidly caught in Fanon's title *Black Skin, White Masks* where the disavowal of difference turns the colonial subject into a misfit: a grotesque mimicry or 'doubling' that threatens to split the soul and whole, undifferentiated skin of the ego. (1994: 75)

As shown below, the participants of this study sometimes construct their identities within a stereotyped 'discourse of homogeneity' while at other times within a 'positive difference' discourse where 'good difference' is celebrated as a form of cultural capital. Bourdieu (1977) and Bourdieu and Passeron (1977), in their theory of cultural capital, theorized that various forms of 'capital' can be accumulated, invested, exchanged and exercised, as well as converted into other forms (Swartz, 1997). Besides cultural capital (cultural goods, services, educational credentials), other forms of capital include: symbolic capital (legitimation), social capital (acquaintances, networks), economic capital (money, property), linguistic capital (language proficiency), and so forth.

Within the context of a predominantly monolingual country, the participants also celebrate the linguistic capital of bilinguality, a signifier closely linked to their ethnic identities, including those participants with limited English proficiency. At other times and in different contexts, the girls were also seen rejecting the position of the 'English-knowing bilingual' or the English expert in the context of their monolingual Japanese peers.

Seargeant (2009) examined the twofold idea of English in Japan where English is taken as a means of communication with outsiders, but also as a cultural symbol of globalization. Makoni and Pennycook (2007) argued for the need to imagine and rethink the role of languages and their historical 'invention' and from there to 'disinvent' and 'reconstruct' languages. Pennycook (2007) problematized the 'myth' of English as an international language in which he established that languages are produced and performed through acts of identity. What is important is 'the multiple investments people bring to their acts, desires and performances in "English"' (Pennycook, 2007: 110–111). Pennycook emphasized the importance of revealing how language is materialized through discourse:

> English is not so much a language as a discursive field: English *is* neoliberalism, English *is* globalisation, English *is* human capital ... the question [becomes] ... what kind of mobilizations underlie acts of English use or learning. (Pennycook, 2007: 112)

Drawing on Bourdieu's (1977) theory of cultural capital, Pennycook's notion of *human capital* may be seen as a resource which can be converted into a fundamental linguistic or cultural capital contributing to an individual's personal worth in the social world. In this study, aside from the various forms of cultural capital mentioned above, I also examine what I refer to as 'intercultural capital'. I define this as a quality, consciousness or proficiency which enables people to glocally communicate well with and understand peoples of other 'different' cultures.

The Participants and Methodology

The participants, who comprise a friendship network, were all born/raised in Japan and were all in the same grade at different schools in a large geographic community in western Japan. Since they were infants, they have had various occasional get-togethers via their non-Japanese parents' social networking. They used Japanese at school and as their first/home language or one of their first/home languages. For this reason not all of them were particularly proficient in English, making two of them (Anna, Sara) 'receptive bilinguals', who while not being very proficient at producing language, nevertheless were able to understand their 'parentese' English. Two others (Naomi, Rina) were highly proficient in both Japanese and English, including high biliteracy proficiency. The English proficiency of the other girls (Hanna, Maya) fell in-between.

Each of their non-Japanese parents (three mothers; three fathers) was born/raised in America, Australia or England. I appear throughout the spoken data as the seventh participant. I position myself – distinct from the participants in terms of both nationality and ethnicity, and generation – as a 'white' American researcher and long-time bilingual foreign resident of Japan where I have spent half of my life, and raised my own mixed-ethnic son.

While I have lived in various locations in Japan over 25 years, I selected this particular site because I was able to find a 'network' of mixed-ethnic girlfriends there in which all of the families had made the educational decision to send their children to local Japanese schools instead of one of several international schools available in the community. They did this in spite of the pricey international schools being within their financial means, as middle-class families. I had lived in the research site on two occasions, totaling six years, and was familiar with the local dialect and culture which helped contribute to the ethnographic aspect of the study and the identification of various discourses affecting the participants.

This study draws on poststructuralist discourse analysis (PDA) (or 'discourse theory') which combines micro-linguistic and macro-Foucauldian approaches (see Baxter, 2010; Kamada, 2008). Adapting Baxter's (2002, 2008, 2010) work in poststructuralist discourse theory, I examine how social practices are connected with multiple relevant discourses and how they are taken up, rejected or changed in particular contexts and interactions with others. PDA is framed in constructionism in which all 'truths' can be challenged and reconstructed or deconstructed. Brubaker and Cooper have criticized the notion of 'identity' as being too ambiguous and 'too torn between "hard" and "soft" meanings, essentialist connotations and constructivist qualifiers, to serve well the needs of social analysis' (2000: 2). In my adaptation of PDA, in an attempt to avoid such ambiguity, I thus refrain from referring to people's identities as 'unfixed' and instead use the notion of 'positioning' within PDA. People take up subject positions for themselves which can be said to be temporarily fixed, with the potential to change depending on social interactions with others. Derrida's (1973) notion of 'deconstructionism' within PDA and which makes up the foundation of discourse analysis, aims to show how the structures formed in discourse, which people take as commonsensical 'truths', are politically produced and promoted by those in power. By 'deconstructing' these taken-for-granted structures, the political processes promoting them can be revealed, such as racism or unequal hierarchical positioning. Human agency comes into play as people can act to challenge and reconstruct dominant ideologies by creating alternative discourses.

This approach included an ethnographic survey of the research site, involving observations and recordings over a long time of language practices, speech patterns, actions and repetitions of topics and lexical items. I used a 'semi-structured interview' format for most of the spoken data collection, although some 'spontaneous conversation' was also self-recorded between participants when I was not present. I used both a descriptive micro-analysis as well as a 'connotative' Foucauldian analysis of the positioning of the participants within the relevant discourses based on the ethnography.

The data were collected in six meetings over several years spanning these girls' early adolescence (ages 12–15) between March 2001 (sixth year, elementary school) and May 2003 (third year, middle school) (see Kamada, 2008, 2010). While most meetings were attended by all six girls, not all girls were present at all meetings. Other data used for the analysis included: audiotape recordings of talk made by the girls, email correspondence with the parents and girls, field notes, individual interviews, and my personal background knowledge. All of the participants used a Japanese dialect indigenous to western Japan. (For a comparative study of mixed-ethnic boys in northern Japan, see Kamada, 2009.)

Hybrid Identity: Unmelted Pot of 'Floating Chunks'

Lorente and Tupas (Chapter 4, this volume) caution about the complacency in which scholars use the term 'hybridity' and they make a good argument about its use as a problematic concept. While I continue to use this term, I do so carefully. I not only highlight the progressive nuances of 'hybrid identity', such as resistance and change, but I also leave open the inclusion of a much more complex and sometimes troublesome nature that also informs the notion hybridity. Drawing on Jameson's (1991) notion of the 'split subject' of 'the third space', Bhabha used the term 'cultural globality' (1994: 216) in describing the tensions and dilemmas of the coming together of the global and the local and the newly created 'in-between spaces'. Bhabha quotes

Jameson in describing how the melting pot notion is being replaced with a model where floating chunks do not disintegrate into the stew. Bhabha writes:

> Hybrid hyphenations emphasize the incommensurable elements – the stubborn chunks – as the basis of cultural identifications. What is at issue is the performative nature of differential identities: the regulation and negotiations of those spaces that are continually, *contingently*, 'opening out', remaking the boundaries, exposing the limits of any claim to a singular or autonomous sign of differences ... where difference is neither One nor the Other but *something else besides, in-between* ... (1994: 219)

This conceptualization of the fragmented in-between 'hybrid identity' is seen being constructed by Anna below. This extract was recorded between two of the girls at a sleepover at Anna's home without my presence. (See Appendix for transcription conventions.)

Extract 1: Shocking Mirror (age 13)

A: yappari jibun ga dondake nihonjin no tsumori demo, mou honma ni 'gaijin' ga daikkirai de, mou jibun wa kanzen ni, nihonjin de, nihonjin maindo de, nihonjin yatte omottemo, kagami o miru to nihonjin jyanaishi, sorega meccha iya jyanai? [...] uun, yappa kagami miru to meccha shokku yana

Extract 1 (Translation)

A: however much I intend to be Japanese, I really hate (being thought of as) 'gaijin' (foreigner), I am completely Japanese with a Japanese mind, but even if I think of myself as Japanese, when I look in the mirror I'm not Japanese, and that's really disagreeable [...] it's just totally shocking looking in the mirror.

Anna's account of the 'disagreeable' feeling of looking at her face in the mirror may be due to the gap she perceived between feeling Japanese and not looking Japanese, and it seems to reflect Bhabha's (1994) account of Jameson's (1991) 'split subject' of 'the third space'. In this short extract Anna used the lexis *Nihonjin* (Japanese person) five times in her rejection of the constitution of herself as *'gaijin'* (foreigner) and instead took up a self-positioning as 'completely Japanese with a Japanese mind'. Drawing on a 'discourse of homogeneity' which denies ethnic diversity in Japan, she negatively positioned her ethnic embodied self as 'the Other'. Anna struggled with her desire to conform to the physiological 'embodiment' of Japaneseness, although she is powerless to change her physicality, as it is something outside of her agency.

In an entirely different manner, another participant, Naomi, was seen as both *rejecting* the constitution of herself as different (Extract 2) and also as *self-identifying* with the notion of difference, but in a 'good' sense (Extract 3). Below, Naomi was comparing how she was differently constituted by her peers in Japan compared with peers in the US during her short trips abroad where she had brief opportunities to attend American schools. She constructed her life in America very positively. When I asked her, in comparison, about how people viewed her in Japan, she responded as follows.

Extract 2: Deconstructing 'Bad Difference' (age 13)

N: here, if they're people I meet for the first time, they're like 'oh my gosh, she's not Japanese', it's like, 'just shut up about it'

Speaking in English, Naomi used a sarcastic intertextual voice to represent Japanese people around her in Japan who try to 'gaijinize' (Iino, 1996) her, 'oh my gosh, she's not Japanese'. She contested being constituted by strangers who turn her into 'the Other' based only on her physical appearance. Within a *discourse of homogeneity*, everyone is expected to be Japanese in Japan and those who are not become 'the Other'. She rejected being positioned as *the marked other* using an ironic voice of how she would hypothetically respond to being singled out and marked as different, 'just shut up about it'. She deconstructed the positioning of *bad difference* by implying an alternate ideology of diversity. Naomi seems to have internalized and observed a greater tolerance to difference/diversity during her short-term experiences in American schools where her mixed-ethnicity was not specifically marked (or named) and was not seen as *strange* or outside of the norm, as in Japan.

Linguistic traces can also be seen of Naomi rejecting and deconstructing a discourse of conformity as epitomized in the Japanese proverb 'the nail that sticks up gets hammered down'. Within a discourse of diversity, Naomi was also implying, 'why can't they just "shut up about it" and accept me as I am'. Within a globalizing discourse of interculturalism, Naomi was able to empower herself based on her ability to draw on her 'outside of Japan' knowledge and experience in order to deconstruct ethnic 'othering' within Japan.

While she rejected the constitution of 'difference' by others above, six months later Naomi claimed and celebrated 'good difference' for herself as she performed nonconformity. We were discussing Naomi's relationships with her school peers.

Extract 3: Celebrating 'Good Difference' (age 13)

1 N: and they are like, 'well you're kind of different, so',
2 L: yeah, do they think that you're really cool?
3 I mean do they want to be friends with you, or do they,
4 N: no, no

5 L: they don't?
6 N: no, I'm like really different from everyone
[...]
9 L: how are you different from them?
10 N: I TRY to be different from them
[...]
15 N: it's funny, but I think they're below me, kind of,
16 because I, I see a lot, a lot more of the world than they do

Naomi again used an intertextual (and probably exaggerated and hypothetical) voice of her classmates 'othering' her, 'well, you're kind of different' (#1). She rejected my suggested construction of her as popular when I asked if her school friends considered her 'cool' and wanted to be friends (#2–3). Naomi empathically answered 'no', positioning herself also as 'really different from everyone' (#6). She made her differentness an asset through her positive self-positioning, 'I TRY to be different' (#10), claiming *good difference* for herself, in her deconstruction of *difference* as *bad*. Later, in stating, 'it's funny, I think they're below me' (#15), Naomi's deconstruction of 'othering' took the form of privileging and placing herself in an elevated position as insider while constituting her Japanese peers as the Other and as outsiders. While positioning herself as separate and different, she also positioned herself within a discourse of interculturalism by implying her greater worldliness and sophistication based on her seeing a lot more of the world than her Japanese peers (#16). While in Extract 2, we examined Naomi's *rejection* of being positioned by others as 'different', paradoxically, here we see her now explicitly constituting her own differentness, but in a reconstituted *good* meaning.

These first three extracts reveal the multi-memberships that these girls assume in their various contexts as they construct, resist and celebrate their hybrid identities. They especially resist being constituted by other people's notions of what they should be. Instead their self-images resemble Jameson's (1991) notion of 'resistant floating chunks' rather than a melting pot of stew.

The following section looks at how meaning is further constructed by drawing on the global capital of bilinguality, which is performed at the local level.

Glocal Language Choice and Identity

As mentioned above, some of the girls were more proficient in English than others. Early in the study, at Maya's first appearance, the girls were seen co-constructing and celebrating the high value of the linguistic capital of bilingualism and the use of English. We had been talking about how some children at school get marginalized for their differences. Maya had been telling a narrative in Japanese about such a girl when I asked if someone could summarize in English what she had said.

Extract 4: Constructing Linguistic Capital (age 13)

1	L:	OK, **chotto matomete,** English
1*		**OK,** *can someone summarize that*, **English**
2	N:	um
3	R:	**Ma, Maya shaberarerno ne**
3*		*Ma, Maya can speak English*
4	L:	**ah, Maya, jya, Maya**
4*		*Maya, well then, Maya*
5	R:	**Maya, du yua besuto**
5*		*Maya, do your best*
6	L:	OK, do your best
7	M:	**iyaa**
7*		*yuk*
8	R:	**gambaru**
8*		*try hard*
9	L:	**OK, gambaru**
9*		*OK, try hard*
10		just sort of say a little bit
11	M:	um, there's a girl
12	L:	uh-huh
13	M:	she's not a bad girl, but everybody thinks that she's so different
	[. . .]	
24	M:	**mm, futsuu ni shabettara**
24*		*if I talk to her as usual*, *then*
25		**if I talk to her as usual then the else**
26	N:	everyone else
27	M:	everyone else will think that I am the stranger too

Naomi and Rina, who were highly proficient in English, had been serving the function of summarizing some of the talk into English during this meeting which was otherwise all in Japanese. When I asked for an English summary, Naomi responded with 'um' (#2), self-selecting to fulfill my request for translation. However, before she could do so, Rina announced that Maya can speak English (#3), positioning Maya as bilingual and implicitly selecting her as the one to perform the translation. It took several turns of encouragement between me and Rina to finally get Maya to speak in English (#4–10). Rina started off in Japanese (#3). Then I also addressed Maya in Japanese (#4) and followed Rina's lead by affirming the selection of Maya to take the floor and summarize her story in English.

Next Rina lent further encouragement to Maya (#5) by use of a phrase appropriated in Japanese as a Japanese-English phrase (*du yua besuto*), but also very clearly an English phrase, 'Do your best'. This kind of structure can be thought of as a Japanese word, created from English origins, rather than as a code-switch into English. Similarly, Higgins refers to 'urban vernaculars' which amalgamate and integrate 'local and global cultural references' (Higgins, 2009: 2). Following Rina, I mimicked her, using the same phrase, but using the English inflection (#6) to further encourage Maya. She faltered at first (#7), but in the end Maya began to speak in English, taking up for herself the position of Japanese/English bilingual.

Although Maya now showed confidence in her use of English, in line #24 she suddenly switched into Japanese for an expression that she was not sure how to express in her second language, English. She was perhaps signaling that her attempt to express herself in English, which followed immediately (#25), was knowingly going to be incorrect. While still communicable to her interlocutors, her English rendition was slightly grammatically off, 'if I talk to her as usual then the else'. To this, Naomi subtly corrected her (#26), which served also to display Naomi's comprehension of Maya's English. To this, Maya, without slowing her pace, incorporated the correction into her narrative and continued to speak on in English (#27).

The importance of this exchange was that when given the opportunity, Maya took up the chance to demonstrate her English proficiency. Along with the other girls co-constructing, she discursively placed value on bilinguality as she 'performed English'. Even though Maya and several other girls were not particularly proficient in English, they all nevertheless positioned themselves and each other as privileged in their possession of cultural and linguistic capital of English proficiency and its attendant high-status position.

Six months later, in the extract that follows, Maya was telling a narrative about her older brother who had put on muscles over the several months while he had been residing with his father in America. Here Maya was responding to my English prompts in English, again offering her a rare opportunity to use her second language as above. Whereas Maya and I are speaking English, Naomi, who is a highly proficient English speaker, interacts throughout using Japanese.

Extract 5: Language Choice and Identity (age 14)

1 M: he, he, he had a bunch of muscles
2 L: oh really?

3 N: (laugh) **muki, muki naru no (?)**
3* *(laugh) he became bunchy, bunchy (?)*
4 L: oh really?
5 N: **bikurishita**
5* *I was surprised*
6 M: really really
7 L: and he's, he's seventeen, you said?
8 M: uh-huh
9 L: uh-huh
10 M: so surprised
11 L: really? how did he get all the muscles?
12 M: um, weight lifting
13 L: weight lifting? oohh, so he must have had a good time, huh
14 N: **yokatta de**
14* *he was happy*
15 M: yeah,
[...]
25 M: and he's going to go the college at North Carolina
26 L: oh really?
27 N: **so nan**?
27* *is that right*?

Rather than *what* is being said, what is of interest here is *how* it is being said and *by whom*. Here all of the alternations into Japanese are by Naomi, a very proficient English speaker, while Maya uses her less-proficient language, English, throughout, ignoring Naomi's cues hinting that it is alright to speak in Japanese.

Maya can be seen constructing and celebrating the linguistic capital of English in her work to 'do English' even though Naomi left open the option to face-savingly switch back into Japanese. Naomi took on the role of linguistic mediator by providing feedback in the context of Japanese, a language which she would normally expect to use when speaking with Maya without the presence of native English speakers. But Maya continued 'Englishing' in order to create and display her linguistic capital of bilinguality, even in its non-perfect form, unthreatened in the company of her mixed-ethnic friends.

Maya, in Extracts 4 and 5 above, and the other girls throughout the data set, were often seen 'doing English' as an extension of their ethnic identities. In contrast to their construction of positive linguistic capital of English, in the next section we see the girls in the act of rejecting the constitution of themselves as 'English-knowing bilinguals' in the face of their Japanese peers.

Contesting Being 'The English-Knowing Bilinguals'

In this section, not only do the girls reject the constitution of themselves as the English experts, but we also see them demonstrating a reflexive and meta-linguistic awareness of intricate linguistic functions of their two languages. This is another form of linguistic capital they can claim and celebrate for themselves which is not easily accessible to their Japanese peers. Hanna starts out using an intertextual voice of a Japanese peer asking her to say something in English.

Extract 6: Pranks and Humor (ages: 13 & 14)

1	H:	**'ne, ne oshite, oshiete, eigo de, eigo de appuru tte ittemite'**
1*		*'hey, hey, teach me, teach me [something] in English, in English, how do you say apple'*
	[...]	
6	H:	**a 'nantoiuno, eigo de' saa, nanka ne,**
6*		*'how do I say that, in English', like*
7		**'anata no koto ga sukidesu' toka na, 'soiu tte nanto iuuno'**
7*		*'I like you', something like that, (they ask me) 'how do I say that (in English)'*
8		so 'I think you are so stupid'
9		**tte na oshieru no**
9*		*is what I teach them to say*
10	N:	(laugh)
11	H:	(in an affected voice) 'I think you are so stupid'
12		**sore toka na, de 'watashi wa tensai desu'** (affected voice) **toka toiu toki wa**
12*		*things like that and 'I'm a genius'* (affected voice) *and, like, times like that*
13		'I am so, I am such an idiot'
14		**toka na oshieta**
14*		*I teach them stuff like that*
15	?s:	(laugh)
16	?:	'I am dumb', 'I am dumb'
17	?s:	(laugh)

Being asked to say something in English by her Japanese peers was disturbing to Hanna as such a request works to shift her from being 'unmarked' and 'like-everyone-else-in-Japan' to being marked and different and foreign. In her work to counter a positioning of difference, Hanna displayed humor in demonstrating her rejection of this positioning in this interaction among her mixed-ethnic peers. Hanna's proficient use of humor is confirmed by Naomi's laughter in line #10. Hanna then provided another example of her Japanese peers asking for an English translation, of 'I like you'. She narrated how she facetiously taught them to incorrectly say, 'I think you are so stupid'. Hanna then proceeded to provide other prankish examples. For 'I'm a genius', Hanna supplied them with, 'I am such an idiot'. Another girl helped to co-construct this act of contestation by offering the rendition, 'I am dumb'.

While the girls used Japanese dominantly here, all of the examples of the English expressions provided in the exchanges with the Japanese girls were produced in English through language alternations of intertextual and affected-sounding voices (#8, 11, 13, 16). In line #1, Hanna's was particularly jocular in her choice of 'apple' as an example of a word she might be asked to translate, because while there is a Japanese word for apple (*ringo*), the English loanword '*appuru*' is also commonly used. Hanna seemed to be sarcastically poking fun at the stupidity of being asked to provide an English translation for a word that is knowingly already English, albeit a Japanese-inflected English loanword.

Even though being asked to speak in English by monolingual Japanese peers could serve to positively position these girls in possession of privileged globalized linguistic capital not accessible to their Japanese peers, here these girls reject being positioned as the 'English-knowing bilinguals' or the English experts. Perhaps what they most reject is being asked to perform a demeaning, meaningless task of producing a string of words incomprehensible to the listener. Simultaneously, they also playfully demonstrate their English knowledge and linguistic capital among themselves through their proficient switches into English and linguistic play-work. They demonstrated their contestation of this humiliating request by providing their Japanese peers with English renditions that were not only incorrect and prankish, but also playful through their proficient use of humor, sarcasm and trickery. Based on the Bakhtinian concept of 'multivocality', Higgins (2009), in her study of Tanzanian bilingual settings, reported on how humor was employed through the use of code-switching in order to allow spaces for multiple presentations of reality, rather than the claim of a single 'truth'.

The next section looks at another aspect of the influence of globalization at the local level, concerning intercultural capital.

Intercultural Capital and Cultural Mixing

The final extract is preceded by Rina trying to recall the sequential details of a television commercial for a language school which we had all seen numerous times. With the girls co-constructing, switching between English and Japanese in her narration of the commercial, Rina introduced into the talk the relatively new concept in Japan of interculturalism (*ibunka*) highlighted in the commercial (see Kamada, 2010).

Through several exchanges, the girls tried to establish the language spoken by the first person appearing in the commercial. Rina took the lead in narrating the sequence of events, first of the appearance of a Japanese person speaking Italian, then an Italian person speaking Japanese. Then, switching into Japanese, Rina narrated the next sequence of a '*kansaijin*' (person from Kansai) speaking French. Since all of the girls are themselves from the Japan region of Kansai and all of them speak the local Kansai dialect, these aspects of the commercial held personal meaning for them, not only as mixed-ethnic and speakers of a world (foreign) language, but also as proud, local provincial Kansai Japanese. Rina switched into English providing a transitional link with 'and then after that', and then alternated back into Japanese to provide an intertextual voicing of a character from the commercial. She used an affected voice imitating an older man, not only in inflection and local dialect, but also in lexicality, '*yaa, ore no youna occhan no na*' ('well, a middle-aged codger like me'). Rina completed the narrative by introducing the final character to appear – a Kansai-dialect-speaking alien from outer space – who she imitated using a local Kansai dialect in an informal register '*ma, ibunka chuuno kana*' ('well, ain't that intercultural'). Drawing on discourses of diversity and interculturalism, issues dealt with in Rina's narration of this commercial were not limited to *ethnicity*, *foreign languages* and *foreign countries* (or *planets*), but also included 'interculturality' of *age* (middle-aged man), *regional locality* (Kansai), *regional dialect* (Kansai Dialect) and *informal registers*. Following this, below, the girls responded to my question asking if they liked the commercial.

Extract 7: Intercultural Capital (age 13)

1	R:	yeah, I think it's good
2	N:	yeah, I like that one.
3	R:	and it says
4		**'hito wa mikake to chigaimasse'**
4*		*'people are different than they appear' (affected in Kansai Dialect)*
5		**to, sore ga yokatta to omou**
5*		*and I thought that was great*
6	L:	uh-huh, uh-huh, uh-huh, why do you think it's good?
7	R:	well because it, I don't know, I just felt kind of funny
8		?: **omoroi na**
8*	?:	*it's interesting*
9	R:	it's funny and it's

10	N:	yeah, you kind of feel happier when you (laugh)
11	R:	yeah
12	L:	uh-huh, uh-huh
13	R:	**'hito wa mikake to chigaimasse' to iu no wa, yappari**
13*		*'people have different appearances' is after all*
14	?:	**ii koto ya ne**
14*	?:	*a good thing*
15	R:	**densha de, ko niramareru,**
15*		*in the train, like, I am scowled at,*
16		**watashi to shite wa sugoi so iu no ga ureshii**
16*		*so I am really happy about that kind of thing (the commercial)*
17	L:	uh-huh,
18		**mmm, mmm, mmm, naruhodo**
18*		*uh-huh, uh-huh, uh-huh, I see*
19	N:	**densha de niramareru no**?
19*		*you were scowled at in the train?*
20	R:	**niramareru to iu ka,** (makes a face, gesture)
20*		*well, scowled at, that is to say (makes a scowling face, gesture)*
21	N:	(laughs) **sore wa wakarun**
21*		*I know what you mean*
22	L:	**nnnn** *(yeah)*
23	H:	**aaaru, zettai niramareru yona**
23*		*me too, I am definitely scowled at*

While Rina's narrative was predominately produced in Japanese and sprinkled throughout with English alternations, I used English to ask Rina's opinion about the commercial, to which she responded in English. With the others co-constructing, Rina celebrated the commercial's explicit message of interculturality. In applauding the promotion of a globalizing discourse of interculturalism produced in a language school commercial on television, Rina positioned herself within this discourse and put value on interculturality. The girls expressed their approval of this mass-media commercial (#1, 2, 4, 7–10, 14, 16) in that it helps to promote the social consciousness of this intercultural discourse throughout society. Switching into Japanese, Rina intertextually voiced several discourses/repertoires from the commercial: 'people are different than they appear' (#4) and 'people have different appearances' (#13). In line #15, Rina offered a real-life example (of being scowled at in the train for looking different) to illustrate how the promotion of a discourse of interculturalism, via the means of a local mass-media distribution route, might help to disseminate an alternative discourse to counter the overarching discourse of homogeneity (where everyone is expected to look the same). Rina applauded the dispersion of this alternative discourse as having the potential to raise the consciousness of people who act to marginalize her on a daily basis in Japanese society, to which Naomi and Hanna both expressed agreement (#21, #23).

Conclusion and Discussion

This chapter has examined the ways in which mixed-ethnic girls discursively create and celebrate intercultural, linguistic, social and symbolic capital through their narratives and interactions in linking their local identities with their global access to resources not readily available to their Japanese peers. It was shown how their hybrid identities are competing, sometimes contradictory and constantly shifting. Within local dominant marginalizing discourses of homogeneity and conformity in Japan, the girls at times struggled to empower themselves. However, at other times in other contexts, within other broader alternative global discourses of diversity and heterogeneity and linguistic/cultural mixing, they were able to empower themselves.

Even the participants with limited English proficiency were able to create positive linguistic capital for themselves – in ways that their Japanese peers could not – on the basis of their access to English via a foreign-raised English-speaking parent and another 'homeland' beyond Japan. The girls took up opportunities to demonstrate their English abilities when given the chance among each other. They worked to constitute themselves and each other as 'owners' of linguistic capital which gave them 'special' access to information and knowledge. In other contexts however, these girls are also seen rejecting the construction of themselves by their Japanese peers as 'the English-knowing bilinguals'. The influence of a global discourse of interculturalism promoted via a television commercial was also seen to have a positive impact on the constructions of their hybrid identities at the local level.

Through a process of struggle spanning their early adolescence, these girls, over time, were able to access a wider array of global discourses, allowing them to assume different and competing local identities and to appropriate and create various forms of intercultural, linguistic and cultural capital in order to empower themselves in the positive construction of their glocally constructed identities.

Acknowledgements

Grateful acknowledgement is made to Multilingual Matters for permission to reprint parts of the analysis and Extracts 1–4 and 7 from Kamada (2010).

References

Baxter, J. (2002) Competing discourses in the classroom: A post-structuralist discourse analysis of girls' and boys' speech in public contexts. *Discourse and Society* 13 (6), 827–842.

Baxter, J. (2008) Feminist post-structuralist discourse analysis – A new theoretical and methodological approach? In K. Harrington, L. Litosseliti, H. Sauntson and J. Sunderland (eds) *Language and Gender Research Methodologies* (pp. 243–255). Basingstoke: Palgrave Macmillan.

Baxter, J. (2010) *The Language of Female Leadership*. Basingstoke: Palgrave Macmillan.

Bhabha, H. (1994) *The Location of Culture*. London and New York: Routledge.

Bourdieu, P. (1977) *Outline of a Theory of Practice* (R. Nice, trans.). Cambridge: Cambridge University Press.

Bourdieu, P. and Passeron, J.S. (1977) *Reproduction in Education, Society, and Culture*. Beverly Hills, CA: Sage.

Brubaker, R. and Cooper, F. (2000) Beyond 'identity'. *Theory and Society* 29: 1–47.

Chouliaraki, L. and Fairclough, N. (1999) *Discourse in Late Modernity: Rethinking Critical Discourse Analysis*. Edinburgh: Edinburgh University Press.

Derrida, J. (1973) *Speech and Phenomenon*. Evanston, IL: North-Western University Press.

Higgins, C. (2009) *English as a Local Language: Post-Colonial Identities and Multilingual Practices*. Bristol: Multilingual Matters.

Iino, M. (1996) 'Excellent foreigner!': Gaijinization of Japanese language and culture in conflict situations – An ethnographic study of dinner table conversations between Japanese host families and American students. Unpublished PhD thesis, University of Pennsylvania.

Jameson, F. (1991) *Postmodernism or, the Cultural Logic of Late Capitalism*. Durham: Duke University Press.

Joseph, J. (2004) Is language a verb? Conceptual change in linguistics and language teaching. In H. Trappes-Lomax and G. Ferguson (eds) *Language in Language Teacher Education* (pp. 29–47). Amsterdam: John Benjamins.

Kamada, L. (2008) Discursive 'embodied' identities of 'half' girls in Japan: A multiperspective approach. In K. Harrington, L. Litosseliti, H. Sauntson and J. Sunderland (eds) *Language and Gender Research Methodologies* (pp. 174–190). Basingstoke: Palgrave Macmillan.

Kamada, L. (2009) Mixed-ethnic girls and boys as similarly powerless and powerful: Embodiment of attractiveness and grotesqueness. *Discourse Studies* 11 (3), 329–352.

Kamada, L. (2010) *Hybrid Identities and Adolescent Girls: Being 'Half' in Japan*. Bristol: Multilingual Matters.

Makoni, S. and Pennycook, A. (eds) (2007) *Disinventing and Reconstructing Languages*. Clevedon: Multilingual Matters.

Pakir, A. (1991) The range and depth of English-knowing bilinguals in Singapore. *World Englishes* 10 (2), 167–179.

Pennycook, A. (2007) The myth of English as an international language. In S. Makoni and A. Pennycook (eds) *Disinventing and Reconstructing Languages* (pp. 90–115). Clevedon: Multilingual Matters.

Seargeant, P. (2009) *The Idea of English in Japan: Ideology and the Evolution of a Global Language*. Bristol: Multilingual Matters.

Swartz, D. (1997) *Culture and Power: The Sociology of Pierre Bourdieu*. Chicago, IL and London: University of Chicago Press.

Appendix: Transcription Conventions

?	(in text) rising intonation, question
(?)	(in text) undecipherable speech
(laugh)	laugh
CAPITALS	loud enunciation
,	(comma) continuing intonation (utterance not completed)
bold print	Japanese transcribed into Romanization (the actual speech) (Hepburn System of Romanization)
italic print	the English translation of the Japanese
regular print	the actual speech in English (not a translation)
(explanation)	explanation or implied speech in parenthesis (not the actual speech)
'quotation marks'	words enclosed in quotation marks indicate quoted speech, emphasized lexis, voice of someone else or self at an earlier time
*after line number	indicates translation of the above line (using the same line number)
[. . .]	ellipsis: omission of one or more lines of the excerpt
? (in transcript speaker column)	unclear which one of the girls was speaking
?s (in transcript speaker column)	unclear simultaneous speakers

Pseudonyms are used for all names: A = Anna, H = Hanna, M = Maya, N = Naomi, R = Rina, S = Sara, L = researcher.

15 Singlish and Hybridity: The Dialogic of Outer-Circle Teacher Identities

Lubna Alsagoff

Introduction

As a theoretical framework that offers a pluricentric perspective on the diasporic spread of English, Kachru's (1983, 1986) Three Circles model makes a clear link between identity and language; in particular, in referring to the ways in which speakers of different cultures have developed new voices in speaking English. Outer Circle or new Englishes, in particular, are seen as testifying to this de- and reterritorialization of language, culture and identity, in which the geographical dislocation of English from its so-called 'native' roots has engendered new ways of speaking. While the model has gained much in terms of insight from this promising premise, Bruthiaux (2003) is right in questioning the explanatory adequacy of modeling language variation simply in terms of a speaker's geographical origin. This criticism should, however, not be seen as leveled against the relationship between language and identity, but rather the way in which identity is conceptualized (for example, see Bhatt, 2008 and also Bhatt, Chapter 7, this volume).

Drawing on the re-conceptualization of identity brought about by post-structural understandings of language, and pioneered in the work of researchers such as Duff and Uchida (1997); Firth and Wagner (1997); Norton Peirce (1995); McKay and Wong (1996); and van Lier (1994), it is necessary to reframe our understanding of identity, from 'a stable structure located primarily ... in fixed social categories', such as gender, age and geographical or national affiliation, to one that is more nuanced and defined more dynamically as 'a relational and sociocultural phenomenon that emerges and circulates in local discourse contexts of interaction' (Bucholtz & Hall, 2005: 585–586). In exploring the potential of a more expansive concept of identity within the Three Circles model, it is, however, necessary to be aware, as Brubaker and Cooper (2000) remind us, that such broad conceptions of identity can see breadth easily falling prey to vagueness. However, the benefits of using identity as a theoretical concept in offering interpretive coherence to the analysis of the discourse which we study in this chapter are clear. Identity offers a lens from which to make sense of the online narratives of the Singapore student teachers which form the empirical focus of this chapter: in particular, identity facilitates an understanding of how the ostensible contradictions in the student teachers' opinions about the English they speak can be better understood as dialogic as they construct and negotiate their professional identities as teachers.

Globalization, Hybridity and Identity

The term hybridity – in particular, linguistic and cultural hybridity – has been increasingly invoked in the research literature across a wide range of academic disciplines, in describing a world where the intensification of the forces of globalization sees people living and negotiating multiple lives and selves, and where language can no longer be assumed to be monotheistically tied to specific cultures, peoples or nations. Yet, the term hybridity, when applied to identity, has had an especially problematic history. While often used descriptively to capture the ways in which migration and an intensely globalized world has necessitated our understanding of identity as plural and unstable, the term has been associated, particularly in colonialist discourse, with strongly discriminatory eugenicist and racist ideologies (Young, 1995). Yet, despite its loaded history, Papastergiadis (1997: 258) judiciously points to the emancipatory potential of negative words, advocating that we not shy away from embracing words with feculent pasts so that we may 'challenge essentialist models of identity by taking on and then subverting their own vocabulary'.

Papastergiadis, in fact, sees hybridity as a 'lubricant' that is able to facilitate opposition to essentialist notions of identity that the self can be quantified in invariable and fixed properties that can define the '"whatness" of a given entity' (Fuss, 1991: xi). This resonates with Bhabha's interpretation of hybridity as a 'third space' – as a mode of articulation, a way of describing a productive, and not merely reflective, interstitial space that is interruptive, interrogative and enunciative (Bhabha, 1994). In articulating the blurring of boundaries, such conceptualizations of hybridity are useful in calling into question established notions of language, culture and identity, and engender new possibilities and new forms of cultural meaning and production that are useful in examining the ways in which English is used across a diverse range of cultural contexts. These promulgate the idea that identity is inherently hybrid, which is also congruent with a perspective of identity seen through a sociocultural lens as multiple, dynamic and shifting, and, critically, as emergent through discourse (Bucholtz & Hall, 2005); harking Stuart Hall's call to move away from 'thinking of identity as an already accomplished fact ... and instead, [think] of identity as a "production", which is never complete, always in process, and always constituted within, not outside, representation' (Hall, 1990: 222). Such conceptions of identity are also premised on the notion that language and identity are 'mutually constitutive', in which language is not simply a reflection of identity but is also instrumental in the constructions and reproductions of identity (Norton, 1997: 419). In such an approach, rather than theorized as a set of a priori essentialized characterizations formed solely on the basis of 'macro-level demographic categories' such as ethnicity, religion or national origin, identity is interpreted more productively as including 'local, ethnographically specific cultural positions' and the 'temporary and interactionally specific stances and participant roles' assumed by speakers in discourse (Bucholtz & Hall, 2005: 592) as well.

The portrayal of identity as hybrid is also congruent with Bakhtin's (1981) notion of multivocality, of language as consisting of heteroglossic voices, often conflicting and contradictory, arising from contrapuntal language flows around centripetal and centrifugal forces. The centripetal represents the homogenizing force of the center while the centrifugal represents the heterogeneity of the periphery. It is in the counterpoint of these contrastive ideologies that linguistically hybrid forms develop as representations and productions of the 'double-voicing' of identities in the liminal third space. These hybrid forms, constituted and constitutive of the complex identities of its speakers, offer speakers, as Bhatt (2008: 182) similarly argues, 'the possibility of a new representation, of meaning-making, and of agency'. It is this double-voicing that aligns theoretically with the recurrent observation made by many scholars that the spread of English as a global language inevitably entails the co-presence of the global and the local (Canagarajah, 2005; Phillipson, 1992). Brutt-Griffler (2002), for example, suggests that a language gains the status of a world language only if it is used and established alongside local languages. Such characterizations of English as both global and co-presently local, in which global ideologies attendant in using English to gain access to international markets are juxtaposed against local cultural orientations which ground and situate English in everyday purposes and contexts of use. An understanding of English as hybrid offers a means of valuing and understanding the ways in which a language as 'supremely' global as English evolves in response to a diverse range of local contexts – it is this co-presence of the global and local that creates a third space which offers speakers of English, typically in the Outer Circles where English is woven into the daily fabric of life, a productive interstice to explore and create hybrid identities.

Yet another key aspect of a sociocultural theory of identity, one which has particular pertinence to the study of postcolonial Englishes, is Norton Peirce's (1995) theorizing of identity as subjectivity, emphasizing identity as situated and embedded in relations of power. Norton Peirce suggests that it is through language that a person negotiates a sense of self within and across a range of sites at different points in time and it is through language that a person gains access to – or is denied access to – powerful social networks that offer opportunities and rights to speak and to be heard (Bourdieu, 1991). Characterized in this manner, socioculturally oriented theories such as Norton's demonstrate that identity can be a powerful tool with which to interrogate the inequalities of power that arise in the spread of English; and especially in the ways in which the norms related to the use of English offer different access to wealth and economic opportunities. Such norms generally create tensions that see speakers needing to balance local desires with global pressures.

Examining Teacher Identity

To illustrate the ways in which identity can more productively explain the dynamics of language variation in multilingual contexts, the meta-narratives of a group of Singapore student teachers are examined in this chapter as they engage in joint co-constructions of their identity as teachers and as Singapore English speakers.[1] Their discourse about the English they speak offers rich grounds to study how identity is intrinsically linked to language use and sense of ownership. The discussion is premised on the belief that language and identity are 'mutually constitutive' in which language is not simply a reflection of identity but is also instrumental in the constructions and reproductions of identity (Norton, 1997: 419). Most importantly, the exchanges among the students, which center on Singlish, the variety of English spoken in Singapore and the focus of ongoing public debate, show how identity is fundamentally hybrid for the group of Singaporean teachers, who ostensibly do not appear to have a consistent or uniform set of beliefs or understandings about the way they speak, and should speak, English.

The discussion thread first opens with the student teachers' positive framing of Singlish (also referred to by the student teachers as Singapore Colloquial English or SCE for short). The initial exchanges establish the common ground for the student teachers, all of whom are Singaporeans. Their discussions focus on personal stories, with the first few exchanges presenting Singlish clearly as a marker of a collective Singaporean identity –Singlish is collaboratively framed as an integral part of what it means to be 'Singaporean' – with a strong emphasis on its role as a cultural identity marker. The construction of a locally grounded identity around Singlish is accomplished in several ways. First, the students use a number of indexical expressions to underscore their ownership of Singlish, for example, 'unique', 'part of the Singapore culture', 'only a true Singaporean' in (1) and (2); 'inborn within Singaporeans' (3), 'unique Singapore flavour' and 'shape the Singapore identity' (4):

(1) Noriza:
Let me start by saying happy 'holidays'. In terms of not travelling to (school:).
Well, personally, I have always feel that Singapore English is a unique language that makes part of the Singapore culture. Usually when we speak Standard Singapore English (SgE) with a blend of local words, without a doubt, only a true Singaporean can understand!

(2) Meilin:
Definitely agree that only a true Singaporean can understand SCE well and use it proficiently. Let's take the particles (lah, lor, hor ... etc) for examples, foreigners who are trying to use them would find it difficult to incorporate them into their speech. Often the attempts would lead to laughter as the pragmatics use of them are distorted. What do you think?

(3) Anu:
Adding on to what Lynn and the rest mentioned, I have come across many foreigners who try to 'imitate' certain Singlish particles such as 'la' and 'lor' to sound more like Singaporeans. Despite their efforts, somehow they do not blend well with the locals' speech. I feel that SgE is something inborn within Singaporeans and therefore is unique. (",)

(4) Mun Lai:
Perhaps it's the invention of such lexicons that adds the uniquely Singapore flavour to our local speech. No doubt foreigners might find them weird, it nevertheless helps shape the Singapore identity.

(5) Li Lian:
I think it is so obvious that Singlish gives people the idea of solidarity, friendship and cool character.

In the students' portrayal of Singlish as a local language, they focus not only on this unifying function of the local vernacular, but also couple this with an articulation of its separatist function. We thus see evidence of 'othering' at work in which non-Singaporeans are referred to as 'foreigners' and are seen as the out-group, as outsiders to Singapore and its 'culture', indicated in the discourse through the contrastive use of possessives such as the first person plural 'we', 'us' and 'our' to refer to themselves as Singaporeans versus the use of third person pronouns such as 'they' and them' when referring to non-Singapore English speakers as in (6) and (7):

(6) Hui Yin:
Foreigners often take some time to understand the true meaning behind our speech acts due to the vocabulary and lexical items that we use.

(7) Idah:
... talking about foreigners trying to imitate Singlish ...
Sometime ago, I watched this local Tamil drama where apart from our local talents, artistes from India were also acting in it ... It was SO exaggerated especially when the Indian artistes used the discourse particle 'lah' at the end of EVERY sentence! What was MORE interesting was they used it with their Indian accent ... it OBVIOUSLY didn't sound Singlish at ALL ... I think that's how they identify us as ... the 'lah' people!

Yet another aspect of the construction of the value of Singlish is in the emphasis of the linguistic capital of Singlish – it is presented and constructed as having value not only to Singaporeans but to foreigners as well. Thus, in the exchanges above, the student teachers consistently describe foreigners desiring to speak Singlish. In (7), a student teacher, Idah, in her discussion of the role of Singlish as a marker of national identity, hints at her sense of pride that even Bollywood movies take an interest in Singlish, thus affirming its value. Other student teachers, Rui Hua and May Li, also express similar ideological beliefs, highlighting the way in which foreigners legitimize and give value to Singlish:

(8) Rui Hua:
yeah. i have an American friend whom i know from an online game ... He thought our language was rather cool. (though he doesn't know

why we use words like lah, siao, meh). Well, i guess Singlish really make us Singaporean unique!

(9) May Li:
I find it interesting how foreigners with Singaporean friends would be interested in the uniqueness of our language ... and it's not for the purpose of fitting in in Singapore as they're not even in Singapore.

(10) Guo Ji:
Yeah it is rather interesting to hear foreigners try to speak like a Singaporean when they are in Singapore. I guess it's similar to Singaporeans who try to speak like an 'ang moh' [Caucasians] when they are speaking to an 'ang moh'... makes sense? haha..

(11) Chin Yee:
yup, I agree that foreigners want to sound like us when they are in Singapore. When in Rome, do as the Romans do, perhaps? But mb they are trying to establish solidarity with us locals, so they would not feel as 'foreign' among us and can integrate into our society better. And also Singlish is KEY when it comes to buying hawker food (and not to get stared at or scolded by the hawker in the process). ;)

In the above exchanges, the student teachers also speak about the 'command' of Singlish as an accomplishment – there is a distinct sense that not everyone can speak Singlish; that only Singaporeans can speak it proficiently. In constructing ownership of Singlish as the sole privilege of 'true Singaporeans', the students appropriate the notion of the 'native speaker', in relation to linguistic inheritance (Rampton, 1995). They subvert and appropriate the use of this concept, used in marginalizing speakers of non-native varieties of English, to instead 'otherize' the dominant group. The student teachers creatively co-construct identities of themselves as 'native speakers', not of Standard English, but of Singlish.

Midway through the discussion, we see the locally oriented ideological positions adopted by the student teachers in the initial exchanges of the discussion forum, however, turn in sharp contrast when these same student teachers move from self-identifying themselves as students and individuals to their institutional selves. In contrast to earlier posts in the forum where student teachers speak of Singlish as 'unique' and 'cool', and portray it as a marker of 'rapport' and 'friendship', the shared discourse in the online discussion shifts in its presentation and constructions of Singlish as 'weird' to foreigners, as an impediment to communication, as leading to 'misunderstanding', and as undesirable:

(12) Hui Ling:
I agree with Noraini and Su Lin that most of what we say can only be heard among Singaporeans like us! Morever, sometimes, the lexical items we use are created by us such as the word cheapo and cheeko. Foreigners may find these words weird.

(13) May Li:
The [Singlish] particles that we use add to their confusion and misunderstandings do happen.

(14) Guo Ji:
I find that, when talking to foreigners, sometimes communication can be problematic, especially when you're trying not to use too much SCE in order to be understood by foreigners. Many years back I was playing pool with a few of my 'ang moh' friends in NZ (at that time i was still learning to play). One of my friends commented that I played quite well for a beginner. I couldn't think of a better word so I just replied, 'I anyhow play one lah!' He just looked at me all confused, wondering what I was trying to say. It was a weird moment … haha …

(15) Hui Yin:
Foreigners often take some time to understand the true meaning behind our speech acts due to the vocabulary and lexical items that we use. The particles that we use add to their confusion and misunderstandings do happen.

There is a distinct shift in sentiment and in the ideological positioning of Singlish. Whereas the positive identification of Singlish aligns with the student teachers' individual local selves, the negative portrayal of Singlish is clearly constructed with a different voice, and aligned with the student teachers' identities as would-be teachers and institutional representatives of the Singapore Ministry of Education, which orients with the value of English as a global language. Hence, as institutional flag bearers, the students now position Singlish as imperfect and undesirable by contrasting 'perfect' English or 'correct' English, on the one hand, with Singlish or SCE, on the other. The contrast sets up the association of Singlish with bad or broken English:

(16) Sharmini:
[My Korean students] used to speak perfect English and now, they have lahs and lors sprinkled all over their speech.

(17) Li Lian:
My concern is that are they able to differentiate between the correct form of English and Singlish? I have a tuition kid who always speaks Singlish and it is so difficult for me to correct him as he acquires Singlish or 'broken' English at home as his 1st lang. Perhaps researchers should also consider children picking up Singlish as first lang and how it may affect the acquisition of Standard English. I believe there would be great insights.

(18) Su Lin:
I think that the children will learn that SCE and SSE have their own time and place. Perhaps now the children are not really exposed to situation that they need to use SSE. Maybe their teacher in the class did not reinforce SSE. However I believe that if the children are being exposed to more formal situations, they will be able to pick up the correct usage of SSE.

Sharmini's characterization of Singlish in (16) as the language of 'lahs' and 'lors' here negatively stereotypes the local variety through reference to its iconic pragmatic particles. Note in particular how this stereotyping contrasts sharply with Idah's earlier reference to Singaporeans as the 'lah' people in (7), in which the focus is on the ways foreigners are positioned as failing at speaking Singlish. Perhaps the strongest indication of the global orientation of these student teachers is in the overt advocating of the use of an exonormative standard of English – what Li Lian (17) refers to as Standard English, and what Su Lin (18) refers to as SSE or Standard Singapore English. Critically, in each of these three posts, the student teachers' voices are as teachers, repositioned as figures of institutional power and authority. Congruent to their constructed global selves, the student teachers talk about Singlish as 'broken' English (albeit in scare quotes). Their voices are transformed by the power of the roles they assume, and the same students, who in earlier posts championed Singlish, are now transformed by these new imagined roles as future teachers. In addition to demonstrating ideological dispositions congruent to a global orientation, the student teachers, in discussing the need to speak and teach Standard English, also show a shift away from informal English usage towards a use of English that is more formal, with fewer local forms.

The discourse of the student teachers exemplifies hybridity in a number of respects. First, they clearly show a meta-awareness of the tensions between the two opposing norms of English, in which a standard variety aligns with their identities as teachers, while the vernacular is representative of their identities as individuals and students. In negotiating their cultural and linguistic orientations towards these competing norms, they exhibit multivocality in interweaving their local selves with their global selves; the student teachers move fluidly between their personal identities as students and their professional selves as institutional representatives of Singapore's Ministry of Education. On the one hand, the student teachers express strongly positive opinions about Singlish – they frame their 'local' identities in relation to the role of Singlish as an identity marker, engaging in discourses that reaffirm and construct these. On the other hand, these same students express negative sentiments about Singlish in voicing concerns about the lack of international currency of local norms. Thus, the same students who champion Singlish are also the very ones who write about it in deprecating terms. Take for example, Li Lian, who in (5) talks about Singlish as cool, and yet describes Singlish as an *incorrect* form of English in (17) when she assumes a teacher's voice. Clearly, the students' imagined future professional identity as teachers is associated with a globalist perspective, and hence uppermost in the student teachers' minds are issues related to the lack of intelligibility and potential problems in communication when using Singlish with non-Singaporeans.

Yet another aspect of the discourse that illustrates the complex interplay of the global and the local is through the student teachers' use of internet-styled features, for example, in the use of lower case letters at the beginning of sentences, emotive icons – for example, (",) – and abbreviated forms such as 'mb' for 'maybe' in presenting their locally grounded pro-Singlish ideological positions. The internet style signals access to and knowledge of the global, but can in fact be seen as an example of vernacularization in resisting centripetal ideologies mandating unitary linguistic standardized norms of English. These bits and bytes of the global vernacular, in utilizing what are traditionally deemed 'non-standard' linguistic forms, serve to disrupt the expected alignments of internet technologies with the global, and instead appropriate these as markers of youth and modernity, emphasizing the power and prestige associated with participation in computer-mediated social networks. The multiplicity and layering of the identity affiliations is evidence of hybridity along a number of dimensions – as student versus teacher, personal versus professional stances, modernity versus tradition, and local versus global.

Hybridity and Teacher Identity

The choice of focus on the analysis of the discourse of a group of student teachers is particularly significant because, as Greene (1981: 12), for example, points out, the process of learning to be a teacher is in fact a process of the making and re-making of identity: 'Learning to teach is a process of identity development ... it is about choosing yourself, making deeply personal choices about who you are and who you will become as a teacher.' Davies and Harré (2001) suggest that identity construction can also be understood as a process of narrative positioning that shows teachers as active agents of their own lives, and of teacher identity formation as a dynamic and changing activity. What is also of significance is Britzman's (1991: 2) observation that the nature of teachers' work is fundamentally hybrid: 'Enacted in every pedagogy are the tensions between knowing and being, thought and action, theory and practice, knowledge and experience, the technical and the existential, the objective and the subjective.' In conceptualizing the tensions inherent in teachers' lives as dialogic rather than simply binary, Britzman in many ways suggests that teachers' lives, and thus identities, can be understood as hybrid, further articulating that although '[t]raditionally expressed as dichotomies, these relationships are not nearly so neat or binary. Rather, such relationships are better expressed as dialogic in that they are shaped as they shape each other in the process of coming to know.'

Thus, although identity is characterized as emergent and fluid, Cohen (2008: 83) points out that teachers are in fact 'not free to perform any identity', and that '... [i]dentity possibilities are constrained by normative beliefs and practices, as well as material conditions, that functionally limit the range of possibilities for a given identity'. Interestingly, Cohen also notes that it is in conforming to the normative expectations associated with particular roles that enables individuals to gain recognition for their work:

> In fact, it is often an individual's ability to conform to the normative beliefs, values, and behavior associated with a particular role identity that allows her or him to demonstrate competence within the role, and thereby to get recognized by (and recognition from) others. (2008: 83)

For English language teachers in a significant number of Outer Circle countries, such norms critically include an expectation that they speak, teach and believe in the sole legitimacy of a so-called 'Standard English', an English that is of international value and currency (see also Snow *et al.*, 2006). These normative expectations assigned to teachers can be understood as a logical consequence of the status of English as an international language of business, commerce, science and technology, and thus regarded by the governments of many nations as an extremely significant form of economic capital; this is especially so in nations such as Singapore that need to maintain their capacity to compete with economically more powerful nations for access to wealthy Western markets. Consequently, such nations see an investment in strong English language skills as fundamental in ensuring that their nation's workforce has strong communicative capabilities in English. Thus, however much English is seen to be local, in having made a home in these different cultural spaces in which it has been spoken and used in a wide range of contexts and over considerable stretches of time, it continues to be significantly shaped by global forces.

In the political macro-discourses of Singapore, it is therefore no surprise that a similar rhetoric regarding the dualistic role that English plays as both global and local language is consistently encountered, with a number of researchers characterizing English in Singapore as 'glocal' (Alsagoff, 2007, 2010; Bokhorst-Heng, 2005; Pakir, 2001), in which speakers are pulled in two opposite directions – the global and the local – and from which two distinctive norms of use have emerged. From the global perspective, English in Singapore is recognized in purely instrumental and utilitarian terms – it is valued for its access to financial and economic markets as well as its status as the language of the internet, science and technology. Since the need to use English, in this perspective, is primarily motivated by, and associated with, a global orientation, importance is naturally placed on an exonormative variety of English that is perceived as guaranteeing global currency and consequently access to international economic and financial markets. In contrast, the local perspective of English sees the language in terms of its emotional ties to the community, and its value as a local lingua franca in fostering social cohesion among the various ethnic groups in multicultural, multilingual Singapore. Since the need to use English is in this case motivated by a local orientation, importance is naturally placed on developing an endonormatively defined linguistic resource that is unique to Singapore – Singlish, the Singapore English vernacular, reflects what it is to be Singaporean, and is a means of expressing local identity/identities. Standard English and Singlish represent two different ideological positions on English and demonstrate the ways in which the centripetal forces of the global are in conflict with centrifugal forces of the local.

Teachers are often implicated in such debates over English (Kramer-Dahl, 2003). Education, seen as instrumental in developing a competitive 21st-century workforce for Singapore, is perceived as key to the economic health of the nation (Gopinathan, 2007). As such, there is a need for teachers, particularly, to ensure that the English they use and teach has international currency. Thus, the use of Singlish by teachers, even informally, in classrooms is something that is strongly discouraged by the Singapore authorities, as the concern is that it will impede students' acquisition of the standard variety of English as well as the development of 'proper' literacy practices. Pakir (1998: 76) argues that the advocacy of an exonormative standard of English for education is 'harmless pedagogic philosophy'. In fact, she suggests that having *only* the exonormative variety as the standard in the classroom is good for teachers, as she sees them being more comfortable with 'guidelines and models and ... happy to place into the system a chosen model' (Pakir, 1998: 76). Pakir goes on to say that teachers can 'either become uncertain in handling norms outside of their immediate reach or remain in blissful ignorance of the difference between the officially sanctioned exonormative standard and the variety in which they typically express themselves' (1998: 76–77). Instead of showing 'uncertainty in handling norms', I argue, based on the analysis of the discourse of the student teachers, that the tension teachers feel between speaking and valuing Singlish as a part of their individual repertoire of identities (what is seen as English, as local) and their institutional roles as teachers which oblige them to 'denounce', is constructed as a hybridity of selves in which multivocalic and layered discourse is built from an interweaving of incongruent contrastive ideological stances. Their discourse demonstrates, as Kraidy (1985: vi) points out, that hybridity is not a single idea or unitary concept; but an association of ideas, concepts and themes that at once contradict and reinforce each other. In particular, the data demonstrate that there is a fluid dialogic in which the local aligns with the student teachers' personal selves while the global is part of their professional identities. Rather than passively accepting their 'assigned identities' (Varghese *et al.*, 2005), the students demonstrate that they instead negotiate such tensions through their discourse, with regard to their ideological positionings of Singlish.

While these opposing opinions expressed by the student teachers in the discussion forum are similar to the debates between the pro-Singlish and anti-Singlish camps described in Bokhorst-Heng (2005), they are far more powerful exemplifications of hybridity because the opposing opinions are in fact expressed by the same students, who in the same breath both champion and disparage Singlish. This ostensible inconsistency and conflict in ideology arises not only from the tension between what the students see as their personal identities as speakers of English in Singapore, and their professional identities as teachers, as institutional flag bearers, but, as Alsup (2003) points out, also as a result of the tension between what the students understand as theoretical truths about the sociolinguistic variation of English and their understanding of the de facto practice in the schools and what they know of the larger national policies. Despite these contrastive viewpoints, and ostensibly inconsistent ideological positions, the online discussion should not be seen simply as linguistic schizophrenia in which the hegemonic and oppressive forces of the center act to constrain teachers. Instead, we see the agency of the teachers in actively negotiating the tensions in the global-local space, by contesting, resisting and transforming the discourses and ideologies of the center.

Pennington's (1992, 2002) discussion of the complexities and heterogeneity of teacher identity as 'not only multiple or hyphenated, but also layered' (Pennington, 2002: 2) resonates with this reading of the interweaving of the multifaceted sets of conflicting ideological positions as hybrid. Pennington sees student teacher identity, in particular, as 'dialogic ... in the sense of invoking and overlaying multiple voices, roles or discourses, including the teacher's past voice as a student, [and] the teacher's current voice as an institutional representative' (Pennington, 2002: 2). Alsup (2006) suggests that only when teachers are able to employ borderland hybrid discourses which enable the multidiscursive articulations and negotiations of contrastive personal and professional beliefs, will teachers be empowered towards developing more robust professional identities. In the Outer Circle countries, such discursive constructions of identity will necessarily entail discussion and negotiation of the norms to which the English being taught is oriented – the global or the local, or as we have seen, hybridity as both.

Concluding Remarks

In this chapter we have explored how identity, as a dialogic between the local and the global, facilitates an understanding of the use of English in the Singapore context. In particular, we see how teacher identity in an 'Outer Circle' context is far from homogenous or unified, where English is, for many speakers, not simply a clearly defined single code or language, but is a fluid metamorphic set of repertoires shifting and changing within the liminal spaces between global and local norms. This chapter has proposed how a more nuanced poststructural understanding of identity enables a richer reading of the conflicts between the personal and professional identities of teachers who speak an English far different from the norms required and whose identities are centered on the interstices of the global and the local. Such conflicts are, as has been shown, more aptly read as hybrid, and understood as being a process of 'becoming' rather than a product of schizophrenic disjuncture. Such a reading of identity as hybrid in such diasporic global contexts enables a richer understanding of the complex and multifaceted ways in which what we see as a single language, viz. English, varies across the cultures in which it is spoken, and across the identities for which it is constituted and constitutive of.

Note

(1) The data for this chapter come from an online discussion forum as part of an ungraded e-learning task in an undergraduate sociolinguistics class I taught in 2008–2009. Although the online forum was meant for the discussion of lexical innovations in Singlish, the student teachers chose instead to focus on their narratives about Singlish. The student teachers gave their consent for the use of this data. They are referred to by pseudonyms.

References

Alsagoff, L. (2007) Singlish: Negotiating culture, capital and identity. In V. Vaish, S. Gopinathan and Y. Liu (eds) *Language, Capital, Culture* (pp. 25–46). Rotterdam: Sense Publishers.

Alsagoff, L. (2010) English in Singapore: Culture, capital and identity in linguistic variation. *World Englishes* 29 (3), 336–348.

Alsup, J. (2003) English education students and professional identity development: Using narrative and metaphor to challenge pre-existing ideologies. *Pedagogy: Critical Approaches to Teaching Literature, Language, Composition, and Culture* 3 (2), 277–280.

Alsup, J. (2006) *Teacher Identity Discourses: Negotiating Personal and Professional Spaces.* Mahwah, NJ: Lawrence Erlbaum.

Bhabha, H.K. (1994) *The Location of Culture*. London: Routledge.

Bakhtin, M.M. (1981) *The Dialogic Imagination: Four Essays* (M. Holquist, ed. and C. Emerson, trans.). Austin: University of Texas Press.

Bhatt, R. (2008) In other words: Language mixing, identity representations, and third space. *Journal of Sociolinguistics* 12 (2), 177–200.

Bokhorst-Heng, W. (2005) Debating Singlish. *Multilingua* 24, 185–209.

Bourdieu, P. (1991) *Language and Symbolic Power* (G. Raymond and M. Adamson, trans.). Cambridge, MA: Harvard University Press.

Britzman, D.P. (1991) *Practice Makes Practice: A Critical Study of Learning to Teach*. Albany, NY: State University of New York Press.

Brubaker, R. and Cooper, F. (2000) Beyond 'identity'. *Theory and Society* 29 (1), 1–47.

Bruthiaux, P. (2003) Squaring the circles: Issues in modeling English worldwide. *International Journal of Applied Linguistics* 13 (2), 159–178.

Brutt-Griffler, J. (2002) *World English: A Study of its Development.* Clevedon: Multilingual Matters.

Bucholtz, M. and Hall, K. (2005) Identity and interaction: A sociocultural linguistic approach. *Discourse Studies* 7 (4–5), 585–614.

Canagarajah, A.S. (ed.) (2005) *Reclaiming the Local in Language Policy and Practice.* Mahwah, NJ: Lawrence Erlbaum.

Cohen, J.L. (2008) That's not treating you as a professional: Teachers constructing complex professional identities through talk. *Teachers and Teaching: Theory and Practice* 14 (2), 79–93.

Davies, B. and Harré, R. (2001) Positioning: The discursive production of selves. In M. Wetherell, S. Taylor and S. Yates (eds) *Discourse Theory and Practice* (pp. 261–271). London: Sage.

Duff, P.A. and Uchida, Y. (1997) The negotiation of teachers' sociocultural identities and practices in postsecondary EFL classrooms. *TESOL Quarterly* 31 (3), 451–486.

Firth, A. and Wagner, J. (1997) On discourse, communication, and (some) fundamental concepts in SLA research. *Modern Language Journal* 81, 285–300.

Fuss, D. (1991) *Essentially Speaking: Feminism, Nature & Difference*. New York: Routledge.

Gopinathan, S. (2007) Globalisation, the Singapore developmental state and education policy: A thesis revisited. *Globalisation, Societies and Education* 5 (1), 53–77.

Greene, M. (1981) Contexts, connections, and consequences: The matter of philosophical and psychological foundations. *Journal of Teacher Education* 31, 31–37.

Hall, S. (1990) Cultural identity and diaspora. In J. Rutherford (ed.) *Identity: Community, Culture, Difference* (pp. 222–237). London: Lawrence and Wishart.

Kachru, B. (1983) *The Other Tongue: English Across Cultures*. Urbana: University of Illinois Press.

Kachru, B. (1986) *The Alchemy of English: The Spread, Functions and Models of Non-Native Englishes*. Oxford: Pergamon Press.

Kraidy, M. (1985) *Hybridity, or the Cultural Logic of Globalization*. Philadelphia, PA: Temple University Press.

Kramer-Dahl, A. (2003) Reading the 'Singlish debate': Construction of a crisis of language standards and language teaching in Singapore. *Journal of Language, Identity and Education* 2 (3), 159–190.

McKay, S.L. and Wong, C.S. (1996) Multiple discourses, multiple identities: Investment and agency in second-language learning among Chinese adolescent immigrant students. *Harvard Educational Review* 66 (3), 577–608.

Norton, B. (1997) Language, identity, and the ownership of English. *TESOL Quarterly* 31 (3), 409–429.

Norton Peirce, B. (1995) Social identity, investment, and language learning. *TESOL Quarterly* 29 (1), 9–31.

Pakir, A. (1998) English in Singapore: The codification of competing norms. In S. Gopinathan, A. Pakir, W.K. Ho and S. Vanithamani (eds) *Language, Society and Education in Singapore: Issues and trends* (2nd edn) (pp. 63–84). Singapore: Times Academic Press.

Pakir, A. (2001) The voices of English-knowing bilinguals and the emergence of new epicentres. In B.Y. Ooi (ed.) *Evolving Identities: The English Language in Singapore and Malaysia* (pp. 1–11). Singapore: Times Academic Press.

Papastergiadis, N. (1997) Tracing hybridity in theory. In P. Werbner and T. Modood (eds) *Debating Cultural Hybridity: Multi-Cultural Identities and the Politics of Anti-Racism* (pp. 257–281). London: Zed Books.

Pennington, M.C. (1992) Reflecting on teaching and learning: A developmental focus for the second language classroom. In J. Flowerdew, M. Brock and S. Hsia (eds) *Perspectives on Second Language Teacher Education* (pp. 47–65). Hong Kong: City University of Hong Kong.

Pennington, M.C. (2002) Teacher identity in TESOL. Paper presented at the Inaugural Meeting of the Association of the Promotion of Quality in TESOL Education (QuiTE), Institute of Education, UK, accessed 2 December 2007. http://www.quality-tesol-ed.org.uk/2002_seminar.html.

Phillipson, R. (1992) *Linguistic Imperialism*. Oxford: Oxford University Press.

Rampton, B. (1995) Displacing the native speaker: Expertise, affiliation, and inheritance. *ELT Journal* 44, 97–101.

Snow, M.A., Kamhi-Stein, L.D. and Brinton, D.M. (2006) Teacher training for English as a lingua franca. *Annual Review of Applied Linguistics* 26, 261–228.

van Lier, L. (1994) Forks and hope: Pursuing understanding in different ways. *Applied Linguistics* 15 (3), 328–347.

Varghese, M., Morgan, B., Johnston, B.L. and Johnson, K.A. (2005) Theorizing language teacher identity: Three perspectives and beyond. *Journal of Language, Identity & Education* 4 (1), 21–44.

Young, R.J.C. (1995) *Colonial Desire: Hybridity in Theory, Culture and Race*. London: Routledge.

16 Enacting Hybridity in the Philippine Diaspora

Corazon D. Villareal

Introduction

This chapter looks at hybridity as *subjectivity*. In particular, it attempts to access the inner state of diasporic subjects through an analysis of their linguistic interactions in the 'location of the everyday' (Smith, 1987). It is concerned with the following questions: How does the hybrid subject develop the agency to manage the diasporic condition? How is language used as an intermediary? In undertaking these aims, the chapter will present the rationale for the project, define key terms, discuss the main theoretical concepts framing its methodology, present and analyze the corpus for the study, then close with a discussion of the meta-linguistic implications of the study for applied linguistics research.[1]

The Philippine Diaspora: An Overview

The diaspora refers to the dispersal of peoples from former colonies to Western countries and their urban centers (Ong, 2004; Walsh, 2003). The Philippine diaspora began largely as a 20th-century phenomenon tied up with American colonization. The influx of Filipino immigrant professionals and students to the US led to the growth of an English-speaking Filipino-American population. The composition and distribution of this diaspora significantly changed, however, from the 1970s up to this first decade of the 21st century, when deteriorating economic conditions in the country brought about by a string of corrupt governments and the market demands of globalization propelled Filipinos to venture overseas. Facilitated by a competence in English, they fanned out to Asia, the Middle East, Africa and Europe, to work as medical personnel, engineers, teachers (mostly English teachers), skilled workers, entertainers, priests and nuns, hotel and restaurant staff, and domestics, among others. Between 10% and 11% of the Filipino population of about 80 million reside outside the country and 70% is affected by migration (Cruz, 2004).

The relationship of the diaspora with their host nations has often been problematic. The diaspora have to contend with the conditional hospitality of their host nations or communities which stipulate restrictions on the guests and thrust them into an inside/outside relation (Derrida, 2000: 77). Studies on the Filipino diaspora revolve around the maneuverings within 'power' and 'resistance' that labor migrants – domestic workers in particular – employ to counter structures of power (see for instance, Abesamis, 1998–1999; Aguilar, 2002; De Guzman, 2008).

This study sites itself within linguistic studies on the Filipino diaspora, a subject on which little has been done, with the exception of Lorente (2007), Manalansan (2003) and De Guzman (2008). Using Bourdieu's framework on symbolic capital, Lorente studies the interactions between agency and structure among Filipino domestic workers in Singapore, while Manalansan (2003: 61) notes that the immigrant Filipino queer's refusal to translate swardspeak[2] into English for non-Filipino gays is laying 'claim to a space no matter how fleeting or limited, in the transnational setting of New York City'. Guzman analyzes the 'emotional textures of migrant lives' through archival sources, public records and personal narratives. However, while these studies on diaspora hover in the sphere of hybridity, the discussions are not framed within the lenses of Filipino migrants themselves – except perhaps for Lorente's and Manalansan's studies. And while agency is seen in the strategies of negotiations, its origins in the introspective space of the diasporic subject are hardly explored.

Hybridity Studies: The Critical Edge

Hybridity studies are of a wide range but of particular importance to this project are those that confront unequal relationships in the political economy of language contact and map routes for resistance. Examples are perspectives on bilingualism as in Bhatt (2008), who analyzes code-switching from Hindi into English in Indian newspapers and identifies this as a site for hybrid subjects; Hinnenkamp (2003), who concludes that code-switching, code-mixing and the stylized forms of immigrant adolescents of Turkish background in Germany are forms of counter-discourse and Woolard (1998), who argues that in delivering simultaneous messages in linguistic contact zones, speakers claim multiple social identities.

Other studies deal with the modalities of technology in a globalized economy. For instance, Shome (2006) examines the virtual diaspora of Indian call center agents; trained to develop an American accent and hide the physicality of their Indian-ness, they reveal a politics of hybridity based on the aural and the invisible – not from body, color and visuality (as previously theorized, for example by Fanon, 1952; Hall, 1988; Cesaire, 2001). Salonga (2011) notes that Filipino call center agents employ play and performance to get around conventions imposed by the corporate hierarchy, yet maintain a functional competence in the global community. Fung and Carter (2006), in a study of computer-mediated communication of 20 Cantonese-English bilingual interlocutors in Hong Kong, observe a hybridity of language 'transcreated' from the interacting factors of modality, technology and cultural diversity. This emerging register is the medium to articulate solidarity and cultural identity.

While these studies demonstrate agency, the motivations and the ideology behind agency are not clear. Since the hybrid situation is fluid, the responses to it may not always be socially transformative but may even support, unwittingly, the status quo (see Bhabha, 1985). If the hybrid subjects are to have a critical awareness of the forces at play in the hybrid experience and respond to this with coherence and consistency, they must be conscious of the cognitive, affective and social factors driving them to understand the complexity of the experience, and from there subvert, resist or even just shield themselves from the host's 'conditional' hospitality. This critical mode is necessary because the diaspora cannot always rely on institutional support from host or home, and must draw from within themselves to manage their hybrid situation. 'Indeed, recognizing the difference within is the basis for being open to a non-suppressive negotiation of differences between people and groups' (Fairclough, 1999: 76). The researcher therefore needs to probe the hybrid's *subjectivity* or inner space.

A Question of Method[3]

But how does one track movements in the subjectivity of the diasporic actors and the process by which they construct and claim agency? The project appears fraught with risks since this goes beyond what can be determined empirically. Yet social difference on which hybridity hinges is seen now 'not only as difference between people but also difference *within* (italics in original); negotiating differences is simultaneously working out who I am or who we are' (Fairclough, 1999: 76). This is consistent with Derrida's thoughts on hospitality encounters between host and guest in sites of hybridity, as interruptions of the *self* (as cited in Westmoreland, 2008: 1) (italics in original). It is significant that for Fung and Carter (2006), linguistic negotiations to cross such differences are 'transcreations', implying interventions by the individual. It is in this broad sense that agency is understood, that is, the conscious deliberate intention to change oneself and one's lived reality. And, if the study of that *within* results in an 'enhanced reflexivity' to new knowledges (with which Giddens (1994) characterizes late modern societies), and to adjustments in social practice, it may be well worth the risk of accessing subjectivity.

The cognitive and affective processes of the subjects are the principal focus for analysis. These will be approached through the *ways of talking* or conversation (Edwards & Potter, 2005, as cited in Ten Have, 1999: 55); turn-taking shall be observed but it shall be extended to the narrators' speaking to themselves and to reacting to what is seen in their field of vision (Goodwin, 1979).

It is not clear how much current interactional linguistic studies (in which we locate conversation analysis) allows for a self-reflexive perspective, especially where power relations are negotiated. Commenting on the celebrated debate between Schlegoff (1999), a known advocate of conversation analysis (CA), and Billig (1999) and Wetherell (1998), advocates of critical discourse analysis (CDA), Van Dijk (1999) notes that the two approaches recognize how text and talk are structured within the confines of social situations. In CA, negotiations within power relations are seen to unfold in the ongoing interaction of the participants. In CDA, contextual features such as power and gender (and in our case, the diaspora) are seen to frame the conversation a priori; once a contextual feature has been identified, CDA explores how it shapes and is shaped by text and talk. However, CA insists that contextualization must not just be presupposed but proven empirically in the details of the conversation. In both approaches, interaction is recorded through a third-party researcher's gaze. It is difficult to know if the speakers and the interlocutor(s) are conscious of the crossings and the negotiations. Neither can the analyst, whose gaze is that of the observer looking in, enter into their subjectivities since the analyst remains apart from the subjects and draws conclusions based only on the conversations.

While hierarchies of power are unearthed and agency enacted, one cannot know if the subjects and the analyst have intimations of the social contexts that drive them, or an alternative reality. Neither do the conversations demonstrate the subjects apprehending that their social realities are often 'naturalized' or taken-for-granted assumptions. Such a realization could come from self-reflexivity which refers to 'the way concepts are mobilized' (Pennycook, 2001: 42–43) and 'a problematizing stance' that acknowledges the limits of knowing (Pennycook, 2001: 8, citing Spivak, 1993: 25).

Thus, CA should be supplemented with a method which not only relates the language to contexts of social relations but proceeds from the subject and the analyst apprehending their hybridity. Here, personal narratives may fill in the missing link. Jerome Bruner, a cognitive psychologist, notes that narrative knowledge is not only the articulation of emotions, but a 'legitimate form of reasoned knowing' (Polkinghorne, 1995: 9). In linguistic studies, narratives have been proven valuable (see Cortazzi's (1994) extensive review). For example, Labov (1972, 1981) analyses the connection between the structures of narratives and their social functions. Narratives contribute to meaning-making. Goffman (1981: 174), for instance, considers personal narratives as 'strips of personal experience', 'replayed' not just to report but to re-experience. Labov (1972) refers to their 'evaluative' function which gives the meaning of the narrative for the narrator, while for Mumby (1993: 5), narratives are sites 'of meaning in which social actors are implicated'.

The chapter utilizes first-hand accounts of narrators struggling to come to terms with diasporic experiences. These are Balde's *Mga Kuwento Mulang Kathmandu* (Accounts from Kathmandu) and Hope Tauro-Batuigas' *Si Ako sa World Wide Web* (I in the World Wide Web). These are taken from Beltran's *Global Pinoy*[4] (2006), a collection inspired by the exodus of overseas Filipinos, the government's globalization program and international developments such as the 'US war on terrorism'. Non-fictional works, like Balde's and Tauro-Batuigas', outnumber fiction. 'Could it be', Beltran (2006: 11) asks, 'that writing on such a topical subject as the "global Pinoy" necessitates a testimonial genre that requires more factuality?'

Manila to Kathmandu: Contemplating Hybridity

The following analysis takes us into the inner space of a Filipino diasporic subject trying to apprehend his experience in hybridity. Balde was a construction engineer in Kathmandu but he hails from Albay in the Bicol region south of Manila. He now writes full time and has become a recipient of many national awards. *Kuwento* recounts his experience from 1988–1997 as a contract engineer with a Canadian firm commissioned by the Nepalese government to repair the runway of the Tribhuvan International Airport in Kathmandu. The account is mainly in Filipino but the language is heteroglossic: English, Filipinized English and Spanish terms are embedded.

> Habang naghihintay sa halo ng ***aspalto***, ang mga ***trabahador*** naming Filipino na hindi sanay sa lamig ay parang mga inakay na nagsisiksikan sa tabi ng ***dyenerator*** at sa darang ng mainit na ilaw. Tila mga ***astronaut***

sa kapal ng kasuotan. Bukod sa ***sombrero*** ay may talukbong pa ang mukha at tainga. Mata lamang ang nakalabas. Malimit ay dalawang ***kamiseta***, isang ***kamisadentrong*** mahaba ang manggas, isang ***dyaket*** at makakapal na ***gwantes*** ang pang-itaas. Ang pang-ibaba ay dalawang magkapatong na pantalon sa ibabaw ng *long john* at tatlong saping medyas sa loob ng *safety shoes.* Itsura ng mga *mummy* sa *Ehipto.* Kung kumilos ay tila mga *zombie* sa sinaunang ***pelikulang*** *horror* – walang *talkies* at *slow motion*. (Balde, 2006: 22) [Bold italics in original]

Direct borrowings from English and Spanish are italicized. A Filipinized orthography and phonology are adopted in words such as *aspalto, dyenerator, pantalon, dyaket* (from English); and *trabahador, kamiseta, kamisadentro, gwantes, medyas, pelikula* (from Spanish).

The narrator interacts with the Nepalese in what he characterizes as broken English. He narrates matter-of-factly and while he notices aspects of Nepali life, he remains uninvolved. He and other Filipinos cannot care less about protracted work as long as the dollars keep on coming. Kathmandu is a bustling tourist spot, especially in November (the best time to climb Mt Everest) when tourists descend from airplanes and even outnumber the Nepalis. Touristy practices are evident: frenzied shopping for gold, precious stones, *thanka* and Buddhist images, bustling hotels and cottages, mountain trekking, river rafting, and so on.[5] Canadians who monitor the project act more as tourists than inspectors.

These signs of modernity appear to adulterate religion. One afternoon the Nepali cook, who learned some recipes from Filipino workers, comes with good news at the staff house:

> *'Sir, I can cook bulalo* (stewed beef bones) *tonight. Plenty of beef with bone marrow'*, sabi niyang nakangisi (he says, grinning).
>
> *'Where did you get beef?'* tanong ko (I asked).
>
> Ipinaliwanag niya sa putul-putol ng Ingles na marami daw kinatay na baka sa isang nayon. Nakabungisngis siya habang nagkukuwento. Napag-alaman kasi ng mga mamamayan na nagkaubusan ng karne sa mga dumagsang turista sa Kathmandu.
> (The cook explains in broken English that many cows were slaughtered in a village when people learned that the beef supply was running out with the influx of tourists. He was grinning while telling the story.)
>
> *'How did you kill the cow?'* nagtataka kong tanong (wondering, I asked).
>
> Lumabas uli ang ngiti niyang galing sa bungal na bibig (Again he broke into his toothless smile).

> *'In Baneswar, sir, very tall clift...we helped the cow commit suicide!'* (Balde, 2006: 21)

While poverty is glaring, the narrator treats it as an administrative concern. One time, the Filipino driver, traversing a narrow street in his Land Rover, runs over a child. The narrator contacts the firm's Nepali agent who strikes a deal with the village council elder: payment to the victim's family equivalent to two years' salary of the head of the family, payment to all members of the council and a monthly salary of not more than six months for the family of the man who consents to imprisonment in place of the driver. The narrator is apprehensive that the company may have to pay the man's salary for life. But the elder assures him that if a cow were killed, the culprit would be beheaded or imprisoned for life. He says further:

> *'It will not happen, Sir. This man, he just come out of jail after six months. And the person killed? He was government employee, he was run over by the Canadian!'* (Balde, 2006: 25)

Events in the country come to a head in 1988, close to the inauguration of the airport, which was also the Filipinos' departure date from Nepal. For some days, in casinos and hotels, the narrator and co-Filipinos sense rebellious stirrings against the government due to widespread poverty, corruption and the flaunting of wealth by the King's ministers. Used to protests in the Philippines during the Marcos years and even in the Cory Aquino presidency, these stirrings do not bother the Filipinos even as they hear talk that money for the airport should have gone to the poor. The ceremony is brief: after reading a short speech, the King leaves briskly with his ministers. However, fully armed Gurkhas in war attire and the military cavalry encircle the airport. The Filipinos hurry back to the staff house in their Land Rover but over the radio they hear of clashes between the rebels and the military forces by the King's palace gate and the spacious grounds of the parliament. They meet rallyists carrying placards with the slogans: DOWN WITH CORRUPT GOVERNMENT! DISSOLVE PARLIAMENT!

Interestingly for the Filipino workers, many rallyists tie yellow bands around their heads and, with their thumbs and index fingers forming an L, they shout CORY! CORY![6] The narrator could not help but join in the shouting while 'the hair on his arms stood on its head' (Nakisabay na rin ako sa sigawan habang nangangalisag ang mga balahibo ko sa braso) (Balde, 2006: 28). Wanting to understand the sudden turn of events, he calls for the company's lawyer when he reaches the staff house. But bloodied Nepalis who worked for them at the airport project seek refuge in the staff house.

The workers recount that many rebels were killed in a bloody battle against the police and other government forces. Luckily the Gurkhas do not intervene. Now, however, the people demand that the King step down and hand over the reins of government to them.

The transformation surprises the narrator. From the lips of workers who would meekly say:

> *'Yes, sir...alright...if you please, sir...Namaste, sir'* the narrator now hears: *'the right to live, to eat, speak...children dying faster than old men...where to go? No place; what to do? Just fight...if we die? Better, than to live like pigs....'* (Balde, 2006: 29)

They debate in broken English with the British-educated Nepali lawyer. The lawyer tells them that communists have instigated the rebellion to dismantle democracy. But the former timekeeper counters:

> *'What democracy is this? If democracy this is, why we cannot speak free? Why no ramro – no good – hospital for sick? No ramro school for children? No ramro pay for workers? Democracy, no ramro!'*
>
> Sagot ng abogado (replied the lawyer): *'Oh, so you want democracy to give you hospital and school and money! Indeed! You want your government to provide you all your needs. Well, in case you don't understand, the government is not a charity ward. What have you done to deserve such bounty? Who are you to make such demands? We don't. My friends, you have to work for it. Like we did...'*
>
> Sabad ng dating opereytor naming ng pison (our former heavy equipment operator butted in): *'You did not – you are born rich'.*
>
> Dugtong ng dati naming tagakalaykay ng aspalto (Added our asphalt mixer): *'With money come from rice we grow! You no call us friends'.*
>
> At mabilis inagaw ng dati naming mensahero (And our former messenger interrupted quickly): *'Friends no make friends slaves'.* (Balde, 2006: 29–30)
>
> ... Nahinuha nilang ang respeto ay hindi nakukuha sa pagkaroon ng mataas na titulo at katungkulan. Nang gabing iyon ay tumitingin na sila ng diretso sa mukha at mata namin. At kung magpapaliwanag ay nagtataas na ng hintuturo, naduduro at tumitigpas sa hangin ang mga palad kapag may argumentong ibig bigyang diin (They discerned that respect could not be earned through titles or positions. That night, they could look us in the eye. And when they argued they would point their index fingers at us and cut the air with their palms.) (Balde, 2006: 30)

The exchange shows in sharp relief differences in their perceptions about the roots of their social predicaments. The workers' assertiveness and the suspension of polite turn-taking sequences ('the heavy equipment operator butting in' and 'the messenger interrupting quickly') indicate their determination to pursue their course of action even in the midst of threats of violent suppression. Gestures such as 'pointing their fingers', 'cutting the air with their palms' and 'looking us straight in the eye' indicate the transformations within their subjectivities (see Goodwin, 1979, on the connection of talk and visual aspects of interaction). The heated exchange is a semiotic seizure of power indicative of continuing violent assertions on the ground.

That communication between the Nepalese and the Filipino and between the workers and the lawyer is in broken English shows the functionality of a register of English in a zone of difference (in ethnicity) and sameness (in sociopolitical realities). A fractured English likewise becomes the medium with which the Nepalese seek to understand realities, transforming themselves in the process. The broken language that appears to break hybridity actually serves to bridge it. Hybridity is enacted as the Nepalese peasants and workers process their course of action linguistically among themselves while drawing from the language of protest deployed by the Filipinos.

For the Filipino engineer, the route to critical awareness is different. Unlike most diasporic Filipinos, the Filipino engineer is not in a subordinate position to a hegemonic host. He is, in fact, esteemed by the less-educated Nepalese workers and considered an equal by the British-educated Nepalese lawyer. His experience is thus a reversal of most hybrid conditions.

The narrator is detached initially, even slightly derisive of his hosts and their traditions; he is in Kathmandu only to earn and to enjoy the exotic. But he sees the poverty and degradation of the people (how, for instance, it was a practice for some to own up to crimes in exchange for measly and temporary income). When the Nepalese take steps to end such poverty and are violently suppressed by the state, he sees a kinship between them and the Filipinos. The experience affects him so much he contemplates the meaning of his experience in a foreign land vis-à-vis the conditions in his home country.

In a conversation with his wife months after his return to the Philippines, he recalls details of that memorable last night in Kathmandu when he gained understanding of the street protests from the debate between the workers and the lawyer.

> Naroon sa pagtatalo niya at ng mga manggawa, nasa kanilang mainit na pagpapaliwanangan, maaninanaw ang suliraning matagal nang nakabaon sa kanilang kinalkihang kaugalian. Kung naroon ka, ay nasaksihan

> mo sana kung paano ang isang napakatandang daigdig ay nangyayaring magising...
> (There in the debate, in their heated explanations, could be gleaned a problem long embedded in the life they had grown up with. Had you been there, you would have witnessed an old world awakening...) (Balde, 2006: 31)

The recollection of the events in Nepal leads him to look into his own home.

> 'At ikaw, ang daigdig na binalikan mo ba'y nagbago na rin?' tanong ng asawa ko na tuon ang titig sa mga mata ko.
> ('And you, this world that you came back to, did it also change?' asked my wife looking at me intently.)
>
> 'Marahil...marahil ay hindi'.
> ('Maybe...maybe not'.)
>
> 'Ikaw ang nagbago....' salo niya.
> ('It's you who has changed....' she interposed.)
>
> 'Kapag nagkaroon ba ng bagong suson ang balintataw ay nangangahulugang nagbago na rin ang kulay ng daigdig?'
>
> ('When the pupil of the eye takes on another layer, does this mean the world has changed colors as well?') (Balde, 2006: 31)

'Manila to Kathmandu' reconfigures hybridity in the postcolonial context. There is no transnational movement to Western geographies; neither does hybridity hinge on the conditions of doubleness of the colonizer and the colonized. Instead, the colonized (both the Nepalese and the Filipino) look into themselves and into each other. Apprehending a sameness in their material conditions, they claim agency – made visible in the hybrid language of protest of the Nepalese and the metaphorical question of the engineer. Yet, while hybridity proceeds from the subjectivity of the individual, from which originates agency, the experiences of the Nepalese and the engineer suggest that hybridity is not just individual. It is part of a complex system in which actors interact with agents both human and non-human, for example, an old world, the repressive apparatus of the state. To quote Marilyn Cooper (2011: 421) in a study of rhetorical agency: '... causation in complex systems is non-linear: change arises not as the effect of a discrete cause, but from the dance of perturbation and response as agents interact'.

Interactive Hybridity

Almost half of Filipino migrants are women, and although there is a mismatch between jobs and levels of education, their numbers have increased along with the attendant problems: the confinement of women workers in socially constructed roles such as care and reproduction, and difficult living and working conditions (Fabros, 2009). An area of concern has been pornography and the mail-order bride trade in cyberspace. This section concerns itself with the human-computer interface as site of hybridity, in particular, the extension of the Filipino woman diaspora to the web. The corpus is Tauro-Batuigas' (2006) *'Si Ako sa Worldwide Web'* ('I in the World Wide Web') and as in the section on 'Manila to Kathmandu', CA is utilized but connections with feminist and media theory are made as well.

The corpus departs from most conversations in that except for a few lines which the narrator recalls were uttered to her by her son and her husband, the conversation is in an informal confessional mode where she takes the reader into her confidence. The mode is symptomatic of her lack of self-importance and aloneness and, not surprisingly, the account segues from her interaction with her reader into that with the virtual. As the narrator turns 40, she is ridden with doubts on her attractiveness and bored with the perfunctory way that her husband treats her. Looking for something different to do, she google searches several words – '40 years old woman', '40 years old women sex life', 'free erotic stories', 'free videos' – becoming progressively aroused as she swings from one website to another. Virtual sex facilitated by text and screen becomes the substitute for the actual pleasures of her body. As Ballard (1991: 55) writes, 'Computers have seduced some users away from face-to-face interactions altogether.'

But as she traipses between the virtual and the real, other realities beyond the safety of disembodied sex intervene. What if her son accesses these? She googles 'Filipina', and notices, to her consternation, advertisements for Filipina mail-order brides, pen pals and nude pictures. The following is an entry on http://manilabeauty.com/:

> *I even encourage you to look at the other sites to compare the quality of the ladies.... You will see how much more selective we really are.*
> *I know many of you are tired of the US or Canadian singles....insincere girls who like to play games or expect constant material gifts. But these Asian ladies are honest, faithful, rarely lose their figures as they age, extremely supportive, and care more about your heart than your wallet.*

Moreover, websites peddle Filipinas engaging in cybersex, as on http://www.filipinbargirls.com. Robot-like, the women follow instructions from chat mates and via the webcam, they perform with sex gadgets like the vibrator, dildo, oil, and so on, for a fee.

The narrator realizes she is herself the subject of her voyeuristic adventure, and her virtual flight to erotica crashes. Lust gives way to rage. 'Bakit ganito ang itsura ko? Bakit ganito and itsura, ang imahen ng ng kababaihang Pilipino sa worldwide web?' ('Why do I look like this? Why this face, this image of Filipina women on the web?') (Tauro-Batuigas, 2006: 35). It is usual to view the virtual either as an escape from reality or as an alternative reality (Saenz, 1996), but here the virtual constructs reality. To this she objects furiously. Upon further reflection, the narrator sadly admits that the virtual image the merchandisers produce is, in fact, an extension of reality since there are now half a million Filipina prostitutes – the highest number in Asia. 'Ekstensyon na rin talaga ang napakalawak na mundo ng hindi naman totoong worldwide web ng totoong mundo' ('The make-believe world of the web has now become the extension of the real world.') (Tauro-Batuigas, 2006: 36). The textual practices and visual images generated on the Filipina on the net merge with a reality borne out by figures. As various realities intrude into the woman's primal computer and the boundaries between the purported image and fact dissolve, hybridity becomes multiple and changing while being enacted in the opposing poles of organism and machine.

In Tauro-Batuigas' account, the medium for negotiating these terrains is primarily textual. 'Sexual experience, like other human experience, is communicated and made meaningful by codes and conventions of signification' (Cameron & Kulick, 2003: 15). Like Balde's, the narrative is mainly in Filipino, but unlike Balde's, intertextuality is explored with global media through references to media personalities like Oprah and Meg Ryan. The narrative is also marked by frequent shifts between Filipino and English: 'O, sige na nga, *exciting* na *gift* iyon considering na sa mga lalaking nakasama ko, itong mama lang na ito ang nakakaalam kung nag-*oorgasm* ba ako o nag-*fake* lang. At take note, 'day, mas magaling pa ko umarte kay Meg Ryan sa pelikulang *When Harry Met Sally*.' [Italics are the narrator's] ('Okay, then. That was an exciting gift, considering that among the men I've been with, he's the only one who could know when my orgasm was real or not. And take note, I'm a better actress than Meg Ryan of *When Harry Met Sally*.') (Tauro-Batuigas, 2006: 32). Filipino speakers code-switch from formal to informal tones to reach out to one another. In this case, however, code-switching is also evidence of the flippant, self-conscious way the narrator copes with a new stage in her life, at least up until the websites jolt her away from a comfort zone and nudge her to move from the personal to the social.

The advertisements on the websites are in Standard English. The narrator understands such English but responds in Filipino like many educated Filipinos, unless they converse with an English-using speaker. It is a Filipino highly resonant with English (as the italicized words in the excerpt above); there are, as well, English words not italicized which blend naturally with the native language. For instance:

> 'Happy Birthday, 'Nay. Magseseven na po. Pasok na ako.' ('Happy Birthday, Mom. It's almost seven. I'm going to school now.')
>
> 'He he he. Hindi ako natatawa. Hay naku! 40. 'Lam mo nang ayaw kong maalala. Insensitive ka talaga. Dahil iyan sa kalalaro mo ng computer games...' ('He he he. That's not funny. Oh! 40. You know I don't want to remember. You're so insensitive. That comes from your playing computer games.') (Tauro-Batuigas, 2006: 32)

Despite the English overheard, which is usually an index of the Filipino speaker's level of education, what comes across is Filipino street language – concrete and palpable, turning lewd and vulgar at times as it articulates body and desire. In contrast to the Standard English, which freezes the Filipina into a sex merchandise, the narrator's Filipino is true and bare, spontaneous and dynamic – through which language we track her subjectivity in process.

Tauro-Batuigas' personal narrative shows the hybrid interaction between woman and web provoking the hybrid response of alienation and liberation. Alienation in the narrator's initial inability to distinguish between bodily desire and machine-generated desire; liberation in the recognition that this machine-text actually holds the woman victim to commodified desire. The experience of hybridity departs from the 'home and away' model in that the narrator never really leaves the physical confines of her room nor does she physically encounter the Filipino diaspora; discernment is reached through virtual interaction and through introspection sited in her subjectivity.

Suspended Hybridity?

While the beginnings of social transformation emerge among the hybrid subjects, these appear to be only a promise since the narratives do not offer a specific course of action. We recall that the engineer ends the account with a metaphoric reflection. In the Tauro-Batuigas account, the narrator browses through other websites which flagrantly expose the Filipina, then reverts to her initial position that these are not the true Filipina: 'Ayoko na talaga!

Hindi ito ang tunay na ako....' ('Oh, no! This is not the real me....'). Alarmed that this day-long rendezvous with virtual sex is an indication of an insatiable sexual appetite, she searches for the term 'maniac'. She finds http://www.manyak.com/, which turns out to be a religious website that lists a series of biblical quotations from the new and the old testaments '...I HAVE SET BEFORE YOU LIFE AND DEATH, BLESSING AND CURSING: THEREFORE CHOOSE LIFE, THAT ...THOU...MAY LIVE. DEUT 30:19...' (Tauro-Batuigas, 2006: 37). Here the account ends.

The solutions both narratives offer to change social conditions are rhetorical. But a sharp ironic edge in the narratives suggests that what appears escapist is actually strategic. The engineer's metaphorical musing harks back to the classic irony of seeing and not seeing in the Oedipal revelations, and resonates with a central concern of critical theory to distinguish between fake and truth, discourse and reality. The housewife resorts to a 'counter deception' by luring the browser to a website on biblical allusions, perhaps a feminist technique to subvert patriarchy in the virtual world. For example, the website http://www.bigbadchinesemama.com bandies itself as a mail-order bride site but it is really a subversion of the mail/male-order bride discourse. It seduces unwitting clients, then hits back at them by displaying a woman with her back to the camera, her right hand with an extended middle finger at the back of her head, thus mocking patriarchal gaze and empowering the woman through a counter-image (Rondina, 2004: 55).

Irony and metaphor are not just literary tools, but part of the cognitive process itself – which is what De Saussure (1983) and Jakobson (1960) would remind us of in their binary linguistic formulations. Moreover, the issue in many instances, according to George Lakoff, 'is not the truth or falsity of a metaphor but the perceptions and inferences that follow from it and the actions that are sanctioned by it' (Lakoff & Johnson, 1980: 158). In other words, the diasporic subject's musings may not directly result in agency, but in its beginnings.

Conclusion: Enacting Hybridity in Linguistic Studies

It is doubtful whether the linguistic researcher, who maintains distance from the subjects of study, can enter into the minds of the subjects contemplating their hybridity. To be privy to this unfolding, the study has deployed CA, along with the autobiographical memoir and the confessional genre. The notion of conversation is broadened from the face-to-face interaction of a speaker with another speaker(s) to that where the speaker interacts with himself/herself or reacts to virtual figures. Such conversations/interactions, moreover, are not confined to two languages or their hybrids (Nepalese-English; Tagalog-English; broken English) as the subjects, in transglossic fashion (to cite García, Chapter 6, this volume), draw upon a whole cultural repertoire to adapt to the fluidity of their communicative situations: body movements, sounds, the visual (placards, L sign), the virtual.

Windows into subjectivity open up because the narratives are the subjects' recollections of past experiences, the impact of which they are continuing to decipher and to articulate in the accounts. The approaches were employed, then, less to track sequencing and turn-taking, or to classify hybridity into types. The purpose was to follow *the process* by which the subjects comprehend the workings of power in their respective diasporic sites. Each is a case study not likely to be reduplicated. As circumstances unfold (Clifford & Marcus, 1966), the subjects move from purely personal interests towards an understanding of the larger situations in the diaspora: the collusion of Nepalese royalty and global agencies to perpetuate poverty among the Nepalese and the merging of capitalist interests and cyber-pornography to oppress Filipino women. It is in this sense of being able 'to read the world' (please see Lorente & Tupas, Chapter 4, this volume) that the subjects' experiences with hybridity have become transformative.

Still, some questions needle. How adequate are autobiographical accounts as windows to subjectivity? How much agency can the hybrid subjects and the researcher enact as global capital's 'predatory mobility' blurs their capacities to apprehend its many forms and sources (Appadurai, 2000: 16)? Could we know that the unrest in Nepal and the Philippines (and, as well, the unrest in our minds) connects with capital and the nation state? Or that the selling of mail-order brides is part of global technologies of 'integration' and 'connectivity'? Indeed, how can hybridity studies be further theorized and enacted to reveal the complexities of the diasporic predicament?

Notes

(1) I thank Topsie Ruanni Tupas for his valuable suggestions on the draft of my chapter and for sharing important materials.
(2) The vernacular code used by Filipino gay men in the Philippines and the diaspora.
(3) L'Eplattenier (2009) uses the term 'methodology' to refer to theorizing the goals of research; and 'methods' to refer to the contexts of the research process, including the research subject and materials. I have this same distinction in mind in this chapter.
(4) Pinoy is the diminutive for Filipino; it is an informal, in-group term used by Filipinos to refer to themselves.
(5) A related study is Francis Lim's (2008), who writes of the shifting subjectivities in the tourism encounters between the Nepalese and Westerners.
(6) These were used during the Aquino-led revolution against Marcos in 1987.

References

Abesamis, M. (1998–1999) Romance and resistance: The experience of Filipino domestic workers in Hong Kong. Unpublished research paper for MA Development Studies, Institute of Social Studies, The Hague.

Aguilar, F.V. Jr. (2002) *Filipinos in Global Migrations: At Home in the World*? Quezon City: Philippine Migration Research Network and the Philippine Social Science Council.

Appadurai, A. (2000) Grassroots globalization and the research imagination. *Public Culture* 12 (1), 1–19.

Balde, A.M. (2006) 'Mga Kuwento Mulang Kathmandu'. In H. Beltran (ed.) *Global Pinoy*, 32, (pp. 20–31). Manila: Cultural Center of the Philippines.

Ballard, J.G. (1991) The pleasure of the interface. *Screen* 32 (3). (Reprinted in Claudia Springer (ed.) (1996) *Electronic Eros*. Austin: University of Texas Press.)

Beltran, H.S. Jr. (ed.) (2006) *ANI. Global Pinoy*, 32. Special Feature on Global Pinoy. Manila: Cultural Center of the Philippines.

Bhabha, H.K. (1985) Signs taken for wonders: Questions of ambivalence and authority under a tree outside Delhi, May 1817. *Critical Inquiry* 12 (1), 144–165.

Bhatt, R.M. (2008) In other words: Language mixing, identity representations and *third space*. *Journal of Sociolinguistics* 12 (2), 177–200.

Billig, M. (1999) Whose terms? Whose ordinariness? Rhetoric and ideology in conversation. *Discourse and Society* 10 (4), 543–558.

Cameron, D. and Kulick, D. (2003) *Language and Sexuality*. Cambridge: Cambridge University Press.

Cesaire, A. (2001) *Notebook of a Return to My Native Land* (C. Eshleman, trans.). Wesleyan University Press.

Clifford, J. and Marcus, G. (eds) (1986) *Writing Culture*. Berkeley: University of California Press.

Cooper, M.M. (2011) Rhetorical agency as emergent and enacted. *Conference on College Composition* 62 (3), 420–449.

Cortazzi, M. (1994) Narrative analysis: State of the art article. *Language Teaching* 27 (3), 157–170.

Cruz, G.T. (2004) Beyond the borders, beyond the margins. *World Mission Magazine*, Special Report XVI (3), March. http://www.worldmission.ph/3March04/MarchSPECIAL.htm#special1 (accessed on 17 June 2010).

De Guzman, O.M.M. (2008) A cultural biography of overseas work: Letters and auto/biographical narratives of women OFWs, 1995–1997. PhD dissertation, University of the Philippines.

De Saussure, F. (1983) *Course in General Linguistics* (C. Bally and A. Sechehaye, ed., with the collaboration of A. Riedlinger; R. Harries, trans. and annotated). London: Duckworth.

Derrida, J. (2000) *Of Hospitality* (R. Bowlby, trans.). Stanford, CA: Stanford University Press.

Fabros, A. (2009) *Revisiting the State of Overseas Filipino Women Workers*. Global South Philippines Program, citing 2009 statistics from NCSO 2009.

Fairclough, N. (1999) Global capitalism and critical awareness of language. *Language Awareness* 8 (2), 71–82.

Fanon, F. (1952) *Black Skin, White Masks* (R. Philcox, trans.). New York: Grove Press.

Fung, L. and Carter, R. (2006) Where East meets West – Dual hybridity in the e-discourse of Hong Kong bilinguals. *Linguistics and Human Sciences* 2 (1), 29–57.

Giddens, A. (1994) *Beyond Left and Right*. Cambridge: Polity Press.
Goffman, E. (1981) *Forms of Talk*. Oxford: Blackwell.
Goodwin, C. (1979) Practices of seeing: Visual analysis: An ethnomethodological approach. In T. van Leeuwen and J. Carey (eds) (2000) *Handbook of Visual Analysis* (pp. 157–182). London: Sage Publications.
Hall, S. (1988) New ethnicities. *ICA Documents* 7, 27–31.
Hinnenkamp, V. (2003) Mixed language varieties of migrant adolescents and the discourse of hybridity. *Journal of Multilingual and Multicultural Development* 24 (1–2), 12–41.
Jakobson, R. (1960) Linguistics and poetics. In T. Sebeok (ed.) *Style in Language* (pp. 350–377). Cambridge: MIT Press.
Labov, W. (1972) *Language in the Inner City*. Philadelphia, PA: University of Pennsylvania Press.
Labov, W. (1981) Speech actions and reactions in personal narrative. In D. Tannen (ed.) *Analysing Discourse: Text and Talk* (pp. 219–247). Georgetown University Round Table. Washington, DC: Georgetown University Press.
Lakoff, G. and Johnson, M. (1980) *Metaphors We Live By*. Chicago, IL: University of Chicago Press.
L'Eplattenier, B.E. (2009) An argument for archival research methods: Thinking beyond methodology. *College English* 72 (1), 67–79.
Lim, F.K.G. (2008) Of reverie and emplacement: Spatial imaginings and tourism encounters in Nepal Himalaya. *Inter-Asia Cultural Studies* 9 (3), 375–393.
Lorente, B.P. (2007) Mapping English linguistic capital: The case of Filipino domestic workers in Singapore. Unpublished PhD dissertation, National University of Singapore.
Manalansan, M.F. (2003) *Global Divas: Filipino Gay Men in the Diaspora*. Durham, NC: Duke University Press. (Reprinted by Ateneo de Manila Press, 2006.)
Mumby, D.K. (ed.) (1993) *Narrative and Social Control: Critical Perspectives*. Newbury Park, CA: Sage Publications.
Ong, A. (2004) Cyberpublics and diaspora politics among transnational Chinese. *Interventions* 5 (1), 82–100.
Pennycook, A. (2001) *Critical Applied Linguistics: A Critical Introduction*. Mahwah, NJ: Erlhbaum.
Polkinghorne, D. (1995) Narrative configuration in qualitative analysis. *International Journal of Qualitative Studies in Education* 8 (1), 5–23.
Rondina, J. (2004) The e-mail order bride as postcolonial other: Romancing the Filipina in web-based narratives. *Plaridel* 1 (1), 47–56.
Saenz, M. (1996) 'Virtual sex'. In C. Springer (ed.) *Electronic Eros* (pp. 80–94). Austin: University of Texas Press.
Salonga, A.S. (2011) Performing English in the Philippine offshore call centers. Paper presented at the Mobility Language Conference, January 2011, Cape Town, South Africa.
Schlegoff, E. (1999) Naivete vs. sophistication or discipline vs. indulgence: A rejoinder to Billig. *Discourse and Society* 10 (4), 577–582.
Shome, R. (2006) Thinking through the diaspora: Call centers, India and, a new politics of hybridity. *International Journal of Cultural Studies* 9 (1), 105–124.
Smith, D.E. (1987) *The Everyday World as Problematic: A Feminist Sociology*. Boston: Northeastern University Press.
Spivak, G. (1993) *Outside in the Teaching Machine*. New York: Routledge and Kegan Paul.

Tauro-Batuigas, J.H. (2006) 'Si Ako sa world wide web'. In H. Beltran (ed.) *Global Pinoy*, 32 (pp. 32–37). Manila: Cultural Center of the Philippines.
Ten Have, P. (1999) *Doing Conversation Analysis*. London: Sage Publications.
Van Dijk, T.A. (1999) Critical discourse analysis and conversation analysis. *Discourse & Society* 10 (4), 459–460.
Walsh, R. (2003) Global diasporas: Introduction. *Interventions: International Journal of Postcolonial Studies* 5 (1), 1–3.
Westmoreland, M.W. (2008) Interruptions: Derrida and hospitality. *Kritike* 2 (1), 1–10.
Wetherell, M. (1998) Positioning and interpretative repertoires: Conversation analysis and post-structuralism in dialogue. *Discourse & Society* 9 (3), 387–412.
Woolard, K.A. (1998) Simultaneity and bivalence as strategies in bilingualism. *Journal of Linguistic Anthropology* 8 (1), 3–29.

17 Reframing the Global-Local Dialectic and Hybridized Textual Practices

Rani Rubdy and Lubna Alsagoff

Introduction

This collection of chapters has brought together diverse research perspectives on the theme of hybridized textual practices resulting from the entanglement of a global language like English with the languages and cultures of local multilingual settings. The volume gives particular focus to how local agents make language choices within this global-local interface to achieve their communicative purposes and to negotiate, re-appropriate and reconfigure their social identities using hybrid linguistic practices. It also attempts to explore why, for instance, social agents make the decisions they do about language, or, to use Makoni and Pennycook's (2007) framework, why they seem to perform identities in the ways that they do. Each of the studies in this volume presents its own take in grappling with this theme; at the same time, all the chapters are united by the common aim of bringing hybrid language practices to the center of discussions about English as a global language. We revisit the contributions to this volume and analyze and synthesize the arguments relevant to this discussion. In particular, we foreground the nexus between the decentering forces and individual agency that come into play in constructing linguistic forms of localization as speakers draw on the global resources of English to produce a fascinating range of hybridity. We discuss the salient features of this interplay between the global and the local as explored by the contributors in relation to the central conceptual issues within the theoretical debate of globalization. In so doing, we draw together critical points and identify common strands that might help illuminate, expand, interrogate and/or challenge current understandings of the notion of textual and cultural hybridity, cast here as the new norm in late-modernity.

The Deterritorialization of Global Cultural Practices and Discourses

Globalization has disturbed the way we conceptualize 'culture'. The tendency to connect the realm of culture to the particularities of place, a stable territorialized existence, called up a metaphor of a mosaic of cultures – with each culture as a universe of shared meanings, radically set apart from every other. Nowadays though, it is impossible to think of culture in such restricted terms as the natural property of spatially circumscribed populations, as cultural interconnections increasingly stretch across the globe, eroding the isomorphism between culture and place. The dislodging of culture from particular or fixed locations in space and time calls up new metaphors of mobile cultures, as suggested by Clifford's (1997) anthropological work on 'traveling cultures'. However, Tomlinson (1999: 2) points out that although 'globalization promotes much more physical mobility than ever before, the key to its cultural impact is in the transformation of localities themselves'. Thus for him, 'the transformation of culture is not grasped in the trope of travel but in the idea of "deterritorialization"'.

The general weakening of the ties between culture and place does not imply that globalization destroys localities, but on the contrary that 'cultural experience is in various ways "lifted out" of its traditional "anchoring" in particular localities' (Tomlinson, 2003: 273), becoming reterritorialized into hybrid forms due to their shifting contexts. Viewed from this perspective, in the case of a translocal language like English, as Blommaert (2003) points out, English does not eliminate the local languages, but enters the repertoire of language users as a resource that fulfills both pragmatic functions (as in vernacularization) and metapragmatic ones. Pennycook uses the term 'transcultural flows' to refer to the ways in which cultural forms move, change and are re-used to fashion new identities in diverse contexts. Transcultural practices therefore 'refer not to homogenization or heterogenization but to alternative spaces of cultural production' (2007: 47). Pennycook in fact maintains that rather than seeing English as an imported language, it makes more sense to consider it as always/already local (Pennycook, 2007, 2010).

Taking this idea a step further and situating her study in East Africa, Higgins (Chapter 2) makes a strong case for English as a local language.

Instead of looking to language as the starting point in understanding hybridity, Higgins uses Appadurai's (1996) framework of 'scapes' or 'flows' and draws on data from the mediascapes of hip hop and advertising, and the ideoscapes of politics and public health education in Kenya and Tanzania to argue that rather than simply adapting English to fit local purposes, hybridity or reterritorialization of English is best explained in terms of both global and local flows within fluid shifting scapes. In other words, the reterritorialization of English in its local contexts involves the '*re-scaping* of already localized language' through various kinds of language-related alterations, as when language that is associated with the spheres of the 'underclass' is 'elevated' to the status of a cool commodity by local mobile phone companies in Dar es Salaam or when hip hop language in East Africa is re-scaped through its affiliation with the ideoscapes of HIV/AIDS awareness in Tanzania. Higgins suggests that hybridity be re-perspectivized as a local phenomenon, by exploiting the *multivocality* (Bakhtin, 1981) of the language to simultaneously index the multiple meanings associated with each scape.

Hybridity as 'Boundary-Subverting', as 'Third Space'

Similar to the idea of the dislocation of culture and place is Bhabha's (1994) concept of *third space*. It represents a space where difference is neither global nor local in orientation, but one that is capable of accommodating the potential incommensurability of differently located identities. The third space then is a critical factor that facilitates the construction of new social identities, and destabilizes and displaces essentialized ones. It shapes, and is shaped by, synthesis of the global and the local, entertaining difference without imposing hierarchy. Akin to Robertson's (1992) concept of 'glocalization', it is in this space that social agents are presumed to have the capacity to synthesize, to transform. The third space is thus a theoretical construct referring to a semiotic space between competing cultural collectives – for example, colonized-colonizer, indigenous-foreign, local-global, traditional-modern – where cultural identity across differences of class, gender roles and cultural values is negotiated, setting up new structures of sociolinguistic authority and new sociopolitical initiatives (Bhatt, 2008). Used in this sense, the third space offers speakers the possibility of a new representation, of meaning-making and of agency.

By providing a mechanism to negotiate and navigate between a global identity and local ones, the third space also allows speakers to (re-)position themselves with regard to new community practices of speaking and writing, creating counter-discourses to the hegemony of the monoglossic discourses and policies favoring standardization and conformity (Bhatt, 2008). The linguistic indexing of this liminal space, of new identity positions, is signaled through discoursal hybridity in texts and interactions: code-switching is one exponent of that hybridity. The mixing of linguistic features in newspapers and commercial advertisements, as specific instantiations of 'mediascapes' (Appadurai, 1996), variation in the more pragmatic aspects of talk (for example, in negotiating politeness, accepting compliments or using terms of address) and creolization are other visible markers of this transformation/hybridity.

The concept of third space is productively explored by Bhatt (Chapter 7) in his analysis of how contemporary Indian women are represented in the news media through the strategic use of Hindi in Indian English newspapers. In this way the linguistic indexicalities of English (new, global, modern) and Hindi (old, local, traditional) are juxtaposed through code-switching to allow for gendered representations to be read 'in-between' traditional-local practices and a global-modern identity. In dynamic tension between the 'traditional-local' and the 'modern-global' a liminal ideological space is created where the two worlds converge and get renegotiated. In effect, Hindi-English code-switching is used as a rhetorical authentication of indigenous gendered practices AND as a form of discursive resistance to such traditional practices and values. In this struggle for a space – between power and solidarity – new, hybrid identities for the modern Indian woman are seen to emerge.

The concept of third space and glocalization once again provides a framework for the examination of hybridized textual practices in Rubdy's (Chapter 3) study of the signage in the linguistic landscape of three cities in the Indian state of Maharashtra. The signage which comprises shop signs, billboards and advertisements, reflect a strategic and creative blending of English with Hindi and Marathi texts and scripts using a range of modalities such as aural rhyming, word play, linguistic puns and intertextuality, all constituting attempts at democratizing the canon of Standard English through processes of localization. Interestingly, much like Higgins' (Chapter 2) multilinguals in East Africa who exploit the *multivocality* of the language to make it fit into the contexts of national political campaigns in Kenya and HIV/AIDS prevention in Tanzania, the highly purposeful, conscious deployment of the stylized hybrid formations in the Indian signage seems to correspond closely to the plurilingual dexterity and creativity of everyday language use among the middle-class youth in multilingual India, strongly suggestive of a de-centering process that subverts the canon.

Roy's chapter (Chapter 9) situates itself within the contemporary Indian film industry to discuss, in particular, 'crossover' films at the turn of the new millennium, as a hybrid product negotiating between two or more cultures, and for hybrid audiences, resulting from the 'transnationalization' of Bollywood. Roy notes that despite having a global audience in view, the filmmaker's liberal use of the local Hindi/Punjabi vernacular in these crossover English language films with no attempt at semantic glossing works as a strategy in using 'the gap between the colonial language and the colonized world to enunciate cultural difference' (p. 156). Although Roy does not explicitly use Bhabha's concept of third space, she interprets the crossover films' refusal to translate Hindi/Punjabi colloquial speech into English for a global audience as a strategy for foregrounding the '"untranslatability" of cultural difference' while countering the transnationalization of Indian commercial cinema via the reassertion of locality. Roy's study, like Rubdy's and Higgins', demonstrates the complex interpenetration of the global and the local (Hannerz, 1990), in which the local becomes more globally integrated and yet does not lose its distinctiveness.

Languages and Cultures as Discrete Forms or Continua?

One of the charges made against hybridity is that 'it is predicated on an assumption that there exist two distinct codes or separate entities which are combined' (Makoni, 2011: 683). The very concept of language mix takes it as a given that languages are discrete identifiable entities, whereas in Pennycook's words, 'languages are always mixed, hybrid and drawing on multiple resources' (2010: 129). In his view, the notion of languages as discrete, stable, monolithic entities with solid boundaries is actually the product of colonial knowledge production. In practice, people draw on a whole range of linguistic resources which cannot be easily pigeonholed as 'separate languages' in their everyday linguistic practices. Parallel to these hybridized linguistic practices are their similarly hybridized sociocultural identities.

Otsuji and Pennycook (Chapter 5) thus reject the notion of bilingual or multilingual code-switching to explain the concurrent use of English and Japanese by the participants in their study. Instead, their focus 'is on the hybrid starting point of mixed linguistic resources, where genres, styles, practices, and discourses are mobilized as part of everyday linguistic interaction' (p. 85). Clearly, they see hybrid language as 'unmarked' ('unremarkable') and not as the 'ramification of the interaction between pre-given discrete "languages"' (p. 83). Thus, it is important to note that as opposed to the concept of multilingualism which suggests the existence of additive separate languages, Otsuji and Pennycook's use of the concept of metrolingualism 'starts with the assumption of mixing and diversity as a given' and focuses on 'how people produce, resist, defy and rearrange linguistic resources in and through local linguistic practices' (p. 85).

In his chapter, Saraceni (Chapter 11) discusses hybridity as a concept that can assume one of the two following senses depending on the orientation one adopts towards the concept of 'language': (a) a particular form of language combining items from two or more languages (language as system); (b) a linguistic amalgam used in language practice where speakers negotiate and draw from a shared repertoire (language as practice). His analysis of textual data from Facebook reveals considerable linguistic hybridity as the network users seamlessly combine the resources of English, Malay and Bahasa Indonesia 'in a borderless linguistic amalgam' in their online interactions without much regard to the 'official' designation of individual words, grammatical patterns or syntactic structures that may signify ascriptions to particular languages. Saraceni's participants express that for them language hybridity is something natural, 'requiring no conscious act of any particular creativity' (language as practice) (p. 203); yet, they also are very conscious of the discrete elements of language mixing (language as system) and are 'particularly sensitive to their symbolic, cultural, and identity significance' (p. 203). Saraceni importantly points out that a 'discussion on linguistic hybridity requires reflections that go deep to the very heart of the concept of language' (p. 202).

Omoniyi (Chapter 12), in exploring data from YouTube and its attendant commentary/discussion, suggests that the internet has created e-borderland contexts which constitute zones of continuity or confluence of linguistic flows and which problematize and call into question the 'binarization of local and global'. Omoniyi suggests hybridity as 'a strategy of creative and resistive divergence from the essentialism of an institutionally recognized International English' (p. 213). He demonstrates how such internet discussion forums that overtly represent established global points of reference associated with the UK and the US are, however, legitimate sites for challenging the status quo by promoting fluid hybrid language forms co-constructed by the senders and recipients that implicitly infuse a local dimension into the interaction. Omoniyi's reconceptualization and construction of the local and global in his e-borderland framework draws on a number of key concepts, including Bhabha's third space and Blommaert's (2007) sociolingusitics of scale. Even then, Omoniyi argues that a review of our analytical tools that goes beyond language choice is needed if we are to successfully unravel the complex negotiations and constructions anchored to histories that are endemic of contemporary language practices.

Much in line with arguments that seek to reorient language not as an abstract object but as a living cultural communication process is García's chapter (Chapter 6). García deconstructs the normalizing monoglossic ideologies within studies of bilingualism, such as that underlying dual language education, as having had the effect of negating the fluidity of bilingual language practices and furthering inequalities in the education of language minorities. She specifically critiques 'the dual monoglossic concepts' of diglossia, as well as the concepts of additive and subtractive bilingualism, which she claims may have contributed to some of the failures that can be observed today in the promotion of plurilingual practices for a global world. García looks at how linguistic hybridity is critically needed as a pedagogy to construct bilingual education that truly reflects the fluidity of language practices and identifications in the 21st century. She suggests that the term 'transglossia' be used to capture the complex dynamism and hybridity of these language practices and advocates a pedagogy of translanguaging in which bilingual students are encouraged to draw on their entire linguistic repertoire and 'use these complex and fluid discursive practices to perform their learning' (p. 112).

Hybridity Co-opted by Capitalistic Interests or Turned to Local Advantage?

Globalization has most often been defined in the mainstream media in economic terms, as the exploitation by businesses of expanded world markets. From a neoliberal perspective, such expansionism involves 'the ability to trade freely across the entire globe, to tap into new markets and take advantage of cheap foreign labor costs' and is seen as a positive development that 'enhances the money-making capabilities of companies' (Seargeant & Swann, 2012: 178). Others consider globalization as something that is having 'pernicious' effects on societies around the world and see it as a combination of economic and cultural imperialism, 'with powerful corporations and countries exploiting resources and workforces across the globe, while simultaneously imposing a bland and standardized cultural impress on diverse local traditions' (Seargeant & Swann, 2012: 178).

These contradictions and tensions are nicely captured by Lorente and Tupas (Chapter 4) in their study of the overlapping global-local discourses in the online website of a company that offers training in teaching English as a foreign language to South Koreans. Their analysis of this website sheds light on 'how hybridity is deeply entangled with the mechanisms of capitalist globalization' (p. 66). In 'selling' English, the website advertises the Philippines as a niche country in the global English language market while glossing over the deep social inequalities that have led the Philippines to historically position itself as a producer of cheap labor, leading the authors to caution that while 'hybridity as third space may be creative, [it is] ... not necessarily transformative or emancipatory, especially because its use can be and has been exploited to advance specific economic agendas' (p. 66–7). They pose critical questions: whenever we examine and analyze linguistic and discursive phenomena 'Who and what hybridizes, for whom and for what purposes?'. And above all, whose interests does it serve?

Continuing in the realm of the marketing power wielded by the media and mediatized texts and their potential exploitation in the service of capitalist goals and corporate market interests, Martin's analysis (Chapter 8) of corporate websites designed for French-speaking audiences exemplifies how English serves not only as a global language of communication in French web advertising discourses but also how through various manifestations of multimodal bilingual creativity such as media disseminated images, languages and music, it helps construct hybrid cultural identities and linguistic practices for French online consumers in the context of virtual marketing. She sees this intermingling of local and global discourses as compelling evidence of hybridity becoming a vital component of the 'glocal' approach to marketing.

Similarly, in discussing the increasing presence of 'hybridized *medialect*' on Korean TV as a combined manifestation of global consciousness and local sensibility, Lee (Chapter 10), shows how the use of English and the ability to hybridize language use by Korean entertainers is positioned as a valuable resource which Korean celebrities mobilize to reprise their roles as entertainers. However, as Lee points out, since English functions as a social stratification variable in Korea, hybridized linguistic practices that provide opportunities for employability and academic success for English-knowing bilingual entertainers and viewing pleasure for bilingual viewers potentially exclude monolingual performers and viewers, thus revealing the close link between televisual content and commercialism. At the same time, while knowledge of English seems to empower Koreans, the lack of knowledge of English seems to marginalize them. These hybridized linguistic practices then either play inclusive or exclusionary roles, including English-knowing bilinguals and excluding English-unknowing monolinguals.

Performing Hybrid Cultural Identity

An important aspect of identities in the present day context of language use is their multiplicity, or what Benessaieh (2010) terms *a plural sense of self*. In sociolinguistics a great deal of research has been conducted on how individuals use language indexically to enact identities and shift frames of reference in conversations and other interactions. This is seen in work on urban practices such as Rampton's (1995) well-known studies on 'crossing' as well as Pennycook's (2007) research on hip hop. Much of this research focuses on how identity is an incomplete and ongoing process and how identities are 'fluid, shifting and strategically negotiated according to changing social contexts' (Canagarajah, 2005: 438).

Studies in the book that address such aspects of fluid, shifting, hybridized identities are those by Kamada, Ooi and Tan, Roy, Alsagoff and Villareal. Kamada (Chapter 14) examines the contested and celebrated linguistic and ethnic 'hybrid' identities of mixed-ethnic adolescent girls of Japanese and white/foreign mixed-parentage who assume a 'third' ethnic identity differing from either of their parents. Within the context of Japan, where ideologies of ethnicity and discourses of homogeneity that conflate 'Japaneseness' with nationality, race, ethnicity, language and 'looking Japanese' continue to persist, the participants in the study express their *glocal hybrid identities* differently in different contexts, 'based on their local experiences within different social rules'. Sometimes they construct English in a positive light celebrating the linguistic capital of bilinguality, and empowering themselves by drawing on their intercultural and global knowledge and experiences; at other times they reject their positioning as 'English-knowing bilinguals' in the face of their Japanese peers to contest this very same identity (p. 249). Made to feel like 'the Other' within the local dominant marginalizing discourses of homogeneity and conformity in Japan, these mixed ethnic girls are able to deconstruct their positioning as *bad difference* by invoking an alternate ideology of diversity, and paradoxically, by explicitly constituting their own differentness within a globalizing discourse of interculturalism to reconstitute *bad difference* into *good difference*. 'Linking their local identities with their global access to resources' [...] allows them 'to assume different and competing local identities not readily available to their Japanese peers to appropriate various forms of intercultural, linguistic and cultural capital to empower themselves in the construction of their glocal identities' (p. 262) and to (re)claim agency for themselves.

Drawing their data from a group of Facebook users of English from Singapore, Ooi and Tan (Chapter 13) investigate the ways in which, 'speakers project different social identities and create different social relationships through their style choices' (p. 226), thus constituting themselves more fittingly as a 'community of practice'. Using 'style' in its multidimensional sense to cover 'a wide range of strategic actions and performances that speakers engage in to construct themselves and their social lives' (p. 226) and combining Coupland's (2007) framework of Identity Contextualizing Processes (ICP) with Ooi's (2001) Concentric Circles Model (CCM), the authors provide an interesting analysis of the way these speakers index specific social and cultural identifications through a range of strategies in the 'glocalization' of

English in Singapore. The versatility with which the Facebook users switch from colloquial or standard English to their hybridized version of SgE-L, which at once includes features from Peranakan Malay, Hokkien Chinese and Bazaar Malay, alongside the use of globalized computer mediated markers and expletives as well as localized markers, illustrates the hybrid ways in which disparate ideologies are negotiated and expressed through the medium of English in Singapore.

Villareal's (Chapter 16) study addresses the performative aspect of identity construction in the context of the Philippine diaspora by probing into the hybrid's 'subjectivity' or 'inner space' through the lens of conversational analysis and a personal narratives perspective. Her data comes from firsthand accounts of two narrators taken from non-fictional writing, as she seeks to catch glimpses into the cognitive and affective processes underlying the interactions of a Filipino contract engineer with Nepali workers in Kathmandu and a Filipina housewife with websites on women and erotica in the virtual world of cyberspace in attempting to gain an understanding of their struggle to come to terms with their diasporic condition. She notes how their narratives are both hybrid and heteroglossic, suggesting that 'while hybridity proceeds from the subjectivity of the individual, from which originates agency..., hybridity is not just individual. It is part of a complex system in which actors interact with agents both human and non-human....' (p. 291) in the process of transforming themselves.

The double vision or plural sense of self that characterizes the life worlds of transnational migrants, borderline communities and diasporic peoples is also exemplified by Roy's study (Chapter 9) of three Indian 'diaspora' or 'crossover' films, mentioned above, in which the characters code-switch with consummate ease between Standard English, Indian English, Hindi and Punjabi to create new meanings alongside cultural nuances animated by the juxtaposition of traditional objects with Western ones. Adopting a postcolonial perspective, Roy interprets these films' refusal to translate Hindi/Punjabi colloquial speech as signifying cultural incommensurability while compensating for the transnationalization of Indian commercial cinema by a reassertion of locality through the localization of the global and the globalization of the local.

Finally, Alsagoff's chapter (Chapter 15) explores the dialogic of teacher identity construction in the dialectic tensions between the co-present global and local (Bakhtin, 1981) – the student teachers who engage in an online discussion forum weave multiple, even conflicting, voices and orientations as they discuss the English they speak and should speak. In negotiating between their ostensibly incongruent orientations towards competing norms in Singapore English, on the one hand upholding global standards of English as would-be teachers and on the other valorizing the local through their identifications with Singlish, the student teachers bring into sharp focus the ways in which the simultaneity of multiple linguistic and cultural identities necessitates a poststructural understanding of identity which understands it as dynamic, multiple and shifting. Alsagoff argues that the analysis of the multivocality of the teachers' discourse demonstrates the dislocations of language, culture and identity that can best be understood as hybrid.

Hybridity's Capacity to Counter Social Inequality

Closely related to globalization's undeniable link with a neoliberal capitalist agenda is the issue of social inequality. Globalization has deepened inequality both within and across different societies. Inequalities involving postcolonial politics and other forms of difference related to race, ethnicity, class, gender and language use are now well established. Asymmetric divisions of labor between 'core regions' and the 'peripheries' in what is known as the 'New World System' reflect deepening inequalities in international relations and many other levels of society (Wallerstein, 2004). For instance, in relation to English, Mazrui (2004) writes about the imbalance in the world's languages at the international level exemplified especially by Africans' 'lingo-intellectual dependency' on English. He considers appropriation as an ideal concept for English – one that has not been achieved in sub-Saharan Africa. Skeptical that hybridity can transform the colonial language, he argues that appropriation remains in the hands of the elite and not in most people's language use. He contends that even in cases where language is transformed into the voice of the people, it is never enough to merely change the language – any linguistic transformations must be accompanied by changes in the social order (cited in Higgins, 2009: 10).

This would mean grounding arguments about the hybrid, fuzzy, shifting, dynamic nature of language within the matrix of socially produced relations of power and power structures. We need to be able to explicate why social agents make the decisions they do about language, or why they perform identities in the ways that they do. 'What are the larger complex, but also very specific and inevitably hierarchical social relations that, for instance, motivate individuals to use a particular dialect, hybrid, creole or standardized language in context A, B, C – *and* not use it in context X, Y, Z?' (Demot-Heinrich, 2011: 399). In relation to our collection of chapters we might ask why is the concurrent use of English and Japanese in the multilingual workplace setting in Australia, described by Otsuji and Pennycook (Chapter 5), unremarkable and oriented to as a normative way of interacting, whereas the self-conscious juxtaposing of these same languages, English and Japanese, in

Kamada's study in Japan (Chapter 14) is seen as indexing conflicting and competing, at times even contradictory, identity positions for their speakers? How do we interpret the linguistic processes in Saraceni's explorations (Chapter 11) of his Facebook users in which the participants appear to seamlessly interweave English, Malay and Bahasa Indonesia in their social network interactions and yet quite clearly continue to perceive them as separate codes? And how do such linguistic choices become marked or unmarked for certain contexts? Similarly, in what ways do the English-Hindi code-mixed instances of word play, allusion and intertextuality in the signage examined in Rubdy's study (Chapter 3) constitute a near-political act of democratizing and dehegemonizing English, dislodging its long history as a niche of the privileged elite in India, while simultaneously opening up global, cosmopolitan resources and imaginaries to the non-English dominant Indian bilingual masses? In contrast, the website of the training organization that offers English language courses to Koreans in the Philippines, analyzed by Lorente and Tupas (Chapter 4) operates in ways that exemplify how the in-betweeness of discourses may at the same time create, sustain, as well as possibly transgress inequalities in the global order.

Viewed from a postmodern framework, it becomes clear that the objects comprising hybridized discourses are not just 'linguistic'. 'The bits of language that are globalized are equally bits of culture and society ... In order to understand language globalization, we need to look at larger semiotic and cultural packages, and a purely synchronic analysis will not do. The packages need to be looked at historically, in their histories of becoming particular signs and dynamically in their use, up-take and re-use sequences' (Blommaert, 2010: 19). Blommaert sees language use in multilingual societies as the performance of identities in relation to the distribution of power-related elements. He explains how proficiency in and access to certain codes can include or exclude people from certain material and symbolic benefits.

Yet, as Williams (1977: 133) notes, '[t]he reality of any hegemony, in the extended political and cultural sense, is that, while by definition it is always dominant, it is never either total or exclusive'. Rather than discussing the subject in terms of a totalizing dominance then, it may be useful to understand hybridity as social practice constitutive of and constituted by sociopolitical and economical arrangements. Kraidy's (2002) distinction between a descriptive, non-evaluative use of the notion of hybridity and a more critical and powerful deployment of the term is relevant to the discussion here. In the first instance, the term is essentially used as a descriptive lens for analyzing the fusion and blending of cultural, textual and discursive/semiotic practices emblematic of contemporary globalization and sociolinguistic phenomena without necessarily giving explicit attention to their wider implications. A critical, evaluative approach towards hybridity, in contrast, offers a more nuanced view of the interplay between cultural and economic processes in an uneven world and the impact of the sociopolitical and historical contexts of language use in understanding how they relate to inequality, poverty, patterns of trade, education and ethical dimensions of the global order. Politically, a critical hybridity theory considers hybridity as a space in which transcultural and transnational communication practices are constantly negotiated in interactions of differential power (Kraidy, 2002: 317). Thus, even as we attend to Clifford's (1997: 10–11) reminder that 'subaltern and non-Western transcultural experiences' are not always signs of liberation, in a postmodern world of globalization where cultural and linguistic authority are being contested, hybridity seems to offer hope for cautious optimism.

Concluding Remarks

This volume has focused on the notion of hybridity within the cultural dynamics of globalization in an attempt to explore the extent of its scope, significance and role as a key area of research in the field of sociolinguistics. In depicting the relationship between English, the language most often associated with global dominance, and the local speech repertoires and/or speech communities, the various chapters in the book have showcased the different ways in which English not only permeates, penetrates and alters the textual and discursive practices of these communities but also their experiences, identities and imaginaries. Their explorations of a rich variety of data have demonstrated the liberating potential of hybridity as much as they have raised awareness of the problematics of the term and the need for further reflection and research as to how to harness the heterogeneity of the concept of hybridity to respond to the challenges of capturing the complexities of contemporary language use. The insights drawn call for an analytical engagement with transnational linguistic and cultural forms if we are to avoid an uncritical celebration of hybridity oblivious to its commodification by capitalist interests. Specifically, with the restructuring of center-periphery relations, we need to rethink how processes of fluidity and hybridity can be freed from their colonial associations of the past which mainly construe hybridity as a weapon of the weak, of a people intrinsically inferior, and reframe it from a postmodern perspective as a specifically constructive, resourceful and empowering response in mediating the pressures of globalization with concrete attentiveness to agency. Hybridity then emerges as a cross-fertilization of languages and cultures within the global-local dialectic by agentive beings who are constantly in search of new social and linguistic resources across borders 'to produce new identities, and assign alternative meanings to the links between identities and linguistic varieties' (Pavlenko & Blackledge, 2004: 27) through linguistic acts of appropriation and negotiation, resistance and transformation.

References

Appadurai, A. (1996) *Modernity at Large: Cultural Dimensions of Globalization*. Minneapolis: University of Minnesota Press.

Bakhtin, M.M. (1981) *The Dialogic Imagination: Four Essays*. Austin: University of Texas Press.

Benessaieh, A. (2010) Multicultualism, interculturality, transculturality. In A. Benessaieh (ed.) *Transcultural Americas* (pp. 11–38). Ottawa: Presses de l'univerisité d'Ottawa, à paraître.

Bhabha, H. (1994) *The Location of Culture*. London: Routledge.

Bhatt, R.M. (2008) In other words: Language mixing, identity representations, and the *third space*. *Journal of Sociolinguistics* 12 (2), 177–200.

Blommaert, J. (2007) Sociolinguistic scales. *Intercultural Pragmatics* 4, 1–19.

Blommaert, J. (2010) *The Sociolinguistics of Globalization*. Cambridge: Cambridge University Press.

Canagarajah, A.S. (2005) Dilemmas in planning English/vernacular relations in post-colonial communities. *Journal of Sociolinguistics* 9 (3), 418–447.

Clifford, J. (1997) *Routes: Travel and Translation in the Late Twentieth Century*. Cambridge, MA: Harvard University Press.

Coupland, N. (2007) *Style: Language Variation and Identity*. Cambridge: Cambridge University Press.

Demot-Heinrich, C. (2011) Review of *Disinventing and Reconstituting Languages* edited by S. Makoni and A. Pennycook, 2007. *Journal of Sociolinguistics* 15 (3), 398–401.

Hannerz, U. (1990) Cosmopolitans and locals in world culture. *Theory, Culture and Society* 7, 237–251.

Higgins, C. (2009) *English as a Local Language: Postcolonial Identities and Multilingual Practices*. Bristol: Multilingual Matters.

Kraidy, M.M. (2002) Hybridity in cultural globalization. *Communication Theory* 12 (3), 316–339.

Makoni, S. and Pennycook, A. (2007) *Disinventing and Reconstituting Language*. Clevedon: Multilingual Matters.

Makoni, S. (2011) Sociolinguistics, colonial and postcolonial: An integrationist perspective. *Language Sciences* 33 (4), 680–688.

Mazrui, A.M. (2004) *English in Africa After the Cold War*. Clevedon: Multilingual Matters.

Ooi, V. Y. (2001) Upholding standards or passively observing language: Corpus evidence and the Concentric Circles Model. In V. Y. Ooi (ed.) *Evolving Identities: The English Language in Singapore and Malaysia* (pp. 168–183). Singapore: Times Academic Press.

Pavlenko, A. and Blackledge, A. (2004) *Negotiation of Identities in Multilingual Contexts*. Clevedon: Multilingual Matters.

Pennycook, A. (2005) Teaching with the flow: Fixity and fluidity in education. *Asia Pacific Journal of Education* 25 (1), 29–43.

Pennycook, A. (2007) *Global Englishes and Transcultural Flows*. London and New York: Routledge.

Pennycook, A. (2010) *Language as a Local Practice.* New York: Routledge.
Rampton, B. (1995) *Crossing: Language and Ethnicity among Adolescents.* London: Longman.
Robertson, R. (1992) *Globalization: Social Theory and Global Culture.* London: Sage.
Seargeant, P. and Swann, J. (2012) *English in the World: History, Diversity, Change.* London: Routledge.
Tomlinson, J. (1999) *Globalization and Culture.* Chicago, IL: University of Chicago Press.
Tomlinson, J. (2003) Globalization and cultural identity. In D. Held and A. McGraw (eds) *The Global Transformations Reader: An Introduction to the Globalization Debate* (pp. 269–277). Cambridge: Polity Press.
Wallerstein, I. (2004) *World-Systems Analysis: An Introduction.* Durham, NC: Duke University Press.
Williams, R. (1977) *Marxism and Literature.* Oxford: Oxford University Press.

Author Index

Subject Index